Stonewall Jackson and Religious Faith
in Military Command

DATE DUE

Stonewall Jackson and Religious Faith in Military Command

KENNETH E. HALL

McFarland & Company, Inc., Publishers
Jefferson, North Carolina, and London

LIBRARY OF CONGRESS CATALOGUING-IN-PUBLICATION DATA

Hall, Kenneth E., 1954–
    Stonewall Jackson and religious faith in military
command / Kenneth E. Hall.
      p.   cm.
    Includes bibliographical references and index.

    ISBN 0-7864-2085-5 (softcover : 50# alkaline paper) ∞

    1. Jackson, Stonewall, 1824–1863 — Religion. 2. Jackson,
Stonewall, 1824–1863 — Military leadership. 3. Jackson,
Stonewall, 1824–1863 — Political and social views. 4. Generals —
Confederate States of America — Biography. 5. Confederate States
of America. Army — Biography. 6. United States — History — Civil
Civil War, 1861–1865 — Religious aspects. 7. Nationalism —
Confederate States of America — History. I. Title.
E467.1.J15H15   2005
973.7'42'092 — dc22   2005004751

British Library cataloguing data are available

On the cover: Stained glass window ©2005 PhotoSpin; *background* ©2005
Corbis Images; Stonewall Jackson ©2005 Corbis Images

Manufactured in the United States of America

*McFarland & Company, Inc., Publishers
  Box 611, Jefferson, North Carolina 28640
    www.mcfarlandpub.com*

For Austen, Evan, and Tiffany

Acknowledgments

I wish to thank Professor Gene Dubois of the University of North Dakota for advice and assistance, especially with the often challenging world of Spanish epic. I am also grateful to Mr. Ron Maxwell for allowing me to visit the set of *Gods and Generals* on repeated occasions. His assistants, including Ms. Jennifer Slatkin and Mr. Michael Atlan, were unfailingly patient and gracious with my requests. Mr. Alan Geoffrian, who was serving as assistant to Mr. Robert Duvall, has also been very gracious. Other people who have assisted me in various ways include Mrs. Niki Pollock of the Special Collections Department, Glasgow University Library; Dr. Judy Slagle, Department of English, East Tennessee State University; Dr. Stephen Fritz, Department of History, East Tennessee State University; Dr. Don Johnson, Department of English, and former Dean, East Tennessee State University; Dr. Ronnie Day, Department of History, East Tennessee State University; the staff of the Stonewall Jackson Headquarters, Winchester, VA; Mr. Jackson Hendricks, Visitor Services Coordinator, Charlotte Museum, Charlotte, NC; Prof. Michael Anderegg, Department of English, University of North Dakota; Ms. Annie Armour, University of the South Library, Suwanee, TN; Ms. Diane Jacob, VMI Archives; Mr. Don Pfanz, Fredericksburg-Spotsylvania National Military Park; Maj. Michael Lynch, National Archives for Military History, Carlisle, PA; Ms. Concepción Ocampos, Prado Museum, Madrid; Mr. Mario Szichman of New York City for suggestions concerning the project. Special thanks to the following members of the cast of *Gods and Generals*: Mr. Robert Duvall; Mr. Frankie Faison; Mr. Patrick Gorman; Mr. Stephen Lang; Ms. Kali Rocha. And, especially, thanks to my wife, Carla, and my children, for their patience with an often impatient author.

All translations in the book are mine unless otherwise indicated.

Table of Contents

Introduction

Despite the existence of numerous biographies of Civil War general Thomas J. "Stonewall" Jackson, none has focused exclusively or even primarily on his status within the tradition of generals fighting for religious motives, or strongly influenced by religious beliefs. A strong case can be made for a "type" of military leader classed as a religious general, or more broadly as a priestly warrior. In these terms, Jackson is one of a long line of military (and often, by extension, political) leaders who have been motivated particularly by religious belief. Aside from their analogous position to Jackson's, these leaders deserve closer study as a group, not least because of their often fascinating personalities. Several of these men are conspicuously "eccentric" or individualistic: Jackson, George S. Patton, Charles Gordon, and D.H. Hill come to mind. Some, Cromwell and Knox for instance, appear less colorful but are no less strong-minded and devout for all that. In some cases, leadership was a mixture of the political and the military: Charles V and Philip II of Spain were monarchs who nevertheless participated in military activities, and Gustavus II Adolphus of Sweden was a ruler who was primarily famed for his soldierly qualities. All these leaders, and others to be discussed in this book, share a combination of religious devotion, or even zealotry, and military forcefulness. Many of them became national symbols; some of them died in untimely fashion; all of them have important tales to tell about the importance of religious faith in the military arena.

Several of these leaders have been the subject of literary and film treatments. In 2003, Stonewall Jackson was presented anew to the moviegoing public in *Gods and Generals*, directed by Ronald F. Maxwell. The film, like the Jeff Shaara novel on which it was based, deals with Jackson as a profoundly religious general who acted on the principles of his faith. It is less straightforwardly martial, or perhaps less of a traditional war film, than was the famous film *Patton*, based on the life of General George S. Patton, Jr., the controversial leader of the U.S. Third Army during World War II. Although this film does present some aspects of Patton's spiritual nature, including his belief in reincarnation, it does not highlight them at the expense of more typical war film elements. It concentrates especially on Patton the individualist, bucking the army establishment, which of course places the film within its period (1970). The emphasis on reincarnation in the Patton film ties into the belief in this phenomenon on the part of Gen. Patton, who also claimed to see battlefield visions. In this respect, he becomes part of a long tradition in epic poetry and romance, in which such visions were staples. Thus, like Patton, the hero of the Spanish *Poema de Fernán González* has dream visions, and the battlefield is visited by saintly warriors (such was also the claim made by one chronicler of the conquest of Mexico).

Unlike the Patton film, the Anthony Mann film based on the life of the Cid, one of the historical-legendary figures discussed in the book, fits the Cid into the national myth of Spain and emphasizes his humanity and his leadership qualities. The Cid film does not shrink from blending history and legend; its combination of these qualities might well remind the viewer at least as much of an American Western (in which field Mann specialized) as of a characteristic Hollywood epic.

Khartoum, the most extensive film treatment to date of another religious general, Charles "Chinese" Gordon, is certainly filmed on an epic scale, but it focuses especially on the unfortunate consequences of political and personal divisions within the British government, as well as the particular traits of stubbornness and touchiness on the part of Gordon, all of which contributed materially to the disaster at Khartoum. The film does not place the religiosity of the general into the foreground, concentrating rather on the military failures against the forces of the Mahdi, who eventually stormed Khartoum and killed Gordon.

In this respect it is unlike *Gods and Generals*, which focuses on the religiosity not only of Jackson but also of Joshua Chamberlain of Maine, who became a legend for Americans after his role in the Gettysburg battle. Chamberlain was also a deeply religious man, albeit of a different background from Jackson. *Gods and Generals*, both film and novel, formulates a contrast between these two leaders as a microcosm of the larger contrast between South and North, both in political and in religious terms. While *Gettysburg,* the previous Civil War film by Maxwell, had concentrated more on the dilemmas presented to Lee by the situation on the battlefield, and on the heroism of the soldiers, both Southern and Northern, who had to fight the desperate battle, *Gods and Generals* tends to exemplify the conflict in the contrast between Jackson and Chamberlain. Like the epic poetry tradition, this film puts forward two champions who embody the virtues and the beliefs of their respective nations. And in this case, the religious beliefs of these two soldiers are emphasized within the context of their views on the war and of their official roles in that war.

The religious, or priestly, warrior has a long tradition in European history and literature, from Friar Tuck to the stern clergymen of Spanish epic. In Stonewall Jackson's own time, religion was a strong factor in the ranks and in the officer corps of both North and South. Religious revivals and devout observance were common during the American Civil War. And, in some cases, men who had served in or studied for the priesthood or the clergy went on to become officers.

One example of such an officer was William S. Rosecrans (1819–98). This Ohio native was acknowledged to be a brilliant if quirky commander whose religious convictions were very strong and public. He often indulged his fascination with Catholicism to the point of probable exasperation on the part of his aides: "Unfortunately for his staff, the general's idea of pleasure was to keep his young aides, with whom he was affable and affectionate, awake all night while he ruminated aloud on religion in general and Catholicism in particular" (Cozzens 18). Cozzens emphasizes the depth of Rosecrans's religious devotion:

> To Rosecrans, the Catholic Church was supreme and infallible; all other theological systems were mere corruptions of the church. The general brooked no dispute on this point. Having embraced Catholicism over the objections of his staunchly Methodist parents while a cadet at West Point, Rosecrans displayed the sort of dogmatism common in adult converts to any faith [Cozzens 18].

Rosecrans seemed nevertheless to hide something of his personality behind a mask of cool intelligence. In his superb *Mountains Touched with Fire*, a study of the battles for Chattanooga, Wiley Sword provides the following picture of Rosecrans's personality:

> Yet there always had been something mysterious and different about Rosecrans. An aura of vanity and perhaps instability seemed to enshroud his outgoing, congenial personality.... To many, he was precisely the general to win the war. To others, he was wrathful, inconsistent, and temperamental. Those not in daily contact with Old Rosy seemed impressed mostly by his restless manner and tireless energy, which was frequently devoted to such minute details as seeing to the proper attire of his men or monitoring camp discipline. Thus, he had become a favorite among his soldiers, who appreciated his sincere concern about their well-being. More-

over, Rosecrans's almost-fanatic obsession for perfection ... was considered as evidence of his great capacity to manage and administrate. ... [I]t was also the mark of a self-consuming eccentric. Lurking behind those "kindly blue eyes" was a penetrating, probing glare, the kind of a look that bordered on the bizarre. Often an able, crafty strategist and a tough, tenacious fighter, Rosecrans, nonetheless, exhibited a peculiar vulnerability — that of the mind [Sword 4].

He had some success as commander of the Army of the Cumberland, especially in terms of discipline and morale. When Rosecrans took command of the army in November 1862, its spirit was low because of the recent warfare in Kentucky. Rosecrans instituted a set of strict disciplinary measures which he applied in an evenhanded manner. For example,

Maj. Gen. William S. Rosecrans, U.S. Army (1819–98). (Courtesy Roger D. Hunt Collection, U.S. Army Military History Institute.)

> Incompetent or otherwise unfit officers were stripped of their rank and marched from camp in the presence of their troops; officers' leave was slashed drastically and all soldiers, officers and enlisted men alike, were required to present written passes on demand when outside their camps [Cozzens 19–20].

Other measures were also taken to improve camp discipline. Cozzens observes that "All of these actions had the effect Rosecrans desired. Morale improved. Being more evenly distributed through the ranks, his brand of discipline succeeded where [General Don Carlos] Buell's had failed" (20).

So Rosecrans had the important virtue of being a

good disciplinarian and organizer, and he was undeniably well above average in intelligence. Nevertheless, he nearly lost his army at Stones River near Murfreesboro, Tennessee (December 31, 1862–January 2, 1863). And he later failed completely at Chickamauga against Gen. Braxton Bragg, losing his nerve and fleeing to Chattanooga with many of his troops. Unlike Jackson, Rosecrans never inspired any mythmakers. An interesting personage nevertheless, he lacked the existential drive so central to Jackson's appeal as a general.

Another "warrior priest" figure, this time on the Confederate side, was Bishop (and General) Leonidas Polk. Polk was a divisional commander under Bragg and then under Joe Johnston until he fell at Kennesaw Mountain during the Atlanta campaign. He was a rather blustery general who was not known as a particularly effective commander. Because of his peculiar status as a bishop who had chosen to fight as a general, however, he became something of a popular icon for some in Southern officialdom and was revered by some (not by all) as a martyr to the cause of Southern independence.

Unlike either Rosecrans or Polk, Jackson became very renowned for his military leadership, and his religious faith was part of that renown. As a "priestly warrior" figure, Jackson shows in this respect more kinship to literary or romance characters like those from medieval and Renaissance epic, and to historical figures like George S. Patton or Oliver Cromwell, than to contemporaries such as Rosecrans or Polk.

The mixing of war with religion is certainly not new. As any student of society knows, men and women have made war over religion, and religion about war, for millennia. War theorists have discussed religious aspects of war and religious theorists (usually moralists) have debated the justice of war.

One would expect, then, that generalship in war and religious conviction or membership would often coincide. Quite evident in the historical record are examples such as those of Joshua, King David, the several Crusader kings, and Oliver Cromwell. All these leaders, and many others, blend religious faith and military generalship.

Generals, or leaders, displaying religious elements fall into several categories. Among these, one of the more obvious is the "warrior-priest," that is, a priest, monk, or other cleric who joins a military or paramilitary organization. In this type, the piquancy is derived from the duality between the seeming man of peace and the visible man of war. Examples of the type include, from legend, Friar Tuck of the Robin Hood cycle; Bishop Jerónimo from the *Poema de Mio Cid*; and Bishop Turpin from the *Chanson de Roland*. From full-fledged fiction, an example would be the priest played by dynamic Scots actor Andrew Keir in the 1965 Hammer film *Dracula, Prince of Darkness* (one of the better Christopher Lee Dracula movies; the sequel to the classic *Horror of Dracula* [1958]).

A second category would be the "priestly warrior," that is, a soldier (in the present context an officer) who is not a cleric but who exercises quasi-clerical functions or who espouses religious aspirations or justifications for his enterprise. Stonewall Jackson would fit into this category, as, in a different way, would Oliver Cromwell and Gustavus Adolphus, as well as Robert E. Lee.

A third category, which fits more precisely leaders such as Cromwell and Gustavus Adolphus, is the military leader at the head of an avowedly religious war, or a war with expressed religious elements: thus, the Protestant vs. Catholic conflict (as with Cromwell and Gustavus Adolphus), or the Christian vs. infidel warmaking of the Crusades, or the revolt of the Maccabees. A soldier like Hernán Cortés, who espoused as his goal the Christianizing of the New World's inhabitants, would be at the edges of this classification, since, even if sincere, his expression of religious motivation was *de rigueur* for Spanish military expeditions into "heathen" territory.

Parallel to the religious warrior categories is the type of the inspired leader, often secular, but driven nonetheless by something like a religious fervor. Spartacus and William Wallace (or rather the Braveheart of legend and film) would be two cases of such fervent inspiration in military leaders that the zeal expressed seems nearly religious.

Further along the spectrum would lie anomalous leaders inspired by a heretical or eccentric religious vision which becomes melded with nationalist or ideological motives. Two examples, very different in time and character but not in strength of motivation, are Joan of Arc and John Brown. A third case would be the leader of the Tai-pings in 19th-century China.

Within the tradition of American military leadership, the religious element is more often muted than in, for example, the Spanish tradition until the 18th century, when the values of the Enlightenment began to supplant those of the Reconquista. Still, even in the U.S. tradition, religious generalship in our meaning of the term is not unknown. At the time of the Civil War, piety was much more commonly and openly expressed among the ranks than now. Even so, a leader like Stonewall Jackson was thought unusual in his strict observance of religious custom, as in his refusal to march or fight on Sunday.

The American cultural tradition does not always trust military men, even if it values their services. Neither does it trust the cleric, seeing in him the danger of the mountebank. Not Torquemada, but Elmer Gantry, is the popular caricature of the priest in America. The combination of the officer and the cleric is therefore doubly suspect, as if the two poles of social control had joined forces. The fear of fanaticism is not far below the surface, and Jackson was tagged with this stigma.

In this connection, an interesting dichotomy is observable between the contemporary attitude toward generals of the first type noted above, the warrior-priest, and the priestly warrior type as embodied in Stonewall Jackson. Leonidas Polk was an Episcopalian bishop who became a not particularly effective general for the South. He was not disparaged, though, for his connection to the church—to the contrary, this was thought an attribute lending soldierly sternness and *virtù* to his demeanor and conduct. In fact, his status as a leader in the church was used to excuse his blustery and overbearing demeanor—he was, after all, the leader of a flock. Contrast this attitude with the treatment accorded Jackson, who was routinely written and spoken of as a crackpot or a fanatic, as if his assumption of religious zeal were somehow inappropriate. General William S. Rosecrans suffered much the same treatment; perhaps his adherence to Catholicism contributed to his being seen as eccentric in a nation filled with Protestants. In any event, Rosecrans was a very religious man, as Wiley Sword explains in trying to understand his personality:

> Of much importance from a psychological perspective was Rosecrans's conversion to Roman Catholicism. Although raised by a staunch Methodist family, young Rosecrans had converted while a cadet at West Point.... Rosecrans had embraced his new faith with great enthusiasm, and he was fond of long discussions about religion. His espousal of the Catholic faith was an "intellectual decision," he conceded, based upon his experimental spirit and a need for "an authorized supernatural teacher." Not only did the devout Rosecrans carry a cross attached to his watch chain, but from his pocket he often withdrew "a dirty-looking string" of rosary beads— obviously well used, noted an observer. Later ... Rosecrans literally adopted a displaced Catholic priest, Father Patrick Treacy, who became his close friend, confessor, and unofficial adviser [Sword 6].

A mistrust of military men (and of government leaders) is not unique to the United States, nor is skepticism concerning the clergy. Still, it is a fact that in the European tradition the military, as an arm of the monarchy, was often identified through its legally constituted authority with the defense of the church. This nexus was especially notable in the history of Spain, where the Catholic Church and the monarchy functioned in an uneasy but legalized synergy during much of the period of conquest and colonization of the Americas.[1] Charles V and Philip II of Spain were both active promoters of Catholicism at home, in Europe, and in the Americas. One of their chief lieutenants, Hernán Cortés, rose from humble origins in the province of Extremadura to become the conqueror of Aztec Mexico and the subject of chronicles and epics. Like Patton and Fernán González, Cortés came to be associated with the epic motif of the battlefield vision. This association implicitly linked him with heroic figures from the Reconquista period like El Cid and Fernán González, who were also depicted as experiencing dreams and battlefield visions or apparitions involving the Spanish patron saint, Santiago de Compostela, and also other important Catholic figures like St. Peter.[2] Like Jackson, but in a very different context, Cortés, and, by extension, his master Charles V, were fitted into a national story promoting the religious and social imperatives of their respective cultures. Such treatment was also accorded the figures of Henry Havelock and Charles Gordon, who were eulogized and nearly sanctified within the context of Victorian British ideology.

Patton, on the other hand, suffered the effects of his vision of warfare, which was retrograde in the context of the mid–20th century, and most particularly at the end of World War II. His martial values fit uncomfortably into the vistas of reconciliation and cooperation between opposed ideologies like capitalism and communism. His quasi-religious view of warfare and of politics, one of struggle, sacrifice, and victory, was not that of a world soon ready to adopt the United Nations charter. Additionally, Patton was a victor in the war, while Havelock, Gordon, and Jackson were associated with defeat, or at least disaster, despite any victories personally linked to them. Unlike them, Patton was not glorified in compensation, as a sort of defense mechanism against defeatist feelings. So, his religious or spiritual pronouncements were seen as unseemly, somehow in bad taste, because the prayers of the Allies were clearly answered and supported; but the devoutness of Gordon or Jackson was seen as an element of their determination to battle against odds which were known with hindsight to have been overwhelming and inescapable.

Some of the warriors of God to be discussed in the book were both victor and glorified, notably Hernán Cortés, but in such cases (his most clearly), the ideological context of the society in which they lived was amenable to such glorification. Jackson was to be glorified most spectacularly by the remnants of the nation which he tried to defend, and although he would not have agreed with all the ideological stances of some of his hagiographers, his postwar image fell chiefly into their hands. His legend, and the legends of other religious generals and warrior-priests, will inform the central thrust of this book.

1

Pro Patria Mori ...

On May 10, 1863, Thomas Jonathan Jackson, aged 39, died from complications following surgery. He had been injured a week earlier, receiving three bullet wounds which necessitated the amputation of his left arm. His attending physician, Dr. Hunter Holmes McGuire, had performed the surgery and was optimistic about his recovery. But on May 8, an infection was discovered which McGuire diagnosed as pneumonia. An illness far too serious for the medicine of the time to treat other than symptomatically, pulmonary infection often led to death, and in light of Jackson's already weakened condition, the prognosis would have been bleak. On Sunday, May 10, his wife and infant daughter were at his bedside, along with some of his colleagues.

Near dusk, the man mumbled some unintelligible phrases and then, clearly but weakly, said, according to those present, "Let us cross over the river and rest under the shade of the trees." Those words were his final utterance.

The place of death was an improvised sickroom near present-day Thornton, Virginia (between Fredericksburg and Richmond). The man, Thomas J. Jackson, was by then much better known by his battlefield nickname, Stonewall. Until his fatal injury and illness, he had been one of the keystones in the Confederate States' military structure. A man of indomitable fighting spirit, he was neither universally liked nor well understood — in fact, he was not universally liked precisely because he was not well understood. "Humorless" and "grim" were some of the nicer adjectives applied to this complex man by his contemporaries. His subordinate and later his replacement as corps commander, Gen. Dick "Old Baldy" Ewell, called him "a crazy old fool" (until he saw the method in the madness).[3] His quartermaster, Joseph Harman, used much more profane expressions about him, which have not survived in verbatim form due to the prudery of the age.

But Stonewall Jackson found many friends and even more admirers when he began, against the odds, to win battles. And he kept on winning, in the process forging an image which was to become legendary.[4]

The Shenandoah Valley campaign in 1861 and 1862 was in large part responsible for his growing legend. This campaign is valued today as a prime example of doing more with less in war. Let one of Jackson's soldiers, present with him in the campaign, speak here, in a passage dealing with the Valley Campaign and its immediate aftermath near Richmond:

> From the time we left Swift Run Gap, about the first of May, we had marched hundreds of miles and fought seven general battles, viz.: McDowell, Front Royal, Winchester, Cross Keys, Port Republic, Cold Harbor and Malvern Hill, besides some smaller engagements and skirmishes, and had defeated and demoralized four separate armies, viz.: Milroy's, Banks', Fremont's and Shield's [sic]; had cleared the whole Valley of the enemy and assisted General Lee to defeat McClellan and banish the foe from before Richmond. We had remained in no camp over three days at one time until we reached Gordonsville; but had marched and fought the enemy, often marching all night and often through rain and mud, and never, during that time, did General Jackson have over twenty thousand men, and often not that. History does not record more brilliant campaigns within the short period of a little over two months than those of "Stonewall" Jackson [Casler 102].

Jackson became a folk figure for many of his men. This bespeaks qualities in the man that were not necessarily immediately apparent. Often thought of as stiff, stolid, and humorless, Jackson was not always or even primarily so. Particularly at home, in the privacy of his living room, he was surprisingly animated. He loved to dance and to bestow charming verbal endearments on his wife. He adored children and could be seen at Fredericksburg cavorting in a most un–Stonewall-like fashion with the little daughter of a friend of the army. His men must well have sensed something hidden in the man, as soldiers often do in their commanders. Casler mentions, for example, that "It got to be a common saying in the army, when any cheering was heard in camp or on the march, that it was either 'Jackson or a rabbit'" (Casler 92–94).[5] Casler also says that the common soldiers were very fond of Jackson, despite his sternness and drive:

> ... the soldiers loved him. Every time he would pass our brigade we would all commence cheering him, to see him raise his cap, show his high, bold forehead, and go dashing by in a gallop. No matter whether it was raining or snowing, the cap would be raised and kept off until he

had passed the whole line [Casler 92].

This combination of Jackson qualities is truly fascinating. His modesty and innate kindness, and, in seemingly total contrast, the almost Saxon ferocity with which he could advocate and pursue warfare against those who were, after all, his brothers, are key to understanding his legendary status. For most Southerners of his time, Jackson was a hero because of his fighting prowess, but he was even more admired for his Christian qualities. His Christian devotion was not, for religious writers of the period like R. L. Dabney and Moses Hoge, in opposition or contrast to his warmaking: quite the contrary, his warmaking under

Lt. Gen. Thomas J. "Stonewall" Jackson (1824–63) at Chancellorsville, 1863. (Courtesy Virginia Military Institute.)

the circumstances of the War Between the States was seen as his Christian duty: "His patriotism was a duty to God. His obedience to the State that called him to the field was made clear and plain to him, as obedience to God. All soldierly duty was rendered as a service to his God" (Smith, J. P., "Religious Character" 8). Jackson is not just another general in the large panoply of Civil War generals, and he is not just another religious general either. For many Southerners, Jackson was a very special hero.[6] And especially for those from Calvinist backgrounds, he was the avenging angel leading the soldiers of God.

What was different about Stonewall Jackson was the warrior side to the man, coupled with the more than flash of real genius— most especially if genius be defined as that singlemindedness that sees simple solutions to complex problems. Jackson's ability to perceive the most direct means of attacking the enemy's soft spot was testified to over and over again. Rev. Moses Hoge comments, for instance, that Jackson had "an almost intuitive insight into the plans of the enemy, and an immediate perception of the time to strike the most stunning blow, from the most unlooked for quarter" (Hoge and Kemper 12). Rev. Hoge adds to this that the general also had, and acted upon, "a conviction of the necessity of following every such blow with another, and more terrible, so as to make every success a victory, and every victory so complete as to compel the speedy termination of the war" (12). Added to this killer instinct was the peculiarly remorseless tenacity which this man of God was capable of displaying.

Jackson's apparent ruthlessness may seem difficult to accept or to explain from a modern perspective. Moderns might expect someone like Patton to be ruthless, for after all he was a conscious ideologist of warfare. One is not surprised to hear of remorseless killings from Quantrill, or Mosby, or Vo Nguyen Giap's regulars. But Jackson will either seem hypocritical, with his pronouncements of Christian faith on the one hand and his statements and acts of nearly wanton killing on the other, or like an unbalanced fanatic cut from John Brown's cloth. He was neither. Dabney provides an intriguing clue to his motivation. He narrates the story of Jackson's comments that the "brave" Federals should least of all be spared. When Col. John Mercer Patton (a great-uncle of George S. Patton Jr.) communicated the deaths of some brave Union soldiers and expressed his "regret" at this outcome, the general asked him why he regretted this. Patton then responded

> that they exhibited more vigor and courage than anything which had been attempted by any part of the Federal army; and that a natural sympathy with brave men led to the wish that, in the fortunes of the fight, their lives might have been saved.

To which Stonewall Jackson "drily remarked: 'No; shoot them all: *I* do not wish them to be brave'" (397).[7]

Rev. R.L. Dabney, who served as an aide to Jackson for a time, comments that Jackson's elliptical style masks much meaning. According to Dabney, Jackson

> meant to suggest reasonings which show that such sentiments of chivalrous forbearance [as expressed by Patton], though amiable, are erroneous. Courage in the prosecution of a wicked attempt does not relieve, but only aggravates, the danger to the innocent party assailed, and the guilt of the assailants. There is, then, a sense in which the most vigorous are the most worthy of death; and the interests of those who wage a just defence prompt them to visit retribution, first, upon those who are most dangerous [397–98].

Related to this attitude of Jackson's is, surely, his rejection of erstwhile friends in the military who had stayed with the Union. Elihu S. Riley cites an instance of this view of Jackson's:

Major Dwight, of the Federal Army, who had been captured in the battle of Winchester, remained a prisoner in that town. Finding that some of the Federal wounded needed some "required conveniences," says General Cooper of the Federal Army, the Major appealed to General Jackson, and in his appeal the Major told him there was an officer in the 2nd Massachusetts, "who is, I believe," said the Major, "an old friend of yours." "Friend of mine, sir?" replied Old Jack, *"he was, sir, once a friend of mine"* [Riley 88].

This peculiar form of religious righteousness may smack to some readers of the notorious Vietnam-era line about "destroying the village to save it"[8]— but it was clearly quite understandable to men of Dabney's and Jackson's background. In fact, the views expressed by Dabney about the Federals cast them as wayward sinners who must be reformed for their own good, much as heretics were "reformed" all too literally in *autos-da-fe*. In view of Dabney's and Jackson's Calvinist beliefs, such expressions of forced reformation are to be expected. These concepts also have a long tradition in Catholicism, forming an important element in the debates about just war during the Crusades. Jonathan Riley-Smith addresses this topic in "Crusading as an Act of Love," where he discusses the 12th-century justifications of the Crusades in terms of love for fellow Christians, for example those living in Muslim-occupied lands (184–85), and also in terms of love for the infidels themselves, who must be reformed.

The just war debate relies heavily on St. Augustine. In several of his works, he established that "just violence required right intention on the part of the imposers of force" (Riley-Smith 185). In terms that foreshadow Reverend Dabney, Augustine discussed violence and warmaking for the purposes of correction:

> many noble and saintly men had in the past inflicted death as a punishment for sins. Those put to death had suffered no injury from it; rather, they were already being injured by their sins… [Riley-Smith 185].

Frederick H. Russell writes that "[t]he die for the medieval just war was cast by St Augustine" (16). Russell summarizes Augustine's general approach to the question of just war:

> Frequent reference to the Old and New Testaments provided Augustine with a means of defeating the doctrinaire pacifism of the Manichean heresy and also with guidance to contemporary Christians who still harbored suspicion of war and military service. Augustine saw in Moses' wars a just and righteous retribution, and compared the punishment of unwilling souls to that dealt a child by a loving father. The just warrior restrained sinners from evil, thus acting against their will but in their own best inter-

est.... Punishment of evil-doers that prevented them from doing further wrong when administered without being moved by revenge or taking pleasure in suffering was an act of love [Russell 16–17].

So, Jackson could be seen in Augustinian terms as a just warrior bringing malefactors—northern invaders—to his side of the fence of righteousness. Beginning most especially with the Valley Campaign, and despite a brief lapse in performance during the Seven Days battles before Richmond, Jackson was to become Robert E. Lee's most valued and trusted subordinate. Although their style of command and their demeanor differed sharply, they formed a relationship of intuitive communication and deep trust which, though not unique in the history of warfare, is relatively rare.

Robert E. Lee, the great commander of the Army of Northern Virginia, had a very different public image from Jackson's.[9] Lee fits rather neatly into Edward Tabor Linenthal's category of the chevalier warrior, the "man on horseback" with knightly characteristics (Linenthal Ch. 1). Even Lee's horse, Traveller, came to be associated with him in knightly fashion, becoming himself a part of Southern folklore, as Marshall Fishwick explains, calling Traveller "Virginia's Bucephalus": "[T]he charger was under constant fire, but he was never scratched. Johnny Rebs told tales about both the man and the horse around their campfires, and much of Traveller's tail was tweaked out by soldiers and souvenir hunters" (Fishwick 153).

Lee was known to his soldiers as a generous, humble man who lived by principle. Their loyalty to him was based essentially on their adoration of him as a father-figure, thus the sobriquet "Marse Robert" and the protectiveness displayed by the men who restrained him from attacking the enemy personally at Spotsylvania by physically holding Traveller back and by refusing to attack until Lee went to the rear. These are the actions of sons restraining a father from a dangerous course of action. The reverse side of the coin was the early nickname for Lee, Granny Lee, an implicit recognition of his status as elder, but also a cross-generic insult pointing to the military qualities he was thought not to have: decisiveness, boldness, and innovation.

Lee was also perceived as a gentleman, a man of nice manners and elegant carriage. And, to complete the knightly portrait, he was universally characterized as very handsome and well-built. His politeness, integrity, and physical bearing gradually made him for many Southerners, and for Northerners as well, the embodiment of Southern cavalier culture and the standard-bearer of the Confederate cause. (Mrs. Roger A. Pryor, in her *Reminiscences of Peace and War*, actually referred to him as "our beloved commander, our Bayard *sans peur et sans reproche*" [205].)[10] Lee's successes and failures in battles were bellwethers of Confederate fortunes, and after his death in 1870 he became central to Lost Cause ideology.

The reasons for Jackson's fame were generally different from those for Lee's. In common with Lee's image was Jackson's reputation for boldness and aggressiveness as a campaigner. But there the images start to diverge. Where Lee was graceful, Jackson was ungainly. Where Lee was courtly and well-spoken, Jackson was often brusque and inarticulate.

These qualities in Jackson were quite apparent to his men. One sketch of Jackson, offered by Confederate Captain John E. Dooley in his *War Journal*, compares him to General Lee. Dooley provides a soldier's perspective on the contrast between the two men, in his description of the troops' reactions to the scene "when the generals pass by":

> It may be either Gen. Jackson or 'Uncle Robert', as the boys call Genl. Lee. If the latter, he is riding, perhaps, with a few aides, dressed in a neat grey uniform, mounted upon a gently moving charger [note the chivalric imagery]. By the plain grey uniform you would simply recognize him as a general. His hair and beard turning grey; his mildly beaming face, large black eyes recognizing all around him; his mouth firmly but pleasingly set, and his whole figure expressing gentleness, dignity, and command. As he passes the admiring throngs they doff their warworn hats and greet his presence with reiterated shouts and most enthusiastic. He answers each burst with a placid smile and with a dignified but most courteous bend of his noble head [...].
>
> Should the attraction of the excited soldiery prove to be Stonewall Jackson, it may be that he passes by at full speed, nearly always in a canter and often covered with dust so thickly as almost to be unrecognizable. Cheer after cheer rings after him, which he acknowledges from time to time by doffing his forage cap or nodding kindly from right to left. But he is glad to be rid of the turmoil and cheering, and often puts spurs to his charger and is soon hidden in clouds of dust [Dooley 62–63].

Capt. Charles M. Blackford also offered an eyewitness comparison between Lee and Jackson, near Richmond in 1862, in a letter dated July 13th. He observed Lee, Jackson, and President Davis together outside the president's house:

> Lee was elegantly dressed in full uniform.... The highest type of the Cavalier class.... Jackson ... was a typical Roundhead. He was poorly dressed, ... though his clothes were made of good material. His cap was very indifferent and pulled down over one eye, much stained by weather and without insignia. His coat was closely buttoned up to his chin and had upon the collar the stars and wreath of a general. His shoulders were

stooped…, and his coat showed signs of much exposure to the weather…. His face, in repose, is not handsome or agreeable and he would be passed by anyone without a second look, though anyone could see determination and will in his face by the most casual glance — much I would say to fear but not to love [Blackford 86].

Other Confederate commanders were not always so prominent in the public mind. At different points in the war, James Longstreet, Joe Johnston, P. G. T. Beauregard, John Bell Hood, and Braxton Bragg were well-known to Southern newspaper readers. But the only commander who attained and kept anything like the status accorded to Lee was Thomas J. "Stonewall" Jackson.

If Lee seemed to epitomize for Southerners of his generation the gentleman-soldier, Jackson did not at first sight appear to incarnate anything soldierly. The Confederate command was very skeptical at first, but their opinion was to change. An apt sketch of their early perspective is provided by Randolph Harrison McKim, a soldier in the Army of Northern Virginia, who refers to the loyalty of Jackson's men to their commander and then provides an amusing picture of the views of the Confederate establishment toward Jackson:

> From the hour when, at the battle of Manassas, General Bee pointed to him and cried to his wavering South Carolinians, "There stands Jackson, like a stone wall!" the rank and file of the army gave him their complete confidence, and were ready to follow wherever he led, and to attempt whatever he commanded. Not so the authorities at Richmond. Not so all the officers of high rank in the field. Generals who had known him at West Point and remembered that his scholastic rank was low, and that only by patient plodding could he keep up with his class, found it difficult to believe that Jackson could be a brilliant soldier. Those also who had known him as the quiet and by no means inspiring professor at the Virginia Military Institute felt the same scepticism. They acknowledged his steadfast courage and his unflinching resolution. Those qualities had been displayed by him in the Mexican War … and now again at Manassas and at Kernstown, but his critics said, first, that he was indeed the man to lead a forlorn hope into the jaws of death, but had not the capacity to command a brigade; and when he had disproved this in battle, they said that he could fight a brigade under the eye of a capable superior officer, but could never fill an independent command, which required strategy and judgment. It will be remembered that, owing to the representations of General Loring [a disgruntled Jackson subordinate], in the winter of 1861, the Richmond authorities so hampered and interfered with Jackson that he wrote his resignation, resolving to enter the ranks as a private soldier, and that it was only with great difficulty he was induced to withdraw it. The prejudice he encountered in high quarters was such that at each step forward that he made

toward military greatness his detractors had fresh objections to make to his further advancement. "He might do to command a brigade, but not a division." Next, "Well, he had done pretty well as a division commander, but could never handle an army independently." It was not till after the brilliant series of victories which he won in the valley in 1862 that the voice of detraction was silenced. And even after that at Malvern Hill, when Jackson ordered a charge, General Whiting was heard to exclaim, "Great God! Won't some ranking officer come, and save us from this fool!" He came! [McKim 90–92].

Although Jackson had an impressive record in the Mexican War, having displayed flashes of the initiative which was to become his hallmark in an artillery attack in Mexico City, his career since the war had been, like Lee's, and like those of other officers like Grant and Sherman, disappointing. Of these officers, only Lee had stayed in the army until the outbreak of the Civil War. Grant had been forced out as a result of financial problems and drinking. Sherman had left the service to pursue private business interests. Jackson had resigned after a disastrous posting at Fort Meade (in Florida) and had taken a position as professor at VMI.

Neither Jackson nor Grant was suited for non-military work, Grant especially not; but Jackson's lack of suitability was somewhat disguised by the fact of his professorship in a military academy. Jackson was at best an indifferent teacher; he did not exactly ignite the classroom because of his insistence on sticking to one approach for teaching, basically a by-the-book rote technique. He did apply himself rigorously to his work, preparing long hours for his classes. Like Grant, Jackson was nothing if not determined and tenacious. With hindsight, one can see in both men's peacetime careers the reasons for their future success. If Grant was a failure in peacetime, it was not for want of trying; in fact, his very doggedness and resoluteness got in his way by keeping him in lines of work for which he was not suited. But these very qualities would later, in the right setting, prove his greatest assets in winning the war. Jackson, similarly, was insistently honest and forcefully industrious, and these qualities would later become central to his success as a commander.

When the Civil War began, however, Jackson was merely another local commander of little importance. His western command, in the Shenandoah Valley, was virtually ignored by Richmond. The focus was on the Washington-to-Richmond corridor, where the first important battle of the war was fought at Manassas or Bull Run.[11] "Because the threat to Richmond posed by Union Gen. Irvin McDowell's troops was perceived as very real, Jackson's army was summoned from the Valley and went into the Manassas battle. At Henry House Hill, Jackson was given the sobriquet that would stay with him throughout his career and after his death. Although some controversy has persisted over the exact intent of the nickname Stonewall, some maintaining that General Barnard Bee (the name's originator) actually applied the tag to Jackson out of frustration at his inactivity, most authorities now agree that the nickname was intended as a compliment to Jackson's steadfastness during the battle (Robertson, *Stonewall Jackson* 835–36).

Jackson himself always averred that the name should apply to the brigade and not to him. This preference is highlighted in Ron Maxwell's *Gods and Generals* (2003), when Jim Lewis (Frankie Faison) comes to apply for a position as Jackson's cook, after the Battle of First Manassas.[12] (The scene was shot at the Stonewall Jackson Headquarters museum, the actual house at 415 N. Braddock St. in Winchester, where Jackson spent the winter of 1861–62. The house once belonged to Col. William Tillman Moore, an ancestor of actress Mary Tyler Moore. The colonel was wounded at Manassas and lent the house to Jackson as a headquarters while he recuperated.) After Jackson asks him, in the course of a desultory introduction, if he knows about the names his men call him (Lewis had said offhandedly about himself that people call him all sorts of things), Lewis mentions "Stonewall." Jackson replies rather solemnly that "That name properly belongs to the First Virginia Brigade, not to me. They were the ones earned it." Laura Morrison Brown, Jackson's sister-in-law (she was his wife Anna's younger sister), wrote that Anna was not particularly enamored of the epithet: "I remember this name was at first distasteful to Mrs. Jackson; she said it was not appropriate to his gentle nature; but she finally accepted it as a badge of honor" (Brown 24).

In any case, by the time Jackson had completed his famous Valley campaign, he had acquired the fame with his men of a determined and brilliant fighter who shared in their hardships.[13] At the beginning of the campaign, he was disparaged by most of the men in his ranks. Allen Tate writes of an example of his men's lack of confidence in him, an attitude which soon began to change. Jackson ordered a march to the west from Winchester to Romney (now in West Virginia). At the outset (New Year's Day 1862) the temperate weather turned much worse, and the men began to suffer from the cold. They did not understand the reasons for the march and did not credit Jackson with much strategic sense (or sense of any kind), so their morale worsened.[14] On one cold morning, writes Tate,

> some members of the Stonewall Brigade, rising, shook off the blanket of snow that had thoughtfully come down upon them while they slept. They cursed the leader that had let them suffer. They said he was mad. The whole

expedition was insane. Then they saw a not unfamiliar figure get up and shake off his snow-blanket; the figure approached them. He called out a pleasant "Good morning!" He had been lying only a few feet away and he had heard them [107].

Tate drives home the moral of the little story: "What kind of man was General Jackson? He had not uttered a word of sympathy for their suffering. He had issued harsh and peremptory orders. But he suffered exactly as they did" [107–08].

Jackson began to gain his men's trust as his little army started to win victories, tying down much larger Federal forces. Tate summarizes the midpoint of the campaign:

> In the fourteen days from May 19th to June 1st, the Valley Army of 17,000 men had marched one hundred and seventy miles. It had put to flight an enemy of 12,500 and, in the whole theatre of war, had paralyzed the activity of 170,000. It had threatened the North with invasion. It had captured property amounting to three hundred thousand dollars, 3,000 prisoners, and 9,000 rifles. At last, surrounded by 60,000 men, it had brought off a large convoy without the loss of a single horse and wagon. It had achieved all this with the loss of only 600 officers and men [154–55].

More successes were to come, and by the end of the campaign, Jackson's men were fiercely devoted to their commander and would endure any hardship to follow him. Anna Jackson, commenting on Jackson's soldiers, provides as well one perspective from the North:

> From the rapidity of his forced marches, Jackson's soldiers were sometimes called his "foot-cavalry." They sometimes marched twenty-five, thirty, and even thirty-five miles a day! A Northern writer said that "Jackson moved infantry with the celerity of cavalry. His men said he always marched at 'early dawn,' except when *he started the night before;* but despite all these 'hardships, fatigues, and dangers,' says one of the 'foot-cavalry,' 'a more cheerful, genial, jolly set could not be found than were these men in gray'" [Jackson 284].

So, Jackson had attained to the kind of unquestioning loyalty granted also to Lee. The methods by which Jackson reached this point vary in some important respects from those of Lee, however. Jackson was generally unforgiving of insubordination, cowardice, desertion, and unwillingness to fight or march, as well as of poor judgment by his lieutenants (but not of ignorance on the part of green troops). He refused furloughs even for extreme family circumstances. He was demanding to an almost inhuman degree of his troops' stamina.[15] Lee could be stern to the point of enforcing summary discipline, but he maintained an image of kindliness despite his recourse to such measures. Jackson was Lee's mirror-image in this general respect.[16] His sternness notwithstanding, Jackson became the object of much affection for many of his men (in much the same way as the combination of sternness and of admiration by common soldiers under one's command was a prominent feature of Gen. George S. Patton's career). A characteristic testimonial is found in one of Capt. Ujanirtus Allen's letters from the lower Valley,[17] on August 15, 1862, just before the Antietam battle of September 17:

> Genl Jackson is a strict presbiterian. My dear he is one of the greatest men living. So brave so pleasant in his intercourse and kind to the soldiers. He is the idol of the soldiers. You never hear a word against him unless, by chance some weary fellow will say that he is marched too hard; but he will invariably add, "I reckon old Stonewall knows what is best, don't think he would march us so hard unless it was necessary." Gen'l Ewell is as brave as the bravest, but is one of these crabed dispeptic kind of fellows. The boys all praise him for his bravery, but you never hear them whiling away the hours around the camp fire with jokes and stories of him as they do of Jackson [Allen 145].

One of Jackson's officers noted the odd similarity of Jackson's authority to Lee's:

> "General Lee is the handsomest person I ever saw.... This is not the case with Jackson. He is ever monosyllabic and receives and delivers orders as if the bearer of a conduct pipe from one ear to the other. There is a magnetism in Jackson, but it is not personal ... no one could love the man for himself. He seems to be cut off from his fellow men and to commune with his own spirit only, or with spirits of which we know not. Yet the men are almost as enthusiastic over him as over Lee" [Davis, B., *They Called Him Stonewall* 12].

Davis provides as well a more detailed physical description of Stonewall:

> Today he wore, as he had since anyone could remember, the old coat of a major, a grimy, dusty, threadbare and single-breasted survivor of the Mexican War, permanently wrinkled into the General's inelegant mold by its sixteen years of service. The most urbane of his officers could describe the General's cap only as "mangy." Now, as ever, it rode far down his nose, the visor all but touching the beard. The coat was stained with the rusty watermarks of years; everything about him seemed in disrepair. So awkwardly did he crouch on his fence that he created the impression that, if he should fall, he might clatter to earth in three or four sections [Davis, B., *They Called Him Stonewall* 10].[18]

What must have struck several observers as odd about Jackson was the machine-like or puppetlike nature of the man. Even the descriptions of his demeanor seem to recall a doll-like quality, particularly the glassiness of the blue eyes and the squeakiness of the voice. An unlikely hero indeed, Jackson certainly did not match with the heroic manliness of Lee or of cavalry star Jeb Stuart. As John W. Schildt notes, "Stuart may have been more dashing, but Jackson was the one with whom the rank and file of the people and the military could most easily identify" (79). John Esten Cooke, the Virginia novelist who also served in Jackson's campaigns, nonetheless evaluated him as heroic after his own peculiar fashion:

> I hate the courtier, and the hero-worshipper, in all his ways....
> And yet I have the faculty of reverence for real worth, largely developed. I never worshipped [a] hero yet — but I take my hat off and bow low to a great and noble soul like Jackson. He is a true "soldier of the Cross" no less than the valiant leader of our armies — and in his person centre the most conspicuous virtues of the patriot and the Christian. They speak of his eccentricities, his awkwardness, his shy odd ways, and many singularities. Let these be granted. There is beneath all this in the soul of the man, a grandeur and nobility, a childlike purity and gracious sweetness, mingled with the indomitable will, which make him what I call him — a real hero [Cooke 49–50].

Like Ulysses S. Grant, Jackson is often presented as "unheroic" in appearance. Repeatedly, he is described as not displaying an aspect proper to a soldier of his importance. With both generals, a motif of near-invisibility is recurrent. A good example regarding Jackson can be found in the work of that purveyor of imagery, poet and southern Agrarian ideologist Allen Tate:

> Early Monday morning, June 23rd, Jackson and his staff-officer rode through the streets of Richmond. *The citizens they passed in the streets gave them no attention whatever.* Jackson, the mysterious hero who went into battle praying, was far away in the Shenandoah. What a figure he must be! There must be something incomparably grand in his presence, the very figure of martial spirit! [164].[19]

Grant experienced directly an instance of his own invisibility. Gene Smith recounts Grant's arrival in Washington on March 8, 1864, to receive his commission as lieutenant general:

> At the desk [of Willard's Hotel] the soon-to-be Lieutenant General Commanding the Armies of the United States asked for accommodations *and was taken for nobody in particular.* The clerk assigned him an upstairs

Confederate monument, 1867, St. David's Episcopal Church, Cheraw, S.C. Written on the monument: "They have crossed over the river and they rest in the shade of the trees." (Photograph by author.)

> room and glanced at the name on the register only when Grant had turned to go. The clerk read "U. S. Grant and son, Galena, Illinois" and called him back to assign the best suite in the house, Parlor A [Smith, G., *Lee and Grant* 173–74].

Grant is not presented as comical in his aspect, as is Jackson; he is typically described in his drabness as grayly epitomizing a rather scruffy Midwesterner: "'an ordinary scrubby-looking man with a slightly seedy look.'" Grant, Earle comments, was "neither a god nor an uncle but a man of terrifying simplicity, so simple that he had to win in the end" (Earle 172). Jackson is similar in his shabbiness,[20] though one might not think of "seedy" (an adjective sometimes applied to Grant) as a quality of his, because it implies a disreputable nature, reminding one of pasts such as Grant's with its drunkenness and business failures. And Jackson is similar as well to Grant in his simplicity — but his is the simplicity of a Puritan warrior.

In his Virginia Puritanism, Jackson continues a tradition of American warmaking. In his study of the image of the warrior in American cul-

ture, Edward Tabor Linenthal stresses the importance of the military heritage in our national background. He traces much of this heritage to a
"western ideology" in which "history is in some sense both 'war' and the
stage on which cosmic conflict is carried out" (Linenthal 1). For Linenthal, the ideology in question "was part of our Puritan heritage" and "transformed most American wars into crusades" (1). Much of the crusade
imagery is directly traceable in turn to the sermons of the Puritans, which

> set the stage for the spiritual battle between Christ and Satan, a battle
> which takes place in the soul. Life was pictured as a pilgrimage and a bat-
> tle; the soul was like a soldier in battle. The preacher "was above all the
> leader of a crusade and holy war," depicting the image of a soldier fight-
> ing for Christ [Linenthal 1].

Robert E. Lee assuredly did not see the Civil War as a crusade in any
traditionally religious sense. Jackson most certainly did. This basic
difference in perspective accounts for the divergence in the military thinking of the two men in an early stage of the war. Lee, as Jackson's superior
(he was chief of staff in Richmond), stressed the need to avoid invading
Maryland if not absolutely necessary (Robertson, *Stonewall Jackson* 234).
Jackson replied that the circumstances required such actions. Robertson
comments:

> One might say that in this early period of the war Jackson saw the future
> more clearly than did Confederate authorities…. This emerging warrior
> was not concerned with the historical principles underlying the … conflict.
> Southern "rights" occupied none of his attention…. Jackson's simple per-
> spective was that Virginia and the South were fighting to maintain an inde-
> pendence against an enemy determined to take it away [234].

So, for Stonewall Jackson, drastic measures were justified. This was
Jackson's famous "'black flag' policy." As Jackson told his wife's brother-
in-law,

> "I … see in this war, if the North triumph, a dissolution of the bonds of
> all society … it is the prelude to anarchy, infidelity, and the ultimate loss
> of free responsible government on this continent…. I always thought we
> ought to meet the Federal invaders on the outer verge of just right and
> defence, and raise at once the black flag, viz., 'No quarter to the violators
> of our homes and firesides!'" [Robertson, *Stonewall Jackson* 234].

According to Jackson, "'The Bible is full of such wars' … 'and it is the only
policy that would bring the North to its senses'" (Robertson, *Stonewall
Jackson* 234). Edward A. Pollard, a prominent Richmond journalist and

Southern "Lost Cause" explicator,[21] wrote in his *Lee and His Lieutenants* that:

> These were not the utterances of a hard heart, or the indication of a cruel disposition. They were nothing more than the expression of the severe and supreme idea of war. Of all high Confederate commanders [note the careful exclusion of Union commanders such as Sherman and Grant], Gen. Jackson appears to have been most convinced of the necessity of fierce and relentless war. He realized fully that it was quite vain to court the enemy with shows of magnanimity, and that the only way to deal with a horde of invaders was by examples of terrour and lessons of blood. Yet no one was more attentive to the proper courtesies of war, and in no breast bared to the conflict resided a finer spirit of humanity. Judgment with him took precedence of the sensibilities, and the commands of necessity were broadly translated into the lessons of duty [Pollard 227].

On the eve of the battle of First Manassas, Jackson is seen praying "hours before dawn." Although this is Sunday and his wife's birthday, Robertson observes that "Jackson would *wield the sword of God* against the infidel who would desecrate his sacred homeland" (259).

Lee and Jackson formed a nearly symbiotic pair, akin to, and often likened to, Grant and Sherman. Of the two pairs, the Confederate one offers more contrast in social terms than does the Union one, which was chiefly a contrast in personalities between the stolid Grant and the mercurial Sherman. Lee and Jackson differ not only in personality but also in social class and moral outlook. The two were complementary in several ways. Lee was a "Cavalier" from tidewater Virginia, a descendant of Lees, Carters, and Custises; Jackson was Scots-Irish, a descendant of immigrants to the mountainous regions of western Virginia. Lee was Episcopalian, and a somewhat reluctant observant; Jackson struggled with his faith before becoming a devout Presbyterian, returning, as did Lee, to his roots: Lee to the Anglican, upper-class tradition, with its emphasis on form and, in its later versions, on reform and social service; Jackson to the Calvinist, evangelical strain of Protestantism.[22]

As Lee's determined and dauntless star lieutenant, Jackson gained fame which would lend to, and in fact entailed, his presentation as an epic hero. Note, for example, the parallel drawn between Jackson and a famous hero of legend, by John Warwick Daniel, in 1868. The reference was to the last words uttered by Jackson, "Let us cross over the river and rest under the shade of the trees":

> How like were his to the dying words of Arthur, the blameless King, as the Poet Laureate [Tennyson] has rendered them: "I am going a long

way / To the Island valley of Avilion, / Where falls not hail, or rain, or any snow, / Nor ever wind blows loudly; but it lies / Deep meadowed, happy, fair with orchard lawns / And bowery hollows crowned with summer sea, / Where I will heal me of my grievous wound" [Daniel, J. W., *Character* 61].

But matters were not always so for Stonewall Jackson. As an instructor at VMI, Jackson, out of his element in the classroom, was subjected to ridicule and taxed with student indifference. Krick summarizes his situation thus:

> His rigidity ... made the ... cadets dislike him. They called him Square Box, a derisive tribute to his imposing boot size, and at times would sneak into his classroom to draw an immense foot on the chalkboard [Krick 60].

A cadet composed a comical poem about Jackson: "'Great Lord Almighty, what a wonder,/Major Jackson, Hell & Thunder'" (Krick 60). These elements combined amount to a mock-epic treatment of Jackson as a sort of Lt. Kije, a useless functionary devoid of imagination.[23]

Jackson's fortunes as epic hero were slow to change. Even when he became commander at Harpers Ferry early in the war, his subordinates and colleagues viewed him as eccentric and foolish, certainly not as heroic. For example, Capt. William T. Poague, in his *Gunner with Stonewall*, presents the men's initial frustration with Jackson's hard-driving and secretive leadership, and includes a specific anecdote about an officer who later changed his opinion of the general. The context is the early march to Romney, Virginia (now in West Virginia), during the Shenandoah Valley campaign:

> In all the war I never had a similar experience — never endured such physical and mental suffering as on this trip. The expedition seemed to everybody to be a dismal failure. Our confidence in our leader was sorely tried. Loring's part of the army was in a state of semi-mutiny, and Jackson was hissed and hooted at as he passed them. This I had from a friend in the Georgia regiment who teased me a great deal about the "crazy general from Lexington."
> The next time I met him — Captain E. P. Howell of Atlanta — he was a most enthusiastic admirer of "the great 'Stonewall'" [Poague 18].

Only with the Manassas battle, where he acquired his nickname, and then with the Valley campaign, did his image become that of a heroic figure in the Confederate epic. For example, John Opie, a cavalryman who served under Jackson (and Lee and Stuart), and who was not chary of his criticisms of commanders, including Jackson when warranted, wrote of Jackson:

Military historians have not rendered unto Jackson the things that are Jackson's; they have not accorded to him the rank upon the roll of military commanders to which his genius and achievements justly entitle him. No history has yet been written [as of 1899] which fully recounts his deeds.... The men who composed the Army of Northern Virginia, and their gallant adversaries who constituted the Army of the Potomac, considered him the genius and master spirit of the war. On many different occasions, while the war was in progress, Federal soldiers said to me, "Give us Jackson, and we will whip you."

Future historians will do justice to his genius, and will rank him with that quartet of the greatest of great men — Napoleon, Hannibal, Caesar and Frederick — with whom, when we consider his limited resources, he ranks as equal in war. The Federal Generals Banks, Shields, Milroy, McDowell, Fremont, Pope, Burnside, McClellan and Hooker will be unwilling but everlasting witnesses to his unconquerable genius.

His Valley campaign has never been surpassed in the annals of war. For conception and execution it is not equaled by the Silesian campaign of Frederick, or the Italian campaign of the young Napoleon.... His subsequent rear attack and defeat of Pope, at the Second Manassas, is unparalleled in war, for both audacity and success [139–40].

Jackson was to become, in the tradition of epic heroes, the subject of a poem, later set to music. This poem was well-known in the Confederacy and, with music, became a sort of anthem for the Stonewall Brigade, as well as a song honoring Jackson. The poem was called "Stonewall Jackson's Way":

> Come, stack arms, men; pile on the rails;
> Stir up the camp-fire bright!
> No growling if the canteen fails:
> We'll make a roaring night.
> Here Shenandoah brawls along,
> There burly Blue Ridge echoes strong,
> To swell the Brigade's rousing song,
> Of Stonewall Jackson's Way.
> We see him now — that queer slouched hat,
> Cocked o'er his eye askew;
> The shrewd dry smile; the speech so pat,
> So calm, so blunt, so true!
> The "Blue-light Elder" knows 'em well:
> Says he, "That's Banks; he's fond of shell."[24]
> Lord save his soul! we'll give him —" Well,
> That's Stonewall Jackson's Way.
> Silence! Ground arms! Kneel all! Caps off!

Ole Massa's going to pray.
Strangle the fool that dares to scoff:
Attention!— it's his way.
Appealing from his native sod,
In forma pauperis to God, —
"Lay bare Thine arm! Stretch forth Thy rod:
Amen!"— That's Stonewall's Way.
He's in the saddle now. Fall in!
Steady! the whole Brigade.
Hill's at the ford, cut off; we'll win
His way out, ball and blade.
What matter if our shoes are worn?
What matter if our feet are torn?
Quick step! we're with him before morn;
That's Stonewall Jackson's Way.
The sun's bright lances rout the mists
Of morning; and By George!
Here's Longstreet, struggling in the lists,
Hem'd in an ugly gorge.
Pope and his Dutchmen![25]— whipped before.
"Bay'nets and grape!" hear Stonewall roar.
Charge, Stuart! Pay off Ashby's score,[26]
In Stonewall Jackson's Way.
Ah, Maiden! wait, and watch, and yearn,
For news of Stonewall's band.
Ah, Widow! read, with eyes that burn,
That ring upon thy hand.
Ah, Wife! sew on, pray on, hope on!
Thy life shall not be all forlorn.
The foe had better ne'er been born
That gets in Stonewall's Way [Palmer].

Commenting on the poem in his edition of *Outlines from the Outpost* by John Esten Cooke, Richard Harwell observes that the perceptive Cooke was not taken in by the fiction, not unknown to authors of epic poetry, that the poem was the creation of an anonymous soldier (thus representing the *vox populi*), and that it was "found" on the battlefield:

"Stonewall Jackson's Way" was written by John Williamson Palmer within the sound of the firing at Antietam. Dated "Martinsburg [now part of West Virginia, but near the Antietam battlefield in Maryland], Sept. 13th, 1862," it was first printed in Baltimore with its origin fictitiously noted, as indicated by Cooke's somewhat skeptical mention that "it was found on the body of a sergeant of the Old Stonewall Brigade [Cooke writes "found they say 'on the body'"]." Palmer was a Southern correspondent for *The New York Times* at the beginning of the war and later wrote for *The New York Tribune* but finished his wartime career in the Confederate Army as a member of General John C. Breckinridge's staff. "Stonewall Jackson's Way" was widely reprinted in Confederate periodicals. It was issued as sheet music in Richmond in 1863 by J. W. Randolph [Cooke 56n2].

After his death and the end of the war, Jackson's myth became, so to speak, set in stone. His legend soon became part of the postwar southern Lost Cause mythology. But he also became part of the national epic for Southerners and for all Americans. He was favorably viewed even in the North at the time of his death: "'In two years [of war], he has made his name familiar in every civilized land ... as a general of rare skill, resource, and energy. He never ... lost the fervor of his piety, or remitted his Christian duties. We think of him now as a noble-minded gentleman, a rare and eminent Christian'" (McCorkle 29). His status as a figure in the national epic is not that of a leading star like Lincoln or Lee, but he is there nonetheless, and his image has been very much present for actual leaders like George S. Patton, who greatly admired him (Nye 89) and who was wont to compare his relationship with his friend Dwight Eisenhower, when they were beginning their army careers, to the relationship between Lee and Jackson:

> Despite the difference in age, service, and experience — Patton was from the West Point class of 1908, Eisenhower the class of 1915 — Patton always regarded the younger man as his future superior in war. Often, talking in his jocular manner, Patton would tell of the days when they would run the next war. "Ike, you will be the Lee of the next war, and I will be your Jackson" [Eisenhower 332].

(Little did Patton know of the irony within his prophecy: not only would Ike lead the Allied forces, with Patton as his most forceful battlefield commander, but Patton, like Jackson, would die adventitiously.) Besides such examples of reverence by actual military men, the treatment of Jackson as epic hero can be seen in various examples of narrative fiction, though only rarely in film, as well as in poetry, songs, and ballads.[27]

Jackson's nickname or heroic epithet, Stonewall, was taken to mean that Jackson was steadfast, determined, and fearless and hard in battle — an immovable object, as it were, when on defense.[28] As noted earlier, Jackson always claimed that the tag was applicable to the eponymous brigade rather than to him personally. Jackson's attending physician during his final days, the young Dr. Hunter Holmes McGuire, noted the general's concern for his soldiers and his preference of the nickname for the brigade:

> By eight o'clock, Sunday night [the day after his wounding], the pain in his side had disappeared, and in all respects he seemed to be doing well. He inquired minutely about the battle [Chancellorsville], and the different troops engaged, and his face would light up with enthusiasm and interest, when told how this brigade acted, or that officer displayed conspicuous courage, and his head gave the peculiar shake from side to side, and he uttered his usual "good, good," with unwonted energy, when the gallant behaviour of the "Stonewall Brigade" was alluded to. He said, "The men of that brigade will be, some day, proud to say to their children, 'I was one of the Stonewall Brigade.'" He disclaimed any right of his own to the name Stonewall. "It belongs to the Brigade and not to me" [McGuire, H. H., M. D., "Last Wound" 407–08].

Historian Robert K. Krick has observed that the nickname as well as his deeds were important to Jackson's image (Krick 62).

The epithet or heroic tag applied to Jackson also contained within it one of the more important facets of the character of the epic hero. This is *sapientia*, one of the qualities in the topos *sapientia et fortitudo*. These qualities are characterized by Francisco López Estrada in his study of the *Poema de Mio Cid* as "las dos manifestaciones propias del héroe completo en la literatura europea [the two manifestations belonging to the complete hero in European literature]" (López Estrada 117).

St. Isidore of Seville (599–636)[29] listed fortitude as one of four virtues associated with "living well." His formulation began with prudence: "Ethicam Socrates primus ad corrigendos conponendosque mores instituit, atque omne studium eius ad bene vivendi disputationem perduxit, dividens eam in quattuor virtutibus animae, id est prudentiam, iustitiam, fortitudinem, temperantiam" (Isidore II.xxiv.5). As Josef Pieper notes in his *Prudence*, the virtue of Prudence, for theologians such as St. Thomas Aquinas, forms the root of the other important virtues such as Wisdom (13–22): "Prudence *'informs'* the other virtues; it confers upon them the form of their inner essence"; and "Prudence is the *'measure'* of justice, of fortitude, of temperance" (19, 18). Thus, Aquinas might say,

> every sin is opposed to prudence. Injustice, cowardice, intemperance are in direct opposition to the virtues of justice, fortitude, and temperance.... Thus prudence is cause, root, mother, measure, precept, guide, and prototype of all ethical virtues; it acts in all of them, perfecting them to their own nature; all participate in it, and by virtue of this participation they are virtues [20].

Later in his study, Pieper summarizes the meanings of Prudence:

> Prudence ... is the circumspect and resolute shaping power of our minds which transforms knowledge of reality into realization of the good. It holds within itself the humility of silent, that is to say, of unbiased perception; the trueness-to-being of memory; the art of receiving counsel; alert, composed readiness for the unexpected. Prudence means the studied seriousness and, as it were, the filter of deliberation, and at the same time the brave boldness to make final decisions. It means purity, straightforwardness, candor, and simplicity of character; it means standing superior to the utilitarian complexities of mere "tactics" [42–43].

Stonewall Jackson clearly displayed these qualities during his military career. His well-known tactical flexibility and seeming suddenness of decision and action would certainly fall under "alert, composed readiness for the unexpected." This tactical flexibility was the result of long study and deliberation, as his planning for the entrapment of General Banks in the Valley showed (Vandiver 219–24). He was certainly ready to accept "counsel," although he naturally reserved to himself the right to make final decisions. He often impressed observers as meditating or considering courses of action; among many such commentaries, Sgt. Howard's is especially useful, because it combines a characterization of his verbal and physical demeanor with an evaluation of him as taking his own counsel: "While very courteous, his words were few and to the point, the voice distinct but rather low.... The habitual expression of his face was that of one communing with his own thoughts and others seldom spoke to him without being first addressed" (Howard 80–81).

Jackson shared this prudent quality with some very good epic company, including among many others the Cid and Achilles. The latter, though not often associated with prudence, did at least spend a lot of his time "communing with himself" and considering his course of action (Dubois). The Cid was generally seen as prudent, though a man of action (that is, a man of wisdom and fortitude); what is of interest here is the terminology employed by the poet about the Cid. When the Cid learns of the outrage perpetrated on his daughters by the Infantes de Carrión (the Princes of Carrión), a beating known as the Afrenta de Corpes, he communes with himself for a time: "Van aquestos mandados a Valençia la mayor; / quando gelo dizen a mio Çid el Campeador, / una grand ora penssó e comidió; / alçó la su mano, a la barba se tomó;" (Menéndez Pidal, *Texto* 1131–32) (Dubois) ["These tidings came to Valencia, and when they were told to my Cid, he thought and pondered a full hour: and he raised his hand and grasped his beard" (Anonymous, *Poem of the Cid* 105)].[30]

Jackson is treated as prudent in the Maxwell *Gods and Generals* within a context, a fierce battle, in which he is often said to be aggressive (which he was) and perhaps even reckless (which he was not). This scene is from the attack on Henry House Hill, during the battle of First Manassas or First Bull Run (July 21, 1861). As the Confederate line faces the Federal artillery and the green troops, full of bravado, itch to attack, the camera shows part of the 33rd Virginia, commanded by Col. Arthur Cummings, starting forward independently and then charging the batteries. Sandie Pendleton, one of Jackson's aides, begins to become a little agitated; but Jackson, more experienced and wiser than he, cautions, "Easy, Mr. Pendleton, easy. It's good to have your dander up, but it's discipline wins the day." This prudence is part of the "Stonewall" compound.

The Stonewall epithet was indeed a critical part of Jackson's casting as an epic hero for the South. The mock-heroic strain in his legend was never far from the surface, however. Nevertheless in several respects, including the descriptions of his clothing, demeanor, and religion, he was not always subject to early ridicule. Even as a major teaching in Lexington he was noticed as a special personage, as Anna Jackson records in her biography of him:

> A Southern lady thus describes the impression that Major Jackson made upon her: "There was a peculiarity about him which at once attracted your attention. Dignified and rather stiff, as military men are apt to be, he was as frank and unassuming as possible, and was perfectly natural and unaffected. He always sat bolt upright in his chair, never lounged, never crossed his legs, or made an unnecessary movement. The expression of his soft gray eyes was gentle, yet commanding, giving you a delightful feeling of the sweetness, purity, and strength of his character. His dress (in times of peace at least) was always in good taste, and faultlessly neat. Everything he wore was of the best material. 'A thorough gentleman' was not exactly the expression to describe the impression first made upon you: it was something more — a title of greater distinction than this must describe him —'a modern knight of King Arthur's Round Table,' would have more properly conveyed the indelible picture he fixed upon your mind. Nothing unworthy, nothing ignoble, nothing of modern frivolity and littleness— any thoughtful observer could have seen, even before the war, that 'Stonewall' Jackson was as true a hero as Bayard, or Raleigh, or Sidney" [Jackson 64–65].

And McHenry Howard, in his memoirs of the war, defended Jackson from the frequent imputations to him of eccentricity. James Robertson notes that "[o]n March 26, 1862, Howard was named an aide on the staff of Brig. Gen. Charles S. Winder," who commanded the Stonewall Brigade during 1862; and thus, "Howard was more than an eyewitness to all of the major battles of Jackson's now-famous 1862 Valley Campaign" (Robertson,

"Foreword" vi–vii). In the course of his description of Jackson, Howard stated that he did not think the general to be especially odd:

> I heard of his habit of raising his arm and hand at times while riding, which has been often told in books, and, among other theories, that it was to promote the circulation which he imagined to be defective on that side, also that it was to invoke a blessing; but I never remarked it as a frequent gesture, although with him often on battle fields, as well as on the march and in bivouac, and I believe the impression that it was a very frequent habit is much exaggerated [Howard 80].

A particularly folksy use of the nickname for Jackson is to be found in a letter from a Georgia soldier to his family, written from Winchester during the retreat from Antietam. The letter of October 1, 1862, written by James Thomas Thompson, of the 11th Regiment, Company H, Georgia Volunteers, also highlights Jackson's special qualities and contrasts him with another folk figure of the war, John Hunt Morgan (later killed at Greeneville, Tennessee):

> When wee fell back out of Md. across the river "Uncle Stone Wall" lay s[t]ill until the Yankies all got over on this side then he picked into them and just slaughtered them…. You can tell the boys that thay may brag on John Morgan, but he cant come up with "Uncle Stone." Tell them he dont Get behind stumps & trees as thay say thay did. We hant got the trees & stumps to Get behind. Thay say he is like a flee. When thay think thay have got him fast & go in to get him out, he is clear Gon & is whiping them somewhir elce. Some of the boys swares "Stone Wall" can kick up the Devil in 5 minutes any time. It dose look like he can hav a fight just when he Gets ready [Austin 52].

Additionally, a very appropriate choice of a horse for this man was to be part of his legend. Like other epic or legendary heroes, Jackson acquired a horse complete with nickname, thus following in the tradition of Alexander (Bucephalus), El Cid (Babieca), and Wellington (Copenhagen), and William III (Sorrel) ("Famous Horses"). Jackson's mount was usually called Little Sorrel, although the general himself called the horse Fancy. The mount was not by any means a magnificent charger like Grant's Cincinnati or a great horse like Lee's Traveller. It was instead a somewhat pudgy creature, albeit a very affectionate and charming one, which might recall Don Quixote's Rocinante[31] in being a sort of mockery of a great warrior's *destrier*. Certainly, Little Sorrel did not fit the traditional image of the horse when associated with the warrior, as detailed by Angel Valbuena-Briones in his article on symbolism in the theater of Spanish dramatist Pedro Calderón de la Barca:

Desde muy antiguo es un símbolo fálico ... paralelamente, indica ... soberbia y orgullo. Este sentido se deriva de la distinción ... que suponía ... el ir a caballo. ... Su ímpetu era temido en el campo de batalla y así ... el *Libro de Job* ... dice: "La gloria de su resoplido es terrible...." [Since very early times it is a phallic symbol and ... passion-evoking ... in parallel fashion, it ... indicates haughtiness and pride. This feeling is derived from the distinction ... that ... riding a horse implied.... Its impetus was feared on the battlefield and thus ... the *Book of Job* ... author says, "the glory of his nostrils is terrible" (Job 39.20) [Valbuena Briones 69].

Neither quality explicated here fits Little Sorrel, who hardly seemed "phallic" or "passion-evoking," and certainly not "haughty" or "proud." Nevertheless, the horse was very sturdy and dependable, like its master; its workmanlike, nonshowy qualities fit Jackson's style quite neatly. The horse was also well-trained by Jackson, as the following anecdote attests:

> The Confederate soldiers would always cheer when either General Lee or General Jackson appeared. The Federals, finding this out, would immediately shell that part of the line where the cheering was going. This made no difference to the Confederate soldiers, such was their enthusiasm for Lee and Jackson, and come what would, nothing could stop them. They could not help cheering. Stonewall Jackson, observing that the enemy shelled where the cheering was, taught Old Sorrel as soon as she heard cheering to run as fast as she could, and I have seen Jackson, as the cheering went on, take his hat off, and put it under his arm, while Old Sorrel dashed down the line" [Riley 27].

Perhaps one could call Jackson's training of his steed to run at the sound of cheering a prudent measure, because although the shelling which usually ensued might not have harmed him or Sorrel, it might have injured or killed men of the brigade. Certainly Jackson showed no fear of shelling or gunfire, as attested by many observers. One of the most piquant accounts of his demeanor under fire can be found in *Outlines from the Outpost* by John Esten Cooke, who reported the "anecdote" as being "told me by a distinguished officer on the staff of one of our Generals, in the battles around Richmond [the Seven Days]":

> On Tuesday, in the hottest of the fight, he [the officer] was sent with a dispatch to General Jackson. As he galloped toward the point where he expected to find him, the artillery fire grew so hot that it seemed impossible for any troops to withstand it. Trees were crashing down every instant, and the air was rendered sulphurous by exploding projectiles. He pressed on and finally was directed to General Jackson. He found him sitting on the side of a road, down which the enemy were pouring their most deadly fire — with round shot and shell ploughing the ground and burst-

ing within a few feet of him — and this was the occupation of General Stonewall and General Hill, who sat beside him. They had a piece of bread each, and one bottle of molasses between them. First General Jackson would break off some bread, pour some molasses on it, and eat it — passing the bottle over to his companion, who did likewise. Then the bottle would be returned, and the same ceremony would be repeated. My informant says, the spectacle was the most extraordinary which he ever witnessed; and indelibly impressed upon his mind the conviction that General Jackson was wholly insensible to fear [Cooke 71–72].

This heartwarming little scene would have played very comically on screen, as it does in the Cooke retelling; perhaps Jackson and Hill were secretly putting on a little show for their observer.

Both Jackson and his horse, who long outlived his master, endured many dangerous episodes, travelling together through arduous campaigns. Anna Jackson, the general's widow, described Little Sorrel (as "Fancy") at some length in her biography of her late husband:

His name of "Fancy" seemed rather a misnomer, for he was anything but a fancy-looking animal; but he was well formed, compactly built, round and fat (never "raw-boned, gaunt, and grim," as he has often been described), and his powers of endurance were perfectly wonderful. Indeed, he seemed absolutely indefatigable. His eyes were his chief beauty, being most intelligent and expressive, and as soft as a gazelle's. He had a peculiar habit of lying down like a dog when the command halted for rest. His

Little Sorrel after the Civil War. (Courtesy Virginia Military Institute.)

master made a pet of him, and often fed him apples from his own hand. General Jackson had several other horses ... but he preferred the little sorrel to them all, finding his gait, as he expressed it, "as easy as the rocking of a cradle" [171].

After the war, Little Sorrel was taken to the North Carolina farm of Anna's father (near present-day Stanley, west of Charlotte), where he lived for many years as a most engaging pet:

> Here he was treated to the greenest of pastures and the best of care, and did excellent service as a family horse, ... and for a long time was the riding-horse of the venerable minister [Anna's father] to his country churches. One of the young Morrisons used to say that Old Fancy (as he was called on the farm) "had more *sense*, and was the *greatest old rascal* he ever saw." He could make as good use of his mouth in lifting latches and letting down bars as a man could of his hands, and it was a frequent habit of his to let himself out of his stable, and then go deliberately to the doors of all the other horses and mules, liberate each one, and then march off with them all behind him, like a soldier leading his command, to the green fields of grain around the farm — a fence proving no obstacle to him, for he could, with his mouth, lift off the rails one by one until the fence was low enough to jump over; so that he was continually getting into mischief. But he was such a pet that he was allowed to do anything; and was often taken to county fairs, where he was an object of as much interest as one of the old heroes of the war [171–73].

Little Sorrel must have learned something about stealth and leadership from his master! The horse's body was later preserved, to be displayed in the VMI museum. Some of Jackson's aura, perhaps, survived through the agency of his horse. Such has been the case with other mounts who came to symbolize or commemorate important events, as the famous example of Comanche, the horse who survived Custer's Last Stand in 1876, as detailed in Elizabeth A. Lawrence's engaging article:

> the badly wounded horse was rescued from the battlefield, nursed back to health, and maintained as an honored member of the Seventh Cavalry until his death in 1891.... Over the years, Comanche has ... taken on diverse meanings at different times and for various groups of people [Lawrence 85].

Like the men associated with them, both Comanche and Little Sorrel became linked in American legend to the events in which they participated. Little Sorrel, in particular, forms an endearing link to the determined general who symbolized for many Southerners, and then for many Americans, fearlessness in the face of superior force.

2

The "Sword of God": Stonewall Jackson and Nationalist Zeal

Had Thomas J. Jackson been so inclined, he could have written his own military biography using Judas Maccabeus as a model. Both leaders died during battles, both were fervent nationalists, and both dedicated their lives to their religious faith.

The life and career of Judas (or Judah) Maccabeus are detailed primarily in two sources: *I Maccabees* and Flavius Josephus's *Antiquities of the Jews*. Judas was killed in battle during one of his army's attacks on the Syrians.

In *I Maccabees* appears the account of how a group of zealous Jews, faithful to the tenets of early Judaism (today they might be termed ultra–Orthodox), rebelled in 136–134 B.C. against the rule of the Seleucid kings, specifically Antiochus Epiphanes, who prohibited Jewish religious practices in order to meld the Jews into his kingdom:

> Then the king wrote to his whole kingdom that all should be one people, and that all should give up their particular customs.... And the king sent letters by messengers to Jerusalem and the towns of Judah; he directed them to follow customs strange to the land, to forbid burnt offerings and sacrifices and drink offerings in the sanctuary, to profane sabbaths and festivals, to defile the sanctuary and the priests, to build altars and sacred precincts and shrines for idols, to sacrifice swine and other unclean animals, and to leave their sons uncircumcised. They were to make themselves abominable by everything unclean and profane, so that they would forget the law and change all the ordinances [Callaway 1.41–50].

These rebels, who came to be known as the Maccabees, probably from the Greek word for "hammer," were led initially by the priest Mattathias. Mat-

36

tathias led the revolt initially because he "not only refused to take the first pagan sacrifice but slew an apostate Jew who was willing to step into the breach" (Grant 28). Mattathias and his sons (five, including Judas) went into the mountains to fight, employing the time-tested stratagem of guerrilla warriors. Mattathias died in battle in 136 B. C., and Judas assumed the leadership.

Michael Grant, in his *The Jews in the Roman World*, evaluates Mattathias as a "prototype" leader for the Jews. He was to become a model for zealous leadership: "Mattathias enjoyed a very special position in the hearts of contemporary and later Jews because he seemed the arch-hero of resistance movements, the prototype of ruthless zeal" (Grant 29). Grant sees him as a latter-day Phineas, a zealous priest from the Mosaic period "who, in defence of monotheism, had seized his spear, attacked an Israelite cohabiting with a foreign woman and pinned them together in death" (29). Here is the Old Testament account of the incident:

> And, behold, one of the children of Israel came and brought unto his brethren a Midianitish woman in the sight of Moses, and in the sight of all the congregation of the children of Israel, who were weeping *before* the door of the tabernacle and the congregation. And when Phinehas, the son of Eleazar, the son of Aaron the priest, saw *it*, he rose up from among the congregation, and took a javelin in his hand; And he went after the man of Israel into the tent, and thrust both of them through, the man of Israel, and the woman through her belly. So the plague was stayed from the children of Israel [Num. 25.6–8].

Judas Maccabeus, a greater military leader than his father but rather less singlemindedly zealous, is, Grant notes, "one of the great military heroes on whom subsequent Jewish nationalists looked back with admiration" (29). A comparison with Jackson is apt in many ways (the chief difference being that Jackson was a subordinate commander, not a national leader): both leaders were militarily brilliant, both led outnumbered forces, and both achieved great victories despite the odds of fighting against a dominating national force.

Just such a comparison was made by Elizabeth Randolph Preston Allan, daughter of Col. John L. Preston, who was important in the history of VMI, and who served on Jackson's staff. She was the wife of Col. William Allan, who served with Jackson and became the author of one of the best studies on Jackson, Lee, and the Army of Northern Virginia (*Stonewall Jackson, Robert E. Lee, and the Army of Northern Virginia, 1862*). In her *Reminiscences*, written for her children, Elizabeth says that "Jackson is said to have studied intently the wonderful campaigns of Judas Maccabeus." She compares the two both in style of warfare and in motivation:

> Judas, like the later leader [Jackson], was fighting to save his home-land, and the discrepancy in men and arms, also, showed a direful parallel. The ancient Book of the Maccabees offers this glowing sentence. "On the eve of battle, Judas gathered his men about him for a final message, speaking not of dangers, nor of strategy, but of *God— of freedom—* and of their *right*. Thus arming them, not with the defense of shield or spear, but with the encouragement that lies in good words, and the valor of a great dream, *worthy to be believed*." Armed with this dream, they went forth, conquering and to conquer; the defender of the Valley led his men thus armed, with the dream of freedom, and their right — to victory [Allan 143–44].

Judas Maccabeus had a second career in the Middle Ages. His military leadership, his rebellion, and his death were all to figure into medieval exemplary narratives. In "The Maccabees as Exemplars in the Tenth and Eleventh Centuries," Jean Dunbabin discusses some of the presence of the Maccabees, especially of Judas, in the medieval exemplary narrative. During the ninth century, Maccabees I and II were dealt with at length, and thereby transmitted in an understandable form to medieval readers, by "the Carolingian scholar Rabanus Maurus" (31). According to Dunbabin, the scholar offered a comprehensive summary and a characteristically medieval exegesis of the books (31–32).

Dunbabin also shows how the collective presentation of the Maccabees in the Old Testament was portrayed in Christian terms by the illumination of a manuscript now called "MS Leyden University" (32–35). He concludes that the monkish illustrators of the manuscript were probably "at St. Gall in the early tenth century," and that the condition of war then prevailing ("Hungarian raids") would have led the illustrators to see in the story of Judas Maccabeus and his men the model of a providential intervention in their own situation. In a passage that could well be applied to Stonewall Jackson, Dunbabin observes of the monks that "[i]n driving home vividly the lesson that God protects those who fight in his name, the monk-artists were also offering a few practical hints as to how warriors might do it" (35).

Dunbabin also discusses a particular example of the political utilization of Judas Maccabeus for some medieval image-making. Because of a conversion due to illness, a nobleman with a violent history, "Arnoul, Count of Flanders," lent his support to "the monastic reformer Gerard of Brogne," in the year 930. In 941, to dedicate the restored abbey at St. Peter's, Ghent, Arnoul published a charter referring to the restoration of the Temple in Jerusalem by Judas Maccabeus (37–38). Dunbabin observes that this appropriation of Judas Maccabeus by Arnoul was very astute, manipulating the biographical, political, and religious content of the hero's legend to suit his own purposes, so that "Arnoul was magnified in finding his own niche within biblical tradition" (37–38).

The exemplary use of the Maccabees gradually became less prominent during the Middle Ages. By the 12th century, the clerical posture had become more distanced and sophisticated:

> clerks tacitly accepted that the old exemplarism was naïve; though they might on occasion employ a Maccabean simile for rhetorical effect, they no longer thought of it as prescriptive. Israel's past had lost its unique meaning [Dunbabin 4: 40].

As far as "the laity" was concerned, though, the clerical shift to "scholasticism was emotionally impoverishing." So, Dunbabin asserts, the laity "began to develop through the medium of epic and romance their own form of exemplarism" (40). Judas Maccabeus remained, however, a "throw-back" to the older imagery; not as "secular" as King Arthur, for example, Judas served as "the defender of Jerusalem against the Saracen foe." And he became "a feudal lord and a crusader" (40–41).

By the 14th century, Judas Maccabeus had taken his place along with the more secularized heroes such as Arthur and Charlemagne in the topos of the "Nine Worthies." This motif, widely distributed except for the Scandinavian and Spanish areas (Loomis 32), was to be found in the arts for about 200 years. Turville-Petre notes its source in a poem from the early 14th century called *Les Voeux du Paon*, by Jacques de Longuyon (Turville-Petre 79).

The Worthies were generally presented in a certain sequence: "Hector, Alexander and Caesar (the three pagans), Joshua, David and Judas Maccabaeus (the three Jews), and Arthur, Charlemagne and Godfrey de Bouillon (the three Christians)" (Turville-Petre 80). Turville-Petre also cites a poem which highlights for our purposes the crusading spirit then accorded Judas Maccabeus. In two lines of the poem, Judas Maccabeus tells of his restoration of God's law to Jerusalem: "For while I was lord of Jurye I maynetened þe ryght, / The land of Moyses allso, from tyme I beganne" [For while I was lord of Jewry I maintained the right, / The land of Moses also, from time I began] (82).

The story of the Maccabees has been retold in several contexts since the Middle Ages. Handel composed an oratorio based on their story. Pedro Calderón de la Barca (1600–81), the great Spanish dramatist, wrote a play (not one of his better ones, alas) called *Judas Macabeo* which centers on a love triangle between Judas, Lysias, and a Jewish girl. More recently, American novelist Howard Fast published the intriguing *My Glorious Brothers* (1948), a book which, like his *Spartacus*, lends a radical cast to the struggle of unfree peoples or classes.

Fast (1914–2003), the prolific author of novels such as *The Immigrants*, had previously written at least two novels dealing with rebellions. These were *Spartacus* (1951), which took Roman history as its starting point to narrate the tragic story of the failed slave revolt led by the near-legendary Spartacus (memorably played in the Stanley Kubrick film adaptation by Kirk Douglas); and *My Glorious Brothers*, which also uses Roman and Jewish historical sources to narrate a rather different story, the rebellion of the Maccabees against the oppressive rule of Antiochus Epiphanes.

The novel is narrated by Simon Maccabee, one of Judas's brothers, who became ruler after the death of Judas and Jonathan. The narrative is conveyed to the reader by the device of a memoir (by Simon) which forms part of an official report from a Roman visitor to Judea, who met Simon and his family when Simon was an old man. Simon's reminiscences begin before the revolt of the Maccabees and end before his own marriage and rulership. Much of the narrative centers around the struggle itself, but considerable space is also dedicated to the family relationships among the Maccabees, including a strong vein of jealousy between Simon and Judas. This jealousy concerns the beautiful Ruth, who was killed early in the revolt.

In the narrative, Simon serves the function of a "witness narrator" who retains a certain critical distance from the events and personalities of the historic rebellion. He is also an unromanticized character who repeatedly tells the reader of his lack of glorious qualities: "I, Simon, the least of all my glorious brothers"; "I, Simon, Simon of the iron hand and the iron heart; I, the least, the most unworthy of all my glorious brothers, the single, stolid, plodding and colorless son of Mattathias" (Fast 94, 207). This unromantic aspect is sharply contrasted to the idealized vision of Judas as a youthful, godlike figure, a David or Adonis type: "Judas stood, tall, slim-hipped, auburn-haired, all in white, trousers and jacket, his long hair blowing—child and father, young and old, a strange mixture of the gentle and the fierce, the humble and the arrogant, the tame and the wild" (Fast 140). The narrative ends with a dream reported by Simon to his wife in which he prophetically sees the Romans conquering the Jews and exterminating them: a nearly accurate vision of the Masada defeat in 66, in which, if the Romans did not exterminate the Jews, they certainly crushed their existence as an independent people. Simon consoles himself with the reflection that his brothers and he had lived and had contributed to the heritage of his people — much as Jackson, Lee (and their adversaries) still live in American historical memory.

The comparison of Jackson to Judas Maccabeus (and by extension to Phineas and other biblical heroic figures) raises the question of the character and nature of heroism in the Bible. Comparison is sometimes drawn between biblical heroes or leaders and those of Western epic. That the Old Testament and Western epic are justifiably comparable is inarguable in some respects, the chief of which is the representation of "national" or "folk" culture in both cases. Furthermore, the appropriation of biblical characters and themes in medieval and Renaissance epic is well known. But comparisons or contrasts between Old Testament heroes and epic heroes can be very tricky. Witness, for example, the claim by Megged that the heroes of Homeric epic, such as Achilles, are "ideally perfect," while "[t]he Patriarchs are in no respect perfect heroes" (Megged 420). This statement is overstated in part, since it glosses over questions such as the well-known hubris of Achilles—certainly a character fault and not evidence of "ideal perfection." As William R. Herman comments in his article on heroism and Milton, "The Hellenic hero ... *need not be morally adequate*" (Herman, W. R., "Heroism" 13). Herman also contrasts the "qualities of individuality, self-determination, and physical courage" of the "Hellenic hero" with those of the typical Old Testament hero, whose "main characteristic is not physical strength but moral strength, permitting him to be obedient to God when all others reject God or the need to be obedient" (13). Megged's claim that "there is not one biblical character who is a replica of another" (Megged 422) is also debatable, given the presence of clear parallels between figures like Judas and Phineas. In fairness to Megged, he does allow that characters like Daedalus have "weaknesses," but he also avers that "not one of them has natural human dimensions; they embody the personification and codification of the human unconscious and are not multi-faceted individuals" (Megged 422). Still, this line of argument seems more applicable to mythic than to epic figures like Achilles, Hector, or Odysseus.

William Whallon, in his "Old Testament Poetry and Homeric Epic," distinguishes usefully between the prose and poetry of the Old Testament. He amends (but also pays tribute to) Erich Auerbach's famous comparisons in *Mimesis* between Old Testament prose (the story of Abraham and Isaac) and Homeric poetry (the motif of Odysseus's scar). He makes the important point that "half of the Old Testament is in prose and the other half in poetry — two broad categories that are not very much alike at all." For Whallon, "the true generic analogue of Homeric epic is ... the poetry, and not the prose" (113). In the course of his argument, he avers that neither in the Homeric epic nor in the Old Testament poetry (but not its prose) do the heroes (Achilles excepted) evince any "change in character, ... nor even any individuality worth talking about." Whallon does not attempt to settle the question of the change of character in Old Testament prose, carefully stating this to be "arguable" (123–25).

Allowing, then, for the distinctions drawn by Whallon, one may follow some of Megged's line of argument as it relates to the transference of Old Testament heroism into the medieval and Renaissance epic. Jackson's image (and those of other glorified generals from history, including Lee) can be better understood in terms of the figuration of the hero in epic, and most especially in medieval and Renaissance epics. The image of the religious general owes much in its outlines and in its character in poetic and fictional treatments of religious generals like Jackson (and Gordon and Lee, for that matter) to medieval saints' lives and to the Christianization of the epic hero in the Arthur cycle, and in other medieval epics such as Le Couronnement de Louis [The Coronation of Louis].

Megged criticizes the medieval treatment of Old Testament and New Testament characters for turning them into plaster saints (Megged 422). He places the heroes of medieval epic into another lineage, that of Gilgamesh and Homer. Both strains, the more robust European epic tradition, and the rather prettified version of biblical heroes, can be perceived in the tradition of hagiographic narratives such as the 13th-century Libro de Alixandre [Book of Alexander] and Vida de Santo Domingo de Silas [Life of St. Domingo of Silas] (ca. 1230), by Gonzalo de Berceo (Del Río 67, 72).

The image of the religious general can be analogized to medieval saints' lives and to the Christianization of the epic hero in the Arthur cycle, as well as in medieval epics such as Le Couronnement de Louis. Other medieval epics with near-sanctified heroes are the Spanish Poema de Mio Cid and the French Chanson de Roland. Sometimes generals themselves have cultivated such parallels, as in Patton's well-known fascination with St. George. More often, however, writers of history and fiction have cast figures like Jackson into Arthurian or Rolandesque molds, or into the configuration of a saint.

One such process in medieval epic appears in Le Couronnement de Louis, a king who was later canonized and sanctified. Gerard L. Brault has illuminated the role of the St. Peter "cult" in the composition of the cycle of poems by William of Orange, of which the Louis is a part. He details the importance of the cult to the Louis poem and to William in particular (102).

Of interest is the prominent role played by a certain relic of St. Peter in the narrative of the poem. This is the arm of St. Peter, which is used by the Pope to bless William before a battle with a giant (Brault 102–03).[32] The St. Peter arm relic is used here as a talisman to give invulnerability to William: "He is allowed to kiss its major joint, presumably the elbow. The Pope makes the sign of the cross with it over William's helmet and against his heart." Brault notes that "it never comes into contact with the tip of William's nose," which he later loses (102–03). At least the consequences are less drastic than with Achilles, who was bathed in the river Styx by his mother, the nymph Thetis, but whose heel was not immersed (Hamilton, E., *Mythology* 201–02).

Like saints, famous leaders and generals have sometimes left relics to their followers or devotees. A notorious example from the 19th century was the shameless use of a war injury for political purposes by Mexican general and recidivist president Antonio López de Santa Anna. Santa Anna, having lost his leg in battle, apparently did not flinch when it was "disinterred [in 1843] from its grave at Manga de Clavo and solemnly reburied in the [national] cathedral." Given the Mexican penchant for corrosive humor, however, the leg was to become an object of derision for many of his countrymen when his political career took a downturn (one of many): "The *léperos* [poor beggars] celebrated the occasion [of his overthrow in 1844] by digging up Santa Anna's leg and trailing it through the streets on a string" (Parkes 207–09).

The case of Stonewall Jackson is quite different from this. When he was wounded on May 2, 1863, his arm had to be amputated. This was done in a hospital tent near the Wilderness. According to Robertson, citing Chaplain Beverley Tucker Lacy's narrative, the chaplain "found the amputated arm wrapped in a cloth and lying outside Jackson's tent ... [and] buried it in the family cemetery of the J. Horace Lacy estate near the field hospital" (Robertson, *Stonewall Jackson* 735, 918n3). The estate was called Ellwood. Later, a vertical marker was installed to memorialize the remains.

This memorializing of Jackson's arm comes very close to a reliquary for a secular saint. Like Peter and other Christian martyrs, Jackson (like Lee) was seen by many in the South as a martyr in the service of a noble cause, not slavery but the upholding of honor and chivalry, or, more prosaically, of states' rights. Whether consciously or not, the preservation of his arm as a "relic" lends weight to his canonization as

Burial site of the arm of Stonewall Jackson.

a "saint" of the Confederacy, and the existence of a reliquary for him (including other items such as his bloodstained raincoat from the night of his wounding) allows him, like Peter in the William cycle, to become a figure (in the sense of a figuration) in the created epic of the South.

Like Jackson, other generals in history have of course been glorified or put into an epic frame. One might think of Napoleon, Wellington, Wallenstein, Caesar. The list becomes less expansive when the component of religion is included. One ancient example of this combination is Judas Maccabeus, who became a figure of epic status in the national history of the Jews. More often, in the modern sense, generals of a religious bent have been thought eccentric, literally off-center, because their perceived overemphasis on religious motives is "off-center" to the secular thrust of society. The Confederacy had in common with the Israel of the Maccabees that both were heavily eschatological in their ideological position; both participated as well in victimhood status, aggrieved and oppressed by "alien" and technologically superior rulers. But in a society more like the "oppressed" of Israel and the Confederate States of America, what of the "religious general"?

Stonewall Jackson was certainly zealous in his prosecution of the war, and he was by all accounts unshakable once dedicated to a course of action. He thought in terms of strategy and tactics, as a trained West Pointer, but nearly as important, he stuck to the last because of his sense of duty. He did not trouble himself greatly about bookish military theories; in fact, James Power Smith, one of his aides, includes in his *With Stonewall Jackson in Northern Virginia* a comment made to Lord Roberts in an interview. This was "the story told of Jackson, that he read only two books in the latter years of his life — the Bible and the campaigns of Napoleon" (Smith, J. P., *With Stonewall* 83). Whether true or not, the story is illustrative of Jackson's salutary simplicity of approach. Even if untrue, the anecdote is important just because it was told about the general: it is clear that he was perceived to be both Biblical and Napoleonic in inspiration. Jackson in fact combined the two perspectives, characteristically, in a remark quoted by surgeon Hunter McGuire:

> "In listening to Jackson talking of Napoleon Bonaparte, as I often did, I was struck with the fact that he regarded him as the greatest general that ever lived. One day I asked him something about Waterloo. He had been over the field, inspecting the ground, and spent several days studying the field of battle. I asked him who had shown the greater generalship of these, Napoleon or Wellington? He said, 'Decidedly, Napoleon.' I said, 'Well, why was he whipped, then?' He replied, 'I can only explain it by telling you that I think God intended him to stop right there'" [Riley 101].

Revealingly, when on his deathbed Jackson's mind still turned to military matters and to the Bible. In a meld of both strains, he asked, according to Dabney, that Smith search out for him (or really, for Smith's benefit) some "models" from the Bible:

> General Jackson now also enforced his favorite dogma, that the Bible furnished men with rules for every thing. If they would search, he said, they would find a precept, an example, or a general principle, applicable to every possible emergency of duty, no matter what was a man's calling. There the military man might find guidance for every exigency. Then, turning to Lieutenant Smith, he asked him, smiling: "Can you tell me where the Bible gives generals a model for their official reports of battles?" He answered, laughing, that it never entered his mind to think of looking for such a thing in the Scriptures. "Nevertheless," said the General, "there are such: and excellent models, too. Look, for instance, at the narrative of Joshua's battle with the Amalekites; there you have one. It has clearness, brevity, fairness, modesty; and it traces the victory to its right source, the blessing of God" [Dabney 714–15].

The "narrative" to which Jackson is referring is found in the Book of Exodus. Here are the relevant verses:

> Then came Amalek, and fought with Israel in Rephidim.
> And Moses said unto Joshua, Choose us out men, and go out, fight with Amalek: to morrow I will stand on the top of the hill with the rod of God in mine hand. So Joshua did as Moses had said to him, and fought with Amalek: and Moses, Aaron, and Hur went up to the top of the hill.
> And it came to pass, when Moses held up his hand, that Israel prevailed: and when he let down his hand, Amalek prevailed. But Moses' hands were heavy; and they took a stone, and put it under him, and he sat thereon; and Aaron and Hur stayed up his hands, the one on the one side, and the other on the other side; and his hands were steady until the going down of the sun.
> And Joshua discomfited Amalek and his people with the edge of the sword.
> And the LORD said unto Moses, Write this for a memorial in a book, and rehearse it in the ears of Joshua: for I will utterly put out the remembrance of Amalek from under heaven.
> And Moses built an altar, and called the name of it Jehovahnissi:
> For he said, Because the LORD hath sworn that the LORD will have war with Amalek from generation to generation [Exod. 17.8–16].

Jackson had it right; the narrative is indeed compact, and it gives credit to God for the battle. But there is something else: Jackson could probably have thought of other biblical narratives equally as pithy and just as humble.

Why this one? Maybe what fascinated him so about this passage was its reference to Joshua.

Whether unwittingly or not, Jackson seems to have hit upon a good biblical analogy to his own attitude and approach to warfare, and to life. Joshua was well known as an effective warrior, whose victories included the fall of Jericho. Easton's *Bible Dictionary* quotes an interesting characterization of this biblical hero:

> The character of Joshua is thus well sketched by Edersheim: "Born a slave in Egypt, he must have been about forty years old at the time of the Exodus. Attached to the person of Moses, he led Israel in the first decisive battle against Amalek (Ex. 17:9, 13), while Moses in the prayer of faith held up to heaven the God-given "rod." It was no doubt on that occasion that his name was changed from Oshea, "help," to Jehoshua, "Jehovah is help" (Num. 13:16). And this name is the key to his life and work. Alike in bringing the people into Canaan, in his wars, and in the distribution of the land among the tribes, from the miraculous crossing of Jordan and taking of Jericho to his last address, he was the embodiment of his new name, "Jehovah is help." To this outward calling his character also corresponded. It is marked by singleness of purpose, directness, and decision.... He sets an object before him, and unswervingly follows it" (*Bible Hist.*, iii. 103) [*Easton's Bible Dictionary*].

First, it is notable that this man underwent a name change, from Oshea, meaning "help," to Jehoshua, meaning "Jehovah is help," and that this happened after his signal victory over Jericho. Like Thomas J. Jackson, whose assistance was critical to the Confederate victory at First Manassas (First Bull Run), and who became immortalized as Stonewall Jackson there, this Jewish military leader is said to have received his immortal name following a crucial battle.

And then look at the characteristics attributed to Joshua. His name is said to epitomize his nature and his conduct: he has recourse to Jehovah for help, and Jehovah responds by giving him important victories. Even more than this, Joshua's own character traits reflect his constancy in searching for help from Jehovah and his courage obtained from this divine source. Again, as Edersheim says, "'To this outward calling his character also corresponded. It is marked by singleness of purpose, directness, and decision.... He sets an object before him, and unswervingly follows it.'"

Most certainly this is a perfect fit for Jackson. It's almost uncanny that he would mention this biblical hero in the very moment of his own serious illness. Maybe he expected to recover and thought that, being so resolved, and being helped by God, he would recover. In any event, his famous motto, "You can be whatever you resolve to be," could have applied to Joshua too. Perhaps, as well, it's no accident that Joshua began as a lieutenant to a military-religious leader, Moses. Jackson served the South's greatest such leader, Robert E. Lee. And, to his own men, Jackson became not only a figure of folklore but a leader glorified in religious terms. Anna Jackson provided an apt characterization of his men's viewpoint on their leader:

> They indulged in jokes *ad libitum* at the expense of each other, their indefatigable leader, and the Yankees. They declared that General Jackson was far greater than Moses. "Moses," they said, "took forty years to lead the Israelites through the wilderness, with manna to feed them on; 'old Jack' would have double-quicked through it on half rations in three days" [Jackson 285].

Another epithet applied by Jackson's men to their leader was indicative of both strains in their view of him: a rather irreverent comic perspective combined with admiration for his sincere piety. This was the term "Old Blue Light," which seems a little mysterious to modern ears.[33] The term referred to a division within the Presbyterian Church in America. Lonn Taylor of the Smithsonian Institution understands "Blue Light" as:

> a fervent and conservative Presbyterian. In the 1830's the Reformed Presbyterians split ... [The more liberal faction was] called "New Lights" and the conservative faction, "Old Lights." ... [which was] jocularly referred to as "Blue Lights," ... from the rhyme with "new" and [from] "true blue."... Jackson, because of ... Presbyterian piety and ... blue eyes, was called "Old Blue Light"... [Taylor].

Capt. Charles M. Blackford, a close observer of Jackson, noted that the "Old Jack" nickname was meant fondly by his soldiers and that he was greatly loved by them: "He is ... a great military genius and has made such an impression on the men that 'Old Jack' is ... a rallying cry and a term of endearment. The army is full of stories about him.... Whenever he is recognized by the soldiers, he is cheered." Nevertheless, Blackford reiterated the reclusive nature of this commander (Blackford 89).

Jackson had an undistinguished career at West Point, finishing midway in his class. He distinguished himself in the Mexican War (1846–48). His fortunes declined after this point, with his nadir reached at Fort Meade, Florida, where he got into a most unfortunate contretemps with his commanding officer. He resigned his commission and ended up as an instructor at VMI, where he was a dedicated teacher in a profession to which he was unsuited.[34] When the Civil War began, he became just another commander on the western front, not garnering much notice until he exploded onto the public scene at First Manassas.

His career now began a vertiginous upward trajectory. His Shenandoah Valley campaign of 1862, intended by Lee as a diversion to keep Lincoln from reinforcing McClellan in front of Richmond, not only achieved that goal but stole all the publicity thunder from other war activities. Jackson and his Stonewall Brigade became household words in both South and North. The name "Stonewall" became feared in the North and thrilled the South. When Jackson returned to Lee's command after the Valley campaign, he went on, after a slow start in the Seven Days battles, to forge an enduring record as an aggressive and inspired tactical leader. His partnership with Lee was one of the great collaborative enterprises in military history. His career ended suddenly with his death by friendly fire in May 1863, during the battle of Chancellorsville.

The rapidity of Jackson's ascent to fame, and his early death at age 39, inevitably bring to mind comparisons with figures such as Alexander the Great (rapid rise, early death), Charles XII of Sweden, and perhaps Napoleon or Charlemagne. With all these men, and others, including "Chinese" Gordon, Gustavus Adolphus, and Judas Maccabeus, Jackson shares the element of a comet-like trajectory. His early death lends itself easily to "what if" scenarios, especially about Gettysburg.[35] But more importantly, the seemingly gratuitous and adventitious nature of his demise, at the peak of his powers, explains much of the fascination with him in mythic terms. This element even lends a peculiar resonance to his status as a religious general, as if he were both professing and living the life and values of figures like Jesus or Adonis.

The nature of Jackson's death has lent itself easily to hagiographic treatment and to generally mythic descriptions of him as a wounded god, as a Christ figure sacrificed for the greater good of the South, and so on. Even though the modern era may deprecate such wide-eyed treatment of a man as a saint or a godlike figure, the fact remains that such treatment of Jackson accounts for much of his appeal and his enduring legacy.

A most curious example of the Southern glorification of Jackson as a "saint" was observed during October 1862 by Capt. Charles M. Blackford, 2nd Virginia Volunteers, Company B, when on picket duty near Harpers Ferry. His picket was close to the home of a railroad worker, "whose young and pretty wife was a great rebel" (Blackford 130). Blackford relates that when Jackson and some of his staff were nearby, the "pretty hostess" observed him intently for a time and then, "she ran into the house and brought out her baby ... and handing it up to the General [Jackson] *asked him to bless it for her*" (131). Stonewall's reaction to this petition may indicate that he was by this time accustomed to such adulation, or it may simply be a characteristic example of his stolid demeanor, but in any case, the

General "seemed no more surprised ... than Queen Elizabeth at being asked to touch for the 'King's Evil.' He turned to her with great earnestness and, with a pleasant expression on his stern face, took the child in his arms, held it to his breast, closed his eyes and seemed to be ... occupied for a minute or two with prayer" (131). Blackford expressed, after the fact, a concomitant desire to memorialize the occasion:

> It was my wish at the moment that I were a poet or a painter, to put the scene in immemorial words or upon an eternal canvas, the picture of him sitting there on his old sorrel.... Around-about the soldiers in their worn and patched clothing, ... while his staff officers sat a little to one side. Then Jackson, *the warrior-saint of another era,* with the child in his arms, head bowed until his greying beard touched the fresh young hair of the child, pressed close to the shabby coat that had been so well acquainted with death.... For the first time it brought to me that this stern, enigmatic man whom I admired, respected but never loved [a commonly expressed reaction of soldiers to Jackson], had another side to him...; that of a tender man of family [131–32].

Like Abraham Lincoln, Jackson died an untimely death. Their careers, thus truncated, have been subjects of historical and fictional speculation. In the case of Lincoln, speculation has centered around his putative future conduct of what came to be called Reconstruction policies.[36] His successor, Vice President Andrew Johnson of Tennessee, was known to dislike the Southern planter class;[37] and many in the South, as well as moderate Northerners, feared that he would institute a radical reign of terror on the prostrate section. Although this did not turn out exactly as feared, still Lincoln's death led to an ascendancy of the Radicals and an eventual imposition of draconian measures on the South. Additionally, these same Radicals were to pursue (some say persecute) Andrew Johnson through the means of an impeachment trial. And Lincoln became a martyr for the Radicals, who exploited his death at the hands of Southerner John Wilkes Booth. The Radicals tried to lay the blood-guilt on the Confederate states in much the same fashion, and with as little justification, just as some elements of medieval Christianity had saddled the Jews with Christ's death. The fact that many Southerners did not hate Lincoln[38] would have made little impression on such demagogues.

Lincoln was assassinated by a fanatical pro–Southern egotist. Stonewall Jackson also died in his prime, but in his case the fatal act was one of friendly fire. The question of his death was not suited for pointed political exploitation, as was Lincoln's. But Jackson's passing was to become a central part of his mythology, and of the Southern myth of the Lost Cause. The undeniable pathos of the wounding and death of Jackson at the early age of 39, and at a critical point for the Confederacy, only lent more solidity to the hagiographic bathos which quickly surrounded the incident and his persona in the South, and also made more credible many of the later claims of Lost Cause proponents.

But Jackson's pathetic death has been the occasion for much more speculation than that put forth by the Lost Cause ideologists. Such events as Jackson's early death are ready-made for authors of alternate history and fiction. No less an authority on Confederate military history than Robert E. Lee speculated sadly on the effect of Jackson's absence from the Army of Northern Virginia's high command when he stated that "'if I had had Jackson at Gettysburg, I should have won the battle, and a complete victory there would have resulted in the establishment of Southern independence'" (Tate 320).[39]

While some treatments of Jackson and the Civil War have followed a speculative path, others have been more traditionally straightforward. Some have dealt uncritically with Jackson as an exemplary Knight Templar of southern independence, for instance John Esten Cooke and the Reverend R. L. Dabney in their several works. Others have criticized his difficult personality (Richard Taylor in *Destruction and Reconstruction*), or have caricatured him (Taylor again). Some authors, like Southern Agravian Allen Tate, have poured into the vessel of "Stonewall Jackson" their own tendentious viewpoint. His military biographers have sometimes tended to accept anecdotes about Jackson's campaigns which have proven to be unfounded. For example, James Robertson criticizes the early and very reasoned study by British military historian G.F.R. Henderson for this type of error. Among the several biographical texts on Jackson, the recent *Stonewall Jackson* by James Robertson (1997) is both the most thorough and the most judicious, taking especial pains to correct errors and misconceptions and to clarify confusion about Jackson's life.

An important perspective on the life of Stonewall Jackson which is solidly grounded in fact is his deep religious faith, specifically his Presbyterianism, which informed his private and public careers. Like all Protestants in the United States, Jackson inherited the traditions of Europe and of the British Isles. In order to understand Jackson and other men similar to him in their faith, their antecedents in the Old World should be examined.

Protestant Roots

Ulrich Zwingli

The career of Ulrich Zwingli (1484–1531), a native of the Zürich region, has been overshadowed by that of his more publicized compatriot

John Calvin.[40] The two men represent divergent strains in Swiss Protestantism. Zwingli's Protestantism was more intellectualized than was Calvin's. Zwingli did not place as much emphasis on the community of the elect as did Calvin, and he was more uncompromising than was Luther with regard to the tenets of Catholicism.

Zwingli was also far more intolerant of dissent from his positions than was Calvin. Although one usually thinks of Calvin's Geneva, with its sumptuary laws and other prohibitions, as the model for later Puritan social experiments, it was actually Zwingli who was the more tyrannical. Also, some of the strictures in Geneva merely codified what was already practice.

In any event, Zwingli became a lightning rod for Cath-

Ulrich Zwingli (1484–1531), engraving, Théodore de Bèze, *Icones* (1580).

olic fear and trembling about Protestantism. He proved to be more or less incapable of the flexibility displayed by Calvin and Luther. His attempt to set up a Protestant republic was eventually blocked by an odd coalition of Catholics and Lutherans, both of whom feared his extremism. He died fighting in battle against Catholic troops. So, Zwingli was in a very real sense a priestly warrior, a man who strove and died for his religious convictions.

Like Stonewall Jackson, Zwingli believed strongly in the concept of a just war. Zwingli was more reluctant as a warrior than was his spiritual descendant from Virginia, but Jackson would surely subscribe to the tenet held by Zwingli that war is especially justified when a sovereign realm is provoked. According to Robert C. Walton,

> It is too much to say that Zwingli advocated complete pacifism in response to what he had experienced, but he came to believe that war was

just only when hearth and home were attacked. Therefore he maintained that unless attacked by a foreign power, the [Swiss] confederacy should remain neutral [DeMolen 77].

Zwingli died in battle, and he may certainly be considered a warrior of God. But like Jackson, he went to war reluctantly. Jackson harangued his troops early in the war, as a scene from the film *Gods and Generals* shows, maintaining that only because of the invasions of their homes by the Northerners were the Virginians responding by force.[41] (He even displayed a wry sense of humor in this speech, averring that Lincoln had asked Virginia Governor Letcher for three regiments to put down the rebellion, and that "we have sent him three"—not exactly the kind of help Abe wanted.) Most of Zwingli's battles, however, were political and doctrinal. His Reformed theology gave way in church history to Calvinist doctrine, which became the basis of Presbyterianism.

As in his harangue to the Stonewall Brigade, Jackson expresses on several occasions in *Gods and Generals* a justification for the war that rests upon the aggrieved status of the invaded South. This justification hews close to Zwingli's position, but it ties in even more directly to Jackson's own Presbyterian background. As John Dall observes, Calvin distinguished sharply between religious and civil authority relative to the church. Dall explains that here Calvin diverges sharply from the Lutherans and the Zwinglians:

> Unlike Luther and Zwingli, who freely surrendered the administrative and disciplinary power of the Church to the civil authorities, whether princely or republican, Calvin attempted to mark off for the Church a sphere of spiritual jurisdiction distinct from the civil; and on the determination of his followers to define and preserve this sphere, irrespective of all difficulties, hangs much of the trouble that fell to the lot of Presbyterianism in later years.

Calvin was in respect of authority rather conventional:

> Calvin does not seek to interfere with or to minimize in any way the scope of the civil power.... [H]e holds that it is the duty of all Christian men to obey whatever lawful rulers have dominion over them. The only circumstances under which resistance, active or passive, is justifiable arise when the commands of rulers clash with the commands of God [exactly this position was taken by many Confederates]. Conversely, it is the duty of rulers to preserve public peace and happiness, and their first care must be for religion and morals [Dall 9: 249].

John Knox

John Knox (c. 1513–72) does not have the profile for moderns of John Calvin or Martin Luther. But Knox was indispensable to the creation of

Scottish Presbyterianism, and thus of American Presbyterianism. The life of Thomas Jackson would have been radically different from what it was without the historical contribution of John Knox.

Knox was born to a family of middling means in Lothian (Reid, W. S., *Trumpeter* 15). He became a seminarian against his father's wishes and, upon reaching adulthood, became a minister of the English church. He gravitated toward the more radical wing of the Church in Scotland, associating himself with critics of the Established Church, most notably with Bishop Wishart.

Wishart attacked the privileges and some of the beliefs of the Catholic priests in Scotland. He ran afoul of a most unsavory and powerful church official, Dean Beaton. The Dean managed to

John Knox (c. 1513–1572), engraving, Théodore de Bèze, *Icones* (1580).

have Wishart burned for heresy (Reid, W. S., *Trumpeter* 30). Wishart's followers, including John Knox, vowed revenge (30–31).

They made their opportunity in due time. Dean Beaton, aware of the threat to his person, holed up in his castle at St. Andrews with armed guards and a brace of followers. Although he could have called in reinforcements once the unrest began, he chose not to do so. The stronghold was breached and a massacre ensued, during which the Dean was killed by the sword of one Melville (Reid, W. S., *Trumpeter* 36–37).

Following the death of the Dean, the authorities rounded up many of Wishart's supporters. Among these was Knox, who was sentenced to the galleys in the service of France. In addition to the severity of galley work, Knox and other Protestants were subjected to special abuse by the Catholic masters, who tried to force them to kiss images of the Virgin.

Knox was released from the galleys after 17 months. Returning to Scotland, he married and began to become important among the Scottish Protestants. He published several incendiary tracts, including an attack on government by women, clearly directed at the reign of Catholic Mary Tudor (Bloody Mary to history). He also published an influential treatise on rebellion. Knox became known especially for his thunderous preaching and his volatile irascibility.

His most lasting contribution to the nascent Scottish Presbyterian Church was his role in the formulation of the Scottish confession. The Confession became the basic text for the Scottish Presbyterian Church, much as the Augsburg Confession had for the Lutherans. Knox is not a figure with a significant accretion of legendary, outsized characteristics, but his importance for Protestantism cannot be ignored.

Oliver Cromwell

Jackson has often been compared to Oliver Cromwell (1599–1658). There is certainly some justice in the comparison, although some of Jackson's strongest partisans have differed with this point. The Reverend R. L. Dabney, of Jackson's staff, for example, offers a full discussion of the two leaders, attacking any comparison between them:

> With all the genius, both military and civic, and all the iron will of the Lord Protector, he [Jackson] had a moral and spiritual character so much more noble that they cannot be named together. In place of harboring Cromwell's selfish ambition, which, under the veil of a religiousness that perhaps concealed it from himself, grew to the end, and fixed the foulest stain upon his memory, Jackson crucified the not ignoble thirst for glory which animated his youth, until his abnegation of self became as pure and magnanimous as that of Washington. Cromwell's religion was essentially fanatical; and, until it was chilled by an influence as malign as fanaticism itself—the lust of power, it was disorganizing. Every fibre of Jackson's being, as formed by nature and grace alike, was antagonistic to fanaticism and radicalism. He believed indeed in the glorious doctrines of providence and redemption, ... but he would never have mistaken the heated impulses of excitement for the inspirations of the Holy Ghost, to be asserted even beyond and against His own revealed word.... Especially was his character unlike Cromwell's, in its freedom from cant; his correct taste abhorred it. Sincerity was his grand characteristic.... His action, like Cromwell's, was always vigorous, and at the call of justice could be rigid. But his career could never have been marked by a massacre like that of Drogheda, or an execution like that of the King [Charles I] [Dabney 113–14].

In any event, both leaders were deeply religious and were motivated as well by a strong sense of local patriotism. Jackson, like Cromwell, was not a member of the aristocracy. And both men were advocates of black-flag warfare, Cromwell even more so than Jackson.

In some important respects, though, the comparison doesn't work. For example, the two men differ in their political stance. The proper analogy between the parties in the English Revolution which began in 1629 and the rebellion of Confederate states in 1861 is between the Cavaliers (the Royalist party of Charles I) and the Confederacy. David Hackett Fischer draws such an analogy in his discussion of "regional cultures" in America: "In defense of their different cultures, the two sections also fought differently. The armies of the north were at first very much like those of Fairfax in the English Civil War; gradually they became another New Model Army, ruthless, methodical and efficient. The Army of Northern Virginia, important parts of it at least, consciously modeled itself upon the *beau sabreurs* of Prince Rupert [who was often cited as a parallel to Jeb Stuart].[42] At the same time, the Confederate armies of the southwest marched into battle behind the cross of St. Andrew, and called themselves 'Southrons' on the model of their border ancestors" (Fischer 860). Some writers have linked the Roundheads (Cromwellians) to the Confederates, because both were insurrectionist entities. But in point of fact, the Roundheads represented a true revolution in the sense that they were representatives of the working classes and the new urban population around London, a nexus that fits the North in our Civil War much more closely than does the Cavalier base, which was, like the power base in the Confederacy, the larger landowners and country squires (Fischer). According to this interpretation, which seems to me very reasonable, one might say that Jackson and Cromwell do not share ends but perhaps, rather, means.

And there is more to the question than this. Disregarding for now the differences between their goals and the motivation of their relations or factions, Jackson and Cromwell share an important feature detailed by one of the 19th century's most widely read and thus influential commentators on the heroic, Thomas Carlyle.

In his *On Heroes and Hero-Worship*, Carlyle studies several historical or semi-historical figures, including Moses, Frederick the Great, Napoleon, and Cromwell, as putative "heroes." Carlyle, often seen as a militarist and even as a protofascist, is ably defended from both charges by D.J. Trela in "Carlyle, the Just War and the Crimean War." One of the leaders discussed by Trela as to Carlyle's treatment of him is Oliver Cromwell. In his *Oliver Cromwell* (1845), Carlyle justifies his subject's black-flag warfare for "reasons" which Trela presents as essential "to understanding his belief in justifiable war." These rationales, Trela says, "derive largely from the characters of Cromwell and the Irish." Carlyle distinguishes between (from his point of view) the relatively marginal Irish and, in Trela's words, the "more civilized and sincere" Cromwell (Trela 3).

Sincerity is important for Carlyle, but, says Trela, it is not enough. Carlyle believes that it must be "coupled with" "elevated piety or devotion." Trela provides Frederick the Great as a contrasting example: he was sincere enough, but he was "sceptical"; in fact he was "sincerely sceptical." But he is not placed on the same high level by Carlyle as is Cromwell. Trela says that what a hero needs is "sincerity coupled with devotion." Furthermore, Carlyle thought of "Puritanism" as "an advance on Roman Catholicism.... Cromwell was a dedicated Puritan" (Trela 3–4).

This emphasis on sincere devotion to one's faith and the added element of Puritanism as laudable for this reason will be seen as very applicable to Jackson as military commander. Other religious-minded generals of the Civil War, with some exceptions, do not measure up well to this standard. Rosecrans might be said to be insufficiently sincere, due to his overweening egotism and ambition, and inadequately devout, because of his high intelligence which led him to skepticism and doubt. Polk was not sincere in the sense of being zealous and forthright enough. Only Lee will compare with Jackson in meeting these criteria.

Jackson has stood out from the other religious general figures of the Civil War because of his special qualities. These include particularly his "everyman" nature, and, paradoxically, his eccentricities which distinguish him from the generality. Like Lincoln, another "quare fellow," as Flann O'Brien might have said, Jackson blends insensibly into folklore because he seems odd in a harmless way. But Jackson's popularity in the South is finally explicable only in terms of two essential characteristics: his indomitable pertinacity and his unfortunate martyrdom.[43]

Jackson, Presbyterian of the South

Although Jackson's image with the public has consistently been one of a pitiless, fanatical, religiously obsessed warrior — again, an obverse of John Brown, with whose image Jackson's has become oddly confused at times — he is more complex than this caricature. Still, it is true that, in order to see Jackson in all his dimensions, he must be approached from the perspective of his religion. As one of his former adjutants, James Power Smith, who after the war had become a doctor of divinity, said of him in 1897,

> Eminent critics are telling us that the campaigns of Jackson will be the study and admiration of military schools for centuries to come. However true that may be, of this we are sure, the religion of Stonewall Jackson will be the chief and most effective way into the secret springs of the character and career of the strange man, who as the years go by is rising into the ranks of the great *soldier-saints* of history — Saint Louis of France, Gus-

tavus Adolphus of Sweden, Oliver Cromwell of England, Stonewall Jackson of America [Smith, J. P., "Religious Character" 3].

And, as writer John W. Schildt observes, Jackson had deep faith in the workings of "divine providence":

> He believed Romans 8:28 to be true.[44] He was simply an instrument in the hands of the Almighty. General [Richard] Taylor and others have alluded to the fact that even when riding he seemed to be praying, or in meditation before a campfire. "Those who rode or walked beside him on the march have told me [Graham] that they often saw his lips moving as if in silent prayer. Before he went into battle he might be found upon his knees... .[45] And when the battle was over, he always recognized it not by his own skill or valor, but by the favor of the Almighty Ruler of whom he had asked the victory, and to whom he bowed again in humble thanksgiving for the victory that had been granted" [Schildt 82].

Jackson's Presbyterianism was of the Scots-Irish type known in the South of the 19th century. This brand of religion was heavily influenced by Calvinism, which grew out of the religious ferment of the Swiss Reformation. During the 16th century, the tenets of what would be known as Calvinism were hammered out in a long and complex doctrinal process within the Swiss Protestant churches. John Calvin established in Geneva a rigid system of Church control which excluded those who did not accept the tenets of Calvinism (Bainton 120–21).[46]

Jackson became a member of the Lexington, Virginia, Presbyterian Church in 1851 after some searching internal debate over the relative virtues of several approaches to Christian faith, including Catholicism. Gamaliel Bradford comments succinctly: "Like a very similar nature in a different sphere, John Donne, he examined all creeds first, notably the Catholic, but finally settled in an austere or sturdy Calvinism" (132). He was brought into the Presbyterian Church by his former Mexican War colleague, fellow teacher, and future brother-in-law (and his subordinate in the Civil War) Daniel Harvey Hill. Hill apparently introduced Jackson in 1851 to a prominent Lexingtonian and Presbyterian church member, John Lyle, who owned a bookstore on Main Street (the "Automatic Bookstore") which, in a manner reminiscent of colonial American or Latin American towns of the early 19th century, served as a meeting place and salon for discussions of politics, religion, books, and town lore and gossip (Lyle 26). Lyle and Jackson "soon became close friends," and "Hill felt afterwards that John Lyle 'was instrumental in arousing a religious interest in Jackson's mind,' as the young officer visited the bookstore regularly and frequently discussed matters of religion with Lyle" (Lyle 26). Note here that Hill qualified this statement about Lyle's importance in Jackson's conversion to Presbyterianism by attributing at least the denomination to be chosen to another possible "influence":

> But even after he [Jackson] had become an earnest Christian, and wished to connect himself with the church, he had no special predilection for Presbyterianism. This was determined by a potent influence, unconscious, I doubt not, to himself. He fell in love with the daughter of a Presbyterian clergyman. Had he known it he would have resisted a bias in his denominational connection from such a cause. But I have always believed that her faith wore new attractions in his eyes, after he had given her his heart [Hill, D. H., "The Real Stonewall Jackson" 625].

In any event, Royster Lyle relates as well that during "late September or early October [of 1851]," John Lyle "introduced Jackson to Dr. White [the pastor of the Lexington Presbyterian Church]," and that Jackson soon became a member of White's congregation (Lyle 26).

As a pre–Civil War Virginia Presbyterian, Jackson was not expected to devote himself to reformism or other social causes. James I. Robertson summarizes the position of the church at that time: "Presbyterian doctrine ... stressed personal salvation and individual morality. The faithful viewed efforts to improve society ... as outside the purview of church members because such activity challenged God's preordained conceptions of earthly existence" (Robertson, *Stonewall Jackson* 135). The roots of the church were in John Knox's Scottish Confession and ultimately in the doctrines of Calvinism.

As a Virginia Presbyterian of his epoch, Jackson was a very active church member. He became a respected deacon and also dedicated much time to teaching black Sunday school sessions. His importation of religion into his generalship was most visible in his refusal to fight and even to march on the Sabbath and in his insistence on holding church services. He was also given to scolding his officers for their language, as in a celebrated incident with Gen. Richard Taylor,[47] although apparently with patience and even good humor, and to pious declarations. And, Jackson mixed warlike and religious imagery in statements about himself. For example, he wrote to his aunt that:

> "The subject of becoming a herald of the cross has often engaged my attention, and I regard it as the most noble of all professions. It was the profession of our divine Redeemer, and I should not be surprised were I to die upon a foreign field, clad in ministerial armor, fighting under the banner of Jesus. What could be more glorious? But my conviction is that I am doing good here, and that for the present I am where God would have me be" [Jackson 60].

Jackson was never really "out of character" in religious, and in military, terms, during his church appearances. During his headquarters posting in Winchester (winter 1861–62), he and Anna became good friends with the pastor of the Kent Street Presbyterian Church, Rev. Dr. James Robert Graham, whose house was only a block away from Jackson's headquarters and whose church Jackson attended. He and Anna actually lived in the Grahams' house for a time during his stay in Winchester.

Graham was pastor of the more conservative of the two Presbyterian churches in Winchester (Holsworth 16). Holsworth notes that "probably" Jackson preferred this Kent Street church, but "he did make several appearances at the town's other Presbyterian church." According to Holsworth, Winchester had undergone a Presbyterian schism, ending up with two churches, on Kent and Loudoun streets (16).

A Winchester resident, Kate Sperry, was present in the congregation when Jackson visited the more liberal of the two churches (the Loudon Street church). Sperry recorded Jackson's visit in her diary for February 23, 1862, including a prayer "offered" by him "when he was called upon": "He bowed his head and prayed, 'O Lord God of Hosts, prevent we beseech thee, the effusion of blood, but if we must fight, give us the victory. Amen'" (16).

But was Jackson really a fanatic in the sense of being a "hard" general? Perhaps he can be understood better by applying some terms used by Robert Jewett in his *Captain America Complex*. These are "prophetic realism" and "zealous nationalism." Jewett defines prophetic realism as follows: "It seeks to redeem the world for coexistence by impartial justice." In Jewett's formulation it "runs" "[a]longside zealous nationalism," which "seeks to redeem the world by the destruction of the wicked" (Jewett 10–11). A fine example of zealous nationalism is to be found in the career of Judas Maccabeus and his followers: "They were convinced that Yahweh was leading them in battle and providing the victories against the mercenaries" (21). Contrasting with the ideology, according to Jewett, was the prophetic realism "set forth by Jesus of Nazareth":

> At the beginning of his ministry he rejected the dream of bringing the messianic kingdom through violence…. He located evil not in the enemy but in the heart of the chosen people itself, exposing the cruelty and callous disregard for life which legalistic self-righteousness had produced…. He worked to alter the stereotypes which made zealous warfare seem necessary…. He warned his fellow countrymen about the dangers of subscribing to the zealot war aims, prophesying that revolt against Rome would bring destruction to Jerusalem… [Jewett 23].

Jewett, in extending his thesis into the modern era, passes through the Civil War period. He sets the zealous nationalism both of the abolitionists and of much of the Confederacy against the prophetic realism of Lincoln (34ff). In connection with the "'militant South,'" Jewett cites especially James W. Silver's study of the effect of the churches on Southern morale: "Every Confederate victory proved that God had shielded his chosen people and every defeat became the merited punishment of the same people for their sins" (37).

Jackson would clearly fit the "zealous nationalist" definition. His advocacy of a "black-flag" policy (not so different, incidentally, from that of Sherman, who was also thought to be unbalanced, just plain crazy, not religiously mad), his employment of Joel-like invective, his admonition to "kill the brave ones," can all be adduced to prove his zealotry. In this zealousness, Jackson is nevertheless only different in degree of emphasis from many other leaders of the Civil War, both North and South. The difficulty with simply adopting the label "zealous" for a soldier with Jackson's determination and persistence is that when one looks behind the drive and the rhetoric, one finds, as with Sherman — so different in character from Jackson — a core of practical rationality, a kind of hard "prophetic realism." Thus Jackson observed that only by being hard will the war be won, and Sherman spoke of the need to make war cruel in order to make it short. These are not the sentiments of unbalanced fanatics. Instead they are the reasoned positions of clear-sighted soldiers who see war in unblinkered terms.

Not exclusively a "zealous nationalist," then, Jackson was also a very pragmatic "prophetic realist." This hybrid quality in Jackson is part of the fascination with his image: the seemingly fanatical zealot who was also so down-to-earth and practical about the necessities of war. Again, he is similar in this regard to Sherman, but Sherman evinces none of the third dimension of Jackson: a religious overtone to nearly everything he did, so that he is easily likened in this respect to Old Testament figures like Judas Maccabeus or Joshua, or indeed to epic heroes like the Cid and to military leaders like Chinese Gordon, and, inevitably though inaccurately, Oliver Cromwell.

Jackson and Civil War Religious Generals

This study includes a focus on the careers of several officers of the Civil War because of the mix of religion and militarism in their lives. Although most Civil War officers and soldiers were religious, figures like Jackson, Polk, and (Daniel) Harvey Hill manifested their religion in particularly striking fashion. This was also the case with some other officers of the Civil War, perhaps less well-known than the three just mentioned, but fervent in their religious conviction nonetheless. These officers are of interest as well because they help to put Jackson into greater relief due to the parallels between his and their faith histories.

One of these generals is William Dorsey Pender of North Carolina. Pender was born near Tarboro, North Carolina,[48] on February 6, 1834 (Longacre 16). He was mortally wounded at Gettysburg, near the Emmitsburg Road, on July 2, 1863 (the second day of battle, during the Confederate push from Seminary Ridge toward the Round Tops). Longacre recounts the fatal wounding of General Pender:

He was standing at the edge of a wood ... when the Union guns across the field began to return Longstreet's fire. Solid shot came crashing

Brig. Gen. William Dorsey Pender, CSA (1834–63). Courtesy of the North Carolina State Archives.

through the treetops while shrapnel and bursting shell exploded just above ground level. Realizing that his perch had become too precarious, Pender turned to leave, but it was too late. A shell burst in front of him, and he went down with his fifth and final wound of the war. On July 18, 1863, William Dorsey Pender succumbed to that wound [185].

Pender died in a fashion befitting his strong religious faith. In his last hours, he requested that an "attendant" write a letter to his wife for him: "'Tell my wife that I do not fear to die. I can confidently resign my soul to God, trusting in the atonement of Jesus Christ. My only regret is to leave her and our two children.' He also wished her to know that 'I have always tried ... to do my duty in every sphere in which providence has placed me'" (Longacre 15).

Like Jackson, Pender was fervently religious. Unlike Harvey Hill and

Polk, though, Pender did not become a Christian early in life. In this regard he was much more like Jackson, who found his niche in Presbyterianism only after long soul-searching. But Pender was different even from Jackson with respect to his faith, because Jackson had joined the church before the war began. Pender's was a battlefield conversion, so to speak, albeit a very sincere one. Pender had no religious education as a child; he "matured in ignorance of the Bible" (Samito 174), a rather unusual circumstance in that era. Pender began to express his growing faith in letters to his deeply religious wife; significantly, his faith was first couched in terms of providentialist convictions regarding the Southern cause (Samito 176).

Pender worked hard at his study of Christianity and was eventually baptized as an Episcopalian (Samito 176). This was a publicly performed baptism which "generated newspaper coverage that he found embarrassing and invasive of his privacy" (Samito 177). Samuel Pender briefly described the ceremony and its aftermath:

> General Pender had been publicly baptized, in August, 1861,[49] in the field near Manassas, by the Rev. A.T. Porter, of Charleston, South Carolina; Colonel Benjamin Allston and General S.D. Lee [Stephen D. Lee, to become important as an artillery commander in Robert E. Lee's army], both of South Carolina, being his witnesses. The publicity given to this by newspaper reporters was so repugnant to his feelings, that, while in camp near Richmond, he rode quietly into the city at night, and was confirmed by Bishop Johns, in St. Paul's church (Pender 234).

Pender became a very committed Christian. He began to sound very Calvinistic for an Episcopalian in his denunciations of the Northern soldiers; for him, now, the Yankees were "a 'drunken rabble' of 'unprincipled villains' fighting for revenge" (Samito 177). This sounds very much like Harvey Hill in its vitriolic phrasing, and not too far from both Hill and Jackson in its sentiment.

Pender was also much like Hill and Jackson in his emphasis on discipline. He was innovative in his approach to discipline, and he was firm and consistent in its application of it. A conscientious commander, he worked his brigade hard:

> From his first days in command, Pender ensured not only that his units were drilled early and often but that they did so in close coordination. His concept of drilling by brigade rather than by regiment or battalion appears to have broken new ground. According to a member of his staff, "other Brigadiers asked him why he did it, and he gave such reasons that they began to follow his example." The basic reason was that the method produced dramatic results. The staffer noted that "it brought his regiments

close communication with each other ... and inspired a confidence and a[n] esprit de corps that made his Brigade a unit in action, easily handled, each regiment relying implicitly on the others, and having unbounded confidence in their General" [Longacre 108–09].

According to Hassler, this stress on discipline was a major factor in his growing respect for his division commander, Maj. Gen. A. P. Hill, who also put a premium on discipline. Pender became a Hill partisan, a fact of his career that was to put him at odds with Jackson, who had a running dispute with Hill during much of the war.

Thus, when Pender hoped for promotion in early 1863, he was not optimistic about his chances because of his "loyalty" to Hill (Samito 188). Samito comments further that there was no love lost on Pender's part for Stonewall Jackson: "[H]e forgets that one ever gets tired, hungry, or sleepy. ... [H]e would kill up any army the way he marches" (Samito 188). Notice, however, that Pender questions neither Jackson's competence nor his integrity. He also perceived his importance to the cause, proffering strongly his hopes that Jackson would not die from his wounds (Samito 189). The distance that Pender felt from his superior appears to have been partly personal (the Hill question) and partly, perhaps, an uncomfortable perception that he shared some of the traits often criticized in Jackson. Pender could be a difficult man, as Longacre observes: "[H]e was ... a martinet; he could be curt to officers and men; at times he appeared egotistical and vain..." (12).

Union Gen. Oliver Otis (O.O.) Howard (1830–1909) was a type of religious general who was in many ways the opposite of men like Jackson and Pender. Although Jackson and Pender were deeply religious, they were not suffocatingly pious. A native of Maine, Howard had a reputation as an excessively pious man, with a hint of old-maidishness—the kiss of death for a commander. Matters were not helped by his unfortunate luck as commander of the Eleventh Corps, which always seemed to be in the wrong place at the wrong time, due to factors not always within his control. He seemed to flagellate himself emotionally to a degree not found even in the deeply religious Jackson or Pender. In his discussion of religious faith in Civil War armies, Gerald Linderman quotes Howard in connection with "failure" in battle. Linderman emphasizes in his commentary on failure in battle and faith in God that it was clear to many Civil War soldiers that "sacrilege" or "faithlessness" might lead to defeats in battle. But the problem for a man like Howard was how to account for reverses in war when one had done all he could to honor God. As Linderman writes, "Key [a Confederate diarist] attributed his survival to his faith in God *and* his constant prayers for God's blessing. Favorable results required that he regularly invoke God's protection in prayer; failure to do so would court calamity. Here, then, was a way of explaining failure while leaving intact the assumption of the power of godliness. The soldier had to do his part, the army its part, the people their part. God is on our side, common reasoning went, and God's Plan is one of goodness, so death and defeat signal only that *we* have not yet met the conditions requisite for its execution" (Linderman 106). Linderman connects Howard's remarks about himself to this mindset; thus Howard: "[T]he pride and haughtiness of my heart is more than pen can tell, but I believe God will school me, by failures when I act without Christ, by disappointments and afflictions, [so] as to bring my miserably foolish soul into full subjection to himself" (Linderman 106–07).

In any case, Howard's reputation with many soldiers illustrates the underside of the "religious general" typology: such leaders were always at risk of being seen derisively or resentfully by their subordinates. Apparently, though, Howard made a good impression particularly on cadets like future Confederate Maj. Gen. Stephen Dodson Ramseur (1837–64), also a religious man who became a commander of great promise: "A new chapter in the religious life of West Point began when Lieutenant Oliver Otis Howard arrived in the fall of 1857. So devout that he expected to leave the army for the ministry, Howard immediately secured permission from Colonel [William] Hardee [later General Hardee, C. S. A.] and the chaplain to organize a social meeting for prayer and conference to be held twice a week during the free half-hour between supper and the call to quarters. A cadet recalled that 'Howard's little prayer meeting' usually included ten to fifteen cadets. All knelt while Howard conducted services consisting of a hymn, a passage from the Bible, and a prayer. Ramseur was one of the prayer leaders" (Gallagher 20).

Unlike Howard, Pender was a soldier well liked and admired by subordinates and superiors, despite his widely known penchant for strict discipline. Samuel Pender writes that with his "winning gentleness of manner.... [H]e won all hearts," and that "[h]is men, from the lowest private to the highest officer, loved him devotedly and lamented him deeply [upon his death]" (235). He was particularly well-eulogized by his immediate superior, A.P. Hill, who, when "asked ... who was the best General of his grade he ever knew, [gave] the reply..., 'General Pender,'" and by Robert E. Lee, who said of him, "There was an officer who never held his proper rank. He ought to have been one of my Corps Commanders" (Pender 235).

Jackson, A Legend Remade: *Gods and Generals*

Stonewall Jackson has been featured less frequently in fiction and in film than have other figures of prominence from the Civil War. Perhaps this is because his personality is quirkier than Lee's, or less expansively American than Lincoln's, or less maniacal than John Brown's. Not long after the Civil War, he did appear as a character in several novels, such as *Surry of Eagle's Nest* (1866) and *Mohun* (1869) by John Esten Cooke (1830–86), and in *The Long Roll* (1911) and *Cease Firing!* (1912) by Mary Johnston (1870–1936) (daughter of Confederate Gen. Joseph Johnston).

Among novels dealing extensively with Stonewall Jackson, the most prominent is Jeff Shaara's *Gods and Generals*.[50] The book is a prequel to the celebrated *The Killer Angels*, by the novelist's late father, Michael. *The Killer Angels* focuses on the battle of Gettysburg (July 1–3, 1863), at which Jackson was not present, having died at Chancellorsville about two months previously. The novel is very effective in communicating the desperate nature of the great battle. The characters highlighted in this novel, about which more will be said later, include Lee and Longstreet, as well as Union officers Winfield Scott Hancock and Joshua Chamberlain.

Gods and Generals was undertaken by Jeff Shaara at the urging of director Ron Maxwell, who had adapted *The Killer Angels* for the screen as *Gettysburg* (1993).[51] The novel opens with Jackson teaching at VMI, where he was an engineering and artillery instructor, and emphasizes in its early pages the awkwardness and otherworldliness of the devout Jackson. Shaara highlights the religious faith of the future general, showing him in earnest conference with his minister at Lexington Presbyterian Church, Rev. White. He goes to the Jackson's Mill region, near present-day Clarksburg, West Virginia, to search for his mother's grave. He avails himself of the services of an old man living near Jackson's Mill who guides him to the gravesite.

The novel also follows the pre–Civil War careers of Lee and Chamberlain, both important to the later events in *The Killer Angels*. All three characters are depicted as rather ill-fitted to their peacetime pursuits, which are all tied to some form of instruction: Lee as West Point superintendent, Chamberlain as Bowdoin College professor, and Jackson as VMI instructor. Implicit is the notion that for these men, who symbolize distinct aspects of the United States's social structure (Lee the career officer, Jackson the ex-soldier, and Chamberlain as academic), war is the rough corrective to a society out of joint, and it will become the norm for these three men.

Like *Gettysburg*, *Gods and Generals* treats the Civil War as a tragic event, or series of events, with an assortment of tragic heroes. Jackson's shadow suffuses the proceedings, with Lee's regret over the absence of his great lieutenant from the field only too evident. *Gods and Generals* deals with Jackson as one of the "gods" of the war whose career follows the Alexandrian heroic trajectory, from obscurity to greatness and fame, and thence through early death to mythic pathos. Jackson's "god" status does not eclipse his own reverence for the God of his Presbyterian faith, however. The "gods" of the title refers not only to the ennoblement of one of the title's "generals" but also to the faith practiced by, most especially, Jackson and Lee, and even to the "gods" pursued by men such as John Brown or, in a different way, Jefferson Davis: the Baconian "idols of the tribe," in this case abolitionism or slaveholding, which result in the tragedy unfolded in the work's pages.

An early scene in the novel shows Jackson, struggling at VMI with his teaching in the face of student harassment, trying to find his place in the spiritual realm through consultations with his minister and friend, Rev. White. The Presbyterian minister advises him to resolve some of his central anguish by searching out his mother's grave in western Virginia. Jackson last saw his mother when she was dying and he was very young, and he has never overcome the loss. So, Jackson travels to Ansted, Virginia (now in West Virginia), where he is assisted by an old man in finding the burial site, which is unmarked and overgrown.

Jackson is presented accurately here, but his character is also drawn with heroic features. He is a figure on a smaller scale than Aeneas or Achilles or the Cid; but like them, he undergoes trials of spirit and of body.

Trials of what kind? Remember, first, that Jackson had resigned from the army after his stubbornness led to very negative consequences with his superior in Fort Meade, Florida.[52] He has undergone a kind of self-imposed exile from his chosen field. Like Achilles, his pride causes him problems; of course, he is unlike Achilles in that Achilles' pride has large consequences for his society. Jackson's pride has limited and private consequences; still, he exhibits a sort of hubris in his apparent self-righteousness over his commander's supposed immoral conduct.

At the novel's beginning, Jackson is also caught by the past. He cannot let go of his mother's death; the implications of his sense of abandonment seem profound, as he is spiritually hampered and even paralyzed. In a sense, he is a prisoner of his family past. Like Aeneas grieving the loss of Troy,[53] Jackson is not free until he begins to think more of the future's possibilities. His visit to his mother's grave is a journey that begins to free him. In his study of the dynastic epic, Andrew Fichter observes that

> The decisive moment in the life of the dynastic hero is that in which he ceases to dwell solely on the tragedy of the past. Such a moment occurs in the elaborate rite of passage in book 6 of the *Aeneid*, where Anchises orchestrates and Aeneas witnesses the pageant of the Roman future. Up

> to this point ... Aeneas seems destined only to accumulate losses and to reenact in various settings his painful exile from Troy [Fichter 6].

Like Aeneas in another setting, Jackson reaches a turning point when he undertakes his journey to western Virginia.

Aeneas shares with the eponymous hero of the 12th-century Spanish epic *Poema de Mio Cid* an essential integrity of purpose and a virtuous courage which will not be shaken by adversity. Aeneas and the Cid must both confront the facts of exile, even if for Aeneas such exile is of longer standing than for the Cid. For both heroes, firmness of purpose will lead to their self-realization. In Homeric terms, the quality of *areté* (loosely, "virtue") is the key:

> The gauge for any hero lies within; it is what Homer calls his *arete*. Like all concepts, *areté* is difficult to define adequately. It is the realization of the person, his excellence, the achievement of his potential, when he becomes what he has within him to be [Beye 59].[54]

One might well apply the same concept to Stonewall Jackson, who even had as a guide the maxim "Be whatever you resolve to be."[55] For Jackson's career as one of the most aggressive leaders of the Confederate Army, the realization of his inner potential was crucial. After his journey "back in time" to his old homestead, Jackson's fortunes begin to change; he soon finds his niche in another military organization, the Confederate army.

When the Civil War begins, Jackson goes with his state of Virginia, as does Lee, and joins the Confederate state army. This incident takes place in the novel after the painful separation scene between the Junkins, Jackson's second family (the old man is the father of his late first wife), and the general. Rev. Junkin has decided that he must leave for the North. A restrained Jackson shows no resentment about the old man's decision. Shaara presents Jackson as a model of silent stoicism. Even more than the long-suffering Cid, who protests vocally about his mistreatment at the hands of King Alfonso VI, Jackson shows only Christian compassion, which he characteristically leaves unspoken: "Jackson watched him go, did not speak, and gave a short prayer: *God please watch over him, he has always been Your good servant*" (Shaara, J., *Gods* 107).

As Jackson leaves their house, a group of cadets are waiting for him. Shaara depicts Jackson addressing the excited VMI cadets as an example of the leader's "reluctant hero" stance. Jackson, the voice of experience and reason in war, tries to deflate the cadets' anxious, unrealistic view of warfare:

"You are all quite eager for a war," he said, and there were whoops, a jumble of hot words and the loud cries for blood. He waited, wanting to tell them, to give them some of the wisdom that had been taught to him only where the blood flows and men scream, the horrible sounds of raw death.

"In Mexico ... I have seen a war. You do not know what..."

But they had stopped listening, heard only each other.... Jackson stepped down, moved through outstretched hands, the deafening cries of a world gone mad, and walked away [107].

Shaara uses Jackson's well-known fear of public speaking to good advantage here by making his interior monologue much more reasoned and eloquent than his fragmented attempt to harangue the cadets. The harangue by Jackson is also quite inarticulate when compared to the polished epic harangues to be found in works such as the *Poema de Fernán González*, which contains an effective and moving such speech. This harangue was given by the hero Count Fernán González, who was an actual historical personage from the 10th century, before the (legendary) battle of Hacinas:

> Mando a sus varones el buen conde llamar,
> Quando fueron juntados mando los escuchar,
> Que el (les) deria que querye la serpyent(e) demost[r]ar,
> Luego de (los) estrelleros començo de fab[l]ar:
>
> "Los moros, byen sabedes, (que) se guian por estrellas,
> Non se guian por Dios que se guian por ellas,
> Otrro Criador nuevo han fecho ellos dellas,
> Diz(en) que por ellas veen muchas de maraui[e]llas."
>
> "A y (avn) otrros que saben muchos encantamentos,
> Fazen muy malos gestos con sus esperamentos,
> De rreuoluer las nuves e (de) rreuoluer los vyentos,
> Muestra les el diablo estos entendymientos."
>
> "Ayvntan los diablos con sus conjuramentos,
> Aliegan se con ellos e fazen sus conventos,
> Dizen de los pas[s]ados todos sus fallimientos,
> Todos fazen conçejo, los falsos carvonientos."
>
> "Algun moro astroso que sabe encantar,
> Fyzo aquel diablo en syerpe fygurar,
> Por amor que podies[s]e a vos (otrros) [mal] espantar,
> Con este tal enganno cuydaron (se) nos tornar."
>
> "Commo sodes sesudos byen podedes saber
> Que ellos non han poder de mal a nos fazer,
> Qua quito les don Cristo el su fuerte poder,
> Veades que son locos los que lo quieren creer."
>
> "Que es [de] tod(o) el mundo en uno el poder,
> Qua [a] el solo deuemos todos obedeçer,
> Ca el es poderoso de dar e de toller,

Atal Sennor com(mo) (aqu)este deuemos nos temer."
  "Quien este Sennor dexa e en la vestya fya,
Tengo que es caydo a(l sennor) Dios en muy gran[d] yra,
Anda en fallimiento la su alma mesquina,
Quantos que assy andan el diablo los guia."
  Tornemos en lo al que agora estamos,
Travajado avemos, me(ne)ster es que durmamos,
Con ellos en el canpo cras mannana seamos,
Todos en su logar as[s]y commo mandamos."
  Fueron a sus posadas, se echaron a dormir,
Començaron las alas los gallos a feryr,
Leuantaron se todos, mis[s]a fueron (a) oyr,
Confes[s]ar se a Dios, (sus) pecados descubryr.
  Todos grandes e chycos su oraçion fyzieron,
Del mal que avyan fecho todos se (a)rrepentieron,
La ostya consagrrada todos la rresçebyeron,
Todos de coraçon a Dios merçed pedieron [Anonymous,
Poema de Fernan Gonçalez st. 472–82].[56]

[The worthy Count ordered his men called together, / when they were assembled he ordered them to listen, / as he would say that he wanted to point out the serpent, / next he began to speak of astrologers, / "The Moors, as you well know, are guided by stars, / they are not guided by God since they are guided by them, / they have made from the stars a new Creator, / they say that through these they see many marvels. / There are others who know many spells, / they make bad signs with their auguries, / by stirring up the clouds and stirring up the winds, / the Devil shows them this knowledge. / The demons gather with their conjurings, / they come to them and make their pacts, / they tell of those in the past all their failings, / all make their councils, the false bewitched ones; / some starry Moor who knows how to enchant, / that devil made to appear as a serpent, / from love that could badly frighten you, / with such a trick as this trying to unsettle us. / As you are sensible you can well know / that he has no power to do evil to us, / for Lord Christ took from him his strong power, / may you see that those who wish to believe it are mad. / Because all power in the world resides in One, / whom alone we must all obey, / for he has the power to give and to take away, / such a Lord as this we well should fear. / He who abandons this Lord and trusts in the Beast, / I hold that he has plunged God into very great wrath, / his mean soul lives in a fallen state, / those who live thus are guided by the Devil. / Let us turn to what is now before us, / we have labored, it is needful that we sleep, / let us be with them in the field early tomorrow, / everyone in his place as we command." / They went off to their dwellings, they lay down to sleep, / the cocks began to beat their wings, / all arose, went off to hear mass, / to confess to God, to uncover their sins. / Everyone great and small made their prayers, / of the bad things that they had done all repented, / all received the consecrated host, / all from their hearts asked for mercy from God.]

Jackson's epic deeds on the battlefield were not paralleled by an epic eloquence akin to this example.

After the attempt by Jackson to calm the cadets, he muses on his motivations for going to war. Here Shaara highlights the religious nature of Jackson's patriotism:

> He walked toward the town, ... thought of his path, his duty to God. He weighed again ... why he would fight, why it was the right thing to do, but all the politics and causes ran together, ... and the one clarity was that God was here, ... had shown him the Path, and the reasons men gave no longer mattered [Shaara, J., *Gods* 107–08].

Besides emphasizing Jackson's devoutness in the novel,[57] Shaara brings out his social awkwardness, a quality shared by other leaders such as "Chinese" Gordon. The historical Jackson was socially awkward, and so Shaara is not inaccurate in stressing this, but once Jackson the man becomes Jackson the novel character, the social shyness is to be seen not merely as one aspect of his personality or as a trait which helps to highlight his fearlessness in battle. Jackson the character is depicted carefully as both devout and socially somewhat inept, and even as somewhat humorless because of his stiff response from shyness. Shaara employs this shyness to good advantage in a scene in which Jackson rides up to Lee decked out in a new dress uniform given him by Jeb Stuart.[58] Lee's bemused reaction at the radical change in Jackson's usual appearance allows Shaara to show the two important leaders interacting as characters in a way which emphasizes not only Lee's poise but Jackson's clear subordination to him. Jackson's Presbyterian humility causes him to apologize for his display, curiously enough by means of apologizing to Stuart for seeming ungrateful:

> Jackson looked up, concerned, said, "Oh, certainly not, sir. Forgive me, General Stuart, but perhaps this was a mistake.... I did not wish to appear grandiose" [Shaara, J., *Gods* 314].

Jeff Shaara considers this a very special scene in the novel for him:

> The scene with the new coat was a joy to write, because it showed another side of Jackson that most people have never seen. I'm not so calculated as to use an attention-getting device to lead the reader to a look at a battle plan. The characters will carry you through the battle strategy with little help from me. After all, if the battle itself is not to be very interesting, nothing I can do will change that. By the time Fredericksburg emerges into the story, you have become acquainted enough with each character to appreciate the gravity of his involvement, and how it affects each one on a personal level. (I hope.) Any time I can bring a particularly

personal touch into the story, it breaks up the seriousness of the larger events. That's important to the reader. Tragedy after tragedy wears people out. By the same token, the death of the little Corbin girl shows Jackson experiencing a different kind of tragedy, and he responds very differently than he would in the thick of battle. It's another wonderful, deeply personal moment that gives Jackson three dimensions [Shaara, J., e-mail to the author].

This scene, in which Lee is comically surprised by Jackson's "display," is actually the opening of a sequence of tactical planning before the battle of Fredericksburg. In a scene also included in Ron Maxwell's film treatment of the novel, Jackson and Lee's other lieutenants at the battle plan their tactics on an unrolled map. When Lee requests input from Jackson, he is surprised at another deviation from the norm, because "Jackson had not built his reputation by defensive tactics" (Shaara, J., *Gods* 315).

Jackson had however built part of his reputation by defensive tactics, at least in the sense that one may combine an offensive strategy with defensive tactics. (For instance, the famous battle in the Ia Drang valley in November 1965 showcased the defensive skills of the U. S. Army's 7th Cavalry Regiment, which had actually begun the battle in an offensive posture.[59]) Similarly, at First Manassas, on July 21, 1861, Jackson displayed both defensive and offensive skills and determination. Shaara deals with the battle obliquely, summarizing it briefly and orienting it towards Lee's perspective. An old man serves as "reporter" of the battle, informing Lee of the rout of McDowell's forces and of Jackson's acquisition of his new nickname (Shaara, J., *Gods* 148–50).

A memorable sequence in the film of *Gods and Generals* was director Maxwell's presentation of the attack on Fredericksburg by Union Gen. Ambrose Burnside's forces on December 13, 1862. This series of frontal assaults on the well-fortified Confederate positions is considered one of the North's worst and most avoidable disasters. Maxwell presents the battle in a series of scenes, including the preparations for the attack at Burnside's Stafford Heights headquarters; the attempts to cross the Rappahannock into Fredericksburg, which were frustrated for a time by the lack of pontoon boats and then by the work of Gen. Richard Barksdale's Mississippi soldiers, who fired on the nearly defenseless Unionists in the boats; the fine scene of the fighting in the streets of Fredericksburg; the order of battle for the ill-fated Union regiments; the assault itself, which came in successive waves; and finally the aftermath, which included a horrifying and frigid nocturnal stay among the corpses of their comrades for many Unionists, including Joshua Lawrence Chamberlain.

The Fredericksburg scenes are mentioned here for their relevance to

Chamberlain, and for another reason: their hidden allusions to the English Civil War and to Oliver Cromwell. Ron Maxwell presents to the audience a display of Chamberlain's oratory (remember, he was a professor of rhetoric, which included classical expertise), in which he harangues his 20th Maine regiment with an extended set of verses about Caesar, Pompey, and the Roman Civil War. These verses derive from Lucan's *Pharsalia*:

> Now had Caesar in his course passed the icy Alpa, and revolved in his mind the vast commotions and the future war. When he had arrived at the waves of the little Rubicon…, the mighty image of his trembling country distinctly appeared to the chieftain in the darkness of the night…. Then did horror smite the limbs of the chieftain, his hair stood on end, and a languor that checked his course withheld his steps on the verge of the bank. Soon he exclaims, "O Thunderer, who dost look down … upon the walls of the mighty city from the Tarpeian rock, and ye Phrygian Penates of the Julian race…, ye secret mysteries, too, of Quirinus borne away…, and Jove of Latium, who dost reside in lofty Alba…, and ye Vestal hearths…, and thou, O Rome, equal to a supreme Deity, favour my designs! With no fatal arms am I pursuing thee; lo! here am I, Caesar, the conqueror by land and by sea, everywhere (if only it is permitted me) thine own soldier even still. He will it be, he the guilty one, who shall make me thy foe!"
>
> Then did he end the respite from the warfare, and swiftly bore the standards through the swollen stream…. When Caesar, the stream surmounted, reached the opposite banks, and stood upon the forbidden fields of Hesperia; "Here," said he, "here do I leave peace, and the violated laws behind; thee, Fortune, do I follow; henceforth, far hence be treaties! The Destinies have we trusted; War as our umpire we must adopt" [Lucan 12–13].

Lucan (Marcus Annaeus Lucanus, 39–65) (Duff ix) was a very widely read poet during the English seventeenth century (Syfret 162). In part this popularity was due to the prevailing literary tastes; but the *Pharsalia* was also very pertinent to the period when Charles I was fighting for his throne (and, as it turned out, his life) against the leaders of the Roundheads, most prominent among them Oliver Cromwell. Generally, in the English seventeenth century, Roman politics and history served as models (Syfret 162).

As Andrew Shifflett says, commenting on the English translation of Lucan by Tom May (1627), "*Lucan's Pharsalia* brought the wars and ideas of Caesar, Pompey, and Cato home to English readers during years when they could relate directly to the experience of civil war" (Shifflett 805–06). Lucan's epic poem deals primarily with the civil war which brought an end to the Roman republic. Julius Caesar (the eventual victor) and Pompey were the principal antagonists.

Lucan wrote at a chronological distance from the events; but unlike Horace, who was an unblinkered Augustan and thus favored authority (Syfret 171), Lucan was less sanguine about political leadership:

> Horace had experienced civil war...; the rule of Augustus promised and gave freedom, stability, and peace.... Lucan ... had seen what came after Augustus and knew that power must corrupt [Syfret 171].

Lucan in fact committed suicide after engaging in an anti–Nero plot (Duff xi).

Lucan's relevance to the English Civil War can be readily perceived in "An Horatian Ode upon Cromwell's Return from Ireland" (1650; see Marvell 294–95) by Andrew Marvell (1621–78). Scholars still debate Marvell's politics— Royalist (Cavalier) or Cromwellian (Roundhead), or indeed, neutral or shifting — but it is a commonplace of Marvell criticism that Lucan's poem served as a partial model for the "Horatian Ode." The source material from Lucan "relate[s] ... Caesar's decision to cross the Rubicon, and the chill dread of the inhabitants of Ariminium as he camped before the town" (Worden 526).

But, according to Worden, the background to the allusion must be explicated (526). Worden believes that Marvell saw in Cromwell a new English Caesar who would "clear the path to empire by defeating the Scots and then moving into Europe to level its monarchies" (534). Thus, Marvell's acquiescence in Cromwell's rule (despite any sympathies Marvell might have personally for the Stuarts) is "patriotic" in nature; Cromwell would "rescue a land torn by civil war" (531).

Unlike Marvell, who is often said to have been a Royalist, albeit on sometimes rickety evidence,[60] Joshua Chamberlain was certainly never considered a monarchist or a sympathizer to the aristocratic ideology of the South. Maxwell and Shaara are at some pains (and sometimes tiresomely so) to demonstrate the innate democracy of this man, who was motivated by the highly Evangelical populism of his New England upbringing. This populist fervor included abolitionist sentiments, which Chamberlain (Jeff Daniels) espouses at some length in the film. So, although Chamberlain's launching into Lucanic speechifying may seem out of place in the film at first viewing, in fact the rhetorical sally is quite apropos and is revelatory of both the best (courage, idealism, stoicism) and the worst (bombast, a touch of the self-righteous) in Chamberlain's character.

Like Marvell, Chamberlain appropriates Lucan for his own purposes. Much as Marvell applied Lucan's presentation of Caesar to the figure of Cromwell, in the apparent hope that the (anti–Royalist) Roundhead Cromwell would restore order to a strife-torn England, so Chamberlain, certainly a latter-day Roundhead in his anti-aristocratic sentiments, implicitly draws an analogy between Caesar at the Rubicon and Burnside's (synecdochically, Lincoln's) forces at the Rappahannock. Of course, with hindsight, it is clear that the crossing of the Rappahannock by Burnside's men certainly did not result in victory; if there was a Rubicon-like moment in the war, for the North, it was more likely Grant's decision to move South rather than to retreat North after the terrible battle in the Wilderness had begun. (Grant's army began the move on May 7, 1864; the moment was retold inimitably by Bruce Catton:

> All along the west side of the road for more than a mile Hancock's men were in position, most of them lying down trying to get a little sleep; ... Warren's corps was on the move, the dark road was all congested, and now here came the whole headquarters cavalcade, riding along with staff officers out in front to tell the men to stand aside and let them through. It was too dark for Hancock's men to recognize any individuals, but they knew the headquarters detachment when they saw it — and suddenly the soldiers realized that the generals were riding south. *South:* that meant no retreat, no defeat, maybe the battle had been a victory after all even though it had not exactly felt like one ... and the men of the Second Corps sprang to their feet and began to cheer, and kept on cheering as long as they had breath for it. For the first time, Grant had won the spontaneous applause of the Army of the Potomac [208].

Be this as it may, clearly Chamberlain's recourse to Lucan is not only politically fitting, it is emotionally in tune. Like the later Chamberlain of *Gettysburg*, the Chamberlain of *Gods and Generals* has great faith in the innate rightness of the Union cause; but he is definitely not a tender-minded optimist. He might well have agreed with Marvell, at a similar moment in English history. To Marvell, the position of England in the mid–17th century was also problematic; as Syfret notes, he worked with "[t]he obvious historical parallel [which] was the civil wars of Rome ... through the eyes of Horace and Lucan" (Syfret 171).

Just as Chamberlain loved the Union and thought the Rebels misguided in their enterprise, even though they might be men of integrity, so did men like Jackson and Lee leave the Union reluctantly, struggling with their consciences and their religious beliefs in the process. One of the central episodes in the path to be taken by Lee took place in the Virginia House of Delegates. The scene that shows Robert E. Lee accepting the command of the Virginia Militia from the Virginia House was shot in Charles Town, West Virginia, in the courthouse. In this case, Charles Town stands in for Richmond, where the actual House met in 1861 to offer the command to Lee.

The location is truly ironic. Not far from the courthouse is the site where abolitionist rampager John Brown was hanged on December 2, 1859. At this hanging, Jackson and his detachment of VMI cadets provided security. (The site is now marked only by a plaque at an ice-cream parlor.) The courthouse was the actual venue of the trial at which Brown was convicted and condemned, in one of the more fateful decisions contributing to the Civil War.

The courthouse is a simply but nicely constructed 19th-century building which had been dressed inside with portraits for the shoot. The "legislators" included among their number some current U. S. senators and other personalities, including retiring Texas Republican Phil Gramm. The scene to be filmed, Lee's acceptance of the command of the Virginia Militia, included the speech by the Virginia Speaker, played by dialect coach Robert Easton. Clearly enjoying his period role, Easton worked through the necessary takes with appropriately ripe flamboyance, introducing Robert Duvall as Lee like a Victorian emcee. After Duvall stepped to the podium, he too worked through several takes, and it seemed that the tightly scripted piece of his role was not especially suited to his famous improvisatory style. Despite some frustration on his part, though, Duvall turned in a compelling performance as a modest but dignified Lee accepting a commission as a reluctant warrior and secessionist.

If Lee's speech was integral to his career in the Confederacy, so too was the battle of First Manassas to the future of Thomas J. Jackson. Ron Maxwell clearly perceived the cinematic possibilities of the Manassas battle and did not treat it as an aside or as a bridge to the later career of Stonewall Jackson. The Manassas battlefield was recreated on a private farm near Staunton, Virginia. As with *Gettysburg*, Maxwell brought numerous companies of reenactors to film the important battle. The battle on Henry House Hill, where Jackson led the fierce counterattack that turned the fight for the Confederates, was recreated with a battery of Confederate Napoleons and a charge by a company of reenactors led by a cavalry dash headed up by Stephen Lang as Jackson. Both the artillery barrage and the cavalry charge required several takes for the proper timing and camera placement. The battle itself was to be augmented with CGI digitizing, but the employment of such technology did not mean that historical accuracy, or approximation to such accuracy, was to be sacrificed or shortchanged. In any event, the battle is one of the important set-pieces of the film version, even if for Shaara it represents mainly a station on Jackson's way to fame.

This scene also gives visibility to one of the more intriguing personalities in Jackson's brigade (and later in his corps), his artillery commander William Nelson Pendleton, nicknamed "Old Penn." This man was a chaplain turned cannoneer who added even more of a religious flavor to the Stonewall Brigade. Old Penn was quite a personality. He was not an especially gifted artilleryman, according to Edward Porter Alexander, important as an artillery leader at Gettysburg and later as a chronicler of the Civil War. Alexander, who *was* a gifted artilleryman, criticized Pendleton's performance at Malvern Hill in a tone of professional understatement that does not diminish the severity of his evaluation:

> Pendleton did not find Lee all day long [at Malvern Hill], nor did any orders from Lee find him. He implies [in his report] that his reserve artillery was not expected to go in until all the division batteries were first engaged. The division batteries were not organized into battalions, and, acting separately, were easily overpowered when brought out, one by one, in the face of many guns already in position. Pendleton's battalions of from three to six batteries each, would have stood much better chances; and while there were not many places, there were two extensive ones, in either of which all of these battalions could have been used — Poindexter's field, and the position on Magruder's right, to which Lee made the pioneers [the engineers] open a road. As matters were, our whole reserve artillery stood idle all day [Alexander 158].

Pendleton was the father of Alexander "Sandie" Pendleton, one of Jackson's more famous aides (played in the film by Jeremy London).

In the film, Old Penn (played by British actor John Castle) is introduced to the viewer as he shows off his battery of four Napoleons. He tells Jackson that he and his men call them "Matthew, Mark, Luke, and John" (an audience-pleaser). This isn't a made-for-Hollywood anecdote. The cannons actually were so tagged. John M. Opie, who was a cavalryman in the Fifth Virginia (a part of the Stonewall Brigade), recounts the role of Penn and his battery in an engagement (Opie's first) very early in the war:

> Then a battery took position and commenced firing at us, when four of our guns, unlimbering, immediately returned their fire. The officer in command of our artillery was a pious old gentleman, an Episcopal preacher, Captain Pendleton, who subsequently became general of artillery. He named his cannon Matthew, Mark, Luke, and John. When he wished a gun to be fired, he raised his hands towards the heavens and exclaimed aloud, "May the Lord have mercy on their wicked souls! Fire!" [Opie 21–22].

The sequence in the film version closes with a meditative scene at the end of the battle in which Jackson and an aide return to the battlefield. Shooting at "magic hour," Maxwell and cinematographer Kees van Ostrum compose a beautiful scene, with the smoke of battle still lingering and mist rising from the field. Of course, the beauty in pictorial terms is to be contrasted with the death and suffering on the field. Jackson goes to a dead soldier and kneels as if to bless him. The clear intent of the scene is to position Jackson as a father-figure and as a spiritual leader, ministering to his men in time of need. On a simpler level, the scene shows another side of Jackson, the private side of compassion and tenderness, which did not often appear in the battlefield context. Stephen Lang, playing Jackson, interprets quite subtly the shift from the tough, clipped style germane to Jackson's generalship on the field to the private, softer side of this difficult role.[61]

On the film set, Stephen Lang often appeared mercurial, seemingly changing in mood from brusqueness to geniality. When not in the middle of a stressful shoot, he is in fact a very urbane, congenial person. He told the author that he went to considerable effort to "stay in character" on set, and that the Stonewall persona was a challenge to maintain. Certainly the ruthless aspect of Stonewall's character must have been draining to portray.

Lang even maintained his stage accent when off-camera, talking on the set with cast, crew, and visitors in the Virginia Highlands twang adopted as close to Jackson's probable accent. As were other members of the cast, Lang was assisted by dialect coach Robert Easton, a very remarkable professional who is expert in the many subtle variations of Virginia dialect.[62] This maintaining of a stage persona is partially, as Lang says, a tactic in keeping an even tone to the performance; but Lang is on to something deeper about personalities like Jackson's (or Gordon's). That something deeper is the need for a man as complex as Jackson to show a certain persona to the outside world in order to protect his hidden vulnerabilities, both for emotional and for professional reasons. Thus, Jackson was gruff and even abrasive with subordinates; he seemed quick to rush to judgment, sometimes fatal judgment, as when he summarily ordered a man shot because he appeared to be a spy. (He was not, and the order was rescinded.) Lang, too, often seemed gruff and brusque, even unapproachable; this apparently was largely attributable to staying "in character."

The tougher side of Jackson, the obverse which rounds out his particular version of religious generalship, is on display in the film most especially at the battle of Chancellorsville. Here, Jackson leads his men in a furious charge against the Federals, part of the famous flank attack which sealed Jackson's fame as an aggressive, farsighted tactician.[63] In the Shaara novel, as the first fury of the charge slows, Jackson's men face a routed line of Federals, where one very young soldier faces them defiantly and is cut down. Shaara places within an interior monologue a famous remark by Jackson which was actually made to some of his soldiers who held their fire at the sight of a courageous Union officer, who thus managed to escape death at that moment:

> now Jackson saw one man, with the face of a boy, still standing, facing the oncoming line. He was trying to reload, and now Colston's men were on him, and the boy was trying to raise the rifle, and there was a flash of steel, the quick rip of the bayonet, and the boy was down. Jackson turned away, the image hard in his mind, thought, We must kill the brave ones, we must kill them *all*[64] [Shaara, J., *Gods* 424].

A strong point of the film adaptation of *Gods and Generals* is the Jackson death scene. This is of course one of the central scenes in the Jackson epic and is derived from eyewitness accounts of the event, including those by Anna Jackson, Sandie Pendleton, and Dr. Hunter McGuire, the attending surgeon. After being wounded on May 2, 1863, and undergoing amputation of his injured arm on May 3, Jackson appeared to be recovering. But by May 8th the signs of pneumonia, or of some comparably serious infection, coupled with extreme debilitation probably from fatigue, were all too evident.[65] His wife, Anna, was informed, as was Jackson, and Anna brought their infant daughter, Julia, to Jackson's bedside on the final day, May 10. This is the scene adapted from the novel and shot with great care by Ron Maxwell.

Maxwell wanted to emphasize Jackson's dignity and nobility in accepting his fate. These qualities were universally noted by the eyewitnesses to the historical scene. So, the film scene was shot with much effort given to eliciting restraint and self-discipline as the governing emotions not only from Lang but also from those attending the deathbed scene, especially Kali Rocha as Anna. The visitors to the sickroom, Jackson's aides Pendleton, Morrison, and Smith, were to rise from their chairs as the overhead camera tracked back to end the scene in a bloom of light symbolizing the transit of Jackson's soul. This effect was perhaps the most demanding because of the precise timing required of the actors. Several takes were required for the timing to be correctly effected.[66]

The death scene is only one way in which Jackson is presented as an epic hero: being mourned by his wife and his "retainers," Jackson will achieve a species of immortality as signaled by the bloom of light at the moment of his demise. Maxwell also treats Jackson as epic material by dealing with the response of his superior to the death of his "vassal" or retainer. The scene in the film when Lee is informed of the death of his loyal lieutenant is also based on the novel's presentation of historical material. In the film, the scene provides an opportunity for Robert Duvall, as Lee, to showcase his mastery of emotional subtlety through minimal gesture.[67] When the news is brought to Lee by an assistant, he momentarily loses control of his public self-possession. Duvall conveys this moment of self-revelation by turning away from the camera to hide the tear welling in his eye but at the same time allowing his voice to break while pronouncing his brief tribute to Jackson.[68]

The death of Jackson deprived Lee of his most trusted lieutenant. He was left with the enigmatic Longstreet and with the sometimes unreliable and infirm A. P. Hill, as well as with Dick Ewell, who was unfortunately bereft of the strong guidance and prodding given him by Jackson.[69] The Confederate cause suffered badly as a result of the loss of Jackson, but the likelihood in any case is that the rebellion would have failed due to lack of resources.

The situation on the Union side was quite different. Grant became the new overall commander of the Union armies, although Meade retained nominal command of the Army of the Potomac. Grant could call upon Sherman and George Thomas (with whom Grant did not get along, but who was stolidly reliable) as well as upon the formidable pepper-pot Phil Sheridan as subordinate commanders. Further down in the command structure, Grant had some excellent assistance; one of the better commanders was Joshua Chamberlain, to whom considerable space is devoted in the Shaara novels. Chamberlain, a former rhetoric professor from Bowdoin College in Brunswick, Maine, had become by 1863 an accomplished regimental commander. He was promoted to brigadier general on the battlefield by Grant himself, the only instance of such promotion during the war. Wounded six times during the war, Chamberlain was to conduct the formal ceremony of the stacking of arms at Appomattox, where his chivalrous behavior in ordering his troops to carry arms as a salute to the dispirited Confederates commanded by Gen. John B. Gordon earned him the respect of his foes. He went on to serve as governor of Maine and to participate in Union remembrance ceremonies during subsequent years.[70] Chamberlain forms a nice counterpoint to Jackson, as a more secularized version of the priestly warrior.

Chamberlain was at first destined for the seminary, or so were his mother's wishes. But he ended up studying languages and rhetoric and became a professor at Bowdoin College, where his lectures showed evidence of his background in religion and in moral philosophy. Both Shaara novels so far considered highlight his philosophical and quasi-religious side, but he is far more skeptical than Jackson, or, for that matter, than Lee.

Jeff Shaara underlines the religious background of the future war hero, noting that his mother had named him in a purposeful manner. His two given names, Joshua Lawrence, encapsulate his hybrid heritage of war and religion:

> His father ... had named him to honor the famous military hero of 1812, Commodore Lawrence, the man forever known for the quote, "Don't give up the ship" [oddly apropos given Chamberlain's last-ditch effort at Little Round Top]. His mother ... preferred the more biblical Joshua, and though both his father and grandfather had been named Joshua, his father had settled on calling him Lawrence... [32].

While not religious in the deep and fervent Jackson manner, Chamberlain, a thoughtful New Englander, does participate in a very Emersonian civil religion, expressing a strong faith in a moral society. The two figures present a useful contrast between New England Puritanism and Virginia Presbyterianism, both of which grew out of the Protestant Reformation but which represent very different lines of development. Chamberlain expresses this faith in a halting address to his class in June 1862, a scene adapted in shortened form in the film version. In the novel, Chamberlain asks his students to consider whether or not basic patriotism is the cause for which many Unionists fight. He decides that the motivation for volunteering in this war is "more than politics, more than Mr. Lincoln, more than some vague principle…. If you believe something is truly important, you have an obligation to fight for it" (Shaara, J., *Gods* 200).

This expression of civic faith is certainly more secular than Jackson's, founded as the Virginian's is upon Calvinist principles. Where Jackson fits the designation "zealous nationalist," Chamberlain would fall into the category of "prophetic nationalism." But both espouse extrinsic reasons for their actions, and both seem to march to a directive outside themselves. Chamberlain, in fact, gives up his teaching post and risks his marriage to leave for an unknown future in the Union army.

His leave-taking in the film from his wife, Fannie (Mira Sorvino), contains the poignant inclusion of a Cavalier poem by Richard Lovelace, "To Lucasta, Going to the Warres."[71] Fannie recites the poem to Chamberlain, lending doubly sly overtones to the scene. In the first place, the poem should be recited by Chamberlain, as the man of the pair, and as the warrior departing to his possible death. Additionally, the use of the poem by Fannie communicates her consciousness of her own private war against her husband's enlistment, which she did not hear of until it was a fait accompli, and which she would probably have opposed. A third and probably unintended irony is the fact that Lovelace was a Cavalier poet, sympathetic to royalism. The poem might have fit better politically in the mouth of Mrs. Robert E. Lee than in the mouth of Fannie Chamberlain, with her "Roundhead" abolitionist, democratic sympathies.

Joshua Chamberlain became a hero to many Americans because of his "everyman" qualities. Stonewall Jackson has been a hero to many Americans, and to many Europeans too, because of his essential decency, his basic Americanness. The film emphasizes these qualities in several scenes.

It is historical fact that Jackson became close to the five-year-old daughter of a woman, Kate Corbin, who provided hospitality to Jackson and his aides and to Lee's general staff. Jackson and the little girl played and talked and the general was seen to be enthralled as she played with paper dolls. In her memoirs, a neighbor of the Corbins, Fannie Adams, wrote not only of the general's affection for little Jane Corbin, but of his warm treatment of another child who lived near his headquarters: "They were great pets with the General.... On one occasion they carried him a basket of apples. When they came back each had a gold band on her hair. General Jackson had taken the braid from his caps—his old one and his new." According to Adams, who was 13 at the time, she also acquired "pet" status from Jackson; he allowed her to "cut off one curl" from his hair (Adams 292–93).

The film improves on these facts. Using a scene when Jackson must decide the fate of some deserters, he is shown whittling a piece of wood. Sandie Pendleton comes into his tent to discuss what to do with the deserters. Jackson is unbending, saying that military justice must prevail because these men are the enemies of the whole Confederacy.[72] The men are then shown to have been condemned and are executed by firing squad. One of them is Willie, who in a scene early in the film had pledged to Jackson to die if necessary for the Confederacy, opposing his father's clear wish that he not enlist. Die he does, but not in the glorious way he would have wanted.

The significance of the whittling becomes clear later on, in a fine example of preparation on the part of Maxwell and Shaara. When Jackson learns that Jane Corbin is ill with scarlet fever, he goes to see her and gives her a little carved angel which he asks her to put on her Christmas tree. This of course might be dismissed by modernist cynics as an example of Dickensian sentimentality, but remember that it's also quite true to the period: these men and women *were* more sentimental in public than people are nowadays.

Jackson is soon informed that Jane has died. He walks over to a tree stump, sits down, and starts weeping audibly. Sandie Pendleton wonders why he's crying when he didn't cry for his dead men. Dr. McGuire says that "He's crying for all of us." Maybe so. Perhaps instead he's remembering his dead child, Mary, and that he fears that he may never see his baby daughter, Julia. In any case, the film does not shrink from showing the very real sentiments actually expressed by this many-sided and much misunderstood soldier (Maxwell, *Gods and Generals*).

Also prominent in the film *Gods and Generals* is the insistent presentation of Stonewall Jackson's human or private side. This is at least unusual in films about Civil War heroes, who tend to be shown in battlefield frame only. Their dilemmas and extra dimensions are normally and conventionally related to their strategy and tactics. But *Gods and Generals*, both novel and film, tries to look through the characters' eyes.[73] And, even when not literally showing the characters' point of view, the film opens up unexpected perspectives on them. Hence, the scene shows Jackson carrying little Jane Corbin "on horseback." While Jackson "bucks" and "whinnies," his men watch in astonished bemusement. Many have never seen this side of any general, much less of the reputedly grim Jackson. Despite his role as a "soldier of God," Jackson did not lose the core of kindness and generosity which had made him so beloved to his family and to many who knew him in Lexington.

3

Other Protestant Warriors

Gustavus Adolphus and General
Muhlenberg, Lutheran Soldiers

Stonewall Jackson is an honored figure in Southern and American legend because of his personal qualities, including his courage, initiative, innate tactical talent, and deep religious faith. Additionally, he is a figure accorded epic status because of his untimely death. Like Jackson, King Gustavus II Adolphus of Sweden (1594–1632) has been revered in his homeland and abroad for his special qualities and has been mourned for his early death on the field of battle.

Gustavus Adolphus became king in 1611 upon the death of his father, Charles XI. Charles had pursued an aggressive foreign policy which had opened up a two-front conflict. A dispute with Poland had inflamed the situation in the East; this circumstance in turn aggravated Denmark's stance toward Sweden in the West because of Danish ambitions in the East. So, Gustavus inherited a potentially explosive situation. He pursued the war with Denmark, which was not a success, and which ended in the Peace of Knäred in 1613. The dispute with Poland was put on the back burner for some time, flaring up briefly in 1617. During the early 1620s, Gustavus was to address the Polish question as his principal foreign policy concern. The vicissitudes of foreign entanglements during the decade led to Sweden's involvement, with Gustavus as military and civil leader, in the Thirty Years War (1618–48). Gustavus was killed in battle in 1632 (Roberts, M., *Gustavus Adolphus* Ch. 3–4).

Gustavus Adolphus of course differs from Stonewall Jackson in the important respect that Gustavus Adolphus was the king of a sovereign nation and Jackson was a military leader, in a somewhat subordinate capac-

King Gustavus II Adolphus (1594–1632) (Reproduction: The Royal Library, National Library of Sweden).

ity, of a would-be sovereign nation. Both were, however, central to momentous events in the history of their countries, and both displayed outstanding military and personal qualities. And both acted from religious as well as military motivations.

According to historian Michael Roberts, division of Gustavus Adolphus's motives into neat compartments of "religious" vs. "military" or "political" is not possible. He notes that little disagreement now exists among historians as to the motivations of a 17th-century leader such as Gustavus Adolphus: "The old controversy about whether Gustavus was animated by religious or political motives has long since ceased to trouble historians. In the world of the early seventeenth century the two could scarcely be disassociated" (Roberts, M., *Gustavus Adolphus* 54). But, continues Roberts, the king was a sincere Protestant, with deep convictions: "His Protestantism was based on education and founded in conviction; his piety was genuine; his sense of confessional solidarity was strong" (54). Still, his commitment to the Protestant faith had to be fitted with his duty to his nation: "The outbreak of the Thirty Years War confronted him with the necessity of making judgements whch should balance the interest of Protestantism against the interests of Sweden.... In 1611 it was clear ... that the first priority must be Poland. By 1628 ... the first priority had become Germany" (Roberts, M., *Gustavus Adolphus* 54–55). So Gustavus and Sweden entered the war, which was to end for Gustavus with his ultimately ignominious death (in spite of his valor) on the battlefield:

> The Swedish left had run into tough resistance, and in an effort to lighten the pressure upon it Gustavus took the Småland regiment of cavalry to that part of the front and launched it in a charge.... Almost immediately, he was hit; his horse carried him away from his escort.... An Imperialist horseman fired a pistol into his back; he fell heavily from the saddle; and as he lay face downward in the mud a final shot through the head ended his life. The body lay where it fell. Enemy plunderers took the King's ring, his watch, the chain which he habitually wore around his neck, and one of his spurs; until at last, stripped to the shirt, the corpse lay half-naked and unregarded, while his riderless horse careered around the battlefield [Roberts 183–84].

Gustavus Adolphus did become a revered figure in Sweden, and he did come to represent in no small part the Protestants' struggle against the Catholics. He was also seen as a soldier's soldier. His conduct on the battlefield and in camp with his soldiers is reminiscent of another great leader, Stonewall Jackson; for example, during the king's battlefield career, "when field fortifications were to be constructed he did not think it beneath his dignity to do his share of the digging." Also like Jackson, the king was

bold to the point of heedlessness (Roberts, M., *Gustavus Adolphus* 194).
He shared as well with Jackson, though not to the degree to which Jackson carried it, the practice of ascetic living: "He did not share the contemporary habit of heavy eating and drinking, though he [unlike Jackson] could hold his liquor when the obligations of hospitality required" (Roberts, M., *Gustavus Adolphus* 194). In summing up the reputation gained by this remarkable king, Roberts writes:

> The mercenary soldiers in his armies certainly did not forget him. In his lifetime he had seemed a comrade as well as a leader; devotion to his person was the main link that bound them together; and after his death he became a legend. His own subjects were in no doubt as to his stature: within a decade of Lützen they were habitually referring to him as "Gustavus Adolphus the Great." No Swedish monarch has been more beloved in his lifetime; none has enjoyed a more lasting popularity with posterity — and even with historians [195].

Like Jackson, Gustavus Adolphus was a very deeply religious Protestant who was nevertheless not a narrow-minded bigot. Several sources on Jackson stress this point. A good example is his widow, Anna Morrison Jackson, in her biography of the general:

> he was the furthest possible remove from being a bigot. His views of each denomination had been obtained from itself, not from its opponents. Hence he could see excellences in all. Even of the Roman Catholic Church [which he had seriously considered joining when in Mexico] he had a much more favorable impression than most Protestants, and he fraternized with all evangelical denominations. During a visit to New York City, one Sabbath morning, we chanced to find ourselves at the door of an Episcopal church at the hour for worship. He proposed that we should enter; and as it was a day for the celebration of the communion, he remained for that service, of which he partook in the most devout manner. It was with the utmost reverence and solemnity that he walked up the chancel and knelt to receive the elements [58–59].

Concerning the Swedish king, Philip J. Haythornthwaite comments that:

> Religion was one of the motivating passions of Gustavus' life. A most devout man without being a bigot, he saw himself as the champion and defender of Protestantism. "A good Christian," he declared, "can never be a bad soldier; and the man who has finished his prayers has already got over the best part of his day's work" [26–27].

Both Jackson and Gustavus Adolphus were to be eulogized, and both were to become inspirations for literary treatment. In the case of the Swedish king, contemporary works were written about him by his "court poet," Johan Narssius. These works "have long lain buried in the dust-heaps of oblivion" (Ahnlund 295).[74] But at the turn of the 20th century, the great Swedish dramatist August Strindberg (1849–1912) was to base one of his historical plays on the life of the king. *Gustav Adolf* (1900) "presents a superb realistic interpretation of the king" as a corrective to the plaster saint "Gustav Adolf of the textbooks" of Strindberg's time (Strindberg viii, 5).

Less famed than Gustavus Adolphus was Peter Gabriel Muhlenberg (1746–1807), a Lutheran pastor from Pennsylvania who rose to become a major general in the Continental army during the American Revolution. Before the Revolution, as head of the Virginians of German descent, Muhlenberg was an active supporter of the Patrick Henry faction, which urged strong measures against the British (Muhlenberg 41–45). The pastor was in fact known for his fiery views as "Peter the Devil" (Van Tyne 56). When the decision was taken to seek independence, he was given a commission as colonel of the 8th Regiment from Virginia. He decided soon afterward to preach a sermon at Woodstock, Virginia, to the members of his far-ranging congregation. This sermon was the "occasion" of "a well-authenticated anecdote" about the new officer-preacher (49–50). Henry A. Muhlenberg sets the scene for the sermon:

> Upon his [Rev. Muhlenberg's] arrival at Woodstock, his different congregations ... were notified that upon the following Sabbath their beloved pastor would deliver his farewell sermon.... Of this event numerous traditionary accounts are still preserved..., all coinciding with the written evidence.... The appointed day came. The rude country church was filled to overflowing with the hardy mountaineers of the frontier counties.... We may well imagine that the feelings which actuated the assembly were of no ordinary kind.... In this spirit the people awaited the arrival of him whom they were now to hear for the last time [Muhlenberg 50–52].

The reverend-colonel arrived, clothed in the robes of his clerical office. The scene to be narrated by his descendant, although evidently authentic, seems straight out of epic tradition:

> He came, and ascended the pulpit, his tall form arrayed in full uniform, over which his gown, the symbol of his holy calling, was thrown. He was a plain, straightforward speaker, whose native eloquence was well suited to the people among whom he laboured. At all times capable of commanding the deepest attention, we may well conceive that upon this great occasion, when high, stern thoughts were burning for utterance, the people who heard him hung upon his fiery words with all the intensity of their

souls.... After recapitulating, in words that aroused the coldest, the story of their sufferings and their wrongs, and telling them of the sacred character of the struggle in which he had unsheathed his sword, and for which he had left the altar he had vowed to serve, he said "that, in the language of holy writ, there was a time for all things, a time to preach and a time to pray, but those times had passed away;" and in a voice that re-echoed through the church like a trumpet-blast, "that there was a time to fight, and that time had now come!" [52–53].

The scene ends in a climax so uplifting that, were it not attested as true, would seem to have been invented from cloth of epic or romance. Thus, continues Henry Muhlenberg's account:

> The sermon finished, he pronounced the benediction. A breathless stillness brooded over the congregation. Deliberately pulling off the gown, which had thus far covered his martial figure, he stood before them a girded warrior; and descending from the pulpit, ordered his drums at the church-door to beat for recruits. Then followed a scene to which even the American revolution, rich as it is in bright examples of the patriotic devotion of the people, affords no parallel. His audience, excited in the highest degree by the impassioned words which had fallen from his lips, flocked around him, eager to be ranked among his followers. Old men were seen bringing forward their children, wives their husbands, and widowed mothers their sons, sending them under his paternal care to fight the battles of their country.... Nearly three hundred men of the frontier churches that day enlisted under his banner; and the gown then thrown off was worn for the last time [Muhlenberg 53–54].

The description is especially reminiscent of epic and its related form, romance, in its insistent use of encomiastic and hyperbolic language. Thus, the point is made that the preacher has a "tall form"; he is a masculine, soldierly figure who fulfills by his physicality and his soldierly calling the topical requisites for *fortitudo*. His plain speaking style is emphasized, and it is noted that despite this plain, straightforward style he is capable of arousing the audience: like Achilles, the Cid, or for that matter Patton, the reverend communicates his emotions through manly means: no effete, flowery oratory for him. Since he is a cleric, the *sapientia* part of the topos is clearly fulfilled, but it is not the *sapientia* of the weak townsman or the cloistered scribe: this man is a seamless mix of *sapientia* and *fortitudo*— the complete epic hero, as it were.

Perhaps one might see a distant echo of figures like Rev. Muhlenberg in the storyline of the Revolutionary War film *The Patriot* (2000), directed by Roland Emmerich and starring Mel Gibson as a composite hero, Col. Benjamin Martin, based in part on the historical leader Francis Marion, the "Swamp Fox," who contributed to the defeat of the British forces by employing guerrilla tactics in the swamps of the Santee River in lowland South Carolina. One of his staunchest allies is the pastor of the town near his plantation. This pastor, Reverend Oliver (Rene Auberjonois) follows the men of his church into the forces of Col. Martin, fighting as an irregular until he is killed during an ambush of the camp of Martin's nemesis, British Col. William Tavington (played by Jason Isaacs and based on the historical Col. Banastre Tarleton). The pastor never exchanges his clerical collar for a military one, unlike Muhlenberg. His church is desecrated by Tavington, who orders the parishioners burned inside it, leading to a reckless fury on the part of Martin's men, including his son Gabriel (Heath Ledger) and the pastor, who then die in the attack on Tavington's camp (Emmerich).

In passing, it is well to note that the image of the preacher "pulling off" the clerical "gown" to reveal the "girded warrior" is strangely parallel to a memorable scene from the Michael Curtiz *Adventures of Robin Hood* (1938) (Curtiz). King Richard the Lion-heart is travelling incognito in England because his brother John (Claude Rains) has usurped the throne during his absence on the Crusades. Richard and his small band are waylaid by Robin Hood and his men. After the usual requests to hand over the loot, Robin (Errol Flynn) engages the (incognito) King Richard (Ian Hunter) in brief conversation about his own loyalties (to Richard) and about the sorry state of the realm. Richard still does not reveal himself. Then, Robin, having learned from his interlocutor (Richard) that the king (Richard himself) is back in the kingdom, orders his men to go to find him and to protect him at all costs. Only then, assured of Robin's loyalty and rather forced by events to drop his pretense, does Richard say that Robin and his men need look no further for the King because he is "right here." Richard dramatically pulls aside his cloak to reveal the coat of arms of Lion-heart — a glorious pop culture moment which nonetheless partakes of epic tradition (with its emphasis on hidden identity and anagnorisis extending back to the *Odyssey*) for its effect, much as does the scene of Muhlenberg's own self-revelation.

Henry Havelock, Victorian Champion

Jackson was sometimes compared to General Sir Henry Havelock (1795–1857) by biographers contemporary to the Civil War. Havelock was a hero for the British public because of his relief of Lucknow during the 1857 Sepoy Mutiny in India ("Havelock" 470). He was admired as much for his Christian qualities as for his soldiering, as the following obituary from *Saturday Review* attests: "While many heroes whose exploits have been on a much larger scale have become mere assemblages of syllables in the page of history, General Havelock's will be reverently spoken, as a type of the Christian soldier" (Pollock 2–3).

One comparison drawn between the two soldiers stressed their Christian nature and dwelt upon the similarities in their tactical qualities. This comparison was made in an 1866 biography of Jefferson Davis and Jackson and will be quoted here in its entirety:

> There is much, too, in Jackson's character, that resembles the pictures which have been drawn of Havelock, who, a few years ago, rendered his name famous by the brilliancy of his military performances in India. Added to a strong religious feeling which was predominant in the character of both these Generals, they alike possessed great activity of mind and fertility of resource, and each exercised over those under his command such a parental sway, that his entire force was ever ready to move almost as one man at the beck of its commander. This is plainly shown in the celerity of movements and in the long and rapid marches which so mainly tended to the greatness of their successes. Each considered that he had a duty to perform — his duty to his country — a duty, however, which in one case was directed to a sectional part thereof, and against the best interests of the entire nation; and the singleness of purpose of each was so great, that he removed every obstacle out of the way which interfered with the proper performance of this duty — never omitting that greater duty of all men, the duty to his Maker; never undertaking any enterprise without first invoking the Deity to guide his steps and to bless his endeavors with success [*Jefferson Davis* 230–31].

Despite such comparisons, opinion about the parallels between Jackson and Havelock was not unanimous. R.L. Dabney disagreed with such parallels, although he did not dismiss the existence of some similarities between the two leaders "in energy, in directness, in bravery, and in the vigor of [their] faith." But Dabney did not believe that Jackson and Havelock were really comparable:

> [Jackson's] spiritual character was far more symmetrical, mellow, and noble [than Havelock's]. His ambition was more thoroughly chastened. He had risen to a calm and holy superiority to all the glitter of military glory, to which Havelock never attained. Had Jackson reared sons to succeed to his name, he would never, like him, have directed them to the bustling pursuits of arms in preference to the sacred office of the gospel ministry. He would have said that, if his sons were clearly called by the providence of God to fight, and even to die, for the necessary defence of their coun-

try, then he should desire to see them brave soldiers; but that otherwise, his warmest wish for them would be, that they might share the honor of winning souls, the calling which he most coveted for himself. Nor had he, either in manners or character, any of that abnormal vivacity which made Havelock as peculiar as he was great. The field on which his military genius was displayed, and the armies he wielded, were so large compared with those of the British captain, that a comparison on this point would be equally difficult and unfair [112–13].

J.F. Pollock, the most recent biographer of Havelock, highlights his Christian piety but distinguishes between Havelock and more fanatical warriors. He sketches the encounter between Havelock and fellow commander Neill,

Henry Havelock

whom he was relieving and superseding after Neill's successful defense of his post against mutiny. Pollock provides the following portrait of Neill and contrasts him with Havelock:

> Lieutenant-Colonel J.G. Neill, Madras Fusiliers, was an energetic and decisive soldier…. He was enthusiastic and impatient, and believed that unhesitant action in itself won campaigns, whatever the odds or the lack of supplies. He was a Godfearing Scot, but like Cromwell [and unlike Jackson, despite the popular misunderstandings about him] inclined to consider himself the Arm of the Lord and the Scourge of God, pretensions which, on the part of any man, Havelock dismissed as un–Christian [Pollock 156].

Neill sounds almost like a caricature of Jackson. Here as well is the justified analogy between Havelock and Jackson: like Havelock, Jackson attributed his victories to God, thinking of himself as a humble instrument — certainly not "the Scourge of God."

With regard to the religious warrior in the Victorian age, the case of Henry Havelock is instructive as both a parallel and a contrast to the case of Stonewall Jackson. Like Jackson, Havelock was adulated in his home country for his piety and courage. But, unlike Jackson, Havelock appears to have been the object of adoration based on rather tenuous evidence. Both men, though, reflect in their public images the mindset of the Victorian period in England and in America.

Olive Anderson expresses significant skepticism about the reverence for Havelock. In her instructive study, she details the increased importance of the Christian warrior-hero in Victoria's England. She notes that the army's low social status started to rise rapidly with the war in Crimea (Anderson 46). This new popularity would have arisen largely from the identification of the middle class with the men in the army and with the values expressed by them. According to Richard Altick, the middle class had become by Victorian times central to British society: "It was the middle-class orientation and code of values that lent the Victorian social climate its discinctive flavor. Its moral ideology … embraced the values to which most Victorians, even including some aristocrats … subscribed" (Altick 28). The middle class, Altick notes, had identified itself closely with the national interest: "Since the middle class regarded itself as the moral heart of Victorian society, … it took the understandable position that what was good for it was ipso facto good for the nation" (Altick 29). Any new notions about the army and about Christian heroism, therefore, would have had their origins or at least their center in the burgeoning middle class. Much the same could be said of the United States at the time, where even in the South the middle class was a strong force.

Anderson shows as well that in Britain at least, the notion of Christian heroism was new for the 19th-century public. She points to the popularity of the *Memorials of Captain Hedley Vicars, 97th Regiment* (1855; by Catherine Marsh and based on the life of an obscure soldier), which "offered professional soldiers biographical proof that a man of their own day could be a zealous Christian" and a worthy military man at the same time, despite his current low social repute (48–49).

The Sepoy Mutiny of 1857 contributed materially to the new attitude towards the British Army. The Mutiny was in part seen as "a challenge to Christianity itself, … as a divine punishment for official compromise with false religions." Niall Ferguson supports this perspective in commenting that the "Indian [Sepoy] Mutiny was … much more than its name implies. It was a full-blown war" (Ferguson 145–46). Ferguson explains that although the mutiny had several causes, the central motive was "their [the Indian soldiers'] essentially conservative reaction against a succession of British interferences with Indian culture, which seemed to—and in many ways actually did — add up to a plot to Christianize India" (Ferguson 146). Therefore it was quite logical for the British public to react to the Mutiny as an anti–Christian rebellion. Anderson concludes that "any commander who decisively castigated the rebels was likely to become a popular hero" (49). Thus the ground was well-prepared for the near-canonization of Havelock, the saintly man of the hour.

Still, as Anderson notes, among several military men of the conflict, he was the only one to receive such treatment. This was evidently due to the fortuitous confluence of the new importance of the middle class, of which he was "patently" a member, and of a moment in Victorian history "when the educated classes were rapidly becoming enthusiastic about mid–seventeenth century puritanism, and about Cromwell and the Iron-sides in particular." Much of this fascination was due to the work of Car-lyle, who had written forcefully and romantically about Cromwell the hero (Anderson 50–51). And, "Havelock's posthumous renown ... contributed to the growing secular cult of a sternly moral militarism," and to the glorification of the "staunchly puritan man of blood" (51).

This image sounds very much like the image of Stonewall Jackson in the South, and, not coincidentally, in England, where he was greatly admired. The chief distinction, of course, is that there was no doubt of Jackson's unique talent; in fact, his Christianity sometimes seemed incom-patible with his famed "ruthlessness" and unforgiving nature in battle. And one does not note generally in the United States the British attitude towards the military as low-life undesirables. The attitude did exist, though. As Drew Gilpin Faust observes, the mixing of virtue and war was not immediately apparent to Southern moral leaders:

> Godly southerners at first feared that the influences might work in just the opposite direction: that battle would prove an impediment to piety. "War is the hotbed of iniquity of every kind," wrote the Reverend Charles Colcock Jones [of Georgia]. The Army had in all ages been "the greatest school of vice" [Faust 68].

The distinction could be drawn that, for the average Briton of the time, a soldier was not a hero because of being a Christian, not a better Christ-ian because of being a hero: he was for many, at least until the Crimea, a soldier or a hero in contradistinction to being a Christian. "Soldierly virtues" was for the English public a self-evident oxymoron. In the United States, however, and especially in the South, a soldierly hero was often such precisely because of his Christian faith and virtue — or at the very least, no essential contradiction was perceived.

The image of Stonewall Jackson was in line with the post–Crimea image of the British warrior-hero, although, one might add, Jackson's persona displayed a crucial element of Presbyterian (Calvinist) hardness that was not always present in the biographies of British naval heroes. For example, these heroes, as in the case of Havelock in the army, were often glorified by Evangelicals such as Baptists, who were of a different religious tradition than their fellow Protestants, the Scots Presbyterians, from whom Jackson drew his inspiration (Hamilton, C.I., "Naval" 388). Much of Havelock's appeal was due to his piousness (Anderson 50). (He sounds like Oliver O. Howard, who was tolerated rather than admired in the Union Army for his obvious piousness.) Jackson was of course well-known for being pious, but he did not force this on others (he did encourage them to the path of faith, however); and he did not cross the line into self-righteousness about temperance and other such causes. His zeal was displayed in Old Testament terms as an avenging soldier of God. Again there is the distinction between Calvinistic Scots-Irish Presbyterianism (the Reformed Church in the United States) and the Evangelical Baptists or Methodists from England, who were much closer to Congregationalism.

The recent film version of Jeff Shaara's *Gods and Generals* highlights the "avenging angel" aspect of Jackson's persona. Jackson refers to himself and the Stonewall Brigade, in a harangue prior to First Manassas, as "wielding the sword of God." His famous and much-debated remarks about the "black flag" (no quarter) policy are included in a scene with Jeb Stuart. And, most memorably, he replies to Dr. McGuire, outraged at the invasion by the North, that the Army of Northern Virginia must "kill every last man of them."

But Jackson's other, more private, side also appears prominently, especially regarding his religious faith. An early example of this in the film is a scene in his home in Lexington, with his wife Anna, just prior to his departure for Harpers Ferry at the beginning of the war. Taking Anna into the parlor, he reads from his "favorite" verse, 2 Corinthians 5.1: "For we know that if our earthly house of *this* tabernacle were dissolved, we have a building of God, an house not made with hands, eternal in the heavens."[75]

This second letter from Paul to the Christians in Corinth followed his "stern letter" (I Corinthians), which scolded the Church at Corinth for "moral laxity" (Filson 265). His second letter was written after the Church at Corinth had seen its error and had been reconciled. This "thankful letter," says Floyd V. Filson, was quite different in tone from the first one:

> Under the circumstances it was inevitable that it [the second letter] should show deep emotion, lay bare the motives and spirit of Paul, and carry the warm note of appeal and affectionate counsel. This is the most personal of all Paul's letters... [268].

The verse read by Jackson relates to Paul's reminder for the Corinthians, in Chapter 4, "of the rich and glorious eternal life that awaits the faithful servant of Christ." Verses 1–10 of Chapter 5 develop the metaphysical contrast between the body as "tent," or "fragile, temporary" home, and "the more durable, *eternal* building or *house* which will come to us as a gift *from God* at the last day" (Filson 326).

Ron Maxwell and Jeff Shaara establish, beginning with this early scene, a running thread of premonitory statements by Jackson about his own death, but always in the context of his deep religious faith. After 1st Manassas, when Jackson's men had stood "like a stone wall" and Jackson himself had been slightly wounded, his aide James Power Smith asks him how he can be so "insensible" in the midst of shells and danger. Jackson replies that his time is fixed by God and that therefore the moment of his death does not trouble him. In a strong echo of Roman stoic values, Stonewall Jackson amplifies this thought with the observation that all men should live this way, and that then "all men would be brave" (Maxwell, *Gods and Generals*).

The premonition thread is nearly at its end at Fredericksburg when Gen. John Bell Hood asks Jackson if he expects to survive the war. (Hood had told A.P. Hill that he expected to be wounded, as the viewer knows he will be, repeatedly.) Stonewall Jackson replies that he does not expect to survive the war, but that he would not want to survive without a victory. This example of Jackson's premonitory mood is not colored with religious commentary, but it fits nonetheless into the adumbration of his death which runs throughout the film.

An instance of Stonewall Jackson's expressed religious faith concerning death which is somewhat tangential to the main narrative is his kindly visit to mortally wounded Gen. Maxcy Gregg of South Carolina, a subordinate who had resented Jackson because of command differences. Jackson comforts Gregg, asking him to forgive and to put "his mind at ease." Gregg responds that he is not a believer, and Jackson says that "I will just have to believe for both of us." After having witnessed Jackson's own death scene, one might recall the Gregg scene, with Stonewall Jackson placed in the position occupied by Anna in the latter scene, as comforter. The two scenes are contrastive in two special respects. Unlike Gregg, Jackson displays a strong Christian faith which leads him actually to welcome being "transported" to another life. Formally, the scenes are interestingly opposed, because in the Gregg scene, Jackson, sitting to Gregg's left by the bed, is clearly the dominant, nurturing force. But in the Jackson scene, Anna is always posed at Jackson's right hand, seemingly to remind the viewer that unlike Jackson relative to Gregg, Anna is not dominant in this

The tomb of Brig. Gen. Maxcy Gregg, CSA, whose epitaph reads: "Mortally wounded at the battle of Fredericksburg, Va. Dec. 13th, died Dec. 15th 1862 aged 47 years. *If I am to die now I give my life cheerfully for the independence of South Carolina. He rests in hope to rise*" (Elmwood Cemetery, Columbia, SC; photograph by author).

scene but is actually comforted by Jackson as she comforts him. Although the Jackson scene follows in its composition the accounts left by those present, the composition of the Gregg scene is more discretionary and is thus a key to the director's intent.

The Jackson scene is easily connected as well to the early scene between Jackson and Anna, where Jackson reads from Corinthians, and also to another crucial scene from the film, when Jackson tells the father of a young 4th Virginia recruit named Willie that, despite the fact that the father is leaving for Pennsylvania, they may meet again in heaven. The reason for the logical connection between this scene and the reading scene is that 2 Corinthians is a central Pauline text relating to faith in eternal life. In fact, the text read by Jackson fits neatly into Paul's assertion of the hope of eternal life, and as well of the hope of the endurance of the individual personality. According to James Reid, "Paul would have dismissed the idea that body and spirit are so related that the life of the spirit cannot exist when the body is gone" (Reid, J., *Second Epistle* 326n). Additionally, Reid provides an intriguing commentary which is oddly apropos to the context of Civil War and death:

> Hugh Walpole describes how such a conviction [of the separation of spirit and body] came to him when he was working with the Red Cross on the Russian front in World War I. "It was here that I learned ... of the utter unimportance of the body by itself. Something seemed to me always to escape at the moment of death that was of enormous value" [Reid, J., *Second Epistle* 326n].

Interesting, too, is the fact that Stonewall Jackson's comments above are made to a man of the cloth who is avowedly pacifist. The Reverend tells Jackson that the nation will follow the path of Europe if the war is pressed. This minister contrasts sharply with the warrior-priest Old Penn (Gen. William Nelson Pendleton) and with the sometime war participant and preacher Chaplain Beverley Tucker Lacy.

Old Penn had an important role in Jackson's Army of the Shenandoah. But Lacy was at least as important as a spiritual leader, and he even participated in the war effort by assisting Lee at Chancellorsville. While Old Penn actually became an officer, Lacy remained a man of the cloth; but each man plays two roles (as did Bishop Leonidas Polk in another theater of the war). W. Harrison Daniel, in "Protestantism and Patriotism" (a chapter from his study *Southern Protestantism in the Confederacy*), details the diverse sets of roles played by clergymen in the Confederate army. Some, like Pendleton and Polk, left the pulpit to become officers (although Polk did carry out priestly duties on a couple of occasions). Some, like Robert Louis Dabney, served as chaplains but were active in a quasi-military role. Lacy would fit into this latter category. Some chaplains, of course, served purely as chaplains. And, conversely, some ministers turned officers, were, like Polk, almost purely officers.

Lacy, as chaplain, is featured prominently in the latter half of the film *Gods and Generals.* He is shown ministering to the dying General Gregg. And he is asked at Chancellorsville to contact a local inhabitant (Mr. Wellford) so that Wellford may show Jackson's corps a path around Howard's right flank.[76] This is the quasi-military participation already mentioned. Finally, Lacy goes to Lee to inform him of Jackson's impending death and to ask him whether he will visit Jackson. Lee responds that he will not, as if he does not wish to admit a terrible eventuality. The potential martyrdom of his great lieutenant was not at all a propitious outcome for the Confederate cause, as far as Lee was concerned. Unlike our next subject, Gen.

Charles "Chinese" Gordon, Stonewall Jackson was most assuredly worth more to his army alive than dead.

"Chinese" Gordon, Victorian Martyr

Perhaps it is a little unfair to Gen. Charles Gordon to compare him unfavorably to Jackson, or to hint that as a martyr he was more valuable than as a living soldier. Gordon was, though, a rather difficult man who seems to have had an inflated sense of himself. Clearly Gordon was a qualified professional soldier who had been involved in several military campaigns, including the Crimea and the Taiping Rebellion in China, before his death in Khartoum, fighting the troops of the Mahdi, in 1885 (Tingsten 457–59). As Tingsten notes, "[a]n unparalleled hero-cult sprang up, releasing a flood of pamphlets, sermons, books. Statues were erected to his memory, memorial windows dedicated to him in cathedrals and in churches...."[77] The dead general was honored throughout England as "a saintly warrior-martyr" (458).

Like Stonewall Jackson early in his career, Gordon showed "little hint of the lasting fame he was to achieve as the transfigured hero and martyr of Khartoum." He was not outstanding as a cadet at the Royal Military College at Woolwich. He had talent as a surveyor and cartographer "but was otherwise sadly deficient in general education" (Tingsten 459). This record parallels Jackson's at West Point, where he graduated as a middling student in 1846 among a class of apparent luminaries including George McClellan, future commander of the Army of the Potomac (graduated second).[78]

Gordon was also like Jackson in being an eccentric "character." Some of their eccentricities differed, with Gordon's being a pronounced tendency to fits of temper and certain prejudices about social life, and Jackson's concerning particularly his health fears. Both were highly and visibly religious men. Both men suffered reverses in their careers due to their often difficult natures. Jackson once let his self-righteousness win out over his better judgment and essentially doomed his future in the pre–Civil War army by making an exaggerated issue of a (probably) small question about his commanding officer's morals at Fort Meade. Gordon's "quirks of character lost for him a hoped-for vacancy in the Royal Artillery and he had to be content with what was in his estimation an inferior commission in the less popular Royal Engineers" (Tingsten 459). Jackson, after resigning from the army, became a professor at VMI.

With both men, religious and military development went hand in hand. Gordon underwent important religious development in Pembroke. The description provided by Tingsten of his stay there sounds uncannily like Jackson's situation in his first months in Lexington, Virginia: "There were no diversions in the small, dreary town, beyond the narrow social life of army folk — dinner-parties, dances, small talk and gossip — in none of which was Gordon interested" (459). Both men were not social butterflies, although they differ here in their motivation: Gordon acted so out of conviction or perhaps plain perverseness; Jackson was shy and stuttering in public. (Like U.S. Grant, Jackson was ill at ease in crowds. Max Byrd, in his novel on Grant, provides a wonderful interpretative description of Grant's demeanor in social settings, in this case during a tribute party late in his career: "Mark Twain emerged from the darkest alcove, next to the kitchen. 'Look at Grant,' he whispered, pointing, 'cast-iron.' And down at the the head table Grant's face was indeed in its famous 'silent' state, which [Nicholas] Trist had seen only in photographs: utterly blank. The orator, whoever he was, wheeled at exactly that instant and stretched out his arms dramatically toward the General, and Grant merely stared straight ahead, motionless as the room rose and cheered. 'Bullet-proof,' Twain groaned, and went away" (Byrd 40). Much of this could have been written about Thomas J. Jackson.)

Jackson eventually joined the Lexington Presbyterian Church after much soul-searching. The minister there, Rev. William S. White, befriended him, and he became a deacon in the church. Gordon "made a friend in one of his colleagues, an earnest and pious captain" (Tingsten 459). These two friends began to take rides in Gordon's coach, talking of "religious matters." According to Tingsten, "[t]his friendship exercised a permanent influence on Gordon's life and thought, awakening in him the mysticism which came wholly to dominate his religious faith in later years" (459–60). In the Crimean conflict which soon broke out (1854), Gordon impressed Captain Wolseley (later to visit the Confederacy and to author a set of reminiscences about the Civil War) as "one of the very few friends I ever had who came up to my estimate of the Christian hero!" (Tingsten 460).

Gordon became the focus of a hero-cult in England. "He was acclaimed nationwide as 'Chinese Gordon' and newspaper dispatches told of his exploits and his personal bravery, as exemplified in his habit of dashing alone and unarmed at the head of his men through breaches in the stockades of the towns they were assaulting." Like many hero-figures in history, fiction, and epic, Gordon "seemed to bear a charmed life as, cheroot in mouth, he waved them on with his rattan cane, which the mercenaries came to regard with superstitious awe and Gordon as a magical symbol, the Wand of Victory" (Tingsten 463).

Gordon's motivation for leading the Ever-Victorious Army against

the Taipings was a mixture of national self-interest and altruism. His reasons for involvement were partly based on military judgment and partly
upon Christian evangelical goals:

> Gordon may be described as a kind of military missionary. Although he
> fought for the "heathen" Manchus against the "Christian" Taipings, and
> saved bodies rather than souls (eighty to one hundred thousand by his own
> estimate), he believed that Christian influence could be brought to China
> through the introduction of Western "progress." Although not consciously
> an evangelist in the usual sense, Gordon, like the medical missionary, saw
> his profession as a means of working God's will [Smith, R.J., *Mercenaries*
> 126–27].

Like Stonewall Jackson, Chinese Gordon tended to mix religious, social,
political, and military rationales for his courses of action.

This tendency was not at all rare in the Victorian age in which both
men lived. Although one was English and the other American, both were
imbued with the spirit of service to society which was so evident in reformers like Dickens[79] and in the crusades for abolition and other causes in the
United States. Houghton comments on the social attitudes of the era that

> In a Victorian like George Eliot, brought up in Evangelicalism and yet
> filled with Romantic ardor, the creed of strict conduct, the renunciation
> of self, and a dedicated pursuit of social duty could become a sublime
> object of passionate devotion [273].

The social activism of the age was marked by a "cult of benevolence" which
in its linking to Christian charity represented "a shift from the older view
of charity as a religious duty." Writing of Dickens, he observes "That Dickens could identify this Romantic benevolence with Christian benevolence
marks the decline of the older and sterner faith on which the latter had
been based" (275).

Gordon and Jackson share their epoch's views on social duty and service. Additionally, both were, as befitting good Protestant Victorians, self-
effacing about their fame. Gordon returned to England from his Chinese
adventure in January 1865 and "was greeted by a nation eager to acclaim him;
but he dreaded the glare of publicity and fled from it" (Tingsten 463). He
would not seek the limelight, due to his exaggerated puritanical modesty,
and so, Tingsten observes, "he gradually and inevitably became a forgotten
man," that is, until his martyrdom in the Sudan some years later (463).

Jackson did not have the opportunity to begin a slide into obscurity
as Gordon did, because he was cut down at the peak of his fame. Still, he
was similarly self-effacing in public. He always claimed, for example, that

the "Stonewall" epithet should apply not to him but to the Brigade. He also became easily embarrassed when autograph and souvenir hunters (or huntresses) accosted him, as in a well-known instance in Martinsburg on September 12, 1862, during the approach to Maryland where the battle of Antietam or Sharpsburg would be fought, when Jackson became the object of what a latter age might call groupies:

> Jackson could not escape a huge crowd of well-wishers and souvenir hunters. Women screamed for locks of his hair and buttons from his uniform. Men wanted to talk and grasp his hand; children by the scores pressed close to gawk and be part of the spectacle. At one point, Jackson told a large assemblage of women bent on getting strands of hair, "Really, ladies, this is the first time I was ever surrounded by the enemy!"
>
> Finally, he retreated to the Everett Hotel and tried to attend to some paperwork.... People rattled doors and swarmed around windows to get a look at him [Robertson, *Stonewall Jackson* 596–97].

In both cases, however, the self-effacement in public may have masked a deeper egocentrism. Jackson was actually anxious for advancement and recognition in the army. He was not a shrinking violet but a professional solder who admitted that he wanted to be noticed. This ambition does not necessarily conflict with the path of a devout Presbyterian, because service to God and man may well include, or even necessitate, social advancement.[80] John W. Daniel evaluated Jackson's ambition as neither mercenary nor grasping: "He was no intriguer or office-seeker, but in whatever field he labored he pitched into obstacles with such 'energy, zeal, and success' that promotion sought him. His was not the selfish ambition of a Caesar — '*aut Caesar, aut nullus*;' it was not envious like that of Themistocles, whom the trophies of Militiades would not permit to sleep; but like that of Washington [a comparison which though apt does not normally come to mind], it was inspired by the consciousness of merit, and chastened by devotion to duty" (Daniel, J.W., *Character* 14).

Gordon was also less self-effacing than he might appear on the surface, or than his mythographers might have liked one to think. One clue to his personality as less than humble is his hot temper — assuredly a mark of a stubborn and ego-driven man (Eisenhower, also self-effacing in public but notably less so behind the scenes, comes to mind). And Gordon's own statements while in China reveal this side of his character. As Richard J. Smith observes in *Mercenaries and Mandarins*, "Gordon was convinced of the righteousness of his cause, and he was equally certain that his leadership was essential to the success—indeed, the very existence — of the Ever-Victorious Army." He quotes a comment by Gordon: "'I can say that if I had not accepted their command I believe the ... force would have been broken up & the rebellion gone on in its misery for years'" (Smith, R.J., *Mercenaries* 127). Smith concludes that

> Throughout the remainder of his career in China, Gordon continued to hold an inflated opinion of his personal importance, an attitude hardly consistent with his periodic threats to resign from the Chinese service. The dilemma was that while Gordon did not want to serve in a position that was "derogatory" to his station as a British officer, he believed that the British government "would be in a fix, if I choose to give up the command, as it has reduced the garrison at Shanghai & would be obliged to augment it again if I left the Force, as the Chinese would not keep it up" [Smith, R. J., *Mercenaries* 127–28].

Following his death in the Sudan, the legend of Gordon grew apace, and so it is no surprise that in the 20th century the film industry would find in him a worthy subject for an epic. This was *Khartoum* (1966), starring Charlton Heston and directed by British filmmaker Basil Dearden (1911–71) (Burton, O'Sullivan and Wells). As do many historical epics, this film colors or edits the facts. Still, *Khartoum* is actually quite accurate in its presentation of details about Gordon's last months and his struggle against the Mahdi (played memorably by Laurence Olivier). The treatment of the Gordon figure in the film is, however, more heroic than the record indicates; and additionally Gordon's religious eccentricities are glossed over in favor of his personal quirks of stubbornness and fatalism. Gordon's oft-noted interest in adolescent boys, which may have been innocent insofar as he was aware, is totally avoided as a topic in the film, although one character, a young Sudanese servant, does play a part in the film and is treated kindly by Gordon.

Under Dearden's direction, Heston plays Gordon as a somewhat cantankerous and contentious military man who is recalled to service in the Sudan. (American viewers at the time would surely have thought of Gen. Douglas MacArthur, who was also cantankerous and contentious, and who had been recalled to active combat status at the outbreak of the Korean War in 1950 and had later been dismissed by President Truman for insubordination.) Gordon is presented, despite his negative demeanor, as a man who has performed heroic service but who has become jaded and wearied by bureaucracy and by counterproductive policy at the highest governmental levels. Little of his private life impinges upon this film in contradistinction to another treatment of Gordon, the novel *The Last Encounter* by Robin Maugham, which employs the device of presenting his putative diaries as evidence of his inner struggles.

Leonidas Polk, Episcopalian Warrior-Bishop

The career of Bishop, and General, Leonidas Polk (1806–64) is instructive in its parallels to that of Jackson. Polk serves as a contrast, however, to Jackson, because unlike Jackson, Polk was an official member of the cloth who became a soldier and who was not a successful general. Those who did glorify Polk chose to overlook his failures and to exalt him precisely because he was a cleric. In Jackson's case, the reverse was often true: some commentators, then and since, have actually side-stepped his religion, as if this were embarrassing, and have focused instead on his obvious military virtues. Although Polk has had his defenders, his detractors have the better of the argument. One of the sharpest of his detractors, historian Grady McWhiney, comes to the brink of calling him the "worst" general of the war (McWhiney 209).

Bishop Leonidas L. Polk, Lt. Gen. CSA (1806–64). (Courtesy University of the South, photograph by Charley Watkins).

Polk was from Louisiana, where he had become an Episcopal bishop before the war. His prewar career included graduation from West Point in 1827 and his subsequent resignation from the army that same year to study at the Virginia Theological Seminary. After serving as "the first Episcopal bishop of Louisiana," he signed on with the Confederate army at the rank of major general in 1861 (Scott 36).

Before becoming a general, Polk as clergyman had been one of the Episcopal bishops who "welcomed secession and urged the adoption of a practice enunciated by Polk concerning prayers for 'those in authority.'" Polk asserted "that it was traditional procedure for this church to be organized along national lines" and suggested that his colleagues direct their clergy to omit from the Book of Common Prayer the words "United States" in prayers for those in civil authority and substitute the name of their state, and, when the state became affiliated with the Confederacy, to use the words "Confederate States" [Daniel, W. H., *Southern* 9].

Polk at least had the courage of his convictions, whatever his other faults may have been. He remained true to his belief in secession when he was offered, while on a visit to Virginia, the position of major general in the Western Department of the Confederate army. Accepting President Davis's offer, Polk, according to W. Harrison Daniel,

did not attempt to combine ministerial functions with those of a general. He did not preach to the troops, and he performed only four ministerial acts during the three years he was in the army.

These acts included the baptisms of Generals Hood and Johnston in 1864, during the Atlanta campaign (Daniel, W.H., *Southern* 31).

The advisability and the propriety of military service by clergymen like Polk was debated in the South. Gardiner H. Shattuck Jr. notes "[t]here is a good deal of evidence to suggest that most Southerners did not want to see chaplains and ministers taking part in the killing of other men" (Shattuck 68). He cites Polk's enlistment as an example of the chagrin felt by many Southerners at such service, and he also says that

The consensus in the Southern churches was that clergy who took up arms were failing to obey their high calling from God, for ministers should be concerned only with saving sinners and never with killing them. Clergymen who used weapons, moreover, defied the cultural norm dictating that the spiritual and ecclesiastical sphere ought to be entirely separate from the secular and political one [71].

Such debates as this one in the South were not new to the Christian churches. As far back as the Middle Ages, clerics had debated the propriety of their members serving as warriors. A technical prohibition was in force against clerics acting as warriors. James A. Brundage notes that

In theory at least, clerics were forbidden to bear arms or to fight in person against Christians or pagans; this point was often reiterated in the most frequently used eleventh-century canonistic collections.... Bishops might not even do auxiliary duty, for example as lookouts against pirates [28–29].

Brundage comments that, in addition to the general prohibition cited above, "Another much repeated canon directed not only that clerics might not take arms, but also that any who were killed in battles or in brawls should not be prayed for and that those who voluntarily took up arms should be degraded and confined in a monastery" (28n99). John F. Benton cites the cases of two bishops for whom the prohibitions became important: "In the early eleventh century, Bishop Hubert of Angers was excommunicated for fighting at his king's command, while Bishop Wazo of Liège did lead troops in battle, but conscientiously did so unarmed" (Benton 241).

The prohibition was not confined to the Roman Church. In his article on the First Crusade, Roger Porges (8) quotes Byzantine chronicler Anna Comnena (1083–1153), the aristocratic author of the *Alexiad*, who, in recounting the warlike actions of a priest on the Crusade, editorialized on his deeds. She commented as follows:

> The Latin customs with regard to priests differ from ours. We are bidden by canon law and the teaching of the Gospel, "Touch not, grumble not, attack not — for thou art consecrated." But your Latin barbarian will at the same time handle sacred objects, fasten a shield to his left arm and grasp a spear in his right.... Thus the race is no less devoted to religion than to war. This Latin, then, more man of action than priest, wore priestly garb and at the same time handled an oar and ready for naval action or war on land fought sea and men alike [Comnena 317 n17].

Anna seems to confuse practice with doctrine, because the Roman Church had a similar prohibition against armed clerics; but at any rate, the case to which she refers is an interesting one. This priest, as Porges points out, was particularly recalcitrant toward the prohibition (Porges 8). Anna tells of him that despite an "armistice [that] was being arranged, [he] did not cease from fighting":

> [he] was far from having had his fill of battle, although he had exhausted the stones and arrows.... He was ready to use whatever came to hand and when he found a sack full of barley-cakes, he threw them like stones, taking them from the sack. It was as if he were officiating at some ceremony or service, turning war into the solemnization of sacred rites [Comnena 318].

Other bishops who very clearly took on the role of warrior were two Spanish prelates, Gonzalo, bishop of Jaén, and Rodrigo Jiménez de Rada, archbishop of Toledo. Gonzalo appears to have been quite the warrior, leading soldiers out against the Moors in support of King Juan II in 1407. A famous set of *romances* commemorates the event; one of them will be cited here which, according to editor Agustín Durán, appears to be the earliest and most authentic, for reasons to be explained shortly.

REBATO DE LOS CRISTIANOS DE JAÉN,
AL MANDO DEL OBISPO DON GONZALO,
CONTRA LOS MOROS DE GRANADA.

Día es de San Anton,
Ese santo señalado,
Cuando salen de Jaen
Cuatrocientos hijosdalgo;
Y de Ubeda y Baeza
Se salian otros tantos,
Mozos deseosos de honra,
Y los mas enamorados.
En brazos de sus amigas,
Van todos juramentados
De no volver á Jaen
Sin dar moro en aguinaldo.
La seña que ellos llevaban
Es pendon rabo de gallo;
Por capitan se lo llevan
Al obispo Don Gonzalo,
Armado de todas armas,
En un caballo alazano:
Todos se visten de verde,
El Obispo, azul y blanco.
Al castillo de la Guardia
El Obispo habia llegado:
Sáleselo á recibir
Mexía, el noble hidalgo:
— Por Dios te ruego, el Obispo,
Que no pasedes el vado,
Porque los moros son muchos,
A la Guardia habian llegado;
Muerto me han tres caballeros,
De que mucho me ha pesado;
El uno era tio mio,
El otro mi primo hermano,
Y el otro es un pajecico
De los mios mas preciado.
Démos la vuelta, señores,
Démos la vuelta á enterrallos,
Harémos á Dios servicio,
Honrarémos los cristianos.—
Ellos estando en aquesto,
Llegó Don Diego de Haro:
— Adelante, caballeros,
Que me llevan el ganado;
Si de algun villano fuera,

Ya lo hubiérades quitado;
Empero alguno está aquí
Que le place de mi daño:
No cumple decir quién es,
Que es el del roquete blanco.—
El Obispo que lo oyera,
Dió de espuelas al caballo;
El caballo era lijero,
Saltado había un vallado;
Mas al salir de una cuesta,
A la asomada de un llano,
Vido mucha adarga blanca,
Mucho albornoz colorado,
Y muchos hierros de lanzas,
Que relucen en el campo;
Metídose habia por ellos
Como leon denodado:
De tres batallas de moros
La una ha desbaratado,
Mediante la buena ayuda
Que en los suyos ha hallado:
Aunque algunos d'ellos mueren,
Eterna fama han ganado.
Los moros son infinitos,
Al Obispo habian cercado;
Cansado de pelear
Lo derriban del caballo,
Y los moros victoriosos
A su Rey lo han presentado [Durán, *Romancero general* 84].

["The Assault of the Christians of Jaen, under the Command of
Bishop Don Gonzalo, against the Moors of Granada"

It is St. Anthony's Day, / That signal saint, / When four hundred worthy men / Depart from Jaen; / And from Ubeda and Baeza / As many more departed, / Lads desirous of honor, / And the most enamored. / In the arms of their girlfriends, / They all go forsworn / Not to return to Jaen / Without changing a Moor into nothing. / The colors that they bore / Are a pendant cock's tail; / As Captain they take with them / Bishop Don Gonzalo, / Armed with every weapon, / On a sorrel horse. / They all wear green, / The Bishop, blue and white. / The Bishop had arrived / At the Guards' castle: / Out to receive him comes / Mexía, the noble gentleman: / "In God's name I beseech you, Bishop, / Not to pass through the meadow, / Because the Moors are many, / They had reached the Castle; / They have killed three of my knights, / Which has given me great pain; / One was my uncle, / The other my second cousin, / And the other is / My most prized little page. / Let us turn back, Sirs, / Let us turn back to bury them, / We will do service to God, / We will honor the Christians." / As they were thus engaged, / Don Diego de Haro arrived: / "Forward, men, / Because they're carrying off my stock; / If it were some villager's, / You already would have taken it from him; / Still there's someone here / Who is pleased at my injury: / It is not fitting to say who it is, / As it is he of the white band." / The Bishop who was listening, / Spurred his horse; / The horse was swift, / He had leaped over a fence; / But when coming out of a ditch, / In view of a plain, / He saw many white shields, / Many red robes, / And many spear points, / Which glitter in the field; / He had placed himself amidst them / Like a steadfast lion: / Of three battles by Moors / He has disrupted one, / Thanks to the good aid / That he has found with his own men: / Although some of them die, / They have won eternal fame. / The Moors are infinite, / They had surrounded the Bishop; / Tired from fighting / He is unhorsed, / And the victorious Moors / Have presented him to their King.]

Durán believes that this ballad is the most authentic of the several concerning this tale, because in some of the others the Christians emerge victorious. In this one, though, the bishop is captured (and maybe killed); Durán argues that

> ningún interés tenia un poeta cristiano que le indujera á atribuir una victoria á sus enemigos, si en realidad no la hubiesen ganado [85n1].
> [no interest on the part of a Christian poet would lead him to attribute a victory to his enemies, if in reality they had not won it.]

He also comments on the identity of the bishop, writing that

> Don Gonzalo de Estuñiga, ó de Zúñiga, obispo de Jaen, á la usanza de su tiempo, fué mas bien que eclesiástico, hombre de guerra y batallador. Antes de abrazar el estado sacerdotal fué casado y tuvo por hijo á Don Alfonso, que floreció en el reinado de Enrique IV y de los Reyes Católicos, como buen caballero y poeta [85n2].
> [Don Gonzalo de Estuñiga, or de Zúñiga, bishop of Jaen, after the manner of his time, was more than an ecclesiastic, a man of war and a fighter. Before embracing priestly status he was married and had a son, Don Alfonso, who flourished in the reign of Enrique IV and the Catholic Kings, as a good gentleman and a poet.]

Rodrigo Jiménez de Rada (1170–1247), "el Toledano," was Archbishop of Toledo from 1209 until his death. He wrote an important chronicle, *De rebus hispaniae* [*Of Spanish Matters*] (first published edition, 1545), and was probably the author of several other historical works. He represented Alfonso VIII of Castile before the Vatican in petitioning for a crusade against the Muslims; this culminated in the famous Christian victory of Las Navas de Tolosa (1212), in which the archbishop participated directly after having taken a lead role in organizing the expedition. He recounts the battle in his chronicle, but his role is muted; as Manuel Ballesteros comments, "Don Rodrigo calla en sus relatos, modestamente, la parte decisiva que tuvo en estos hechos" (70) [Don Rodrigo silences in his narratives, modestly, the decisive role he played in these deeds]. Ballesteros takes up the banner for the archbishop, though, asserting that

> Don Rodrigo es, pues, el gran factor de la victoria, que sin él no hubiera sido. La presencia de ánimo del gran arzobispo empuja a los guerreros en todo momento y los anima con su ejemplo [78].
>
> [Don Rodrigo is, then, the great factor in the victory, which would not have taken place without him. The presence of mind of the great Archbishop pushes the warriors at every moment and animates them with his example].

Ballesteros fixes the role of Rodrigo at the front line from the beginning of the expedition:

> Alfonso VIII, generalísimo de las tropas, llevaba a su lado la impresionante figura eclesiástica de don Rodrigo, que, llevando indumentaria militar, ostentaba las insignias de delegado pontificio, con la cual calidad tomaba parte en la expedición [66].
>
> [Alfonso VIII, commander-in-chief of the troops, brought at his side the impressive ecclesiastic figure of Don Rodrigo, who, wearing military accoutrements, displayed the insignias of a pontifical delegate, in which capacity he was taking part in the expedition].

Note that here Rodrigo, although officially at the battle as a papal legate, also wears military attire, thus neatly combining the roles of priest and warrior.

It is also clear that, according to Ballesteros, the king and the archbishop exchanged dialogue on an epic level at a crucial point in the battle, when the Moors had penetrated the Christian ranks, causing many of the Christians to break ranks and flee. Ballesteros attributes the following remarks to "history"; whether or not they are typical interpolations is less important than the fact that they cast the archbishop in a heroic light, revealing the high position accorded him by history (or legend):

> En este momento Alfonso VIII y don Rodrigo intervienen con la retaguardia y la batalla recobra su aspecto anterior tras el diálogo celebre que nos ha trasmitido la historia: *Arzobispo, yo y vos muramos aquí;* a lo que responde éste: *De ningún modo, señor, antes aquí mismo venceréis al enemigo.* El ejército flaqueante tornó a embestir con fiereza y eficacia, volvió

> a repetir golpe sobre golpe contra la peña almohade [At this moment Alfonso VIII and Don Rodrigo intervene at the rear and the battle recovers its former aspect through the celebrated dialogue that history has transmitted: *Archbishop, may you and I die here;* to which the latter responds: *By no means, sir, instead right here and now you will vanquish the enemy.* The wavering army turned to battle with fierceness and effectiveness, repeated again and again blow after blow against the Almohad rock] [Ballesteros Gaibrois 76].

As such examples show, the cleric as warrior was not an unknown circumstance during the medieval period: "Though militant ecclesiastics, who violated canon law by the bearing of arms, were comparatively rare, many powerful churchmen retained sizeable bodies of household knights and it was not uncommon for them to lead forces to the host or to direct military operations" (Strickland 73). Medievalist historian Marc Bloch notes that "the type of warrior prelate — those 'good knights of the clergy,' as one German bishop called them — was to be found in all periods" (Bloch 347). In his *Spanish Catholicism: An Historical Overview*, Stanley G. Payne observes that medieval Spain, with its battle against the Moors, was home to an especially militant clergy:

> Spanish frontier conditions may have made some problems worse in the peninsula than elsewhere. Clerics at all levels took part in military campaigns against Muslims, creating the famous typology of the medieval prelate "a Dios rogando y con el mazo dando" (praying to God and striking with the mace). Many of the Spanish clergy thought nothing of wearing weapons as part of their actual costume, a practice that took many generations to eliminate [29].

And Menéndez Pidal comments that "El obispo guerrero es un tipo abundante en la Edad Media [...] recuérdese á Odón, obispo de Bayeux, en la conquista de Inglaterra, ó á don Rodrigo de Toledo en las guerras fronterizas, y en la memorable batalla de las Navas; ó al obispo de Jaén, don Gonzalo, cuyas proezas contra los moros granadinos se cuentan en la *Crónica de don Juan II*" (877) [The warrior bishop is an abundant type in the Middle Ages ... remember Odo, bishop of Bayeux, in the conquest of England, or Don Rodrigo of Toledo in the frontier wars, and in the memorable battle of Las Navas, or the bishop of Jaén, Don Gonzalo, whose feats of prowess against the Moors of Granada are recounted in the *Chronicle of Juan II*]. Marianne J. Ailes in her study of the *Song of Roland* remarks, concerning Bishop Turpin, its priest-hero,

> That the archbishop [Turpin] is depicted urging military service and even engaging in war is for us problematic. Indeed, in brandishing a sword

Turpin does go beyond what was considered acceptable for clergy in the Middle Ages; under church law he should only have carried blunt weapons [Ailes 9].

Ailes qualifies this statement, however, by noting that "men such as Bishop Odo, depicted in the Bayeux tapestry wielding a club and encouraging his troops at Hastings, were important members of a feudal hierarchy, leaders of an aristocratic society geared for war" (9). Perhaps the medieval society of Turpin and Odo wasn't so far after all from the South of Bishop Polk.

In addition to the debate over clerics in armor, there was the other, potentially more divisive question mentioned by Shattuck, the separation of church and state, a bone of contention all too familiar to present-day Americans. Evidently the Confederacy did not wish to throw out this doctrine along with the erstwhile union with the North. Shattuck cites the example of such a strongly religious general as Stonewall Jackson upbraiding "a chaplain who advanced into the battleline." According to Shattuck,

> Jackson believed that chaplains belonged in the rear of the army where they could attend to the work to which they had properly been called. All Jackson wanted his chaplains to do was pray for the success of the Southern cause [Shattuck 70–71].

One must state in Polk's favor that he tried to maintain the dividing line between his status as a divine and his work as a soldier. Polk's problems as a soldier did not stem from this dichotomy so much as from his personality traits.

The late Thomas Connelly, in his fine two-volume study of the Army of Tennessee, establishes Polk as problematic from the very beginning of his command, which began on July 12, 1861. Polk was to assume "temporary command" in the West until he could be relieved by Gen. Joseph E. Johnston. Connelly writes that even in Polk's brief two-month stint as army commander, "he managed to create enough problems to plague Johnston in the fall of 1861 and the Army of Tennessee for the entire war" (Connelly 46). Among these problems was a "feud" Polk conducted with one of his subordinates, Gideon Pillow (a veteran of the Mexican War and a very contentious and vainglorious man). Connelly also notes that "Polk … began to exhibit a sullen aloofness which would hamper cooperation between Johnston and the bishop in the fall and winter of 1861–62" (Connelly 46). Moreover, Polk failed to provide adequate defenses for his department; and he showed intemperate leadership by invading neutral Kentucky. Connelly sums up Polk as a less-than-adequate military man:

During his temporary command, Polk exhibited personality traits which would later prove injurious to the Army. To the casual observer [such as many of his defenders], Polk was a distinguished soldier who was idolized by his troops. True, Polk did present a striking appearance, and he was extremely popular with his men. Yet there was another side to his character that was dimly visible in the summer of 1861, only to emerge in full view when Johnston took command. On the one hand, Polk was the humble, sacrificing bishop who buckled the sword over his clerical robes out of a sense of duty to his fellow Southerners. But he was also a man of little military experience who could be stubborn, aloof, insubordinate, quarrelsome, and childish. As a bishop, Polk had been trained to lead; but, as a soldier, he never learned to follow. Beginning with Johnston, Polk would treat his superior officers in a manner that smacked of insubordination. Until his death in 1864, the bishop often chose to obey his commander only when it pleased him to do so. Yet throughout his career in the Army of Tennessee, Polk had a remarkable ability to evade the blame for situations that were the result of these flaws in his character. He knew how to manipulate Johnston, who was easily dominated by his old West Point roommate. He also knew how to play on the sympathies of another old schoolmate, Jefferson Davis, and to use his own popularity to combat Braxton Bragg's constant accusations that he was insubordinate — accusations that were probably true. With such a personality and with amazing abilities to escape responsibility, Polk in 1861 was the most dangerous man in the Army of Tennessee [46–47].

Polk was to be deeply involved in the disputes between Johnston and his subordinates after the Confederate retreat from Chattanooga in 1864. Polk was accused, especially by General Hardee, of having instigated the revolt against Johnston which led to the unfortunate appointment of Gen. John Bell Hood to the command of the Army of Tennessee.

Bishop Polk was killed by a Union cannonball on Pine Mountain, Georgia, during the Kennesaw Mountain engagement. Like Jackson and Patton, he died in an unforeseen and untimely fashion. (Like Jackson, Polk was exposed to needless injury against common-sense judgment.) Polk was accorded martyr status by some of his admirers. His friend and fellow religious, Stephen Elliott, pronounced his eulogy in Augusta, Georgia, declaring him to be "a Christian warrior" (12). As with the death of Jackson, the demise of Polk served also as an occasion for ministers like Elliott to admonish the North for its lack of godliness and to paint the South as a nation engaged in a holy war:

> If we consider it [the war] a mere struggle for political power, a question of sovereignty and of dominion, then should I be loath to mingle the Church of Christ with it in any form or manner. But such is not the nature of this conflict. It is no such war as nations wage against each other for a

balance of power, or for the adjustment of a boundary. We are resisting a crusade — a crusade of license against law — of infidelity against the altars of the living God — of fanaticism against a great spiritual trust committed to our care. We are warring with hordes of unprincipled foreigners, ignorant and brutal men, who, having cast off at home all the restraints of order and of belief, have signalized their march over our devoted country by burning the Churches of Christ[,] by defiling the altars upon which the sacrifice of the death of our Saviour is commemorated, by violating our women, by raising the banner of servile insurrection, by fanning into fury the demoniac passions of the ignorant and the vile! [Elliott, S., *Funeral Services*, 16–17].

In a manner oddly similar to the outsized eulogies of relatively minor figures like Havelock,[81] Elliott's tribute is wildly hyperbolic:

Full of heroic purposes as he leaped into the arena of life — purposes always high and noble, even when unsanctified — he has been made, by the overruling hand of God, to display that heroism in the fields which Christ his Master illustrated…. Oh! how many records has he left with God of heroic self-devotion, of which the world knows nothing; records made up in silence and in darkness…! The world speaks of him now as a hero! He has always been a hero, and the bloody fields which have made him conspicuous are but the outbursts of the spirit which has always distinguished him [24–25].

Elliott attributes to Polk characteristics which must have seemed either amusing or annoying to most who knew him.

At such a distance from the events of the war, to understand the true import of incidents and of commentary by participants or observers is a risky business. (Witness, for instance, the lively debate over the true meaning of Bee's "Stonewall" remark.) Perhaps, though, the reader may perceive the strange double meaning implicit in Joseph Johnston's lament when Polk was killed at Pine Mountain: "I would rather anything than this!" The standard interpretation of this exclamation has been as grief or regret at the death of a fine soldier and comrade. But what if Johnston (of whom Polk was no friend) had meant something else by his cry? One possibility might be that Johnston feared accusations by Polk's friends that Johnston had carelessly or negligently exposed the bishop to enemy fire by being too visible on the mountain. Or Johnston might have feared that Polk would become a martyr figure and that this status would only lend more visibility to his own detractors. In any event, Johnston's remark does seem a little odd: would he really "rather anything than this"? What if "anything" had meant being under Polk's command? Maybe "anything" would be preferable, indeed, if it meant having Polk transferred out of his command.

Daniel Harvey Hill, Irascible Christian Soldier

Like Stonewall Jackson, Daniel Harvey Hill of North Carolina (1821–89) was a deeply religious general. Both Hill and Jackson were well known for their strongly held religious views, and both were also reputed for their odd personal quirks. In Jackson's case, the personality traits most often noted besides a general sternness and taciturnity were some behavioral tendencies labelled eccentric, like gesticulating strangely, following peculiar diets, and talking to oneself: crank behavior, in short.

The oddness of D.H. Hill was perhaps more difficult to pin down, but if Friedrich Nietzsche had observed this man, he might have applied to him one of his favorite epithets, "dyspeptic." Indeed, Hill often seemed sour, indisposed, peppery, and vinegary. He was renowned (unlike Jackson, who preferred stony silence to verbal disapproval unless words were really necessary or unavoidable) for his very sharp tongue and his scant patience with fools and knaves. Edward A. Pollard wrote of Hill that "His personal eccentricities, his literary whims, and his adventures in the English language [of which Pollard did not always approve], furnished a stock of curiosity and amusement in the war. He had the somewhat equivocal reputation of a man who 'had peculiar notions'; he was frequently charged with insubordination; but doubtful as were some of the parts of his military career, he was a grim and obstinate fighter..." (448).

Hill suffered from ill health, as did Jackson, although Jackson's ill health was sometimes psychosomatic or emotionally driven ("hypochondriac"); while Hill's appears to have been due to real physical irregularity. He had suffered a back injury and apparently had developed a spinal deformity or disc problem which caused him a great deal of pain, particularly in damp weather. Hardly a prescription for hearty good cheer!

Hill was very devout. This religious adherence, of the southern Presbyterian variety, is readily seen in his letters to his wife, Isabella. For example, after his first battle in the Civil War, at Big Bethel Church on June 10, 1861, he thought of a religious link to the fighting:

> "It is a little singular that my first battle in this war should be at *Bethel*, the name of the church where I was baptised and worshipped until 16 years old. The Church of my Mother, was she not a guardian spirit in the battle averting the ball and the shell. Oh God give us gratitude to Thee and may we never dishonor Thee by a weak faith" [Bridges, *Lee's Maverick* 28–29].

As a matter of fact, Hill and Jackson married sisters, two daughters of respected North Carolina minister and Davidson College president Robert

Morrison. But unlike Jackson, for whom marriage to Mary Anna Morrison appears to have been a relatively untroubled path, Hill had some difficulties in his life with Isabella. These problems do not seem to have been minor ones, but neither were they so serious as to endanger the marriage. They appear to have been more along the lines of a running disagreement about Hill's being in military service. Much of this must be gleaned from inference, as Hal Bridges says, because little of Isabella's correspondence to Hill has survived (nor did much of Anna's to Jackson). In any event, Isabella was a good companion and correspondent for Hill, and they shared deep religious beliefs.

Lieut. Gen. Daniel Harvey Hill, CSA (1821–89). (Courtesy of the North Carolina State Archives).

Hill's demeanor in battle, like Jackson's, was widely noted as nerveless. Hill biographer Hal Bridges ties this quality in Hill to his strong faith in God:

> This extraordinary courage, this absolute fearlessness in battle, distinguished Harvey Hill in an army and a war in which brave men were legion. It was the quality most often mentioned when other soldiers spoke of him. It seemed to flow effortlessly from his deep religious faith.... Whatever he did, whether he was praising his God, criticizing his commander, or risking his life to encourage his troops, he did it with a thoroughgoing intensity that set him apart, and often produced intense reactions in others [Bridges, *Lee's Maverick* 154].

In line with this intensity was Hill's hostility towards the Yankees. Before the war, Hill had written an algebra textbook (*Elements of Algebra*, 1857) which contained whimsical and sometimes nasty and racist examples and exercises. Much of the whimsy and the nastiness was directed at the North. In his article on the textbook, Hal Bridges cites several examples of Hill's humor at the expense of Yankee cowardice, hypocrisy, and moneygrubbing. Some additional examples will highlight Hill's religious perspective, and additionally some citations to which Bridges alludes will be examined in full (221). Bridges refers to Hill's lampooning of Northern religious intolerance (such as witchcraft trials), and of course Hill was trying to level the playing field with reference to Northern criticism of Southern slaveholding, that is, Southern oppression of minorities. According to Hill, the Yankees were just as guilty of oppression and intolerance, as this example about the Salem witch trials, alluded to but not quoted by Bridges, will illustrate:

> 14. In the year 1692, the people of Massachusetts executed, imprisoned, or privately persecuted 469 persons, of both sexes, and all ages, for the alleged crime of witchcraft. Of these, twice as many were privately persecuted as were imprisoned, and 7 17/19 times as many more were imprisoned than were executed. Required the number of sufferers of each kind?
> *Ans.* 19 executed, 150 imprisoned, and 300 privately persecuted [Hill, M. D.H., *Elements* 151].

The reader is left to infer that the North has just as much, indeed more, blood on its hands than the South, and that the crimes of the North — and especially of the Puritan New Englanders, where abolitionist fervor was to be the strongest — had been going on longer than slavery in the South.

A rather different slant on Northern society is presented by another exercise dealing with religious sectarians. For Yankees who would criticize the South as full of religious cranks who defended their Calvinist view of social and moral issues, Hill offers the following riposte:

> 39. In the year 1853, a number of persons in New England and New York, were sent to lunatic asylums in consequence of the Spiritual Rapping delusion. If 14 be added to the number of those who became insane, and the square root of the sum be taken, the root will be less than the number by 42. Required the number of victims.
> *Ans.* 50 [Hill, M.D.H., *Elements,* 319].

The "delusion" to which Hill refers was associated with the movement of spiritualism, which became very popular in the mid–19th century in the North. R. Laurence Moore writes that this fad can be traced to "March 31, 1848, when Margaret and Kate Fox professed to discover an intelligent force behind the unexplained rappings [the "Spiritual Rapping" to which Hill alludes] which ... had disturbed their family's ... cottage in Hydesville, New York" (Moore, R.L., "Spiritualism" 478). According to

Moore, within three years of the New York incident, the fad hit the Americans and Europeans (474). Furthermore, of especial interest to an observer of Hill's persuasion would be the section of American society to which this fad most appealed, including many "prominent people": "Many ... abolitionist leaders believed in spirit voices as strongly as ... the wickedness of slaveholding [for Hill, one would presume, two equally fallacious beliefs]" (Moore, R.L., "Spiritualism" 474). From the perspective of mathematician Hill, the spiritualism sweeping the North was but another example of the irrationalist strain which he was at pains to highlight in his attacks on Yankees. If the North is irrationalist at its base, and particularly in its abolitionism, since many abolitionists followed the spiritualist movement, then its charges against the South are *ipso facto* vitiated.

For Hill, the irrationalism and inconsistencies of the northern antislavery movement went right along with its hypocrisy, and that hypocrisy could be perceived in the North's historical attitude toward the indigenous inhabitants of this continent. One of his more pointed attacks on Northern hypocrisy appears in the following exercise:

> 36. In the year 1637, all the Pequod Indians that survived the slaughter on the Mystic River were either banished from Connecticut, or sold into slavery. The square root of twice the number of survivors is equal to 1/10th that number. What was the number? *Ans.* 200 [Hill, M. D. H., *Elements* 318].

Notice that Hill introduces the motif of "slaughter" as well as of enslavement into this example, as if to say that the North is worse than the South, because the South has not been accused of killing off most of a race before enslaving many of its survivors.

The algebra textbook was not the only forum used by Hill for his strong opinions. In the late 1850s, Hill published two books dealing specifically with religious topics. In one of these, *Consideration of the Sermon on the Mount*, Hill expressed his opposition to Catholicism within a discursive milieu. His rebuttal of Catholic doctrine is sometimes rather muted, as in the following passage from his exegesis of verse 8 of the Sermon, which begins "Blessed are the pure in heart," and in which connection he discusses the "renewed" moral cleanness of the reformed sinner:

> The renewed man has now the more difficult task of restraining his depraved appetites and desires.... His body is now the temple of the Holy Ghost, and must not be defiled. Every evil thought must be suppressed, every unholy inclination subdued. No outward cleansing by a mummery of religious forms [as, Hill suggests, in Catholicism], but the attainment of holiness of heart must be the great end of his existence [15].

The Presbyterianism of D. H. Hill is easily perceived in such passages, with their emphasis on interior as opposed to exterior purity. Hill expands, in another section of the book, on the theme of Catholic religious observances. Here, he addresses the topic of "repetitions in prayer":

> Our Saviour then does not condemn repetition *per se*, but that repetition which claims merit because of its much speaking... . Such as that of the Roman worshippers, who repeat the same salutations to the Virgin over and over again. In a Catholic book of devotions, in our possession, almost every sentence closes with "Ave Maria." [Hill then quotes from a text called *Brown's Exposition*:] "It is curious to observe the identity of character of false religion in all its forms—heathenism, corrupted Judaism, and corrupted Christianity. The poor deluded Romanists are in the habit of repeating the Lord's prayer and the salutations of the Virgin in a language [Latin] they do not understand; and of expecting that by the frequent repetition of these, which they number by counting a string of beads [note the none-too-subtle implication of "heathen" practice, as if the Catholics were unconverted Native Americans], they are to obtain deliverance from the greatest evils, and the possession of the most important blessings" [Hill, M.D.H., *Consideration* 65–66].

Hill did not have far to go, then, to arrive at his vitriolic attitude toward the Northern invasion of the South. He expressed this in terms not too far, either, from those of Southern clerics like Robert Louis Dabney. In the context of Hill's generally acid attitudes, though, such sentiments as the following ones, from a Hill letter to "a [Philadelphia] publisher friend" of January 15, 1861, may take on an unforgiving, even vengeful tone:

> I have told you all along that our people would not submit to Black Republican[82] rule. We will not have a party to reign over us, who have sought in every way in their power to foment insurrection and murder. If you had lain down night after night, incited by this most internal [sic: infernal?] party: If you had contemplated as often as I have done the butchery of wife and children through the agency of these same fiends, you would not wonder at our determination to die rather than have our bloodthirsty enemies rule over us.... Ask yourself in the presence of God if the South is not right in her determination to resist to the last extremity. I care nothing for your personal liberty bills, and nothing for the value of Negro property. The few slaves I own, I love, and I know they are devoted to me. But I would give them up, if it were right, at any moment. I care however, to defend my wife and children from assassination and I will feel that in taking up arms against the Black Republicans, I am engaged in the holiest of causes. Do your people think that we have no natural affection, and that we will permit a government over us, whose avowed policy is

murder? "The barbarism of slavery" has not destroyed our love for wives and children, and we will defend them to the death [Herran 59].

The caustic attitude of this general toward his foe was not lessened at all by the action of the war. Unlike Jackson, who was forceful and ruthless when necessary but who harbored no venom towards his enemy, Hill was positively acid. Pollard quotes his report of the battle of Fredericksburg, a great Southern victory. Again, Pollard highlights Hill's "literary exploits" which betrayed his prejudices: "In his official reports he carefully eschewed the ordinary style of such documents, and worried the War Department with conceits and puns to which they were little used in the literature of the war. The enemy he officially designated as 'Yankees,' sometimes 'infernal Yankees,' occasionally 'the pirates and scoundrels.' Of an attempt of the Yankees to cross the river at Fredericksburg..., he wrote to the War Department: 'Finding the fire too hot for them, they fled back to town, where they were sheltered from Carter's fire. Hardaway continued to pelt them; and to stop his fire (as is supposed) the ruffians commenced shelling the town, full of women and children. The town was partially destroyed, but a merciful God kindly protected the inoffensive inhabitants.... Finding that Hardaway's fire did not slacken, the pirates fled down the river. From Yankee sources we learned that the pirates lost six killed and twenty wounded. Whether they over-estimated or under-estimated their loss I do not know. *They sometimes lie on one side, and sometimes on another'*" (Pollard 455–56). Once, Pollard writes, Hill called the Union "'Army of the Pamunkey' [the name of a river near Richmond]" or "'*the Monkey Army'*" (456). Few would call D.H. Hill magnanimous in victory, or chivalrous toward his enemy.

After the war, Hill stayed in the limelight as a defender of the Southern cause. He launched a journal in which his forceful and articulate prose expressed the now-familiar view of Southern military excellence:

> In 1866, ... Hill began publication of *The Land We Love*.... Hill concentrated ... on ... Confederate military prowess. Man for man, he argued, the Confederate forces were superior to those of the Union. Only lack of resources and lack of foreign recognition prevented the South from permanently establishing a new nation [Starnes, R.D., "Forever Faithful" 178].

Hill was reared in a strict Presbyterian family. Although he was of a lower class than was his wife, Isabella (Herran 11–12), both were brought up in this strait-laced milieu. Orthodox Presbyterianism of the Scotch-Irish variety (Hill and Isabella were both Scotch-Irish) discouraged drinking, card-playing, and dancing.

Patton, Protestant Anachronism

General George S. Patton Jr. (1885–1945) was one of our most idio-syncratic warriors. He is justly famed for his aggressive tank tactics and for his familiar, yet authoritative, way with his men. His relief of the besieged pocket of Bastogne during the Battle of the Bulge in December 1944 has entered American legend. Patton is renowned for his blustery profanity and his irreverence toward stuffy authority. He was also much touted for his showiness of dress and his generally flamboyant demeanor. He was known to enforce strict regulations about proper Army dress but allowed himself a certain license, most notably in his choice of firearms: twin ivory-handled .45s. As with so much about this unique man, this bit of ostentation became distorted, in this case perhaps maliciously, with the claim being repeated that he wore pearl-handled revolvers, an imputation of decadence that he characteristically repudiated, as related by his nephew Fred Ayer: "One legend … which was and is totally incorrect and

nonfactual was that Uncle George … carried a pearl-handled pistol, either re-volver or automatic. He took great care to point this out to me. 'Goddammit, Bowser, my guns are ivory-handled. Nobody but a pimp for a cheap New Orleans whorehouse would carry one with pearl grips'" (Ayer 73). Less famous but just as important to his image is his mystical religiosity, a great part of which revolved around military legend.

Like Stonewall Jackson, Patton had a public image which hid much of his pri-vate reality. But, unlike Jack-son, Gordon, or Gustavus Adolphus, Patton lived in the age of media: radio, newspapers, the publicity machine, advertising. So Pat-

Gen. George S. Patton Jr. (1885–1945) (Cour-tesy Patton Museum).

ton's image, much more than Jackson's or even Gordon's, was easily fashioned for a public receptive to heroics and "candoism." Patton was certainly operative in setting up this image.

But the image of the tough, resolute warrior, which contained elements of truth, had another face: the vulnerable, dyslexic man with a very private need for affection. Patton once told his nephew Fred Ayer that he felt an obligation to live up to his own image: "Yes, I know, people ask why I swagger and swear, wear flashy uniforms and sometimes two pistols. Well, I'm not sure whether some of if it isn't my own damned fault, but, however that may be, the press and others have built a picture of me. So now, no matter how tired, or discouraged, or even really ill I may be, if I don't live up to that picture my men are going to say, 'The old man's sick, the old son-of-a-bitch has had it.' Then their own confidence, their own morale, will take a big drop" (Ayer 203).

Patton was also a man who had strong if rather unorthodox religious convictions. If these beliefs were not as off-center as they may seem to viewers of the film *Patton*, where the general seems to believe himself reincarnated, still they were not traditionally devout or pious in the common acceptance of these terms.

Certainly apart from Patton's religious beliefs was the fact of the general's verified roots in Civil War Virginia. His great-uncle John Mercer Patton was commander of the 21st Virginia Infantry under Stonewall Jackson in the Valley but had to leave the service from ill-health (Blumenson 20–21) and was killed at Winchester. Another great-uncle, Waller Tazewell Patton, commander of the 7th Virginia, was killed at Gettysburg on July 2, 1863, in Pickett's Charge (Blumenson 21). (The death of this Patton relative was depicted in the Ron Maxwell film *Gettysburg*, with Ted Turner playing the Confederate officer.) And Patton's grandfather, George Smith Patton, became commander of the 22nd Virginia as a colonel and was killed in the battle of Cedar Creek in September 1864 (Blumenson 21). All three men were justifiably heroic for their families, and Patton seems to have internalized the notion that he was destined to follow in the footsteps of these illustrious ancestors. In fact, he thought to surpass them, believing as a recent West Point graduate that he would one day become a great general, leading armies of men, as of course he did.

Patton became a student of military history and theory. He read extensively, as his surviving library shows, in military biography, autobiography, and theory. He seems to have come home again, so to speak, by highlighting in his reading a military maxim of the commander of his ancestor: "Always mystify." Perhaps Patton was intrigued by Stonewall Jackson because of his family history, but more likely he was attracted to a kindred warrior spirit.

Both commanders were leaders of men rather than devisers of theories.[83] Both generals favored attack over defense, and both were feared for their aggressiveness and rapid thrusts. Both were often perceived as tyrannical and merciless toward error, although in Jackson's case, this was only true with officers or with men who failed to try their best, and in Patton's case, some of the tyrannizing was for show.

Both men professed religious convictions, and it is clear that Stonewall Jackson's were more profound in the traditional sense. But one should not ascribe all of Patton's religiosity to mere showboating or to eccentricity. Like Jackson, but in a way all his own, Patton felt himself chosen for a particular and important role.

In other ways, though, the two leaders were quite different from one another. Patton's religious background was Episcopalian, and as D'Este notes, he was "devout." His family, a formerly wealthy one, had fallen on leaner times until his marriage to rich heiress Beatrice Ayer. Patton's grandfather was the California icon Don Benito Wilson, whose huge ranch, named for his wife, Yorba, once encompassed Orange County. Part of it is now the Los Angeles suburb Yorba Linda. Thomas Jackson could claim no such illustrious ancestry. His grandmother had been a penurious Scots-Irish immigrant, and his father, though of some importance locally near Clarksburg, (later West) Virginia, was not at all wealthy. And Jackson was a Southern Presbyterian, belonging to the Reformed Church, which was very anti–Latitudinarian, that is, opposed to the kind of liberal "latitude" countenanced in the Episcopalian (Low Anglican) Church.

Patton was not a Jackson-style Presbyterian, but he was a very Protestant leader nevertheless. He was especially "Protestant" in the moral sense. He was not at all tolerant of cowardice: he criticized and attacked other generals whom he saw as lacking in "guts," that is, moral courage. He was ferociously anti–Bolshevik and pro–Anglo-Saxon. Patton's moral fervor was essentially anachronistic. He maintained that he had been born in the wrong century, and he lamented the corruption of older values— essentially Protestant ones of individualism, integrity, courage.[84] So he was very much, in this respect, like Jackson, Gordon, or Havelock. He fits into the category of "religious generalship" in the same way that these leaders do, and that a captain as ancient as Judas Maccabeus does: all were deeply conservative in respect to national and religious tradition, even bordering at times on the atavistic in this regard.

Notwithstanding the differences between Jackson and Patton, the tank commander was a spiritual cousin of the Civil War general in more ways than one. Militarily Patton was a "front-line" commander, as was Jackson;[85] he was also a believer in risky, bold, aggressive attacks, and in ruthlessness toward the enemy. As Patton stated on many occasions, his soldiers must kill the enemy in order to avoid being killed. He was no bloodthirsty killer; on the contrary, he saw, as did Jackson, that softness in battle led to more death, and that a clear-eyed view of war demanded a lack of squeamishness about dealing death. As his famous set-piece in the 1969 film *Patton* (the opening speech, a roughly accurate composite of his standard stemwinder) put it, "Now I want you to remember that no bastard ever won a war by dying for his country. He won it by making the other poor dumb bastard die for his country" (Schaffner).

Not only in soldiering but also in religion and spirituality was Patton a kin of Jackson's. Several observers close to Patton attested to his strange mixture of blasphemy (not a Jackson trait) and piety (a most Jacksonian trait), and those who knew him also aver that he was a deeply religious man.

Patton's brand of religion, like Jackson's, was a deeply embedded facet of his character. His religious faith, Episcopalian officially, was complicated by his belief in reincarnation. Patton debunkers may have scoffed at his claims of being reincarnated, but given the peculiarly sincere nature of Patton's character, which not even his detractors have denied, and the almost naïve way in which he was wont to express himself on many occasions, there is little reason to doubt his own belief in his reincarnation pronouncements. Furthermore, the reincarnation belief was a common thread in his family and was more or less taken for granted among them. And, though of course one cannot prove or disprove such claims, Patton did seem to have a strange tendency to recall places in which he had never before set foot. Patton biographer Carlo D'Este discusses his beliefs about reincarnation at length in his chapter "Past and Future Warrior Reincarnate" (320–28). Among other episodes in Patton's life involving reincarnation, D'Este cites accounts related by Patton to friends and family. One might tend not to believe these, since they are related by Patton himself— perhaps he made them up or dreamed them. But one account was related by Ruth Ellen Patton, the general's daughter. On a trip during the interwar period to the Civil War site of the Wilderness battles with a German officer friend, Gen. Friedrich von Boetticher, and Patton's family, who typically participated with Patton in mini-reenactments of famous battles, the following chilling episode took place:

> While we were lining up and receiving our orders, we noticed a group of tourists with a guide. Georgie [the family's nickname for Patton] was gesticulating and explaining the battle, and one old gentleman with "pork chop" whiskers was … obviously intrigued. Georgie finished his speech by saying that he was General Early [that is, playing the role of Gen. Jubal

Early, Confederate brigade commander] and would be with his aides on a nearby rise of ground. General von Boetticher, who had the book they were using, pointed out that General Early had been in another part of the battlefield, and he and Georgie began to discuss it. The old gentleman could stand it no longer and broke in, saying, "The young gentleman [Patton] is quite right; General Early was on that nearby rise. I was in that battle, [on the Union side] ... and, gentlemen, we ran like hell!" Georgie looked at him calmly and said, "Of course, General Early was on that rise; I saw him there myself." General von Boetticher methodically corrected the text of the book [325–26].

Patton's nephew, Fred J. Ayer, recounts in his biography of Patton (*Before the Colors Fade*) that the general professed to him his sincere belief in the reincarnation phenomenon. On this occasion, after Patton had read from the *Iliad* and had talked "of the distant past," Ayer asked him if he "really believe[d] in reincarnation." Patton responded:

I don't know about other people; but for myself there has never been any question. I just don't think it, I damn well know there are places I've been before, and not in this life. [He then relates his version of the amphitheater anecdote, detailed in the film:] For instance, when I took over my first command in France, at Langres, a young French liaison officer met me and offered to show me around since I had never been there before. For some reason I said, You don't have to. I know this place. I know it well. Of course he didn't believe me. But to make a long story short, I told the driver where to go in the small, typical French city — almost as if someone were at my ear, whispering the directions. I took him to what had been the Roman Amphitheater, the drill ground, the Forum, and the Temples of Mars and Apollo.... I even showed him correctly the spot where Caesar had earlier pitched his tent. But I never made a wrong turn. You see, I had been there before" [Ayer 94–95].

Concerning Patton's degree of piety, he was, as in other matters, a walking contradiction. He is renowned for his colorful profanity and brash irreverence. But the other side of this coin was that Patton was "a devout, tithing, church-going Episcopalian" (D'Este 309)[86]:

Religion played a large role in Patton's life. He not only believed in God and, in particular, a god of battles who served as his protector, but in a conception of religion in which God was personalized and not some obscure, invisible spirit to which one prayed in church. Nevertheless Patton found comfort and solace in churches. Former NATO commander Gen. John R. Galvin tells the tale of a German cleric who, as a young priest in 1945, came upon Patton in a medieval church in Bad Wimpfen am Berg ... "Patton was doing a most unusual thing for a man of such reputation.

The warrior, with notebook and pencil in hand, was calmly sketching the stained-glass windows" [D'Este 324].

D'Este, contrasting Omar Bradley's low-key style with Patton's flamboyance, called the latter "the mercurial Patton who might curse one moment and the next get down on his knees to ask for God's help" (465).[87]

Patton did in fact compose a poem (he wrote quite a few) whose final lines illuminate the warrior-priest side of his personality. The poem's title, "God of Battles," is obviously indicative of his chosen vocation; its concluding lines neatly encapsulate Patton's professed melding of war and religiosity: "Make strong our souls to conquer, / Give us the victory, Lord" (Nye 147).

The "God of Battles" may have seemed to Patton to have sent assistants to help him along in the pinch. Patton related a visionary experience on the battlefield in World War I. On September 26, 1918, near the town of Cheppy, Patton and some companions were approaching the source of German gunfire when they actually began to be fired upon. After they managed to dig in and their tanks drove up and beyond their position, Patton called for his men to advance with him. As they were going over the top, they were pinned down by machine-gun fire. As Patton told the story later,

> [I] felt a great desire to run, I was trembling with fear when suddenly I thought of my progenitors [his soldier ancestors] and seemed to see them in a cloud over the German lines looking at me. I became calm at once and saying aloud, "It is time for another Patton to die" called for volunteers and went forward to what I honestly believed was certain death [Blumenson 113].

Patton's vision actually links him to other warrior figures from history and epic. Whether or not such visitations were real, imagined, or invented, the fact remains that Patton perceived himself as part of a warrior tradition that included figures such as Hernán Cortés and the warriors of Charlemagne from the *Chanson de Roland*. Cortés told of seeing the patron saint of Spain, Santiago (St. James) de Compostela, hovering over the battles of the conquest of Mexico (Weckmann 140n38).

This apparition on the battlefield in Mexico was disputed even in its own time. The debate is presented in "The Equine Strategy of Cortés," by Robert Moorman Denhardt. While Cortés's rather adoring biographer Francisco López de Gómara accepted and repeated the tale, a man who was on the scene, Bernal Díaz del Castillo, was more skeptical. Following the López de Gómara account, taken from the Spanish author's *Historia de la conquista*, Denhardt observes that "Cortés, ... when he heard of the vision, used it as a means to encourage his men to fight. The apparition appeared as a mounted man, in the form of San Diego [Santiago], the patron saint of Spain" (Denhardt 552).

At first, the apparition seems to have been a concrete one — a mounted soldier from Cortés's ranks (a certain Francisco Morla). But the fact of his appearance was disputed by Cortés himself, who indeed appears to have "encouraged" his men to believe that the horseman was the saint in person. López de Gómara recounts that, after the Spanish appeared to be losing the battle,

> A esta sazón llegó Cortés con los otros compañeros á caballo.... Dijéronle lo que habian visto hacer á uno de caballo, y preguntaron si era de su compañía; y como dijo que no, porque ninguno dellos habia podido venir ántes, creyeron que era el apóstol Santiago, patron de España. Entónces dijo Cortés: «Adelante, compañeros, que Dios es con nosotros y el glorioso sant Pedro.» [The Spanish then win the battle.] ... No pocas gracias dieron nuestros españoles cuando se vieron libres de las flechas y muchedumbre de indios, con que habian peleado, á nuestro Señor, que milagrosamente los quiso librar; y todos dijeron que vieron por tres veces al del caballo rucio picado [Morla] pelear en su favor contra los indios, ... y que era Santiago, nuestro patron. Fernando Cortés más quería que fuese sant Pedro, su especial abogado; pero cualquiera que dellos fué, estuvo á milagro, como de veras paresció; porque no solamente lo vieron los españoles, mas aun tambien los indios lo notaron por el estrago que en ellos hacia cada vez que arremetia á su escuadron... [López de Gómara 64–66].

> At this point Cortés arrived along with his companions on horseback.... They told him what they had seen a man on horseback do, and they asked if he was one of his company; and as he said no, since none of them had been able to come before, they believed he was the apostle Santiago, patron of Spain. Then Cortés said, "Forward, men, for God is with us and glorious Saint Peter." [The Spanish then win the battle.] ... Our Spaniards offered not a few thanks when they found themselves free from the arrows and the mob of Indians, against whom they had fought, to our Lord, who miraculously had seen fit to free them; and they all said that three times they saw the man [Morla] on the spotted gray horse fight on their behalf against the Indians..., and that he was Santiago, our patron. Fernando Cortés would rather that he were Saint Peter, his special advocate; but whichever of them he was, he appeared there by a miracle, as it truly seemed; because not only did the Spaniards see him, but even the Indians noticed him by the havoc he wrought upon them every time he struck their squadron....

Díaz del Castillo was less credulous than some of Cortés's men. This hardtack old soldier, who wrote his *Verdadera historia de la conquista de la Nueva España* [*True History of the Conquest of New Spain*][88] more than

50 years after the events, was according to his own account spurred to its writing by his weary anger at seeing the constant glorification of Cortés, at the expense of the common soldier like Díaz del Castillo, by apologists like López de Gómara. The old soldier's practicality and skepticism are evident throughout his narrative, and so it should not be surprising that, as Denhardt writes before providing his own translation of some of the relevant material, "Díaz specifically differs with Gómara concerning the appearance of the vision of Saint James" (554). Díaz del Castillo's comments are masterly in their seemingly unschooled irony:

> Aqui Es donde dize françisco lopez de gomara, que salio françisco de morla En vn caballo rruçio, picado, antes q̃ llegase Cortes con los de caballo, y que Eran los santos Apostoles señor Santiago, o señor san pedro … y pudiera ser q̃ los que dize el gomara, fueran los gloriosos Apostoles señor santiago, o señor san pedro. E yo como pecador, no fuese dino de lo ver lo que yo entonçes vi y conosçi fue a fran.ᶜᵒ de morla En un cavallo castaño, que venia juntamente con cortes…. E ya que yo como yndino, no fuera mereçedor de ver A qualquiera de aq̃llos gloriosos apostoles, alli En nra conpañia Abia sobre quatroçientos soldados, y cortes y otros muchos cavalleros, platicarase dello, y se tomara por testimonio, y se oviera hecho vna yglesia quando se poblo la villa, y se nonbrara la villa de santiago de la vitoria, o de san pedro de la vitoria, … y si fuera Ansi Como dize El gomara harto malos cristianos fueramos, q̃ Enbiandonos nro señor dios, sus santos Apostoles, no rreconoçer la gran md. q̃ nos hazia, y rreverençiar cada dia Aq̃lla yglesia [Díaz del Castillo 1:94–95].
>
> [Here is where Francisco López de Gómara says, that Francisco de Morla {the supposed horseman from the Spanish army} came forth on a gray, spotted horse, before Cortés arrived with men on horseback, and that they were the holy Apostles St. James, or St. Peter, … and it could be that those who Gómara says, were the glorious Apostles St. James or St. Peter. And that I as a sinner was not worthy {note the mock self-deprecation} to see what I saw and knew then was Francisco de Morla on a chestnut horse, who came up together with Cortés…. And since I as one unworthy, was not deserving of seeing any of those glorious apostles, there in our company were more than four hundred soldiers, and Cortés and many other horsemen, it would have been talked of, and it would have been credited as testimony, and a church would have been built when the town was settled, and the town would have been called St. James of Victory, or St. Peter of Victory…, and if it were as Gómara says we would be quite unworthy Christians, who, our Lord God sending us his holy Apostles, would not recognize the great mercy that He was bestowing upon us, and would not revere that church every day.

The alleged visions of Santiago during the Conquest fit into a Spanish tradition concerning Santiago, the warrior saint. According to legend

the body of St. James the Apostle had been brought to Spain after his execution in 44, and had been interred near the village of Compostela. During the Reconquest, interest in the supposed burial site was revived when
it was rediscovered "early in the ninth century, perhaps about A.D. 814,"
by a bishop named Teodomiro of Iria (Kendrick 17–18). The cult of St.
James, or Sant' Yago (Santiago) grew until its "triumphant conclusion" for
the medieval Spaniards "with the story of the apostle's personal appearance on earth in the ninth century at Clavijo," during a legendary battle
(Kendrick 18–19).[89] Kendrick writes that the saint "had come to help the
people in a battle in which, so we are told, the Christians of free Spain
won a decisive victory over the Moors" (19–20). This battle was recounted
by the Spanish king Ramiro I, who had supposedly initiated the battle to
end a shameful forced "annual tribute" to the Moors of "one hundred
Spanish virgins" (21–22). According to his narrative, the expedition against
the Moors went badly for the Spaniards, who hid out in Clavijo. Kendrick
summarizes the events which supposedly ensued:

> Night fell, and then a wonderful thing happened. St James appeared to
> the sleeping king [Ramiro] in a dream and announced that he had been
> specially commissioned by Jesus Christ to take Spain under his protection,
> … he went on to promise Ramiro victory on the following day in a bat-
> tle in which the apostle said he himself would take part. The king was
> assured that the casualties on the Christian side would be almost negligi-
> ble, and that in any case the fallen would rank as martyrs…. Ramiro lis-
> tened attentively to this ghostly encouragement, and when morning came,
> … the Christians, now in good heart, descended into the plain and the
> famous battle of Clavijo began. And St James appeared at the head of the
> Spanish army, visible to all, as he had promised, and so inspired the
> Spaniards that the Moors were hopelessly overwhelmed and routed. About
> 70,000 of the infidels were killed. It was in this wonderful victory, so
> Ramiro said, that the Spanish army used for the first time the battle-cry
> *Adjuva nos Deus et Sancte Jacobe.* May God and St James come to our aid!
> [Kendrick 22–23].

Santiago also appeared in other Castilian epics; sometimes his appearances were combined with those of other saints or important national
figures, including dream apparitions, a common motif of epic and legend.
Thus, Santiago appeared to the hero of the 13th-century epic *Poema de Fernán González*, along with San Millán and a saintly monk named Pelayo (at
different places in the poem). J. P. Keller summarizes the dream apparitions experienced by the count:

> Pelayo appeared … and promised that he would come with Santiago
> and a heavenly host [in the coming battle with the Moors]…. Then San

Millán [San Millán de la Cogolla, patron saint of a monastery in Navarra] appeared ... and promised that he would come with Santiago.... On the third day of the battle, ... Santiago came with a heavenly host and turned the threatened loss into a victory [Keller, "Hunt" 255].

In this instance, Santiago appears on the battlefield in person, as it were; the incident is taken as truthful and well-attested, unlike the debate which surrounded the apparition to Cortés. In fact, the Moorish enemies of the count show "great amazement at these sudden reinforcements"; this reaction "is stressed first and more completely than the encouragement they inspire in the Christians" (Davis, G., "National Sentiment" 61):

> [The Moors] Veyen duna sennal tantos pueblos armados,
> *Ovyeron muy grand miedo, fueron mal espantados,*
> De qual parte venian eran marauillados,
> Lo que mas les pesaua que eran todos cruzados.
>   Dixol Rey Almançor(re) [the Moorish King]: "Esto non puede ser.
> ¿Dond(e) (le) Recreço al conde atan fuerte poder?
> Cuydaua yo oy syn duda (de) le matar o prender,
> E a con estas gentes el (a) nos acometer" [Anonymous, *Poema de Fernan Gonçalez* st. 553–54].[90]

> [{The Moors} see at a signal so many armed men, / *they felt very great fear, they were badly scared,* / they were greatly astonished at the place from which they came, / which most worried them as they were all intermixed. / Said King Almançor: "This cannot be. / Whence came such strong power to the Count? / I was eager today without doubt to kill or seize him; / and {now}with {his} people he is to strike us."]

Incidentally, the poem is not lacking in other "supernatural" events, as Keller points out in his article on the organization of the poem. In trying to demonstrate the importance of the symbolic number three in the poem, Keller places the appearance of Santiago along with two other extraordinary events during the count's battles against the Moslems:

The first was the opening ... of a chasm which engulfed a rider and his steed.... The second was the appearance of a "fiery serpent" in the sky.... Our poet-monk used these ... signs [and the appearance of Santiago] to work out part of his purpose of showing the hero as God's chosen instrument against Islam [Keller, "Structure" 243].

Witnesses to the Cortés visitation seemed at the time to be a little hard to find. Gómara's account could be, and was, criticized for its reportage of fantastic events. Such attacks would not have fazed the author had he been writing an epic with no pretensions to verisimilitude. So, in untroubled manner, a 14th-century poem from Spain features a secondhand appearance of Santiago. This is the *Poema de Alfonso Onceno* [*The Poem of Alfonso the Eleventh*], which probably used the *PFG* as one of its sources. The scene quoted above was replayed in the 14th-century poem, but in this instance "the event is not presented by the poet as happening ... but only [reported] by the King of Granada in his lament after the defeat of Gibraltar" (Davis, G., "National Sentiment" 61).[91]

So it is clear that Patton's battlefield visions had ancestors: this type of vision was a commonplace of epic and romance.[92] Patton may indeed have seen such a vision; probably he was susceptible to such visioning because of his reading and of his family background, imbued as it was with legends about his ancestor soldiers.

Patton's reported vision during World War I was to become part of his self-proclaimed legend. Patton was to make a career in the army, culminating in his promotion to four-star general and in the creation of many more anecdotes about this singular man who has been so often misunderstood as nothing more than a blustering, strutting warmonger. Like Stonewall Jackson, Patton maintained within him a very private identity which was frequently attested to by his intimate associates and which differed greatly from his public image. Neither man seems to have allowed his warrior persona to vitiate his domestic personality, although certainly the public deeds of these men often interfered with the private image.

4

Catholic Warriors

El Cid

The exploits of the historical warrior Rodrigo (or Ruy) Díaz de Vivar (d. 1099) are narrated, and embellished, in a series of poems and chronicles which appeared beginning in the 12th century. The most well-known of these works, the *Poema [or Cantar] de Mio Cid* (often dated, though not without controversy, at ca. 1140), compares very favorably to the French epic *Chanson de Roland* or to *Beowulf*. Its origins and sources are still the subject of debate, but one can say that a cleric wrote down the poem more or less as it now exists around the date of 1140. The Cid has also been the subject of plays, most famously *Le Cid* (Pierre Corneille, 1636) and the *Las mocedades del Cid* (Guillén de Castro).[93] The fine American director Anthony Mann (known especially for his tough-minded and psychologically sophisticated Westerns with James Stewart) helmed a "Hollywood epic" about the Cid, starring Charlton Heston and Sophia Loren, in 1961.

The Cid is a figure of interest in the present context because of his image in myth and legend rather than because of his strictly historical characteristics. The historical Rodrigo was involved in the fighting between Moors and Christians and among Christians themselves during the unsettled 11th century in the area of Al-Andalus (the Arabic name for the southern part of what is now Spain; thus, Andalusia, the name of the present-day state in Spain). As Richard Fletcher writes, the Cid was a man of flexible loyalties: "Rodrigo ... was as ready to fight alongside Muslims against Christians as vice versa. He was his own man and fought for his own profit. He was a mercenary soldier" (Fletcher, R., *Quest* 4). Fletcher cautions against extreme evaluations of the Cid resting on such terms as "mercenary": "In modern Anglo-American usage the term 'mercenary' carries

Cid statue, Burgos (www.aytoburgos.es)

pejorative overtones. It is true that the mercenary soldiers of today—for example, in post-colonial Africa—are not a very savoury bunch. Their eleventh-century predecessors may have been equally unappealing: we must not romanticise the Cid." Fletcher emphasizes, however, that his own work employs the word "mercenary" "in the neutral sense of 'one who serves for pay.'" So, the Cid "was a professional soldier. He was a highly successful one, too; more so than many, less so than a few" (4).

As Fletcher also observes, shifting loyalties were not at all uncommon in the period. One don't necessarily have to be as hard on this hero as is

Barbara Matulka when, following 19th-century scholar Dozy, who had written an influential but unfavorable study of the Cid, she dismissively snarls, "The Cid Campeador of history was hardly more than a border ruffian, a typical mediaeval freebooter, who sold his services now to the Christians, then to the Moors" (Matulka 1). But it must be remembered that the process of mythmaking, especially in the hands of the clerical author or authors of the *Poema de Mio Cid*, led inevitably to a romanticized, idealized version of this man, who was cut to the measure of an ideology befitting an anachronistic (because not present at the period of the Cid) Spanish nationalism.

With this important caveat in mind, one can examine the *Poema de Mio Cid* and other works about the Cid for indications of just how this hero functions as a Spanish national and religious symbol. In general, the Cid fits the outlines of a medieval Christian hero. He is usually seen as embodying the virtues of piety, courage, and loyalty (especially on the private level). He is nevertheless subject to powerful poetic treatment by the author of the *Poema de Mío Cid*, as Colin Smith comments; in this instance some of the Cid's qualities as listed by Smith are cited: "He is not merely highly skilled in battle, a fine general and utterly loyal.... He is a loving husband and father, a skilled lawyer, an eloquent speaker at court. He is extremely devout.... His respect for, and trust in his King are not ... absolute but depend ... on circumstances" (Smith, C., "Did" 528–29).

Norman Schafler contends that the "unity" of the *Poema de Mío Cid* itself has often been seen as centering upon the figure of its hero. For Schafler, "[t]he only constant in the Cid's behavior is his adherence to the heroic ideal of *sapientia et fortitudo*," and this complex forms the foundation of "the other ideals the critics have seen embodied in the character of Rodrigo" (44).

Ernst Robert Curtius, whose discussion of the *sapientia et fortitudo* topos is cited by Schafler, does not focus on it exclusively in terms of its Christian uses, but he does provide a summary of its derivation. (A topos is a "commonplace" of discourse, that is, a commonly accepted motif found in literature, like *carpe diem*.) Curtius points especially to the importance of St. Isidore of Seville, a medieval polymath famed for his early etymological studies, in the development of the classical formula into a Christian topos:

> The entire development which leads from Homer to Dares and Fulgentius reaches its conclusion in what Isidore of Seville (d. 636) has to say about the epic: "It is called heroic song because it tells the deeds of brave men. For hero is the name given to men who by their *wisdom and courage* are worthy of heaven" (*Et.*, I, 39, 9). "Sapientia et fortitudo"— in Isidore's

formula Homer's ideal of the hero combines with Hesiod's teaching. The reception of the hero into "heaven" was an idea already known to the ancient Greeks. But Isidore's formulation provides room for the Christian ideal hero of the eleventh century. The knights who, like Roland and his comrades, fell in battle against the infidels were also "worthy of heaven" [Curtius 175].

Schafler presents several examples of the *Poema de Mío Cid*'s implicit casting of the Cid in terms of this topos. He observes that this "exemplary hero" communicates morality to the reader, "and ... *sapientia et fortitudo* is ... important ... in the presentation of his character" (49).

In particular, the presentation of the Cid in terms of this topos is linked directly to his Christian hero status. As Curtius has shown, the *topos* was integral to the "Christian hero" motif in the Middle Ages. Again, though, one must bear in mind that the Cid of this poem was decidedly not the Cid of history, *pace* Menéndez Pidal and the tradition that he so magnificently represented. Thus, R. A. Fletcher writes of the Cid in the context of the Reconquest:

> The Cid was certainly not ... a national and Christian hero in the struggle to liberate Spain from Islam. Legend has rendered him unique in Spanish history: but it is important to remember that he was merely the most skilful and successful, by no means the only man of his type [Fletcher, R.A., "Reconquest" 36].

The treatment of the Cid as epic hero included, as one would expect, accoutrements like heroic epithets and special named weapons (the swords Tizón and Colada) as well as a charger (Babieca). Babieca is an important adjunct to the Cid legend, as he accompanied the Cid on many campaigns and even developed a legend of his own. He was even dealt with in mock-epic terms in Miguel de Cervantes's *Don Quixote* (Part 1, 1605, Part 2, 1615), whose prologue contains a comic verse dialogue between Babieca and Rocinante, the broken-down steed of Don Quixote. In a more serious vein, a ballad subsequent to the *Cantar* was to present Babieca as carrying the dead body of his master into battle, thereby frightening the enemy and winning the battle for the Cid's men. (This legend was used in the final scene of the Anthony Mann film *The Cid* with Charlton Heston.) Babieca was also presented as a talking horse in the ballad "Romance del rey moro que perdió a Valencia" (usually known by its first line, "Helo, helo, por do viene"). The relevant passage is: "Do la yegua pone el pie, / Babieca pone la pata. / Allí hablara el caballo, / bien oiréis lo que hablaba: /—¡Reventar debía la madre, / que a su hijo no esperaba!" [Where the mare puts her foot, / Babieca puts his hoof. / Thus had the horse spoken,

/ hear well what he said: / "The mother deserved to burst, / who did not wait for her son!"] (Anonymous, *Romancero del Cid* 155).

Although Babieca was usually treated as a worthy mount for a great hero like the Cid, his name has caused some puzzlement, being sometimes interpreted as less than flattering. Such an interpretation would strengthen his likeness to Jackson's Sorrel. The comic or disparaging interpretation of the name Babieca is summarized as follows by Stephen Clissold, after the account in the *Crónica del famoso cavallero Cid Ruy Díez campeador* (1512):

> There is little ... that we know of Rodrigo's [the Cid's] early life beyond his family origins, his social status, and the boyhood spent amongst border forays and at the King's court. But where history is silent, poetry and legend have much to say. They relate that Rodrigo had a god-father, a good priest called don Pedro de Pernegas, or more familiarly, Peyre Pringos— Fat Pete —from whom he once begged the gift of a colt. The boy was taken into the paddock and told that he could choose whichever he fancied. Rodrigo stood at the gate as the herd was driven past, but made no move until a mare cantered by with a scraggy colt [actually, says the *Crónica*, "muy feo e sarnoso," 'very ugly and mangy' {fo. II} (López de Velorado)] at her side. "That's the one for me!" he exclaimed, and his god-father let him have his choice, though gently chiding him as a *babieca*, or booby, for picking out such an ill-favoured beast.[94] Rodrigo was unabashed [an early sign, no doubt, of his heroic tenacity]. The colt would turn out well, he declared [prophecy or farsightedness, familiar to the epic tradition, as was the porous wall between the qualities of master and animal], and Babieca should be his name. The prophecy was amply fulfilled; the prowess of Babieca became as legendary as that of her master [Clissold 26–27].

Julius II: Soldier Pope

Pope Julius II, who held that office from 1503 until his death in 1513, has come down to posterity as "the warrior pope." He came to the papacy during a particularly contentious period of its existence. The papacy was embroiled in the unbelievably labyrinthine struggles of Italian politics, and this was nothing new, but additionally the Papal army was threatened by the new nationalism of states such as France and Spain. The latter country had been unified only within the past generation or so, and it was newly militant because of its spectacular success in crossing the Atlantic to found one of history's largest empires. Spain, France, and Germany (at that time, the Holy Roman Empire) were fighting for possession or control of the Italian peninsula; and of course each power wanted either to diminish or to exalt papal strength as that might serve their own cause.

When the reign of Julius began, the papacy had only recently been involved in several internecine squabbles on the peninsula. Also, an abortive attempt by Charles, the late king of France, to invade Italian territory had been resisted by papal troops. All this cost the papacy money, of course, as did the lavish style of living to which some of Julius's predecessors had been accustomed. Julius was thus confronted with another serious problem, financing the papacy's administration and self-defense (Shaw 139–40). This set of challenges helps to explain the "bunker mentality" often displayed by Julius.

But Julius was also a very complicated man. Born Giuliano della Rovere in the village of Albissola, not far from Savona, probably in 1445 (Shaw 10), he was no stranger to high-stakes politics. His uncle Francesco had been Pope Sixtus IV. The della Rovere family was of some importance in Italy, and Giuliano was given opportunities which allowed him to become a cardinal at a relatively young age.

As one of the more prominent cardinals in Italy, Giuliano, who adopted the title Vincula, was quickly to become deeply involved in politics. He became known as a shrewd political combatant who was possessed of a greatly feared temper, but who could generally be relied upon as a man of his word. He fell afoul of Pope Alexander VI, one of the infamous Borgia family from Cataluña, and as a result he spent much of that pope's reign in exile from Rome. Following the brief term of Alexander's successor Pius III, Vincula was elected pope and took the title of Julius II.

In an age when popes practiced power politics on a European stage, commanding armies by proxy with some frequency, the title of "warrior pope" would seem fitting to many holders of the papal office. Julius can lay especial claim to the epithet, however,

Pope Julius II (1445–1513; reigned 1503–13) (Raphael, *Pope Julius II,* woodcut, 1511–12, © National Gallery, London).

because of his longstanding role in military matters—he had helped to defend Italy from the French — and because of his direct, front-line participation in an important battle in Italy during his reign.

Christine Shaw ties the "warrior pope" epithet to Julius's "famous campaign against the Baglioni of Perugia and the Bentivoglio of Bologna in 1506 [these were two Italian ruling families]" but also observes that "[t]he campaign was just the climax of a concerted effort to pacify the Papal States, and to reform and stabilize the government of its cities, which had been under way since the first year of his pontificate" (140). The task that Julius set for himself was more than daunting, because the history of the Italian peninsula had long demonstrated the depth and the impenetrable complexity of the feuds and changing alliances between and within city-states like Perugia and Bologna. Despite Julius's frequent employment of cynical political tactics, and his evident self-interest, he was truly dedicated to advancing the institutional fortunes of the papacy. He was concerned with ensuring that the papacy would be, at a minimum, *primus inter pares* in the political composition of Italy.

In 1506, Julius decided to head a military force against the cities of Bologna and Perugia, where two families (the Bentivoglio and Bagliano, respectively) had proven recalcitrant to papal control. He informed the cardinals of his decision and left on August 26 (Shaw 152). As events unfolded, Julius did not have to resort to a hot war; the mere presence of the pope and his troops at the city gates was enough to elicit surrender, or at least a form of compliance, from the offending cities.

The decision to lead the forces, however, was truly extraordinary for a pope. Although canon law had theoretically prohibited clerical participation in warmaking, this prohibition had often been violated. Even popes had violated it, at a distance, but not, as Shaw notes, in person, at the front: "For a cardinal to lead or accompany a military expedition was commonplace, virtually normal practice [although, of course, not legally permissible]. For a pope to do so, was unheard of. Julius's martial behaviour was one of the features of his pontificate that most upset his critics" (149). This action by Julius led to much resentment. An example of this backlash, as Shaw points out, came from Desiderius Erasmus, the great Dutch Catholic humanist and church reformer, who, "[i]n his satire *Julius Exclusus*," "portrayed the pope arriving at the gates of heaven at the head of an army, demanding to be admitted, only to be turned away by St. Peter" (149). Although the cardinals raised no protest at the pope's action against the two cities (Shaw 152), clearly the watchdogs of papal ethics, like Erasmus, were severely displeased.

These criticisms by Erasmus were to be followed, in connection with another pope, by Spanish humanist Alfonso de Valdés. Also perceived by some as grasping for power not merited by him, Clement VII, though an altogether different personality from Julius, was to be attacked by Alfonso in his *Diálogo de Mercurio y Carón* and in *Lactancio y Arcediano* (*Diálogo de las cosas acaecidas en Roma*) for opposing the putatively rightful and legal proceedings of Charles V, Holy Roman Emperor. Pope Clement VII would certainly, and with much justice, have seen the matter differently, since Charles had sanctioned the infamous Sack of Rome in 1527; but Alfonso cast the disaster which befell Rome in that year as providentially ordained because of the iniquity into which the city had fallen (a synecdoche for the general decrepitude of the church for reformers like Valdés).[95] Clement was certainly no warrior, as Judith Hook explains: "Clement VII was not a man of vigour, nor was he cast in the heroic mould of a Julius II…. At the most basic level of his personality Clement was a sophisticated intellectual…. It was the same intellectual quality which often made Clement appear indecisive" (Hook 26–27). He was far from leading troops into battle — and he lacked the Borgia-like capacity for intrigue possessed by Julius.

Pope Julius II extended his fame as a soldier-pope by his important role in the League of Cambrai. He was in fact reluctant to join the league, chiefly because of his suspicion of the other partners; but he did have strong reasons for joining this alliance against Venice, which had appropriated some of his lands and had repeatedly annoyed him (Shaw Ch. 8). As Kelly Sowards puts the matter of Julius's willingness to sign on with the league, "While it can be argued … that Julius was responsible for forming and breaking the League of Cambrai, he was not wholly responsible and the league was actually initiated against his wishes" (Erasmus 115 n34). Although Julius's own forces did not achieve the eventual victory over Venice, he did receive the benefits of that victory, including a spectacular humiliation of the Venetian ambassadors, who performed an obeisance to him at the Vatican (Shaw 242–43).

The pope was also to lead the siege on the town of Mirandola during the Ferrara campaign in 1511. This siege became an important element in the story of Julius the warrior, not least because of its later connection with the work of Michelangelo. Shaw writes that "Those who were with Julius at the siege of Mirandola and saw him undaunted by cold and wind and snow and artillery fire, knew that they were witnessing a legend in the making" (270). This incident is summarized by Friedrich Gontard:

> As it continued to snow [at Mirandola], the commander-in-chief [Julius] took up his quarters in the kitchen of a monastery. But almost at

once it was struck by the enemy's cannon-balls, and two of the pope's sta-
blemen were killed. His next billet was similarly bombarded. The
monastery lay within a gun-shot from Mirandola. What did that matter?
The Mirandolans ought to learn to shoot straighter.... Sword in hand, the
old man handled his companies so as to spare them fatigue.... What was
wanted was a breach in the walls, through which they could storm the
town. A cardinal suggested it would probably be better to let Mirandola
pay tribute, to save the town and its inhabitants the horrors of plunder-
ing. The old man in armour shook his head. "If Mirandola surrenders, I
will let it be sacked...." But General Fabricius persuaded the pope to take
the garrison prisoner. Mirandola did not have to be stormed, for it capit-
ulated on 21st January. While the gate defences and street barricades were
being dismantled, the sixty-eight-year-old pope clambered on a wooden
chest and had himself hoisted to the top of the wall [360–61].

Julius was renowned for his short temper and for his calculating political nature. With regard to his demeanor, authors Loren Partridge and
Randolph Starn, in their study of Raphael's portraiture of Julius, offer the
following overview of some contemporary observations of the pope:

> Through the worst of times Venetian ambassadors saw the pope as
> "strong," as "above all others *fortissima*." For Machiavelli [who accompa-
> nied Julius on his attack on the city-states], Julius remained "violent,"
> "audacious," "unstable," "hasty," "rash." Other contemporaries agreed that
> the pope was "choleric." This quality was hardly exhausted by a raging
> tongue. "What is more, he pushes and punches someone, cuts at someone
> else ... with so much choler that *nihil supra*," wrote one witness of
> the famous siege Julius led in person against Mirandola in January 1511.
> These violent scenes— one thinks of psychoanalytical discussions of "prim-
> itive rage"— were interrupted by periods of brooding, of half-spoken solil-
> oquies, of plans or reasons changed without warning. "The pope has
> a mind all his own, and its depths cannot be fathomed" [Partridge and
> Starn 5].

Michelangelo also experienced the pope's gruffness and mercurial temperament, as *The Agony and the Ecstasy* shows at length. One instance cited
by Gontard will serve to illustrate not only Julius's temperament but also
his preoccupation with posterity and his warlike image. Julius required of
Michelangelo that he "commemorate the conquest of Bologna" with a large
statue of him ("three times life-size"). But the project did not work out
well, not least because of the pope's parsimony. Still, Michelangelo had a
"clay model ... ready by the end of February [1507]. When Julius saw it,
he asked the meaning of the raised arm.... Michelangelo replied: 'It threat-
ens the Bolognese if they don't obey.' Then he asked: 'What would you
like in the other hand, a book or a sword?' Julius growled: 'What's the use

of a book? Give me a sword. I don't hold with all this scribbling. I'm no scholastic'" (Gontard 364–65).

The model did not survive, as Gontard notes, though Julius's belligerent reputation did. The 1965 film adaptation of Irving Stone's *The Agony and the Ecstasy,* directed by Carol Reed, features Rex Harrison as an acerbic and demanding Julius and Charlton Heston as an earnest Michelangelo.

But Julius was also known for his bonhomie and for a sometimes surprising generosity. His intricately structured personality was notable as well for its optimism in the face of probable defeat, and for his strength of purpose, as Shaw evaluates him in his response to the Cambrai crisis:

> But Julius had one great personal strength, which sometimes could, on its own, counterbalance all the weaknesses of his position. He never knew when he was beaten. Certainly, there were times when he was discouraged, times when he was afraid, but the slightest fresh hope of favourable circumstance would restore his spirits and his confidence and he would once again be predicting the downfall of his enemies and the triumph of the Church. His refusal to admit defeat was rooted in his own character, his obstinacy and courage, and his sheer animal spirit, as well as in his physical strength and endurance; but he was also fortified by his belief that he was about God's work. Many people, from his time to our own, find the concept of a pope fulfilling the will of God by leading an army hard to accept, but Julius was quite sincere [224–25].

The warmaking of Julius, although really differing only in degree from that of other popes such as Sixtus IV, led to opprobrium and satirical attacks. The satirical treatment of Julius owes a great deal to the Renaissance age in which he lived, when the dialogue form, the epigram, and the pamphlet were becoming sharp weapons in the hands of masters such as Desiderius Erasmus, Alfonso de Valdés, and Ulrich von Hutten. Unlike the relative tolerance granted figures like General Polk, who combined in his person the religious and the military spheres, the treatment of Julius was often scurrilous—but, fortunately for history, clever and witty as well.

A major example of the satires dealing with Julius was the *Julius Secundus Exclusus e Coelis* (translated as *Julius Excluded from Heaven*). This dialogue was circulated anonymously not long after the death of Julius but was quickly attributed to Dutch humanist Desiderius Erasmus (Sowards, J.K., "Erasmus" 3), who just as quickly and consistently denied authorship of the piece. Researchers have generally agreed, however, that Erasmus was the author, and that he probably had good political reasons for denying his authorship.

Erasmus had several motives in writing the satire, according to Kelly

Sowards. One reason was his longstanding anti-war position. Another was his reformist stance toward the Catholic Church. Erasmus "argues against the notion of the papacy as an absolute monarchy and for ... the community of believers. He attacks the wealth and secularism of the church" (Erasmus 32). For Erasmus, Julius II embodied the sorry state of church affairs in his time. Most especially, Julius was to be compared invidiously with St. Peter, the founder of the church through the apostolic succession. Erasmus, therefore, drew

> a contrast between Julius II ... and the ... apostolic character of St. Peter; a contrast between Julius the contemporary vicar of Christ and the scriptural image of Christ himself; and a contrast between the ... reality of the present church and the ... of primitive Christianity [Sowards, J. K., "Introduction" 31].

In the dialogue, Erasmus opposes St. Peter to Julius II, who is accompanied by his Genius, a kind of patron deity derived from pagan tradition, and implicitly tying Julius to Roman emperor Julius Caesar. Peter represents on the one hand the ideal of the apostolic succession, and on the other he serves as gatekeeper preventing unworthy souls from entering heaven. (This dialogue is a sort of obverse of Alfonso de Valdés's *Diálogo de Mercurio y Carón*, in which Mercury assists in bringing condemned souls to Charon at the Styx.)

Peter repeatedly dismisses Julius's claim to enter heaven. He especially rebuffs him for his adoption of a military role:

> To begin with, what monstrosity is this: while you wear on the outside the splendid attire of a priest, at the same time underneath you are altogether horrendous with the clatter of bloody weapons? [Erasmus 48].

After such diatribes, the Genius frequently comments ironically, fulfilling the function of a corrective chorus. He usually pokes fun at Julius, or cuts him down to size, as for instance when Julius claims still to be pope because the cardinals have not chosen a new pope yet. The Genius comments, "How he still dreams the dreams of the living!" (50). The Genius figure was related to the ancient Roman and Hellenistic household divinities (in Rome, *lares* [MacCormack 132]), but it had become, as E. C. Knowlton shows, an "allegorical figure" by the time of the Renaissance (Knowlton, "The Allegorical Figure Genius") (Knowlton, "Genius as an Allegorical Figure"). In the ancient Roman Empire, or "in antiquity" generally, "the existence of the divine was frequently expressed in terms of divine pairs or associates." As MacCormack also shows, though, "pairs were formed not only so as to link together divine beings, but also to link the divine with the human." MacCormack explains that this pairing could and did have definite political and propaganda uses in connection with, for instance, "the different cults of the emperor and of his genius" (MacCormack 131–32).

By the time of the Middle Ages, according to Denise N. Baker, the Genius had taken on the primary character of a "tutelary" deity or being. This quality was chiefly transmitted to the Middle Ages, and thence to the Renaissance, by Apuleius in his *De deo Socrates*. She says that "[b]y classifying Genius as daemon Apuleius identifies him as one of the secondary gods who act as mediators between heaven and earth" (282). She cites a relevant passage (quoted here from the translation by Stephen Harrison):

> These the Greeks have endowed with the name of *daimones*, bearers of prayers upwards and benefits downwards between the inhabitants of heaven and earth, who, moving to and fro, carry petitions from men and aid from the gods, acting between the two as a kind of go-between and bringer of blessings [Apuleius 200].

She concludes that Apuleius "emphasizes Genius's tutelary role," because he "does insist that Genius is a good daemon, perfected in virtue, and synonymous with the best desires of the human soul" (Baker, D.N., "Priesthood" 282). Other classical and postclassical writers, such as Vergil and Martianus Capella, postulated the existence of types of genii, including a "good genius" or "'guardian spirit'" (Starnes, D.T., "Figure" 234). And, Starnes discusses the presentation of genii by Erasmus in his *Adagia*:

> He notes that the ancients attribute to each man two genii, which we call demons.... One of the genii attempts our destruction; the other seeks to aid us.... Erasmus notes the parallel ... to the good angel and the bad angel among theologians [Starnes, D. T., "Figure" 237].

The Genius of the *Julius Exclusus* appears to fall largely under the "good" rubric, although it is not devoid of malice. It is however, a mouthpiece of morality, even if ironically expressed. The figure actually seems in this case more like the *gracioso* type later to be seen in Spanish Golden Age drama,[96] which in turn was a cousin of the *servus* character of Greek and Roman New Comedy (Menander, Plautus, Terence). The *servus* often deflated the pretensions of his master by making loud asides to the audience, by intriguing and scheming, or by otherwise providing a comic commentary on the frequently stuffy and unimaginative masters. Erasmus adapts this technique to his dialogue, with notable efficacy.

A key passage in the dialogue concerns Julius's warmaking as opposed to Peter's own violence, detailed in scripture (John 18:10, as Sowards notes [Erasmus 119 n46]). Sowards observes that this is one of the few places in the piece in which Peter has the tables turned on him. The contrast between Julius's and Peter's motivations and ethos could not be clearer. Asked by Peter why he wears "armor," Julius retorts, "As if you didn't know that the supreme Pontiff possesses both swords; ... or else perhaps you would want a man to wage war naked" (Erasmus 55).

Later in the dialogue, Peter expresses Erasmus's vision of the ideal pope (which of course was far from his view of Julius), following the traditional Catholic view of the pope as the chief representative of Christ on earth (Erasmus 61). Erasmus also inserts into the dialogue some pointed criticism of one of Julius's stated motivations in opposing the French and the Council of Pisa, which was convened by some dissident cardinals to try to get rid of Julius (Erasmus 129 n75). Sowards writes that Julius managed to thwart this effort through "diplomacy" (Erasmus 130–31 n81), but presumably he would have resorted to open force if necessary. In any case, Julius had referred to the French and other foreigners as "barbarians" intruding in Italian affairs. Erasmus has his Julius character rehearse some of these remarks; and in a display of hubris, Julius maintains that he only "used them as friends ... so long as I needed their services," and that finally, "it remained for me to act the true Julius and remove all that barbarian scum from Italy" (72). The reference to "the true Julius" is meant of course to link Julius II to Julius Caesar, a characterization the pope never would have accepted and which he did not advance; in any case, once again, the exchange between Peter and Julius allows the Genius to offer pithy remarks criticizing the hypocrisy of the pope's use of the term "barbarians" because of the "hodgepodge" ancestry of the inhabitants of Italy (72). In an extremely scurrilous conclusion to the exchange, Julius comes across as mercenary on top of being warlike (in addition to his previously self-drawn image as intolerant of foreigners). Julius tells Peter, "I would be eager to embrace Indians, Africans, Ethiopians, and Greeks, as long as they pay cash" (72–73).

Erasmus has Julius stick to his best (or worst). At the end of the dialogue, Peter tells Julius that he should be able to "build yourself a new Paradise." But Julius responds that he will simply attack Peter's gates. Because, as Erasmus has it, in a double barb at Julius, new allies will soon be nearby to assist the "warrior Pope." According to Julius, "within a short time scores of thousands of men will be butchered in battle and join with me" (90).

Erasmus also attacked Julius and his ilk in the more famous dialogue *Praise of Folly* (*Encomium moriae*). Here, the digs at the pope are implicit, as he is not named. In the more generalized satire of *Praise of Folly*, Julius is only a secondary topic. He appears within a passage where the narrator attacks the warmongering of the church hierarchy. The paragraph alluding to Julius is useful for the present study. The annotator of the translation used here says that "the reference [in the paragraph] to 'decrepit old men' alludes clearly to Julius II, who was over 60 when he acceded to the papacy" (Erasmus of Rotterdam 181 n119). Here, then, is the selection with the reference to Julius:

> Moreover, since the Christian Church was founded on blood, ... they continue to manage its affairs by the sword as if Christ ... can no longer protect his own people.... War is something so monstrous that it befits wild beasts rather than men, ... so impious that it is quite alien to Christ; and yet they leave everything to devote themselves to war alone. Here even decrepit old men can be seen showing the vigour of youths in their prime [perhaps a reference to Julius's spirited presence at Perugia], ... not a whit deterred though they turn law, religion, peace and all humanity completely upside down. And there's no lack of learned sycophants to put the name of zeal, piety and valour to this manifest insanity, and to think up a means ... for a man to draw a murderous sword and plunge it into his brother's vitals without loss of the supreme charity which in accordance with Christ's teaching every Christian owes his neighbour [Erasmus of Rotterdam 181].

Charles V: Catholic Warrior-Emperor of the Renaissance

A militant Catholic, though chronologically belonging to the late Renaissance in Spain, Charles V, Holy Roman Emperor, and Charles I of Spain (reigned 1516–56), was the first Hapsburg ruler of Spain. Charles can easily be considered a religious warrior, despite having usually commanded by proxy rather than fighting with his troops (with one notable exception, in 1547), because of his religious motivation. If he did not display the fervent and obsessive qualities evinced by his son Philip, of whom more later, still Charles was very consciously a standard-bearer for Roman Catholicism of the Spanish variety. Heinz Schilling, who observes that, despite the fact that "Charles's personal religiosity ... remains more hidden than obvious," his pursuit of public religious objectives was central to his career, also cautions:

> to chastise him ... as a dour defender of papal Catholicism would be a mistake. The Emperor ... compelled the pope to agree to ... Reform.... Charles was not a fanatic... [Schilling 435].

Charles was decidedly Renaissance in his outlook, if the exercise of power politics be a measure, and he had to manage a very unmanageable empire and nation. But he was always committed to the extension of Catholic power. Furthermore, as Frances A. Yates writes, Charles was always aware of the divine basis of his power:

> Deeply imbued with the Hapsburg religious temperament, he bore himself with modesty in his great position and with a profound sense of responsibility to the divine powers whence he believed that he held it.... Charles's own attitude towards his office revived respect for the religious side of the imperial dignity [24].

Nowhere was this commitment more vividly displayed than in the conquest of the cultures of the New World. In this enterprise, no one better represented the peculiar Spanish combination of religion and warmaking than did the king's devoted servant, Hernán Cortés, the conqueror of Mexico.

Cortés has often been portrayed as the model of the Renaissance courtier. Nowadays courtiers may be thought of as effete, overrefined weaklings, something like the sycophants depicted in the Michael Curtiz *Adventures of Robin Hood*. But the meaning of the term was quite distinct from this in the Renaissance. The model of the Renaissance courtier was codified in a literary work, *Il corteggiano* by Baltasar Castiglione. This work was essentially a manual of courtly procedure. Like Machiavelli's *Il Principe* in the political arena, *The Courtier* laid out maxims for the good servant of the ruler. Although Cortés would not have been familiar with the Castiglione work, he was certainly a good example of the kind of courtier (who did not have to be physically present at the court to be termed such) portrayed in the book; and of course what Castiglione did was basically to put into literary form and to idealize elements of widely perceived practice.

Essentially an independent contractor as conquistador, while still loyal to the crown, Cortés had considerable flexibility in financial and tactical terms in carrying out his enterprise (and, of course, he took the fall if he failed in his project). But from the royal perspective in one particular he must toe the line: the conversion of the *infieles* (heathens or infidels) to Catholicism.

Many cynics (then and since) have sneered at the protestations of religious sincerity by men such as Charles and Cortés. Was not conversion of the pagan, after all, nothing but a pretext for exploitation? Despite the undeniable facts that exploitation did occur, and that the motives of many participants were less than pure, the cynics miss the essential point: that for Christians of the period, conversion and commerce were not at all incompatible. Our 21st century, presentist viewpoint may make them

Charles V, Holy Roman Emperor, and Charles I, King of Spain (first Hapsburg ruler of Spain; reigned 1516–56). Titian, *Charles V at Mühlberg*, Oil, 1548, courtesy the Prado, Madrid.

seem so, but Charles V, a cynical politician if one ever lived, was nonetheless quite determined in his push to spread the Catholic faith to the Americas, and his motivations were not wholly economic or political. As William D. Phillips Jr. and Carla Rahn Phillips comment in their *The Worlds of Christopher Columbus*, the religious motive for conquest must not be underestimated, in concurrence with the perspective of the present study:

One prime motive for European expansion, reiterated by nearly all of the early explorers, was a desire to spread Christianity. To the current cynical age, religious motivation is difficult to understand; it is much easier to assume that missionary zeal merely served to justify a lust for gold and glory. Yet Christian religiosity had extraordinary power in Europe in medieval and early modern times, touching virtually every aspect of human life. Europe had spawned generation after generation of charismatic preachers, who inspired and exhorted Christians to lead a good life and fear the consequences of sin.... Only a few decades after Columbus died, Martin Luther and other great religious figures of the sixteenth century would lead their followers away from the Roman Catholic Church in search of a reformed spirituality.... In this atmosphere, one of the oldest impulses in Christianity — the desire to send missionaries to nonbelievers—came to play an important role in European expansion [Phillips and Phillips 38–39].

Such motives were also operative, it seems, with his principal lieutenant in the project, Hernán Cortés. To make the point more specific in terms of Spain and Cortés, recourse may be had to an earlier authority, Francis A. MacNutt, who published an edition of the Cortés letters in 1908:

> Sixteenth century Spain produced a race of Christian warriors whose piety born of an intense realization of love for a militant Christ was of a martial complexion, beholding in the symbol of salvation, the cross, the standard of Christendom around which the faithful must rally, and for whose protection and exaltation, swords must be drawn and blood spilled if need be. They were the children of the generation which had expelled the last Moor from Spain [after 1492] and had brought centuries of religious and patriotic warfare to a triumphant close in which their country was finally united under the crown of Castile. From such forbears the generation of Cortés received their heritage of Christian chivalry. The discovery of a new world, peopled by barbarians, opened a new field to the Spanish missionary zeal, in which the kingdom of God was to be extended and countless souls rescued from the obscene idolatries and debasing cannibalism which enslaved them. This was the white man's burden which that century laid on the Spaniard's shoulders [Braden 18].[97]

Cortés exhibited his Christian motivation very clearly during the famous episode of the cleansing of the temple in Tenochtitlán. This temple, known today as the Templo Mayor and only recently excavated (it is now a museum containing spectacular artifacts), was the shrine of Huitzilopochtli ("Hummingbird of the Left"), the warrior-god peculiar to the Mexica or Aztecs. Cortés and some of his men ascended the tower of this temple in the presence of the still-reigning Moctezuma, and Cortés, horrified at the sight of the idols and the blood from sacrifices, ordered the idols cast down and the temple cleansed. One of his soldiers, Andrés de Tapia, provided a full eyewitness account of the incident. His account is joined here at the moment when Cortés ordered that the temple be cleansed: "[Cortés said to the interpreters]: yo quiero que aquí donde tenéis estos ídolos esté la imagen de Dios y de su Madre bendita, y traed agua para lavar estas paredes, y quitaremos de aquí todo esto. [Here where you have these idols I wish to have the images of the Lord and his Blessed Mother. Also bring water to wash these walls, and we will take all this away.] When the priests refused to accede to his demands, Cortés threw down a gauntlet of faith threatening "de pelear por mi Dios contra vuestros dioses, que son nonada" [to fight for my God against your gods, who are a mere nothing].

To this picture of Cortés as a Levite, or a Maccabee, cleansing the temple of its defilement, Tapia adds an image of Cortés as a Moses or Samson. The conqueror seems to become more than human, as if literally inspired by the Holy Spirit. Impatient, Tapia says, that the cleansing proceed, Cortés began the task himself: "tomó con una barra de hierro que estaba allí, y comenzó a dar en los ídolos de pedrería; y ... juro por Dios que es verdad que me parece agora que el marqués saltaba sobrenatural, y se abalanzaba tomando la barra por en medio a dar en lo más alto de los ojos del ídolo, y así le quitó las máscaras de oro con la barra, diciendo: «A algo nos hemos de poner por Dios»" (Díaz, Tapia, Vázquez, et al. 110–11) [he took up an iron bar that was there and began to smash the stone carvings.... I swear by God that, as I recall it now, the marqués leaped supernaturally, and, balancing himself by gripping the bar in the middle, he reached as high as the idol's eyes and thus tore down the gold masks, saying: "Something must we venture for the Lord"] (Tapia 43). The editor of Tapia's chronicle notes most appositely that the last statement by Cortés, "correcta y expresiva, dice mucho sobre la psicología del español renacentista. Cortés, cristiano militante, estaba dispuesto a sacrificar la vida en aras del cristianismo; pero ello no lo impedía aprovechar los beneficios ocasionales que podía reportar su pía beligerancia" [correct and expressive, says a lot about the psychology of the Renaissance Spaniard. Cortés, a militant Christian, was ready to sacrifice his life on the altar of Christianity; but this did not prevent him from taking advantage of the occasional benefits that his pious belligerence could bring him] (Díaz et al. 111n107).

Although Charles V was an observant, loyal Catholic, this quality did not prevent him from practicing characteristically Renaissance politics. He is often styled "Renaissance" precisely because of his manipulative, cynical, and often coldhearted approach to diplomacy and war. He ruled in an age of the expansion of European perspectives, and he practiced a statecraft appropriate to the age, although not always successfully. He fostered the great expeditions of Cortés and Pizarro, and these conquerors acted in the entrepreneurial spirit of the Renaissance, without neglecting, however, the constant mandate to Christianize the Indians.[98]

Like many other European monarchs, Charles generally put affairs of state before affairs of religion when the two collided. One of his recent biographers comments that "Charles's real interest ... lay in politics and war to the exclusion of almost everything else" (Maltby 129). So, like monarchs as disparate as Henry VIII of England and his distant predecessor Henry II (who had Thomas à Becket murdered), Charles saw fit to countenance one of the great crimes in religious history: the sack of Rome, beginning May 6, 1527 (Hook 162).[99]

So Charles, like his son Philip, can be viewed as a type of "priestly warrior" even though he generally commanded from the rear echelons. In fact, both monarchs took care to be portrayed in armor, with stern martial countenances. The most famous portrait of Charles, by Titian, came about as a result of the direct participation of the Emperor in a military campaign. This was the culmination of his struggle against the Protestants generally situated in what is now Germany, and termed by Karl Brandi "a group of Protestant Estates, who, taken as a whole, represented a national principle" (549). After defeating the principalities of the Danube, Charles was confronted with the continued resistance of the Elector of Saxony, John Frederick. On April 24, 1547, a battle was fought at Mühlberg between the imperial forces, led in person by Charles, and the Protestant forces under the command of John Frederick. Charles led the crossing of the Elbe River to get at the forces of the elector, on the other side; as Brandi says about the fight for the ships left on the bank by the elector, "The Emperor himself was present in person, encouraging his Spanish soldiers to incredible deeds of valour" (568). After the river was crossed, the battle became "a hot pursuit" of the elector's forces, because the imperial forces were so much larger. In the final confrontation once the forces again met, "the Elector himself was slightly wounded and taken prisoner." He was taken to Charles for an unpleasant interview, during which "Emperor and Elector were each mounted and fully armed." Charles treated him disparagingly. Brandi sums up the victory and its aftermath as very important for Charles:

> Charles's scornful words are sufficient proof of the triumph which warmed his heart. This April 24th, 1547, was one of the most glorious days in all his life. He had striven for this victory with all that he had, ardently and obstinately, sacrificing to it his health and his repose, his safety and, if need be, his life. He had taken part in the crossing of the Elbe, and joined

in the battle at evening. To please his allies, he commissioned Titian to paint the great portrait of him as the victor of Mühlberg. He is shown, mounted on his charger, in full armour, his general's scarf over one shoulder, his lance in his hand, the insignia of the Golden Fleece glinting against his breastplate [Brandi 568–69].

The battle of Mühlberg was a celebrated instance of Charles's direct participation in war, but it was not the only example. Charles had previously fought in a more demanding battle, the attempt against Tunis in the fighting against the Turks in 1535. Charles decided to push on to Tunis after besieging and taking La Goletta. In July 1535, Charles and his troops set off toward Tunis through hot and dry country. They were opposed by the fierce Chaireddin Barbarossa, who fought harassing actions against them to keep them from water supplies.

Barbarossa was an independent operator "acting in the Ottoman interest," rather like Francis Drake for the English (Rose 577). Rose paints this "corsair" as the terror of the Mediterranean:

> In one voyage, he went from Tunis via Sardinia and Sicily to Genoa, which he attacked and plundered; then on to Messina, where he ... burnt eighteen barges. He ... was welcomed ... at Constantinople ... and was mourned in 1546 as the "Chief of the Sea" [577].

The Christian troops finally defeated him and took Tunis. In the battle, "an ill-conditioned mêlée," the Spanish ruler took a very direct and courageous hand:

> Charles himself was in the thick of it; later it was said that his horse was killed under him and one of his pages at his side. But he himself never boasted of these things [Brandi 367].

Even though Charles himself may not have flaunted his victory, he was hailed for it in literature anyway. As Roger Aikin explains,

> when ... Charles V attacked Tunis in 1535 his victory was compared to those of the two Scipios over Carthage, ... and, like them, Charles merited the appellation "Africanus." Charles' exploits were celebrated in triumphal processions and in a panegyrical book by Pompeo Bilintano, *Carlo Cesare V Africanus* (Naples, 1536) [Aikin 215].

Charles was highly conscious of his "image." Schilling sums up the Charles V presented to the public and to posterity as "a consciously composed imperial image, developed on classical models, but also reaching into mythology and Christian salvation-history" (437). Charles's military enterprises had an inescapable core of religious motivation. His religious preoccupation was clearly to be seen in his final letter to his son, who was soon to rule as Philip II.

Historian Roger B. Merriman comments that the letter shows "the Hispanicization ... of Charles's originally dynastic point of view" (490). Part of this conversion to Spanish perspectives was religious; it "reveals a truly Spanish zeal" which had grown in Charles (Merriman 490). The letter of "advice" to Philip reflects these concerns:

> Amad a Dios sobre todas las cossas y servidle devotamente: hazed Justicia ygualmente a todos. Tened cuydado que la Inquisicion sea bien exercitada y que so color della no se haga agravio a nadie [Merriman 491].
> [Love God above all things and serve Him devoutly: do Justice equally to all. Take care that the Inquisition be managed well and that under its auspices no outrage be committed against anyone.]

Charles V's public image was in fact closely linked during the Renaissance with his role and importance as Christian emperor. His election as emperor in 1519 was surrounded by prophetic imagery and conversation: he was, according to Marjorie Reeves, the center of a "constellation of prophecies" (359ff). A complex set of prophecies from the Middle Ages was to culminate in a perspective which saw Charles as a second Charlemagne, as the man who would blend the religious and imperial (Christian and Roman) "traditions" into one powerful amalgam for the energetic 16th century: "on Charles V's career the prophetic expectation of both traditions—the Lily [religious] and the Eagle [secular]—became focused" (Reeves 363). This visionary complex found its epitome for such interpreters in the Sack of Rome in 1527: "The Sack of Rome in 1527 by the armies of Charles V was a major prophetic event. It fulfilled so dramatically the prophecies of the King-Chastiser who should destroy Rome that it was difficult not to see it in this context.... the Catholic German interpretation of these events separated the forces of Antichrist, represented by the Protestants and the Turks, from the work of chastisement and renewal which belonged to the Last Emperor: the Sack of Rome confirmed Charles in this role." The expedition against Tunis was also seen in a prophetic light (Reeves 368). Charles V's self-professed role as guardian of the traditions of Rome, both religious and imperial, thus acquired mystical and prophetic underpinnings. Such interpretations were still current at century's end, according to Reeves: "The two great figures of medieval political prophecy, the *Rex Romanorum* and the *Rex Christianissimus*, the Eagle and the Lily, still confront each other at the end of the sixteenth century" (Reeves 386): in other words, during the reign of Charles's son, Philip II.

King Philip II: Royal Priestly Warrior

Philip II of Spain, the second Hapsburg ruler of that country, whose reign lasted from 1556 to 1598, may seem an unusual choice for treatment as a religious general. He was most unmilitary in appearance and manner, seeming, especially in later life, more like a hermit obsessed with Catholic rectitude and with governmental details than a warrior of God. Closer examination, however, shows that Philip's complex personality, as well as his unique historical position, make him an intriguing exemplar of the priestly warrior.

John Lynch offers a succinct description of Philip's bearing:

> Physically Philip II had few reserves. Fair-haired, of rather less than medium height, erect of carriage, his eyes permanently reddened from overwork, he did what he could to nurture his strength, especially by his austerity of life and careful sleeping habits, but his constitution was gradually weakened by asthma, stone, and gout. His resources of mind and spirit, however, were immense. Emotionally he was completely attuned to the exercise of power, and by any standards his sang-froid was phenomenal.... Yet he was far from insensitive; he had a cool head but not a cold heart. To his family he was utterly devoted [Lynch 172].

Philip did not command any armies in the field, as did other kings like the Lutheran Gustavus Adolphus. He was nonetheless the driving force behind a series of wars between Spain and Protestant powers which, though certainly political and economic in character, were often primarily religious in motivation, as were many of Philip's actions in governing his realm:

> Religion pervaded all aspects of Philip's life and work.... In making political decisions which affected his own conscience he invariably consulted his religious advisers.... One of the essential features of his character was his high sense of justice.... But he also believed that his sovereignty gave him the right to execute private and secret justice, beyond the cognisance of any authority except God. This belief led him to acts of savage and arbitrary despotism [Lynch 172–73].

His "belief" in "his sovereignty ... beyond the cognisance of any authority except God" also led him into a checkered series of diplomatic and military adventures.

Among these conflicts, three stand out for our consideration. These are: the series of expeditions against the Ottomans, culminating in the great Spanish naval victory at Lepanto (1571), where Miguel de Cervantes, author of *Don Quixote*, lost the use of his hand; the severely destructive

wars in the Netherlands, where the duke of Alba gained tyrannical noto-
riety in his repression of the Protestants; and finally, the most well-known
conflict for English-speaking readers, the ill-starred Grand Armada of 1588
against Elizabeth I's Protestant England.

Philip had inherited his realm from his father, Charles I of Spain,
who had also held the title (as Charles V) of Holy Roman Emperor. Charles
abdicated the title of emperor in 1556, and so Philip became solely the
king of Spain. But Spain had acquired a vast and unwieldy overseas empire
with the recent conquest of Mexico (then called New Spain, 1521) and of
the Inca Empire (1532), as well as with the exploration of the interior of
present-day Central and South America, of the Pacific Coast, and of the
Caribbean islands. So Philip had a huge empire to administer, and with
it came not only wealth but imperial ideology.

Back in 1492, a grammarian and ideologue named Antonio de Nebrija
had published the first grammar of Castilian.[100] The importance of his
grammar went far beyond the theory and practice of the Spanish language.
Nebrija, a perceptive ideologue, saw that a burgeoning empire needed an
official language; so he understood that Spanish (Castilian) should be that
language. And his model for an empire, with an official language, was none
other than ancient Rome. This made historical sense for more than one
reason. After all, Spain (as Hispania) had once been an important Roman
colony (two renowned Roman writers, Seneca and Martial, were natives
of the colony); and Castilian was a Romance language (like French, Portuguese, Italian, and Rumanian) derived from Latin. So, Spain had obvious links to the ancient empire. And, by analogy, if Rome, with Latin as
its language, had been the great empire and civilizing force for the ancient
world, so Spain, with Castilian as its language, would be the great accul-
turator for the 16th century. As Nebrija wrote, language and empire have
gone hand in glove: "que siempre la lengua fue compañera del imperio; e
de tal manera lo siguió, que junta mente començaron, crecieron e
florecieron, e después junta fue la caida de entrambos" (Nebrija 97) ["language was always the companion of empire; and language followed it in
such a manner, that together they began, grew and flourished, and afterward together came the fall of both"].

Hidden within all this pretty historical play was a kernel of hard ideological matter: Rome, as everyone knew, had fallen, but in its place there
had grown and flourished the empire of Christ on earth, the Holy Roman
Catholic Church. So, if Spain was to take the place of Rome in the modern world, by implication it would be on an equal or at least a parallel
footing with the Vatican. Spain would be the arm which would enforce
adherence to Catholic orthodoxy; she would bear the light of Roman

Catholicism in a world filled with Protestants, Turkish Muslims, and "heathen" natives.

Precedents had certainly been set for crusades against the infidel, beginning with the First Crusade in 1097. More recently, a very famous and powerful ecclesiastic from the reign of Philip's great-grandfather, Fernando, had conducted in person a "crusade" against the Muslims of North Africa. This was Cardinal Francisco Jiménez de Cisneros (1436–1517), who had served as confessor to Queen Isabel and had been one of the most influential figures of the 15th century. He had even served as regent for two years (Kamen, *Spain* 4). Kamen summarizes his influence and prominence, calling him "[t]he most outstanding collaborator of the Catholic Kings":

> [Cisneros was] Isabella's confessor from 1492, archbishop of Toledo from 1495, regent of Castile from 1516. The personal austerity, extreme religious zeal and unswerving dedication of the cardinal coincided perfectly with the queen's own ambitions. He shared with Isabella an ardent wish to convert the infidel, and his intolerant policy towards the Granada Moors in 1500 was approved by the queen.... This crusader against Islam — to whom, in his own words, "the smell of gunpowder was sweeter than the perfumes of Arabia"— was also an enemy of the Jews.... A strong supporter of religious discipline, he was ruthless in pursuit of unity and order among the Franciscans [47].

As Kamen mentions, Cisneros led successful military expeditions against the Moors in 1505 and 1509 (47). It is the 1509 expedition which best fits our outline of the religious warrior, since Cisneros led it in person.

This was the expedition against the stronghold of Oran in North Africa (later to be the scene of the landings of Operation Torch in 1942, when Allied forces landed on the beaches and Patton began his World War II career). Cisneros biographer Erika Rummel says that "Cisneros' missionary spirit and military fervour against the Muslims culminated in the expedition of Oran, a venture which he himself financed and organized" (35). After some years of frustration, Cisneros was finally able to reach "agreement" with Fernando on financing the expedition (36–37). Among the details of financing and command was the important provision that Cisneros would lead the campaign as its "Capitán General"; his direct involvement in all phases of the enterprise occasioned "ill feelings between him and the military commander [Pedro Navarro—rather like a Bradley to Cisneros' Eisenhower]," and "[s]oldiers, too, commented that 'the world was turned upside down': generals were praying and prelates preparing for war" (Rummel 36–37). When the expedition landed in Africa and began to march toward Oran on March 17, 1509, the defenders were "caught ... by surprise"; the fortress soon surrendered after some fighting (Rummel 37).

Rummel quotes from two major sources, a letter of Cazalla, the bishop of Troy, who accompanied the cardinal, and who seems to have provided the more unadorned version of events; and the account of "Cisneros' biographer, Gómez de Castro," whose version is, according to Rummel, "highly rhetorical" (37–38). Although perhaps less authentic insofar as the historical facts are concerned, the Gómez version of the expedition is true to the spirit of Cisneros, Rummel concludes; she provides a pas-

Philip II, King of Spain (1527–98; reigned 1556–98) Sofonisba Anguisciola, *Philip II*, Oil, before 1582, courtesy the Prado, Madrid.

sage of Tacitean interpolation which is worth quoting at length because it illustrates the mindset of the cardinal. This is a harangue apparently given to the soldiers by Cisneros, dressed "in his ecclesiastical robes":

> Knowing your zeal to engage in this holy war, in which both the glory of God and the welfare of our country are at stake, I wish to be a witness to your bravery and noble spirit now that the die is cast, as the proverbial phrase goes. For many years you have heard the message over and over again: The Moors are ravaging our coasts; they are dragging our children into slavery; they are disgracing our wives and daughters; they are insulting the name of Christ. For a long time now you have longed to avenge these evils and crimes ... the mothers of Spain, prostrate before the altars of God, have entreated the Most High to bless our undertaking. They are now anxious to see you return in triumph. In the eye of the mind they see us breaking the chains of their captive children, and restoring them once more to their loving arms. The longed-for day has at length arrived. Soldier, behold before you the accursed land, behold the proud enemy who insults you, and is now thirsting for your blood. Prove to the world this day, that it has not been lack of courage on your part, but only the want

of a fitting opportunity to avenge the wrongs of your country. As for myself, I wish to be the first in facing every danger; for I have come here with the resolution to conquer or to die with you, which God forbid. After all, is there a better place for the priests of God than the battle-field, where soldiers are fighting for their country and religion? (*De rebus gestis*, 279–80) [Rummel 38–39].

With such precedents as this crusading expedition in his family background, Philip had been reared to be a monarch suited to the mission of Christianization. He brought to his reign as well the particular, personal characteristics of stubbornness, obsessiveness, and a seemingly infinite patience with his own slowness in making decisions (Williams 40, 45).[101] As Patrick Williams observes, when Philip had launched himself and Spain (more or less the same thing) on a course, he could not or would not change it. Despite having instituted disastrous policies in the Netherlands, Philip stayed the course:

> It was the fundamental flaw of Philip's kingship that once he had committed his prestige to a position he found it impossible to retreat from it. Consequently, he was prepared to extend and deepen his commitments rather than be seen to retreat from them and in doing so to diminish the majesty of his kingship [Williams 116].

He was in many ways, as David Howarth says, a limited man, but no one could say that he lacked courage, determination, and dedication. He worked inhumanly long at his many bureaucratic tasks, refusing to delegate to others work that would have been better left to them, and he decided early in his reign that he was going to fulfill the mission of Spain as Catholic standard-bearer for Europe (Howarth 28–31).

These qualities and decisions led Philip and Spain into the series of wars mentioned above. The first series, against the Turks, was at times beset with defeats (as with the disastrous enterprise headed by Juan de la Cerda, duke of Medina Celi in 1560 [Williams 97–99]), but at other times had great success.

Philip shrewdly avoided involvement in one disastrous expedition against the Moors. This was led by the ill-starred King Sebastian (Sebastião) of Portugal. This ruler qualified in his own right as a religious warrior and deserves some space in our study. His rashness serves as an instructive contrast to Philip's renowned prudence.

Sebastião was born on January 20, 1554, and was a prince of the Portuguese house of Aviz. He was related to Philip II through his Hapsburg forebears, and he came to the throne of Portugal in 1557. During the rule of his regents, he was reared and educated both "as an absolute monarch of unlimited power" and also as a militant Catholic. One of his regents, his uncle, the cardinal Dom Henriques, "contrived to surround his nephew with Jesuits." So, the young prince "grew up among priests, Jesuits and courtiers whose sole theme was the dread omnipotence of God and his Vicar at Rome and the glories of the Royal House of Portugal" (Bowen 122–23). This tutelage resulted in his belief that he was "supreme and invincible, the special favourite of God," and perhaps also contributed to his general stubbornness and willfulness, his inability to listen to counsel (Bowen 123). He was also adept at military arts and was enamored of stories of knights—in short, of novels of chivalry (Bowen 125). Bowen sums up his mature character as king: "When he had reached his twentieth year Dom Sebastião had become in morals and manners a monk, in disposition and body a warrior, in soul and mind a visionary, and in everything an arrogant and obstinate tyrant" (126). Not surprisingly, the young king decided to embark on a crusade to North Africa. He asked King Philip II of Spain for aid in the enterprise; and here one sees the essential contrast between the two kings: although quite as fanatical as Sebastian, Philip was also an experienced and cautious monarch. Philip consulted with his trusted and capable commander, the duke of Alba, and Alba advised against involvement in such a risky enterprise. So Philip stalled the young king, preferring to keep him on the line in an attempt to hook him into a marriage advantageous to his own designs of eventually acquiring the realm of Portugal. Meanwhile, Sebastian turned to a Moorish ally, the deposed sultan of Morocco, with whom to make common cause in ousting the deposer. Terms were agreed upon, financing obtained, and an expedition was fitted out, which left Portugal on June 24, 1578, headed for Tangiers. The enterprise resulted in the battle of Alcacer-el-Kebir, or

King Sebastian

Alcázar, on August 4, 1578. The battle was an unmitigated disaster for the Portuguese, who lost many of their nobility. The king was killed after he obstinately refused repeated offers of clemency from the enemy, including an offer of safe passage to Tangiers which was chivalrously extended to him by "[t]wo Saracen cavaliers" (Bowen 161). Sebastian charged into the midst of the Moorish troops and was killed (Bowen 149–67).

Despite Sebastian's futile attempts at chivalry, his needless sacrifice became legendary. He was the subject of several ballads and later became mythified into an ideological complex called "Sebastianism." The ballads characteristically take the rough edges off the manner of his death, converting it into a glorious ride to defeat, much as Custer's ignominious defeat was converted into American myth.[102] One of the ballads even features a survivor of the main battle who tries to convince King Sebastian to retire from the field rather than face certain death. After Sebastian calls his idea "cowardly," the Spaniard attacks the Moors singlehandedly, and Sebastian follows his example by leading his remaining men into a futile charge (Durán, *Romancero general* 222–23).

Sebastianism was an important component of the ideology of "certain late sixteenth and early seventeenth century writers [in Portuguese] who looked to the eventual restoration of Portuguese independence" (Roberts, W. H., "Figure" 309); Portugal had come under the control of Spain after the death of Sebastian.[103] The great Portuguese poet Luís de Camões (1524–80) apostrophized the king and his sacrifice in the masterpiece *Os Lusíadas* (1572) in stanzas 6–18 (Camões 2). The "Sebastian legend" became a prominent topic also in the early 20th century, finding its way into the work of writers of the stature of Fernando Pessoa. In his edition of a collection of Pessoa's poems, F.E.G. Quintanilha summarizes the importance of Sebastianism, which

> is a patriotic and mystical movement originating at the death of King Sebastian.... The legend that the king would come back created this movement, which has been treated literarily ... since 1580. It was the inner strength of the Portuguese people during the sixty years of the Spanish occupation (1580–1640) [xxxi n2].

Sebastian had tried to enlist Philip's aid in his crusade to North Africa. Philip declined to participate in such a risky venture. But he was not always averse to risk. The greatest victory of Philip's reign was the naval battle of Lepanto in 1571, fought against the navy of Selim II, successor to Suleiman the Magnificent. At the head of Philip's naval forces was Don Juan de Austria, and as a result of the unexpected victory, Turkish (Muslim) power was perceived as vulnerable for the first time. As Williams notes, Philip grew immensely in public stature:

> In 1565 he had saved Malta from a full-scale onslaught and now he had surpassed even that triumph, defeating the Turk in the largest naval encounter the modern world had seen. He was now without question the greatest monarch in Christendom [109].[104]

Lepanto was a bright spot in Philip's uneven career as proxy military leader. The wars in the Low Countries were to be his darkest moment, darker even than the more famous disaster of the armada. The reader has seen how Gustavus Adolphus fought to maintain and to defend Protestant power in Europe. Philip was fighting (or sending others to fight) to maintain and extend Catholic power in the very recalcitrant Netherlands.

The battle for religious allegiance in the Netherlands came to involve a fierce struggle between the Huguenots, a Calvinist sect, and the Catholics. Both the Spanish and the French became deeply involved on the Catholic side, while the chief leader for the Protestants was William of Orange, who was to play a larger role in future European politics. Against the advice of his more cautious councillors, Philip decided to make an example of the Netherlands, or perhaps just to draw a line in the sand to hedge out the Protestants. He sent the duke of Alba to "pacify" the turbulent province, and the duke carried out one of the clumsiest and most draconian repressions in European history. This religiously motivated enterprise on the part of Philip became an excuse for cruelty on the part of Alba, and the entire episode provided more fuel for the Black Legend already popular in England and other Protestant nations because of Spain's real, supposed, and manufactured excesses in the New World. Williams sums up the Netherlands enterprise, including the financial problems incurred in management of the province, as "misgovernment on an epic scale" (133).

Surpassing the Netherlands disaster in its scope and implications for Spain's future (though not perhaps in its moral wrongness) was the ill-conceived notion of invading England with the Gran Armada Invencible. Many factors contributed to the failure of the enterprise, among them technology and supply problems, but one of the most important factors was the behind-the-scenes inflexible direction of the project by Philip.

Characteristic of Philip, for example, was his appointment of the duke of Medina Sidonia to command the great expedition. A lifelong landlubber who clearly stated (and courageously so, as Howarth explains [23–25]) that he was not suited for the command,[105] Medina Sidonia bore much of the blame that should have been laid on Philip's shoulders (Howarth 244).

In any event, the armada proved to be the strategic low point of the King's career as a backseat general.

The failure of the armada led Philip to retreat still further into his personal and spiritual (not to mention political) isolation. He became more and more monkish, secluding himself in his baroque palace, El Escorial, and subjecting himself to ever-increasing religious rigors. He might almost be said to harken back to the warrior-monks of earlier ages, or perhaps to reflect St. Ignatius of Loyola, whose Jesuits were "warriors of Christ" in rhetorical terms, except that those monks were generally more worldly than Philip became. After Philip died, Spain was to follow a long path of economic and political decline.[106]

Warrior Priests from Epic and History to the Movies: Jerome, Turpin, Friar Tuck, and Bishop Sandor

Composers of epic as well as chroniclers have evinced continuing interest in warrior-priest characters. Much of the fascination with this character type must be attributable, at least in the medieval period, with the prohibition in canon law against clerics carrying weapons. Thus, those clerics who were the exceptions (that is, who actually engaged in warfare or fighting) must have appealed to the "carnivalesque" side of the medieval spirit.[107] The priest who bore arms, according to this interpretation, would be an outlaw figure and would therefore interest the chronicler or the epic cantor, who both followed and shaped the popular fondness for outlawry.[108]

The other side of this coin, though, would be that the cleric when armed might be seen as supporting the social order, especially if he participated in a crusade or if he aided the ruler. This contradiction with the outlaw image should surprise no one familiar with medieval society and its paradoxical sentiments.

This division between the perceptions of the medieval warrior-priest plays itself out in the ambivalent treatment of these characters as heroes. On the one hand, a character like Jerónimo from the *Poema de Mio Cid* is perceived as heroic because he upholds Spanish values as embodied in the person of Mio Cid Ruy Díaz. But his very association with Díaz is problematic, since technically Díaz is an outlaw or at the very least an outcast. (He was under sentence of banishment from Castile because of a disagreement with King Alfonso VI.) Turpin, from the *Chanson de Roland*, is less problematic, since Roland is an undoubted champion for future ruler Charlemagne, but Bishop Turpin still transgresses clerical commandments by carrying weapons.

Turpin in fact is a good example of the warrior priest who exercises both functions equally.[109] He exhorts the Frankish troops to battle against their foe, a battle in which he will participate:

> Archbishop Turpin, some way across the field,
> Spurs on his horse and gallops up a hill.
> With these solemn words he calls upon the Franks:
> "Lord barons, Charles has left us here;
> For our king we must be prepared to die.
> Help us now to sustain the Christian faith.
> You will have to engage in battle, as you well know;
> For you see the Saracens with your own eyes.
> Confess your sins, pray for the grace of God;
> To save your souls I shall absolve you all.
> If you die, you will be blessed martyrs
> And take your place in paradise on high."
> The Franks dismount and kneel upon the ground;
> In God's name the archbishop blessed them.
> As penance he orders them to strike [Anonymous, *The Song of Roland* 65].

Turpin is also "the first to start the battle" (Anonymous, *The Song of Roland* 76). The archbishop will die in battle along with Roland, Oliver, and their companions.

One sees a full-fledged example of the priest as outlaw in the character of Friar Tuck, from the Robin Hood legends. Like Jerónimo, he is associated with an outlaw or outcast who is evidently the true hero of the piece and the carrier of *virtù* for the nation. This may clearly be seen in the famous Michael Curtiz film *The Adventures of Robin Hood* (1938), with Errol Flynn as Robin, and very obviously maintaining the British home front against usurping Normans and their quisling allies. Michael E. Birdwell writes that this film

> used the mother country's past as an allegory for modern concerns. *The Adventures of Robin Hood*'s evil Prince John, the Norman pretender to the throne of England in Richard the Lion-Heart's absence, abused his Saxon subjects just as Hitler did his own people.... Lusting for power, the Norman invaders try to impose their form of order on Saxon England. Robin's followers ... represent the ideal democratic community — the Merry Men — who work together and love life in spite of the hardships. Film historian Ina Rae Hark considered the sequence in which Prince John's henchmen capture Robin and display him chained from head to toe as a symbol of freedom in bondage; it pointed to the possibility all humanity faced if fascism were allowed to continue in the world unchecked [Birdwell 68].

Eugene Pallette's unforgettable Tuck is presented immediately upon his first appearance as characterized by disreputableness: he is clearly overweight, thus having indulged in the cardinal sin of gluttony; and he displays other cardinal errors: sloth, avarice, pride. The viewer is not at all surprised, therefore, when he is challenged by Robin's men, who presume to rob him, thinking him a rich cleric who probably supports King John (the usurper, played inimitably by Claude Rains), that is, the authority in the realm, as one would expect a cleric to do. He won't stand for such treatment, and he opens his habit to reveal a Tuck-sized sword with which he proves quite adept in a duel with Robin. (One of Robin's men warns him that "that priest is one of the deadliest swordsmen in the realm.") By the flourish of revealing his sword he foreshadows his camaraderie with Robin, since monks and priests do not carry weapons without becoming outlaws (at least in theory).

Tuck, a fictional character in all likelihood, could in the real world, and probably in the make-believe one too, have been charged with a violation of canon law. At the very least, the protections against attack which were afforded him by canon law, as a putatively unarmed priest, could have been withdrawn.

Just this did happen to a priest during the First Crusade in which Richard I Lion Heart (the king of the Robin Hood films) participated. This incident concerned a bishop named Philip of Beauvais, who was imprisoned by Richard in 1197 upon the capture of the castle of Milli. Philip appealed to Pope Celestine "on the grounds that Richard was holding an ecclesiastic prisoner, not that the refusal to ransom him was contrary to a 'law of arms'" (Strickland 47). But the pope refused to force his release: "The pope's response — that he would only request, not demand, Philip's release — was equally dependent on an essentially ecclesiastical stricture: Philip had been caught in combat when in flagrant violation of the canonical prohibition on the bearing of arms by churchmen" (Strickland 47). The case was discussed in a *quaestio*, a type of medieval brief in canon case law, which is summarized by James A. Brundage:

> In resisting the attack ... it is held that he was acting legitimately [in self-defense] in his secular capacity.... Secondly it is argued that the respect due to the bishop's office forbids that he be made a slave of his captor. Likewise, ... the bishop ... must not be detained in captivity [443].

The case of Friar Tuck is useful at this point because he is a legendary figure with some possible origin in fact, and so he illustrates the transformation wrought upon historical outlaw figures when these characters enter legend, carnival, myth, folklore, and fiction. He is also a very popular and much-revisited hero in the Robin Hood tales, and as such he makes several different appearances on the stage of fiction. Finally, he is certainly a warrior-priest character, and as such he is another counterpoint to Stonewall Jackson, a man whom history, fiction, and legend have also transformed for the present day.

Like Robin Hood himself, the origins of Tuck are much debated. One line of argument ties him to historical outlaw who, according to one account, masqueraded as a priest — a tautologous situation indeed, since the outlaw would become an outlaw once again, playing the role of a priest carrying weapons illegally. The specific references to Tuck as an outlaw are summarized by Jeffrey Singman:

> The earliest reference to Tuck's name occurs in 1417, when Henry V issued a commission to arrest one assuming the name "Frere Tuck" and other evildoers of his retinue who had committed various "murders, homicides, robberies, depredations, felonies, insurrections, trespasses, oppressions, extortions, offenses, and misprisions" in Surrey and Sussex.... The next year he issued another commission to inquire into reports regarding one "Frere Tuk" and his followers, who had entered parks, warrens, and chases in Surrey and Sussex, "hunting and carrying off deer, hares, rabbits, pheasants, and partridges, burning houses and lodges for keeping the parks, and threatening the keepers." ... In 1429 a pardon was granted to this wrongdoer, in which he was identified as a chaplain named Robert Stafford of Lyndefeld, Sussex [Singman 82].[110]

Another line of inquiry links Tuck (and Maid Marian) to the May Games celebrations, where Robin Hood plays formed part of the annual festivities. The scholars who favor this interpretation see Tuck, and Marian, either as characters from the 13th century (for instance the Tuck of the outlaw legend) who were imported into the May Games, thus combining the historical argument cited earlier and the folkloric aspect of these characters; or, Tuck and Marian are understood as totally invented folk figures from much earlier than the 13th century who were merged into the Robin Hood legend.

A third interpretation identifies Tuck with the Robin Hood tale of the "Curtal Friar," and this is in fact the line which was picked up in the 19th century and which became part of the present-day Hollywood Robin Hood tradition. (In the 1938 Curtiz film, Robin actually refers to Tuck as a "curtal Friar.") It is worth noting that one of the most important authorities on English ballads, including the Robin Hood legends, F. J. Child, cautions against identifying the Curtal Friar too closely with Tuck.[111]

Field observes that the present-day image of Tuck was more or less established by about 1560:

> In the play *Robin Hood and the Friar,* ... Robin's battle with Friar Tuck provides the scene for the expression of virulent antimendicant senti-

ments.... To the extent that the play presents a favorable side to Tuck, it is hardly for traditional clerical or mendicant virtues [such as poverty or charity], but rather for his prowess in love and war [Field 13].

Tuck is not a stern warrior-bishop figure. On the contrary, he is normally represented as "merry" or "jolly," and his motivation is not especially religious. He is most different from a figure like Jackson insofar as his sternness, or lack of it, is concerned. But on closer inspection, one can see that he represents a debased crusader figure without the rough edges now often sanitized for appeal to children. Furthermore, at least in the very familiar Curtiz film version, Tuck (Eugene Pallette) is a more complex figure with regard to religion and morality than might be commonly presumed.

Pallette's Tuck is certainly no ascetic, stern, Spartan Stonewall Jackson or Oliver Cromwell. After a lusty swordfight with Robin Hood, he is invited to join Robin's band with promises of hearty viands awaiting him. He is also notably acerbic, responding to taunts by Little John (Alan Hale Sr.) and Will Scarlett (Patric Knowles) with mock threats ("to let air into that empty head"). And, while not particularly blasphemous, he is not noticeably reverent either.

But Tuck in this film is not irreligious, nor is he really immoral or antisocial. Although he is not shown performing sacramental duties, that is, mixing his roles as priest and warrior, he does show important concern for the rightness of Robin's cause. In a pivotal moment of the film, and one which helps to save it from being a mere adventure romp, Marian (Olivia de Havilland) comes to the inn where Robin's men are hiding out. She wants to help Robin to escape from his date with the hangman after his capture at the film's centerpiece archery contest. Some of the men are very skeptical of her claims to want to help Robin, because she is associated with the Norman oppressors. But Tuck steps in and asks her if she is a good church member. When she responds affirmatively, he asks her to swear by the Virgin Mary that she really wants to help Robin. When she does so, Tuck is transformed instantly into a deeper character: he becomes solemnly authoritative and caring, providing strong cohesiveness for the resistance against unjust authority.

Another treatment of the Tuck character, from the 1991 *Robin Hood: Prince of Thieves*, downplays somewhat his specific warrior characteristics, although it does not eliminate them. His belligerence is highlighted by his kicking Robin Hood and then biting him: this Tuck is more primitive than the sword-wielding Friar of the Curtiz film. The 1991 Tuck is more visibly gluttonous and bibulous; he seems rather of a Sherwood W. C. Fields. The role was very ably filled by comic and actor Michael McShane.

McShane's Tuck is captured by Robin Hood's men in a reprise of a scene from the Curtiz version which concerned not Tuck but another priest who was the butt of antimendicant sentiments from Robin's men, who robbed and ridiculed him. The 1991 film blends the corrupt priest and Tuck motifs of the first film; nevertheless, McShane's outsized performance brings the Tuck features into the foreground.

This Tuck is not only gluttonous and bibulous, but also blasphemous. The film includes the *de rigueur* battle between the friar and Robin, but the fight begins after Tuck falls off the cart he drove into the forest (he runs into a tree branch after kicking Robin in the face and driving off to escape). Robin (Kevin Costner), standing over him, asks him, "Do you yield?" Tuck shouts, "I'd rather roast in Hell!" and bites Robin on the leg (Reynolds Ch. 20). The scene cuts to Tuck hauling the cart along, in another reprise not only of the Curtiz film but of the legend itself, which included the motif of Tuck being forced to carry Robin across the river. He soon joins the band, where one of his pastimes is instructing the Merry Men in the art of brewing beer.

The McShane Tuck is more than this Rabelaisian character, though. Like Pallette's Tuck, this friar has a seriousness about his calling that is not readily apparent. It becomes evident near the end of the film that this Tuck will not tolerate certain kinds of behavior from his brethren. (Like Abbot Sandor, he may blaspheme and shock, but there are limits.) While Robin is fighting the sheriff (Alan Rickman), Tuck bursts into the room where the corrupt bishop is hiding. This bishop had countenanced all the evil deeds of the sheriff, including a forced marriage-rape of Marian (Mary-Elizabeth Mastrantonio). The bishop (Harold Innocent) tries to appeal to Tuck's churchly solidarity: "Brother Friar, you would not strike a fellow man of the cloth." Tuck replies:

> No. No, I wouldn't. In fact, I'll help you pack for your journey. [Loads gold into the bishop's arms.] You're going to need lots of gold to help you on your way.... . Here's thirty pieces of silver to pay the Devil on your way to Hell! [He pushes the bishop from the upper-story window] [Reynolds Ch. 43].

Friar Tuck is a well-beloved figure in the Robin Hood tradition. This popularity has contributed perhaps to the presence of warrior-bishops in quite other contexts. An odd example is the inclusion of a warrior-bishop character in a vampire film, the Hammer Studios Christopher Lee vehicle *Dracula: Prince of Darkness* (Terence Fisher, 1965). Perhaps this is not too surprising after all, because the church and medicine (usually represented by Dr. Van Helsing) are allied in vampire tales against the dark malevolence of Dracula and his servants. Generally, though, the priest is an auxiliary to the doctor and the vampire hunters (the warriors, in the wider context of the present study). In this film, however, the priest supplants the Van Helsing character. He also partakes of the warrior role, thus combining the functions of priest, doctor, and warrior in the film narrative.

This warrior-priest who will lead the vampire hunter band like a "general" makes his first appearance to them (but not his first in the film) at one of the standby settings in Dracula movies, the inn of the village, which provides a relatively safe haven from dark spirits. The film is a sequel to the very successful *Horror of Dracula* (Terence Fisher, 1958), in which Christopher Lee made his striking debut as Dracula, and Peter Cushing his equally impressive debut as Van Helsing. *Dracula, Prince of Darkness* did not include Cushing among its cast (although later Hammer films did). Lee reprised his role, and the very imposing Andrew Keir, a fine Scottish actor, played the warrior-priest role of Father Sandor.

As Sandor, Keir lends an air of gruff authority and of impatience with foolish superstition and other folderol which allows his role to bridge the gap between science and religion by emphasizing his pragmatic rationality.[112] Upon his first entrance in the film, he is established as a most unusual monk. A village girl who died under ambiguous circumstances is about to be staked as a vampire. In the nick of time, Sandor rides into the scene from the forest, dressed in his habit and carrying a very threatening-looking rifle, from which he fires a shot into the air. After shouting "Barbarians!" at the villagers, he berates the local priest who was about to exorcise the girl, telling him, "You shame the cloth you wear," and says roughly, "I will bury her" (in sacred ground). When the priest remonstrates with him, Sandor responds: "You are an idiot, Father. Worse than that, you are a superstitious, frightened idiot." Thus, Sandor is established for the viewer as a monk who carries weaponry and who certainly does not shrink from a fight.

Our monk's next scene takes place at the inn, with a partial reprise of Van Helsing's appearance at the local inn in *Horror of Dracula* (Fisher, *Horror of Dracula*). In this case, Sandor comes into the inn from outside in very blustery weather, interrupting a somewhat boisterous social gathering which includes some English travellers, who will become the focal point of the film. Sandor shows the irreverent side of his makeup by proclaiming the pleasures of "a warm posterior" and a "mulled claret" by the inn's fireplace. He explains his rifle to one of the English tourists (Charles) in a whimsical manner:

Another of my earthly vices. Each time I leave the monastery I bring this with me. The brethren think it is a bundle of prayer books for the unfortunate heathen I meet in my travels. I'm sure they truly believe that the venison I bring home from time to time drops dead by itself.

And, when Charles (Francis Matthews) asks him about his "flock" at the inn, he responds derisively and even repeats audibly for the benefit of the inn's denizens, "I wouldn't tolerate them!"

But Sandor is also shown as fatherly and solicitously concerned as he tries vainly to talk the group of tourists out of visiting Karlsbad, the location of Castle Dracula (at least in this film):

You may think me an eccentric old cleric and not much credit to my cloth. Perhaps I am. I enjoy shocking people's susceptibilities. But I can be serious. And when I tell you not to go to Karlsbad, I want you to take note. [Fisher, *Dracula: Prince of Darkness* Ch. 3].

Later in the film, when Dracula has attacked Charles's wife, Diana (Suzan Farmer), in the monastery, Sandor cares for her as a substitute physician, first cauterizing her wound (a vampire bite on her wrist) and then calling for one of the other monks to bandage the wound. Here he combines Van Helsing's function as medical doctor with his own priestly duties. Not long afterward, he performs the rite of exorcism (staking, actually) and of absolution on Helen (Barbara Shelley), Charles's sister-in-law who had been made into a vampire by Dracula. By performing such rites, then, and in a peculiarly campy way, perhaps, Sandor mixes his roles as warrior (vampire-fighter) and priest, reminding one of the prohibitions by the church against such conduct and of the reticence on the part of clerics like Bishop Polk of Civil War fame to carry out their religious function during their active military service.

Sandor is also careful not to stray too far from his monastic code. Near the end of the film, which contains the usual tracking-of-Dracula-to-his-lair sequence, Charles and Sandor chase Dracula's carriage, which contains his coffin and one holding Diana, and is driven by Clove (Philip Latham), Dracula's human servant. Charles and Sandor head off the carriage, and Charles implores Sandor to shoot Clove. Sandor demurs and hands his rifle to Charles, stating that even he cannot bend the rules so far as to kill a human being (an already dead vampire is presumably a different matter). After Charles dispatches Clove (in self-defense), the carriage lurches off to the castle, where Dracula will be destroyed in an interesting manner. Sandor, noticing running water under ice on which the count is standing, shoots the ice until Dracula falls in and drowns, not being able to pass through running water. The method of Dracula's elimination rather sophistically preserves the monk's ethical strictures, since he does not shoot him directly and since, at any rate, Dracula is already dead. Here is yet another echo, in a very pop culture context, of the canonical prohibition against clergy carrying weapons intended to be used in war or conflicts with other people.

Jerome, the bishop from the *Cantar de Mio Cid*, was a historical figure who may well have violated the "anti-weapon" canonical prohibition. Jerónimo de Perigord became bishop of Valencia in 1098, according to Menéndez Pidal (875) and accompanied the Cid on his campaigns, according to the poem. Jerome not only participates in battle but asks the Cid for the privilege of landing the first blows—but only after officiating at mass:

> el obispo don Jero*m*e la missa les cantava; / la missa dicha, grant sul- tura les dava: / «El que aquí muriere lidiando de cara, / »préndol yo los pecados, e Dios le abrá el alma. / »A vos, Çid don Rodrigo, en buena çin- xiestes espada, / »hyo vos canté la missa por aquesta mañana; / »pídovos un*a* don*a* e seam presentad*a*: / »las feridas primeras que las aya yo otor- gadas.» / Dixo el Campeador: «desaquí vos sean mandadas» [Menéndez Pidal, *Texto* 1089 ll. 1699–710].
>
> ["Bishop Jerome sang the mass/ with the mass finished, he fully absolved them: / 'From anyone who dies with his face to the enemy, / I take away his sins, and God will receive his soul. / For you, Cid don Rodrigo, who put on his sword in a good hour, / I sang a mass this morning, / and I ask of you a favor and hope that it will be given to me: / please grant that I strike the first blows.' / The Campeador said: 'let them be sent to you.'"].

The bishop is as good as his request. Menéndez Pidal, paraphrasing the poem, comments that "he gets his fill of fighting" ("se harta de lidiar" [847]). The poem employs typical epic hyperbole in recounting his exploits: "quando es farto de lidiar con amas las sus manos, / non tiene en cuenta los moros que ha matados" (Menéndez Pidal, *Texto* 1092 ll. 1793–95) ["when he has his fill of fighting with both hands, he loses count of the Moors he has killed"]. Notice that the poem refers to his fighting with both hands, subtly implying that he had no hand free for signing or for other religious ritual. In another of the bishop's battles, also mentioned by Menéndez Pidal, the bishop appears "well armed" and ready for the battle against the Moor Búcar: "Afevos el obispo don Jero*m*e muy bien armado *estave*, / Parávas delant al Campeador, ...: / «Oy vos dix la missa de santa Trinidad. / »Por esso salí de mi tierra e vin vos buscar*e*, / »por sabor que avía de algún moro matar*e*" (Menéndez Pidal, *Texto* 1115–16 ll. 2368–76) ["Bishop Jerome came there very well armed, / He stood before the Campeador, Then the bishop, Don Jerome, came along, fully armed, stood in front of the Campeador, ... 'Today I said for you Mass of the Holy Trinity, / For this I departed my land and came looking for you, / on account of the urge that I had to kill some Moor'"]. Notice that Jerome mixes his two roles quite openly, as the poem indicates by the neat device of twinned motives for his coming to see the Cid: to say mass and to look for Moors to kill.

Jerome's friend and leader the Cid was to have a role in legend, even after his death, in killing Moors.

> Miéntras se apresta Jimena
> Con algunos de los suyos
> Para partir de Valencia
> Con el silencio noturno,
> Y los nobles castellanos,
> Mas valerosos que muchos,
> Con fingidas alegrías
> Velan los soberbios muros;
> Alvar Fañez de Minaya,
> Don Ordoño, y Don Bermudo,
> Para la batalla aprestan
> Del Cid el cuerpo difunto.
> No le visten la loriga
> Que él en las lides trujo,
> Por cumplir lo que mandó
> En su postrimero punto.
> De pergamino pintad
> Le ponen yelmo y escudo,
> Y en medio de dos tablones
> El embalsamado bulto,
> Y de un cendal claro verde
> Vestido un tabardo justo,
> Al pecho su roja insignia,
> Honor y asombro del mundo.
> Unas calzas de colores,
> Guarnecidas de dibujo,
> En lienzo crudo pintadas,
> Y ellas son de lienzo crudo.
> El derecho brazo alzado,
> Al ménos cuanto se pudo,
> En la mano su Tizona

El limpio fierro desnudo.
D'esta guisa le aprestaron,
Y cuando aprestado estuvo
Pavor les dió de miralle,
¡Tal se muestra de sañudo!
Trujeron pues á Babieca,
Y en mirándole se puso
Tan triste, como si fuera
Mas razonable que bruto.
Atáronle á los arzones
Fuertemente por los muslos,
Y los piés á los estribos
Porque fuesen mas seguros.
Y á la lumbre del lucero,
Que por verle se detuvo,
Con su capitan sin alma
Salieron al campo juntos,
Donde vencieron á Búcar
Solo porque á Dios le plugo,
Y acabando la batalla,
El sol acabó su curso
[Durán, *Romancero general* 570–71].

[While Jimena hurries / With some of her people / To leave Valencia / With the nocturnal silence, / And the Castilian nobles, / More valorous than many, / With pretended joy / They guard the proud walls; / Alvar Fáñez de Minaya, / Don Ordoño y Don Bermudo, / For battle they prepare / The dead body of the Cid. / They do not put on him the cuirass / That he wore in contests, / To comply with what he ordered / At his final moment. / They put on him a helmet and shield / Of painted parchment, / And between two boards [they place] / His embalmed corpse, / And with a bright green sendal / Dressed in a closely fitting tabard, / On his breast his red insignia, / The honor and wonder of the world. / Some colored stockings, / Adorned with designs, / Painted on rough canvas, / And they are made of rough canvas. / With his right arm raised, / At least as much as they could, / In his hand Tizona / The clean naked blade. / In this manner they readied him, / And when he was prepared / It made them afraid to look at him. / So fierce did he look! / Next they brought in Babieca, / And when Babieca looked at him he became / So sad, as if he were / More a rational being than a brute. / They tied the Cid to the saddle / Tightly by the thighs, / And his feet to the stirrups / So they would be more secure. / And in the light of the morning star, / With their captain without a soul / They sallied forth to the field together, / Where they vanquished Búcar / Only because it pleased God, / And with the battle ending, / The sun finished its course.]

From this source was taken the scene which ends *El Cid* (1961), starring Charlton Heston in the title role (Mann). This was an internationally produced project, the idea of producer Samuel Bronstein, and was directed by American filmmaker Anthony Mann (1907–67) (Basinger). The aura of the dead leader is used by his followers to frighten the Moors, almost as if the Cid were Santiago himself being carried into battle as a standard. This legend is derived from the ballad tradition surrounding the Cid. In fact, one of the Cid ballads has it that the Moors seemed to see a horde of "threescore thousand warriors" headed by a knight on "a great white charger, / His blazing sword in hand" (Daugherty 156). The force of this leader translates into a talisman which serves as inspiration to his erstwhile followers as much as it represents a threat to his enemies. Mann actually stated to an interviewer that this scene, which serves as the ending of the film, set up the whole movie for him:

> I started with the final scene. This lifeless knight who is strapped into the saddle of his horse ... it's an inspirational scene. The film flowed from this source. I rediscovered the landscape and climate of my westerns and, in addition, I had Charlton Heston [Willemen 19].

Much as Stonewall Jackson's followers invoked his name in a highly reverential fashion, the Cid's body was treated in the tradition as a kind of relic in which resided the power to win battles.

El Cid, incidentally, can plead relative innocence to historical distortion to the extent that the true history of the Cid is still debated; but it is the case that the Cid film actually relies more heavily on the ballad tradition and on the Guillén de Castro play *Las mocedades del Cid* [loosely, *The Young Cid*] (adapted by Corneille for *Le Cid*) than on the *Poema* itself. Its employment of the ballad tradition, as in the important scene noted above, saves it from being just another costume epic with meager anchoring in folk culture. *PMC* scholar Matthew Bailey favorably evaluates the film's historicity: "The movie is based on a variety of Spanish sources, among them the story line from Guillén de Castro's play. Some creative liberties are taken, but for the most part Rodrigo's *mocedades* and especially the love between the hero and Jimena provide the dramatic tension that sustains the movie" (Bailey 98). While the choice of Heston to play the Cid adds its own resonance to the role, because Heston was a seasoned interpreter of "epic" roles, the fact that Mann directed the film is no less significant. Mann had updated the Western formula by adding to it psychological depth: in other words, Mann had repackaged the American epic for audiences. An important Mann signature is, as Douglas Pye has written, the "doubling" of the hero. Instead of the more traditional hero-villain dichotomy, the positive and the negative aspects of the main character are extracted and divided between two main characters who represent "the hero and villain constructed as versions of each other or as bound in a mutually defining relationship: two sides of the same coin" (Pye 170).[113] In Mann's Westerns, James Stewart (the hero) was often "doubled" by his "shadow" figure, played twice by Arthur Kennedy. The difficulty for the hero lies in facing his own negative side and in thus reaching a complete humanity. Marc Jancovich refers to a similar process within the Cid character when he observes that the Cid is a "divided" character who is "unable to resolve the conflict between his public responsibilities and his private desires" (Jancovich 95). Jancovich also notes that the Cid is forced by his role "to literally stand in for God," and that he "is ... presented ... as Jesus Christ himself" because "He even has to go through the act of dying and resurrection to achieve his mission" (96). This treatment of the hero as a Christ analogue might remind the reader of the perspective taken by Lost Cause advocates on Jackson after his death, when he was "brought back to life" as a symbol of the lost aspirations of the South. Jackson was also very sensitive to the division between his public persona and his private, inner life — the ruthless soldier of the Confederacy was the forgiving and quiet man about home. Unlike the Cid of the Mann film, Jackson appears to have "resolved" this conflict by hewing ever more closely to his duty to God and to the South. Despite the strains this imposed upon him, his marriage seems not to have undergone serious stresses because of its basic closeness and strength. Although modernist interpreters of his record may criticize his "image," Jackson deserved his fame and the postwar reverence accorded him. He was indeed a dedicated soldier, and he was also a sincere Christian and a man devoted to his family.

5

Conclusion

The melding of religious motivation and soldierly or military drive and effectiveness has been a central feature of the lives of the historical and legendary figures presented in this volume. The keystone of the study, Lt. Gen. Thomas J. "Stonewall" Jackson, C. S. A., became a legend in his own time. But he never forgot his simple religious faith, murmuring even as he was administered anaesthetic before the amputation of his arm, "What an infinite blessing" (Robertson, *Stonewall Jackson* 736). And when his wife told him that he would not live out the day, on May 10, 1863, and that he would soon "be with the blessed Saviour in His glory," Jackson responded weakly that "I will be an infinite gainer to be translated" (Robertson, *Stonewall Jackson* 751). Like Jackson, the other leaders studied here display strong religious faith, although not all of them were as singlemindedly devout as was Jackson; some, of course, are fictional or legendary characters, but their presentation features a vivid religious thread underpinning their motivations and conduct.

In some cases, the religious element was a motivator toward nationalist expansionism. Charles V, Philip II, and the Cid exemplify this type of religious warrior, in whom nationalism or patriotic fervor and religious faith work side by side, neither being allowed (for the most part) to outweigh the other. In rare instances, such as that of King Sebastian, both impulses ran amok and resulted in imprudent actions and disaster. Many of these leaders, including even the ill-starred Sebastian, became the focus of legends which became part of national mythology or, in the case of General Patton, of institutional folklore and of popular culture. But although some achieved wide fame, none has really had the impact on American folklore and culture that one can see in the career of Stonewall Jackson. In the fine words of Frank E. Vandiver, Jackson became an icon with more than national appeal:

Stonewall Jackson rose from uncomfortable obscurity to be a people's hero, a nation's shining hope. He proved a hero who never failed. As he led that "incomparable infantry" through victory after victory, Jackson's fame increased. His nobility of character, his unaffected piety, his strange personal habits— all these things became the treasured possession of the Southern people. Finally they would become the heritage of America and the world [1].

Notes

1. For useful overviews of the complex cooperative relationship between crown and church in Spain during the 16th century, see John Lynch, *Empire and Absolutism: 1516–1598* (vol. 1 of *Spain under the Habsburgs*) (New York: Oxford University Press, 1964), Ch. 8, esp. 236–48; and Stanley G. Payne, *Spanish Catholicism: An Historical Overview* (Madison: University of Wisconsin Press, 1984), 44–52.

2. The term Reconquest denotes the period from 711 to 1492, during which the Christian principalities or kingdoms of the Iberian peninsula fought to regain control of the peninsula from the "Moorish" or Islamic conquerors who had entered from North Africa in 711.

3. According to Anna Jackson, "When asked once what he [Ewell] thought of [Jackson's] generalship in this [Valley] campaign, he replied, in his brusque, impetuous manner: 'Well, sir, when he commenced it I thought him crazy; before he ended it I thought him inspired'" (Jackson 287).

4. A measure of Jackson's public stature at the time of his death can be seen in the report of his passing written by his brother-in-law, Confederate major gen. Daniel Harvey Hill, and found in the *Official Records*:

No. 20.Goldsborough, May 26, 1863.

The department commander announces the well-known fact of the death of the great and good Jackson, not merely in order to pay a tribute to the illustrious dead, but also to incite the troops to imitate his example. His name has been identified with almost all the great battles of the war, and his genius and courage have been the chief elements in Southern success and Yankee discomfiture. The eagle glance and iron will of the great commander were happily united in him with the patient, uncomplaining endurance of the common soldier.

His wonderful battles have contributed largely to our independence, and his great fame has shed a halo of glory over his beloved South. But his virtues as a man will be as fondly remembered by his country as the brilliant deeds of his military career. He has taught us that he who most fears God the least fears man; that the most exalted courage may be associated with the modesty of the shrinking girl; that the lips which were never defiled with ribaldry and profanity could cheer on most loudly amidst the roar of cannon and the clash of arms. His whole life was a rebuke to the intriguing, the selfish, the cowardly, the vulgar, and the profane.

The pure man will be loved as much as the heroic soldier will be admired in the future ages of the republic.

Let us drop our laurel upon his bier, but remember that we may best honor him by striving day and night, and with

175

his unwavering trust in God, to secure the independence for which he gave his life.

D.H. HILL, Major-General
[Hill, D.H., "General Orders, Hdqrs. Dept. of North Carolina, Number 20." 1073].

5. In a rather similarly familiar treatment of his commander, Capt. Ujanirtus Allen of the 21st Georgia, with Jackson in the Valley, wrote home on June 12, 1862, that:

I presume we will rest here for a few days and then will be away, away, like a meteor and fall upon the anemy [sic] at some exposed point — dealing such a blow as will remind him that the "Valley fox" Stonewall Jackson is again at his old pranks. I wish that I had time to give you a description of the phisic [sic] of this genious [sic], the pride of the whole army and terror of his anemies [sic] [Allen 106].

6. John H. Worsham, in his memoir, *One of Jackson's Foot Cavalry*, sums up Jackson's renown:

It was in battle that the men showed their great love for, and confidence in, General Jackson. His old soldiers had implicit confidence in him. How many times his old command wished him back to lead one of his furious attacks on the enemy. The South produced many generals of great ability; but for brilliancy and dash, the world never saw Stonewall Jackson's equal [103].

Loyalty to the memory of this general is still in evidence among descendants of his men. An impressive example of this continued memory was witnessed by the present writer when visiting the set of *Gods and Generals* in September 2001. The incident took place with the surprise appearance of Stonewall Jackson's great-granddaughter and great-great-granddaughter on the "Manassas" set, near Staunton, Virginia. Mrs. Courtney Creech, the great-granddaughter, was surprised to find that a film was being shot at that location (she and her daughter found the signs for *Gods and Generals* rather by accident), and when she

asked what the movie was and learned that it was a Civil War film, she identified herself. She was immediately escorted to the set and became the cynosure of the afternoon. Besides her introduction to members of cast and crew (especially to Stephen Lang), she met some of the re-enactors. One of them was almost in tears as he asked to shake her hand. He told her that he had an ancestor who fought with Stonewall and that meeting her was a very great honor.

Such an incident has nothing to do with Hollywood, with pop culture; it is not manufactured like Elvis mania, or the product of fantasy wish-fulfillment. Here those of us present saw an instance of present consciousness touching the past and of the astounding endurance of the power of Jackson's personality.

7. This Colonel Patton was one of the famous Gen. George S. Patton's ancestors. Col. Patton was killed in 1864. Possibly referring to this account among others, Riley comments as follows, and gives what he terms "the correct version":

Col. Edwin L. Hobson, of the 5th Alabama Regiment, gives the correct version. It is:
"The occurrence was at the battle of South Mountain, September 14, 1862; Col., then Major, Hobson was in command of the 5th Alabama, Rode's Brigade. Colonel John B. Gordon had been placed by General D. H. Hill, the division commander, to prevent a flank movement by the enemy. The enemy was steadily advancing on the line of Rode's, and, at a distance of 100 yards, menaced a charge. An officer, mounted on a white horse in front, was impetuously urging them onward.
"The potent incident was manifest to Major Hobson, and in the crisis, he felt the necessity of removing the officer. He at once selected skilled riflemen to 'pick him off.' This was unerringly done, and at his fall the enemy hesitated, were checked, and the fortunes of the day were changed.
"Subsequently, and not long before the battle of Sharpsburg (some com-

ment having been made on the sacrifice of the gallant officer), states Colonel Hobson, an officer from General Jackson came to him with the 'compliments' of General Jackson and the message: 'Tell Major Hobson, I want the brave officers of the enemy killed off. Their death insures our success. Cowards are never in the front; the skulkers flee.'" — *Southern History Magazine*, Vol. 25, p. 105. [Riley 98–99].

8. According to *Bartlett's Familiar Quotations*, the saying is anonymous: "It became necessary to destroy the town in order to save it. *Attributed to an American officer firing on Ben Tre, Vietnam [February 8, 1968]*" (784.6).

9. Stephen Lang's comments on the differences between the images of the two leaders are apropos here:

> We think of Robert E. Lee as benign in some way. Part of the reason he's kind of as well liked in the North as he is in the South is because there's a tremendously patriarchal, grandfatherly kind of aspect to Lee. Jackson presents something quite different, it seems to me. It's a more complicated form of myth. Because if you reduce Jackson to qualities, simplify him, you're going to come out with words like a tremendous ferocity, with almost a zealotry in terms of both religion and war, you're going to come out with self-discipline to the nth degree. Well, these are qualities that are extremely intimidating, you know? We don't embrace them quite as easily as Babe Ruth had a huge appetite for food and could swing a bat. Jackson is slightly uncomfortable in a way [Lang].

10. Pierre du Terrail, known as Bayard from his family holdings, lived from 1476 to 1524. He was known as a model of chivalry, and was killed, ironically though fittingly from a historical perspective, by a firearm, during a battle against Spanish troops at Biagrassa:

> On both sides of the road which the retreating army [the French] had to traverse the Spaniards had placed in ambush a large force of arquebusiers. It was a weapon which Bayard held in detestation; for while skill and courage were required to wield a spear or sword, any skulking wretch could pull a trigger from behind a stone. From one of these hated weapons he received his death. As he was retreating slowly, with his face towards the foe, a stone from a cross-arquebus struck him on the side. He instantly sank forward on his saddle-bow, exclaiming in a faint voice, "Great God! I am killed." ... It was the hour of sunset, April the 30th, in the year 1524 [Smith, H. G., *The Romance of History* 137, 163–64].

11. Civil War battles are sometimes known by two names, as in the case of the Manassas battle. The Union usually named battles according to the most important waterway nearby, thus for the North this battle would be Bull Run. The Confederacy usually followed the name of the nearby town in naming the battle, thus for the South this battle would be Manassas. Similarly, the great battle of September 17, 1862, would be named Antietam by the North (after the creek running through the battlefield) and Sharpsburg by the South.

12. Jim Lewis may have been a slave (Robertson believes that "[a] good case can be made that Lewis was a slave whom Jackson hired from his owner," although he also notes that "[s]ome writers have classified Lewis as a freedman who volunteered to become Jackson's valet" [290]). Frankie Faison said that in the film "We approached it that he was a freed man" and that "he came to him [Jackson] looking for a job, jobs were scarce, you know, and any kind of job, that ... had some sort of prestige [to] go along with it was certainly a welcome job" (Faison).

13. Randall Allen and Keith Bohannon, in their edition of the letters of Capt. Ujanirtus Allen, a soldier with Jackson, comment appropriately here, including observations by one of Jackson's Georgia soldiers:

> Stonewall's victories in the Valley in 1862 raised the morale of southerners discouraged by bad news on other fronts, and Jackson's men looked upon their leader with newfound awe. James Cooper Nisbet, one of Ugie Allen's fel-

low officers in the 21st Georgia, voiced undoubtedly universal sentiments when he wrote to a friend at the close of the campaign, "Without tents and often with short rations, we cheerfully move whenever our glorious leader orders." Jackson, he added, "like old Frederick the Great, fights to win, and will win or die" [Allen 86].

14. His men were experiencing Jackson's well-known secretiveness about his plans. Among the many who commented on this aspect of his campaigning was Gen. John B. Imboden, who served under Jackson and later under Lee:

> Jackson's military operations were always unexpected and mysterious. In my personal intercourse with him in the early part of the war, before he had become famous, he often said there were two things never to be lost sight of by a military commander: "Always mystify, mislead, and surprise the enemy, if possible; and when you strike and overcome him, never let up in the pursuit so long as your men have strength to follow; for an army routed, if hotly pursued, becomes panic-stricken, and can then be destroyed by half their number. The other rule, never fight against heavy odds, if by any possible manœvring you can hurl your own force on only a part, and that the weakest part, of your enemy and crush it. Such tactics will win every time, and a small army may thus destroy a large one in detail, and repeated victory will make it invincible" [Imboden 2: 297].

15. Imboden notes, though, that there was a secret to the success of Jackson's forced marches, so that the stamina of his troops could be replenished:

> His celerity of movement was a simple matter. He never broke down his men by too-long-continued marching. He rested the whole column very often, but only for a few minutes at a time. I remember that he liked to see the men lie down flat on the ground to rest, and would say, "A man rests all over when he lies down" [Imboden 2: 297–98].

And, in fairness to Jackson, it should be noted that he was bound by his own rules: since he did not allow furloughs for his men, he would not take one himself, as his gentle rebuff of his wife Anna's request that he visit Lexington for the holidays attests.

16. Randolph Harrison McKim provides a clear summary of the distinctions perceived between Jackson and Lee. After describing Jackson's disciplinarian and rough-hewn appearance, McKim writes:

> In nearly all these respects he was a contrast to Gen. Robert E. Lee, who was elegant in person and handsome in features, a superb rider, the very beau ideal of a soldier, urbane, also, and gracious in manner, with a native dignity which stamped him as a king of men. He had also the rare gift of a rich and melodious voice, which alone would have marked him out in any company. While no man, not even Jackson, could have been a more lion-hearted and aggressive fighter than Lee, yet he lacked the other's strictness and severity as a disciplinarian. It has been said of him that he was too epicene, too gentle, and indeed, if he had a fault as a commander, it lay in that direction. There were occasions when more of Jackson's sternness and inflexibility in dealing with his generals would have been conducive to success on the field of battle.
>
> These two great soldiers were types respectively of the Puritan and the Cavalier. Jackson was a Presbyterian, with many of the Puritan's characteristics. He was Oliver Cromwell, without his selfish ambition. Robert E. Lee, on the other hand, was a devout and loyal son of the Episcopal Church, a Cavalier in bearing as he was in blood, but with a simplicity and purity of character that was certainly not characteristic of King Charles's gallant and dashing leaders. But though they were thus men of very different types, they completely trusted and understood one another, and formed a combination that was well nigh irresistible. Lee regarded Jackson as his right arm, while it is on record that Jackson said of Lee that he was the

only man he would always be willing to follow blindfolded [93].

17. That is, the northern end of the valley.

18. Jackson's description uncannily resembles the mechanical awkwardness of Samuel Beckett's comic characters (for example, Molloy). In fact, Henri Bergson, in 1900 (Sypher vii), approximately two generations after Jackson's time, specified the comic as the mechanical: "*The attitudes, gestures and movements of the human body are laughable in exact proportion as that body reminds us of a mere machine*" (Bergson 79).

19. In his essay on Carl Sandburg's biography of Lincoln, Joseph Auslander compares the Sandburg work with those of other poet-biographers, including Allen Tate. He accords Tate's work on Jackson only limited praise, asserting that it "is little more than a brilliant account of battle scenes and military movements" (656). Apparently Auslander chose to downplay passages such as the one just quoted, in which Tate most certainly interprets with a poet's eye. And, of course, no biography by an American poet can hope to compare in scope and grandeur with Sandburg's work.

20. This generalized view of Jackson was not, however, universal. Alexander Robinson Boteler, who was with Jackson at Fredericksburg, and in fact shared a tent with him, contributed the following observations of the commander in his tent in the very early morning hours: "Lighting the candle he began to write at the table, which stood near the foot of the bed and in a position that enabled me as he sat by it to study his handsome profile, to which, by the way, none of the pictures do justice" (Boteler 81).

21. In his article on the Southern Historical Society and the Lost Cause, Richard D. Starnes summarizes the role of Lost Cause authors such as Pollard and R. L. Dabney, noting their defense of Lee and his men as opposed to the disastrous machinations of the politicians, including President Davis (178).

22. Fischer comments that:

The "right wing" of the British Reformation was the party of Anglican Episcopacy which favored an inclusive national church, a hierarchy of priests, compulsory church taxes and a union of church and crown. Its worship centered on liturgy and ritual, its theology became increasing Arminian in the seventeenth century, and its creed was defined by the Book of Common Prayer. This denomination was specially strong in the south and west of England. It was destined to dominate Virginia for more than a century.

Next to the Episcopalians on Britain's spectrum of religious belief were Presbyterians. They also favored a strong national church, but one which was ruled by strong synods of ministers and elders rather than by bishops and priests. The theology of Presbyterianism was Calvinist; its worship centered on preaching and conversion. The Presbyterians were numerous in North Britain, where they made much use of evangelical field meetings and prayer meetings. They became very strong in the American backcountry [795].

23. Stephen Lang, who played Jackson in *Gods and Generals* (2003), commented that Jackson's "performance" as a VMI professor was "mythic: "there were … mythic aspects to his performance at VMI…. [N]obody makes myths like students do. And of course his performance at VMI was so singular and so … alternately amusing and frustrating to students that it took on qualities of a myth" (Lang). Lt. Kije was the "hero" of a charming piece of satiric music by Russian composer Serge Prokofiev.

24. The unfortunate Gen. Nathaniel Banks bore the brunt of much of Jackson's strategic brilliance during the Valley campaign.

25. A reference to pompous Gen. John Pope, soundly defeated by Jackson at Second Manassas.

26. Gen. Turner Ashby, a favorite cavalry commander of the Valley Army, was killed June 6, 1862, while leading a headlong charge against the Federals (Robertson, *Stonewall Jackson* 428–29).

27. Regarding the topic of the treatment of Jackson in film, and of his fame as different from Lee's, Stephen Lang commented that "I think that Jackson has been

protected kind of by the mists of the Shenandoah Valley, to a large extent," and that a peculiar kind of immortality has nevertheless accrued to Jackson in the Shenandoah region: "But all I can say, and this is a sense I have is, that he has been — he's been protected, he's been waiting to be uncovered, I think. You know, when you talk to the people in the Shenandoah Valley, which I did a lot, in Lexington, and Staunton, and Winchester, a lot of times they talk as if Jackson and the brigade just left town an hour ago. It's almost as if he's out there now, you know, on the back roads and everything, the foot cavalry marching along. That's different than Lee" (Lang).

28. For a full discussion of the controversy, and the probably definitive word in Jackson's favor, see Robertson (835–36).

29. Isidore, "bishop of Seville ... served as adviser to kings and as the spiritual and intellectual guide of the Spanish hierarchy. Though not a creative genius, he was a man of great learning and broad intellectual interests with a great enthusiasm for the wisdom of the past. A prolific writer, his works include the *Regula monachorum...*, the *Liber Sententiarum*, a clear and systematic summary of theology, and the *Liber de officiis ecclesiasticis*, a manual of instruction for the clergy.... St. Isidore exercised his lasting influence on the Middle Ages through his *Etymologiae*, the first of the medieval encyclopedias. In twenty books he set out to summarize for the benefit of future generations the learning of the ancient world.... Although he has often been ridiculed for giving fanciful or capricious etymologies for words, Isidore's achievement in synthesizing human knowledge both religious and secular, Christian and pagan, is nonetheless remarkable. He provided the European Middle Ages with an indispensable instrument which made it possible for untold thousands over many centuries to acquire the rudiments of learning" (O'Callaghan 85–87).

30. Unless otherwise noted, as in this instance, all translations in the book are my own.

31. The Spanish name is a joke: the horse was a "rocìn" [nag] "ante[s]" [before] and is now to be a glorious charger, which of course it is not.

32. In the course of his presentation of the appearances of the arm in the poem, Brault notes that "Arm reliquaries are first attested in the eleventh century" (103).

33. One example of the application of the "Blue Light" term to Jackson is found in the memoir by VMI graduate John Wise: "He was deeply interested in church work, being a typical blue-light Westminster Presbyterian [that is, a Presbyterian adhering to the Westminster Confession]. He was strict in his attendance at church and active in all church work" (Wise 143).

34. Testimonials abound as to his basic unsuitability to the teaching profession, although he did approach it with much dedication. It is noteworthy that an officer under Jackson's command, who had been a cadet studying under him at VMI, recorded his impression of the change in Jackson when he again became an army officer at Harpers Ferry:

> He knew exactly what ought to be done and how it should be done. There was no wavering in opinion, no doubts and misgivings; his orders were clear and decisive. It occurred to us at the time that Jackson was much more in his element here, as an army officer, than when in the professor's chair at Lexington. It seemed that the sights and sounds of war had aroused his energies; his manner had become brusque and imperative; his face was bronzed from exposure, his beard was now of no formal style, but was worn unshorn [Gittings 22].

35. Thus novels such as Douglas Gibboney's *Stonewall at Gettysburg*.

36. Similarly, following the assassination of John F. Kennedy in 1963, some, most famously Oliver Stone in his *JFK*, have engaged in speculation regarding his intentions in Vietnam. Stone would have it that Kennedy planned to withdraw American forces, and that therefore interests in the United States intelligence structure who wished to continue our presence in Southeast Asia plotted and carried out his assassination.

37. Johnson spent much of his life in Greeneville, Tennessee, in the eastern part of the state, where Unionist sympathy was high.

38. For evidence of this point of view in the South, see *The Image of Lincoln in the South* (Davis, M., *The Image of Lincoln in the South*).

39. John H. Worsham offered a straightforward commentary on the emotional and military effect of the loss of Jackson:

> What a loss to the Confederacy! What a loss to the Army of Northern Virginia, and to its commander, Lee, who said he had "lost his right arm." What a loss to his corps. Never more will his sword flash in the enemy's rear, nor will he see his banner floating in one of his fierce attacks on their flank, nor will he hear the wild cheers of his men as they drive everything before them. In my humble opinion, the army never recovered from the loss of Jackson [Worsham 102].

And Edward A. Moore, in his The Story of a Cannoneer under Stonewall Jackson, comments:

> The mortal wounding of Jackson and his death on the tenth more than offset the advantage of the victory [Chancellorsville] to the Confederates. His loss was deplored by the whole army, especially by General Lee, and to his absence in later battles, conspicuously at Gettysburg, was our failure to succeed attributed. In fact General Lee said to a friend, after the war, that with Jackson at Gettysburg our success would have been assured — a feeling that was entertained throughout the army [Moore 177; emphasis added].

Additionally, see Freeman, Robert E. Lee 3:161, for discussion and sources. According to Freeman, Lee "concluded that it was the absence of Jackson ... that made the Army of Northern Virginia a far less effective fighting machine at Gettysburg than at Chancellorsville." Freeman cites two postwar conversations in which Lee offered his perspective:

> Not long before his death, in a long conversation with his cousin Cassius Lee of Alexandria, the General said that if Jackson had been at Gettysburg he would have held the heights [probably Cemetery Hill].... And one afternoon,

when he was out riding with Professor White, he said quietly, "If I had had Stonewall Jackson with me, so far as man can see, I should have won the battle of Gettysburg."

Freeman concludes, as have many before and since, that Lee was correct: "That statement [by Lee] must stand. The darkest scene in the great drama of Gettysburg was enacted at Chancellorsville when Jackson fell" (Freeman 3: 3:161).

40. Calvin, actually a Frenchman, lived most of his life in Switzerland. Zwingli was a German Swiss.

41. The North as invader motif was very common throughout the Confederacy. One example from a Tennessee regimental chaplain serves to illustrate this typical viewpoint: "A dreadful war having sprung up between the North and South, the North having marshaled their thousands to invade and lay waste our beautiful land, subjugate the people and rule with a rod of iron. After mature deliberation and much prayer, I felt it to be my duty to give assistance to the country where I had been nurtured and where the bones of my ancestors reposed" (Deavenport 35). A much more florid formulation of the topic is to be found in the Confederate poem "The Lone Sentry" by James Ryder Randell, which deals with an anecdote about Stonewall Jackson: "Brothers! the Midnight of the Cause / Is shrouded in our fate; / The demon Goths pollute our halls / With fire, lust, and hate. / Be strong — be valiant — be assured —/ Strike home for Heaven and Right! / *The soul of Jackson stalks abroad,* / And guards the camp to-night" (Wharton 79; original emphasis).

42. German-born Rupert (1619-82) was a dashing cavalry commander for King Charles I in the English Civil War. Rupert's defeat at Naseby (June 1645) led to his eclipse as the royal commander, but he cut a figure that has become enduringly chivalrous and, as Trevor-Roper observes, a symbol of futile striving against the tide of history:

> ... Prince Rupert ... [was] famous ... as the most brilliant and dashing of Charles I's generals, the inventor, almost, of the cavalry charge.... In spite of Rupert's brilliant actions, Charles I

lost the war; and I am afraid that ... in this sense ... Disraeli ... described a ... colleague as "the Prince Rupert of parliamentary discussion" [Trevor-Roper 5].

43. The latter fact distinguishes him sharply from Cromwell but is paralleled by leaders such as Gustavus Adolphus, Judas Maccabeus, and Gordon, as well as fictional and legendary figures such as Roland and Arthur.

44. Romans 8:28: "And we know that all things work together for good to them that love God, to them who are the called according to *his* purpose."

45. A characteristic such scene appears in Ron Maxwell's *Gods and Generals.*

46. These tenets, selected from Calvin's *Institutes,* are: "Total Depravity or Total Inability; (2) Unconditional Election; (3) Particular Redemption or Limited Atonement; (4) Irresistible Grace; (5) The Perseverance of the Saints" (Steele and Thomas 11–12).

47. This took place during the Valley Campaign, near Winchester. Ordered by Jackson to take a ridge, Taylor's men came under hot artillery fire, and Taylor reacted hotly himself. Here is his account:

Many men fell, and the whistling of shot and shell occasioned much ducking of heads in the column. This annoyed me no little, as it was but child's play to the work immediately in hand. Always an admirer of "Uncle Toby," I had contracted the most villainous habit of his beloved army in Flanders, and, forgetting Jackson's presence, ripped out, "What the h__ are you dodging for? If there is any more of it, you will be halted under this fire for an hour." The sharp tones of a familiar voice produced the desired effect, and the men looked as if they had swallowed ramrods; but I shall never forget the reproachful surprise expressed in Jackson's face. He placed his hand on my shoulder, said in a gentle voice, "I am afraid you are a wicked fellow," turned, and rode back to the pike.

This incident is excerpted and commented in Robertson 407.

48. Tarboro is northeast of Raleigh, in the sandy farmland on the way to the Outer Banks. Pender is buried in the cemetery of the Calvary Episcopal Church. His family was prominent in the region.

49. Samito (176) gives the date as October 7; Longacre (70–71) as October 6.

50. Among novels featuring Jackson are *Stonewall* (John J. Dwyer), *Turn of Glory* (Al Lacy), and *A Bullet for Stonewall* (Benjamin King).

51. Maxwell's adaptation of *Gods and Generals* was released in 2003.

52. Dabney omits the details of this incident, noting that Jackson did not illuminate him on it.

53. After making these observations, the author noticed in Wayland Fuller Dunaway's *Reminiscences of a Rebel* that the author sets up a parallel between Jackson and another hero of Troy. Referring to Jackson's wounding at Chancellorsville, Dunaway remarks: "Alas! As when Hector fell the doom of Troy was sealed, so with the death of Jackson the star of the Southern Confederacy declined" (69).

54. Another definition of the concept is provided by William Sale in the context of Book I of the *Iliad*: "The central concept [of the Book] is *geras,* the prize of honor, an object — material or human — granted by society to various of its members in token of their *areté,* which in the heroic world meant excellence on the field of battle, in combat with the sword, spear and shield" (89).

55. For a good presentation of the concept of *arete,* see Werner Jaeger, *Paideia,* vol. 1, Ch. 1, "Nobility and Arete." Jaeger emphasizes that for the Greeks, the notion of *areté* is chiefly aristocratic in application. He also notes that "its oldest meaning is a combination of proud and courtly morality with warlike valour" (Jaeger 5). Despite Jackson's lack of aristocratic background, the term fits him in respect of his nobility of spirit. Jaeger notes that "In Homer, the real mark of the nobleman is his sense of duty. He is judged, and is proud to be judged, by a severe standard. And the nobleman educates others [as did Jackson] by presenting to them an eternal ideal, to which they have a duty to conform" (Jaeger 7).

56. In the passage quoted, superscript note numbers in the original have been eliminated.

57. Importantly, though, Shaara does not demonize the man. As he commented,

> I'm not sure what the "historical" Jackson is. Each era has its own conceptions of these characters, and Jackson is no exception. Today, many view him as a religious zealot, bordering on lunacy. If there is one difference between my characters in general and those portrayed in history books, I try to look beyond anyone else's conception of his deeds, his behavior, his "traits," and try to find how the character saw his own world. The events in my stories are, as much as possible, told from the point of view of each character, told the way they might have told the same story. That's my goal. I don't think historians ever try to capture that sense of first-person storytelling- It simply isn't their job to do so [Shaara, J., e-mail to the author].

58. The relationship between Jackson and Stuart appears to have been unique in terms of Jackson's willingness to laugh at himself. Confederate soldier John Wise comments that:

> General Jeb. Stuart was about the only one of the generals who took liberties and poked fun at General Jackson. Jackson admired him greatly, and Stuart heartily reciprocated. Their characteristics were quite different, except that they were both devoutly religious. Stuart was a jolly, singing, laughing soldier and Jackson as grim as a pot on a fire. He would stand ridicule from Stuart, but from nobody else [144].

59. As Col. Moore (Mel Gibson) notes in *We Were Soldiers* when informed that his Air Cav regiment will be renumbered from the 1st Cavalry to the 7th, Custer's ill-fated regiment was the famous 7th Cavalry. The film also plays on the analogies, with, among other things, Moore studying a famous print of the Custer massacre, and Sgt.-Maj. Basil Plumley (Sam Elliott) referring disparagingly to Custer.

60. Gerard Reedy comments, "If we omit the doubtful 'An Elegy upon the Death of my Lord *Francis Villiers*,' ... there is no evidence that Marvell was ever a Royalist, that

is, was ever in sympathy politically with those who rallied to the standard of the King" (29; 139).

61. Lang had previously played Babe Ruth, Ike Clanton, and General Pickett. He is a very thoughtful and studious actor who teaches acting classes at the famous Strasberg school in New York.

62. He played the role of the Speaker of the Virginia Assembly who offers the command of the Virginia Militia to Robert E. Lee.

63. In his *Reminiscences of a Rebel* (1913), the Rev. Wayland Fuller Dunaway, who was with the 40th Virginia, provides a brief first-hand account of the charge, with a charitable observation about the routed Union troops:

> Late in the afternoon of Friday, May 1, our brigade had marched up from Fredericksburg and halted in striking distance of the Federal army. What could we expect but that in the morning we should be waging an assault upon its fortified position? Instead of that Jackson led us with the rest of his corps around the front of that position until we struck the road on the Orange side of Chancellorsville. We were now on Hooker's right flank, having marched quickly and silently fifteen miles over a rough and unfrequented road. The sun was sinking toward the western horizon when our lines of attack were formed on both sides of the road and at right angles to it. Immediately the onslaught began, silent, rapid, resolute, Heth's brigade being on the north or left side of the road. We had not proceeded far before we struck Howard's corps all unsuspecting and unprepared. Their fires were kindled for cooking supper, and dressed beeves were ready for distribution among the companies. They fled before us, strewing the ground with muskets, knapsacks, and other accouterments. Whoever censures them for running would probably have acted as they did, for our charge was as lightning from a cloudless sky. On the way we crossed a little fram [sic], and as I passed the dwelling I saw several ladies who were wildly rejoicing [66–67].

64. The Colston referenced here is Raleigh Colston, who later fought at Gettysburg. He is buried in the Confederate officers' section of Hollywood Cemetery, Richmond. With reference to the aggressiveness displayed here by Jackson, Capt. J. W. Randolph, who was an aide to Jackson, wrote of the flight of the Federals that

> At one time during the evening a young officer, wild with enthusiasm, dashed up to the General crying, "General they are running too fast for us, we can't come up with them." "They never run too fast for me, sir," was the immediate response.

And his aggressiveness was contagious:

> And thus onward rushed pursuers and pursued, down the road toward Chancellorsville. Now and then Jackson would press his horse to a gallop and dash to the front, and whenever he appeared the troops would break ranks and rush around him with the wildest cheers I ever heard from human hearts [Randolph 5].

65. A recent study of his final illness concludes that he probably did not die of pneumonia but rather of what was then called "pyemia," an infectious condition that would now be called sepsis or septicemia; in other words, Jackson died of blood poisoning due to an infection in his amputated arm (Rozear and Greenfield).

66. In the finished film, the "bloom" effect was cut, leaving a slow fade-to-black as a transition to the scene showing the funeral caisson being drawn through the Lexington streets. The dolly out is preserved, however, lending the feeling of a "view from eternity" to the scene.

67. Thanks to Alan Geoffrian, Duvall's assistant, for this characterization of Duvall's special talent.

68. The Rev. William Mack Lee, who had been General Lee's cook during the war and left an autobiography (after the fashion of the time, reproduced in black dialect), provided a moving description of General Lee's reaction to the death of his lieutenant:

Lee Wept Over Jackson's Death.

> "I have even seed him cry. I never seed him sadder dan dat gloomy mownin' when he tol' me 'bout how Gineral Stonewall Jackson had been shot by his own men.
>
> "He muster hurd it befo' but he never tol' me til' nex' mawnin'.
>
> "'William,' he says ter me, 'William, I have lost my right arm.'
>
> "'How come yer ter say dat, Marse Robert?' I axed him. 'Yo ain't bin in no battle sence yestiddy, an' I doan see yo' arm bleedin'.
>
> "'I'm bleeding at the heart, William,' he says, and I slipped out'n de tent, 'cause he looked lak he wanted to be by himself.
>
> "A little later I cum back an' he tol' me dat Gineral Jackson had bin shot by one of his own soljers. The Gineral had tol' 'em to shoot anybody goin' or comin' across de line. And den de Gineral hisself puts on a federal uniform and scouted across de lines. When he comes back, one of his own soljers raised his gun.
>
> "'Don't shoot. I'm your general,' Marse Jackson yelled.
>
> "'Dey said dat de sentry was hard o'-hearin'. Anyway, he shot his Gineral an' kilt him.
>
> "'I'm bleeding at the heart, William,' Marse Robert kep' a sayin'" [Lee 9].

69. John Wise sums up the command relationship between the two:

> General Ewell served with Jackson, and Jackson thought very highly of him, altho [sic] no two men could have been more utterly different. Toward the close of his life, Ewell became very religious himself, but in those days he was far from the Puritan type. General Ewell once told me that on a certain occasion Jackson, in a burst of enthusiasm for something he had done, said, "Ewell, that was well done, and I don't see how a man of your habits and who uses language like yours can do his work so well" [Wise 144].

70. The success of The *Killer Angels* and of *Gettysburg* led to a good deal of visibil-

ity for Chamberlain, who was a nearly forgotten figure previously, at least outside Maine. As is the case nowadays with any historical figure who receives renewed scrutiny, Chamberlain's "myth" has been the object of some debunking, revolving both around his admittedly contentious character and the truth of his claims about Little Round Top. Jeff Shaara has little patience with such fashionable debunking:

> I followed my father's portrayal of Chamberlain, and I agree that my father took a decidedly heroic view of the man. But, contrary to the annoying litany from some modern historians who try to dispute the man's heroism and the magnitude of his accomplishments, I refuse to fall into the "bash Chamberlain" school. What he accomplished at Gettysburg was extraordinary, and all true. Was he the only hero? Of course not. Was he responsible for the victory? He made a significant contribution. How that contribution is measured is how some people get their books published these days. I prefer to look at the man through the telling of his own experiences, from his own point of view. In addition, I rely on Ulysses Grant to help out. I really don't care what modern biographers are digging up to soil the man's overall character. I avoid that kind of nonsense with all my characters, Lee, Grant and Jackson included. If there is an audience who wants nothing but rough edges, or who delights in seeing a man's flaws more than his accomplishments, then they can read someone else's work. They won't find it in mine. Does this mean I'm being naíve or too gentle in my dealing with the characters? That's for readers to judge. I don't believe so. As I said above, I'm trying to tell these stories as the characters themselves might have told it. I really don't pay much attention to anyone's more "modern" analysis. And, by the way, there is not one scene with Chamberlain that is not authentic, not one conversation that could not have happened. Certainly I use license with regard to conversations and mental monologue. These are after all, novels. But no truth

was sacrificed, and I defy any academic to dispute that with facts that show otherwise. (Obviously this is a point that's a bit touchy with me). But I get awfully tired of backlash and revisionism from those who are simply trying to make a name for themselves in the academic community [Shaara, J., e-mail to the author].

71. To Lucasta,
   Going to the Warres.
   I.
Tell me not (Sweet) I am unkinde,
That from the Nunnerie
Of thy chaste breast, and quiet minde,
To Warre and Armes I flie.

   II.
True; a new Mistresse now I chase,
The first Foe in the Field;
And with a stronger Faith imbrace
A Sword, a Horse, a Shield.

   III.
Yet this Inconstancy is such,
As you too shall adore;
I could not love thee (Deare) so much,
Lov'd I not Honour more [Lovelace 18].

72. Col. "Chester" French, an aide to Lee and Jackson, relates a story reminiscent of this one which shows Jackson at his most unbending (although French does not disapprove of his attitude). French tells of how, when two men were condemned for desertion, their commander, Lt. Col. Walker, went to Jackson "to intercede" in their behalf:

> As soon as Jackson seemed to be somewhat at leisure, Walker approached him and submitted his petition for mercy [French was listening not far away, while resting "under a large tree some fifteen or twenty steps from the Adjutant General's table, which was in the open air within a few feet of the General's tent"]. God deliver us! I never saw such feeling displayed by "Old Jack," before nor after [this was early in the Valley Campaign]. While Walker was telling his tale of sorrow, the gaze of the General was fixed on him as if his eyes would pierce him and read his innermost thoughts. He opened not his

lips, but it seemed as if every feeling of his soul was roused to its utmost tension, and when the tale was ended, he turned as an enraged lion upon him and drove off the astonished officer, declaring in a stinging, hissing tone, "Sir! Men who desert their comrades in war *deserve* to be *shot!*—and *officers* who intercede for them *deserve* to be *hung!*"

After he told Walker, "Mr. Walker, I advise you to resign," Jackson did a most characteristic thing: "Looking at the retiring officer for a moment, his head fell forward on his breast, and he walked into his tent "to talk with God." French observed that Jackson spent the rest of the day in his tent, presumably praying and meditating on his difficult burdens (18–19; original emphasis).

73. Jeff Shaara stressed this in a communication with the author:

> If there is one difference between my characters in general and those portrayed in history books, I try to look beyond anyone else's conception of his deeds, his behavior, his "traits," and try to find how the character saw his own world. The events in my stories are, as much as possible, told from the point of view of each character, told the way they might have told the same story. That's my goal. I don't think historians ever try to capture that sense of first-person storytelling — It simply isn't their job to do so [Shaara, J., e-mail to the author].

74. This poet, whose vernacular name was Johannes van Naarssen (1580-1637), produced works on Gustavus Adolphus including *Gustavus soecis, tragoedia* (1633). Rare editions of his work may be found in the Hollis Catalog of the Harvard University libraries.

75. Jackson's calming influence on his wife is the focus here, but note should be taken of the strength of this remarkable woman. As Kali Rocha, who played Anna Jackson in *Gods and Generals*, comments on the relationship between Anna and Thomas:

> I think spiritually certainly they together were very devoted to God and that was a big unifying factor between the two of them. But also she was devoted to him. And her love for him and her understanding of him I think as a sort of eccentric man [were] also extremely powerful. So I think she had a real understanding of who he was ... in the world. And I mean, it sounds dramatic to say, but ... maybe she had an understanding of who he would be in history. Because I never got the sense, at least in my reading of it, this may be projection, that she would insert herself or her own needs into his path [Rocha].

76. The path, and the site of the Wellford home, are preserved today at the Chancellorsville Battlefield Park.

77. Lee was similarly treated, with memorial windows at the church he attended during his latter years in Richmond (St. Paul's Episcopal).

78. For an illuminating study of this important West Point class, see John Waugh, *The Class of 1846* (Waugh). [Thanks to Pat Falci.]

79. For Dickens and other Victorian reformers, see Houghton (274ff).

80. Jackson's ambition has been overstated as a motive for his actions, most notably by Royster in *Destructive Warfare*. Royster maintains, not very convincingly, that Jackson created the image of Stonewall Jackson, rather like a present-day pop culture hero or a politician dressing up his image. This line of argument is characteristic of "presentist" historians, to borrow Roland's term, and of other debunkers: such metafictional or metahistorical sophistication on the part of Jackson, Lee, or any of the figures of the time seems improbable (excepting showmen and mountebanks such as Buffalo Bill Cody, into whose class I would not place Jackson and Lee). In any event, it is true that Jackson had his eye on the public and on his superiors rather more closely than is commonly thought. But this ambition was subordinated to Jackson's religious faith, according to Dr. Hunter McGuire:

> Ambition! Yes, far beyond what ordinary men possess. And, yet, he told me, when talking in my tent one dreary winter near Charlestown, that he would

not exchange one moment of his life hereafter, for all the earthly glory he could win [McGuire, H., "The Memory of 'Stonewall' Jackson" 9].

John Dall's comments in his entry "Presbyterianism" in *Encyclopedia of Religion and Ethics*, edited by James Hastings, shed light on the only apparently contradictory nature of such ambition in a deeply religious man:

> The morality which accompanies the Presbyterian form of Church government and the Calvinist form of doctrine is quite distinctive. It might be logically expected that a profound belief in the sovereignty of God, in election and irresistible grace, would fill the individual with a deep sense not merely of his insignificance but also of his helplessness, and would conduce to a fatalism destructive of all energy and activity. But in Calvinism we find the same paradox as in early Islām, viz. that a creed apparently inimical to all human activity has animated men to the most prodigious efforts. Calvin and Knox, and others of the same faith, when they considered themselves merely as men, were the humblest of creatures, giving God the glory for all that they did and were; but, when they considered themselves as instruments in the hands of God, they were filled with a sense of their usefulness in the world that made them marvels of energy and even of arrogance. Like Paul, they valued themselves little, but they magnified their office. This combination of personal modesty with diligence and fiery energy has always been characteristic of the best Calvinist morality [Dall 9: 269].

Finally, the comments of Stephen Lang, who played Jackson in *Gods and Generals*, are apropos here: "I think that Jackson himself was so caught up in the minutiae of living, the details of running a brigade and a corps, that I don't think he paid the least bit of attention to it [his image]. I think it would have been something of anathema to him as well, because I think that Jackson's own sense of humility, his own consciousness of all glory, all creation, on a moment to moment basis, is due to God" [Lang].

See the characteristically balanced comments by Robertson (xv). Bowers interprets Jackson as struggling even in his Mexican War days with his ambition, which he presumably viewed as a sin of pride:

> If the Lord intended him for garrison duty, so be it; perhaps it was His way of curbing Jackson's excessive ambition. Some youths worry about excessive carnal desire, sloth, aimlessness. Lieutenant Jackson fretted — as he would later at higher rank — about his rampant ambition. He kept it well hidden, as others do lust, throughout his life [Bowers 63].

81. In his biography of Havelock, the Rev. William Brock quotes a nearly hagiographical eulogy presumably delivered at the hero's funeral:

> "There gleams a coronet of light around our Hero's brow,
> But of far purer radiance than England can bestow;
> He takes his place among his peers. His peers! And who are they?
> Princes of yon celestial spheres, whom angel hosts obey.
> The heralds have made search, and found his lineage of the best.
> He stands amid the sons of God, a son of God confess'd!
> He wears a glittering, starry cross, called by a monarch's name;
> That monarch whose 'Well done' confers a more than mortal fame.
> Victorious first at Futteypore, victorious at Lucknow,
> The gallant chief of gallant men is *more* than conqueror now;
> For his whole life was one stern fight against so fierce a foe,
> That only superhuman might avails to lay him low.
> And he possess'd a talisman, thro' which he won the day;
> A blood-red signature which kept the hosts of hell at bay.
> The banner under which he serv'd can never know defeat,
> And so he laid his laurels down at his Great Captain's feet.
> There rest thee, Christian warrior, — rest from the two-fold strife —

The battle-field of India, and the battle-field of life!

Rest in the presence of thy Lord, where trouble may not come,

Nor thy repose be broken thro' by sound of hostile drum;

There, where no scorching sun beats down on the unshelter'd head;

Where no pale moon keeps mournful watch over the silent dead!

And when, in God's good time, this page of history shall be turn'd,

And the bright stars be reckon'd up which in its mid night burn'd,

Then shall the name of Havelock, the saintly, sage, and bold,

Shine forth engraven thereupon in characters of gold!" [Brock 288–90].

82. "Black Republican" was a disparaging characterization of antislavery Republicans often used by militant Southerners or Southern partisans.

83. Patton was certainly no slacker as a theorist, as his pioneering work in the field of tank combat demonstrates. The point here is that he was no armchair theorist. As he maintained repeatedly, theory must give way to practical application on the battlefield.

84. In the film *Patton*, the character Steiger, an adviser to Generals Rommel and Rundstedt, calls Patton "a 16th-century man" and tells General Jodl, Hitler's adjutant, that "Patton is a romantic warrior lost in contemporary times."

85. For examples of this command type, see John Keegan, *The Mask of Command* (Keegan).

86. Martin Blumenson, in his biography of the general, provides confirmation that Patton was religiously observant during World War II. Describing Patton's routine while waiting in 1943 for the Mediterranean invasion to begin, he writes: "Despite newspaper reports of his profanity and lack of godliness, he attended Episcopal services every Sunday" (194).

87. The portrayal of Lt. Col. Hal Moore by Mel Gibson in *We Were Soldiers* plays on this kind of dual image and perhaps owes something to the famous persona established by Patton. Gibson, as Moore, prays in the base's church at Fort Benning before departing for Vietnam. He offers a very devout prayer for his men and in particular for one of his soldiers, praying with him. Then, in a moment that may be as much Mel Gibson as Hal Moore, he delivers in his inimitable manner the following punchline:

Oh yes, and one more thing, Dear Lord. About our enemies? Ignore their heathen prayers and help us blow those little bastards straight to hell! Amen again [Wallace Ch. 4].

In the commentary for the DVD version of the film, director/screenwriter Randall Wallace said that the prayer scene was fictional but was based closely on the characters of the two men. He also noted that the little punch line seemed to him very much in character for Hal Moore.

88. Nueva España (New Spain) was the colonial name for the region which later became Mexico after independence from Spain in 1821.

89. Although the ninth-century setting of the battle and its circumstances cannot be verified, it is probably true, according to Claudio Sánchez-Albornoz, that a battle was fought at the location between Christian and Moorish forces, albeit at a different period and without the supernatural accretions (Sánchez-Albornoz 94).

90. In the passage quoted, superscript note numbers in the original have been eliminated.

91. Visions of battlefield apparitions are common to other cultures. One example of the many sightings of another famous saint, St. George, is cited by John Matzke, "from the English poem *Richard Coeurdelyoun* [Richard Lionheart] of the end of the XIII century.... After the capture of Acre Richard marches along the road toward Caïpha, and a battle takes place in which Saint George aids the English army.

Kyng Richard was almost ateynt,

And in the smoke nygh adreynt.

On his knees he gan doun falle;

Help! to Jesus he gan calle

For love of his modyr Mary;

And as I find in hys story,

He seygh come St. George, the knyght,

Upon a stede good and lyght,

In armes whyte as the flour,
With a croys off red colour.
Alle that he mette in that stounde,
Hors and man, wente to grounde;
And the wynd gan wexe lythe,
Sterne strokes they gynne to kythe.
When Kyng Richard seygh that syght,
In herte he was glad and lyght."
[Matzke 450].

92. Emilie Bergmann comments on the role of prophecies, which normally included visionary experiences, in her study of the Lope de Vega poem *La hermosura de Angélica* (1602):

Ex post facto prophecy in medieval epic and romances, relating events of past history with relation to the time of writing, but future to the narrative, is a common device which can be combined with ecphrasis in the form of a dream vision, symbolic configuration, or prophetic revelation [276].

George Kurman, in his "Ecphrasis in Epic Poetry," defines ecphrasis as "the description in verse of an object of art" [1].

93. The Corneille play drew heavily on the earlier Spanish work; see, for example, Rogers (210). Pierre Corneille (1606-84) was one of France's greatest classical dramatists (*European* 198). Guillén de Castro y Bellvis (1569-1631) was an important dramatist from the Spanish Golden Age. His play on the Cid was published in two parts. The first part, dated between 1612 and 1618, is the more famous of the two and was the basis for the Corneille play (Bruerton 150; Martel and Alpern 324).

94. Martín de Riquer, in his "Bavieca, caballo del Cid Campeador, y Bauçan, caballo de Guillaume d'Orange," *La leyenda de graal* 227-47 (Riquer), casts doubt on this interpretation of the name as applied to the Cid's horse, but arrives at no firm conclusion to refute it.

95. A brief summary of the Sack and of the role of Valdés in the aftermath is provided by John E. Longhurst in his English edition of Valdés's dialogue: "The Christian world was shocked in May, 1527, by the news that the forces of ... Charles V had invaded ... Rome.... Not only had the imperial armies ... invaded the Holy City, but ... had subjected it to nine months of occupation and pillage" (Longhurst 1). In the same passage, Longhurst notes that Alfonso de Valdés was the most effective voice in defense of the action, which he argued was needed to cleanse the city of clerical wrongdoing.

96. Edwin B. Place provides a succinct perspective on the *gracioso*, noting that the character type "provides comic relief ... by making witty, humorously nonsensical, calculatedly stupid, or whimsically extravagant speeches" and through his actions, which include "parodying his master's love affair" and "showing cowardice." Place also observes that "the *gracioso* gives advice to his master, sometimes to the extent of providing considerable plot motivation" (257).

97. Note also these comments by J. H. Elliott regarding the unfolding of the Conquest:

The conquest of America ... proved to be a highly complex process, in which men at arms did not always call the tune. If at least initially it was a military conquest, it also possessed from its earliest stages certain other characteristics which began to predominate as soon as the soldiers had achieved what they could. It was accompanied by a movement aimed at spiritual conquest, by means of the evangelization of the Indians. It was followed by a massive migration from Spain, which culminated in the demographic conquest of the Indies [Elliott, J.H., "The Spanish Conquest and Settlement of America" 189].

98. The conquerors diverged sharply in their observance of such mandates, or rather in their apparent sincerity with regard to carrying them out. A good case can be made for Cortés's relative sincerity, while no one ever accused Pizarro of sincerity except in pursuing gold and fame.

99. Hook, *The Sack of Rome*, Ch. 11, details the events of the Sack.

100. Castilian, or *castellano*, the form of Spanish spoken in Castile, was the native dialect of Isabel I. Because of her prominence as queen, Castile grew to dominate the

Spanish peninsula, becoming the center of royal authority. Its particular dialect thus became standard Spanish in the peninsula, although variants based on other dialects of Spanish became standard in the Americas.

101. For amplification of these points within a balanced perspective, see Gregorio Marañón, *Antonio Pérez* (14–20).

102. One of the ballads, translated by J. G. Lockhart as "The Departure of King Sebastian," highlights the chivalric, one might say Ivanhoe-like, image of the King:

I.

It was a Lusitanian Lady, and she was lofty in degree,
Was fairer none, nor nobler, in all the realm than she;
I saw her that her eyes were red, as, from her balcony,
They wandered o'er the crowded shore and the resplendent sea.

II.

Gorgeous and gay, in Lisbon's Bay, with streamers flaunting wide,
Upon the gleaming waters Sebastian's galleys ride,
His valorous armada (was never nobler sight)
Hath young Sebastian marshalled against the Moorish might.

III.

The breeze comes forth from the clear north, a gallant breeze there blows;
Their sails they lift, then out they drift, and first Sebastian goes.
"May none withstand Sebastian's hand — God shield my King!" she said;
Yet pale was that fair Lady's cheek, her weeping eyes were red.

IV.

She looks on all the parting host, in all its pomp arrayed,
Each pennon on the wind is tost, each cognizance displayed;
Each lordly galley flings abroad, above its armèd prow,
The banner of the Cross of God, upon the breeze to flow.

V.

But one there is, whose banner, above the Cross divine,

A scarf upholds, with azure folds, of love and faith the sign:
Upon that galley's stern you see a peerless warrior stand,
Though first he goes, still back he throws his eye upon the land.

VI.

Albeit through tears she looks, yet well may she that form descry,
Was never seen a vassal mien so noble and so high;
Albeit the Lady's cheek was pale, albeit her eyes were red,
"May none withstand my true-love's hand! God bless my Knight!" she said.

VII.

There are a thousand Barons, all harnessed cap-a-pee;
With helm and spear that glitter clear above the dark-green sea; —
No lack of gold or silver, to stamp each proud device
On shield or surcoat — nor of chains and jewellery of price.

VIII.

The seamen's cheers the Lady hears, and mingled voices come,
From every deck, of glad rebeck, of trumpet, and of drum; —
"Who dare withstand Sebastian's hand? what Moor his gage may fling
At young Sebastian's feet?" she said. —
"The Lord hath blessed my King" [Lockhart and Southey 110–11].

103. In her study of the Madrigal conspiracy of 1594-95, which featured one Gabriel de Espinosa who impersonated the late Sebastian, Mary Francis Brooks highlights the postmortem commentary in Portugal on the fate of that nation and on Sebastian's role in that destiny:

The national phobia of Portugal had become a reality; Portugal was swallowed up by Castile. The easiest explanation for this situation, which had developed in the short time of three years, was the disastrous expedition to Africa [headed by Sebastian]; nevertheless, the same blind loyalty which kept the nobles from obstructing Sebastian's march to certain destruction also prevented the country, after the battle, from laying the responsibility where it belonged, on the shoulders of the young king. Instead, the general belief was that Portugal's defeat was the will of God, divine punishment for the sins of the nation. Some chroniclers defend Sebastian as a monarch and as a person; others condemn him as a fanatical, irrational despot; but all indicate that he and his expedition to Africa were the instruments used by the Almighty to humble the proud Portuguese [Brooks 34–35].

104. Notice how Williams subtly implies that Philip is the actual commander of the forces at his disposal, when in fact he did not command from the front. Of course the blame or credit for the policy and the strategy would ultimately be his, but nevertheless the shift from Don Juan, the actual commander, is telling: Williams, at least, perceives Philip to be the virtual commander of these forces, as if he were actually on the field but commanding from the rear.

105. We might recall Ambrose Burnside's similar protestations to Lincoln before his appointment in 1862 as commander of the Army of the Potomac.

106. Many historians have seen this decline as nearly unique to Spain, or at least as more pronounced in Spain than in other nations of the period (see Kamen 25, 48). Henry Kamen, revising some earlier views of Spain's economic woes in the 17th century, sees the problem at least in part as a local example of a wider economic trough in the period (48).

107. In his groundbreaking study of Rabelais, Russian critic Mikhail Bakhtin connected the special appeal of writers such as Rabelais and Cervantes to their cultivation of the "carnivalesque" style, which he derived from the raucous and irreverent medieval carnival. For Bakhtin, the carnival represented the upending of society and thus the relaxation of norms:

> The suspension of all hierarchical precedence during carnival time was of particular significance. Rank was especially evident during official feasts; everyone was expected to appear in the full regalia of his calling, rank, and merits and to take the place corresponding to his position. It was a consecration of

inequality. On the contrary, all were considered equal during carnival. Here, in the town square, a special form of free and familiar contact reigned among people who were usually divided by the barriers of caste, property, profession, and age. The hierarchical background and the extreme corporative and caste divisions of the medieval social order were exceptionally strong. Therefore such free, familiar contacts were deeply felt and formed an essential element of the carnival spirit. People were, so to speak, reborn for new, purely human relations.....

> This temporary suspension, both ideal and real, of hierarchical rank created during carnival time a special type of communication impossible in everyday life. This led to the creation of special forms of marketplace speech and gesture, frank and free, permitting no distance between those who came in contact with each other and liberating from norms of etiquette and decency imposed at other times. A special carnivalesque, marketplace style of expression was formed which we find abundantly represented in Rabelais' novel [Bakhtin 10].

108. For the close connection between the Robin Hood ballads and popular sympathy for outlaws, see Maurice Keen, *The Outlaws of Medieval Legend* (London: Routledge, 2000), Ch. 11 (Keen 145–73).

109. Comparing Turpin to Oliver, Gerald Herman notes the positive qualities of both, and sums up Turpin's image as follows: "He ... is admired ... mostly for his military qualities.... we have the portrait of the ideal priest, as conceived by an eleventh-century ... aristocracy, ... someone who fights for Christ with deeds instead of just words." Herman also highlights the distinction between the warrior Oliver and the warrior priest Turpin, who "joins to the military perfection of the knight the dignity and sanctity of the priest" (Herman, G., "Why Does Olivier Die Before the Archbishop Turpin?" 380–81).

110. See also Field 13, for a brief discussion of the presence of Tuck in the early Robin Hood tradition.

111. See the full discussion of the Friar Tuck background in Dobson and Taylor (158–59).

112. Keir brought similar qualities to his leading role in the underrated *Quatermass and the Pit* (*Five Million Years to Earth*, USA title) (1967), in which he plays the skeptically humane scientist in a battle against psychic evil (Baker, R. W., *Quatermass and the Pit [Five Million Years to Earth]*).

113. "In the film's symbolic structure, the villain can become a projection of forces within but repressed by the hero." Pye applies this structure to "Mann's films," specifically his Westerns (Pye 170).

Bibliography

Adams, Fannie Lewis Gwathmey. "Reminiscences of a Childhood Spent at Hayfield Plantation near Fredericksburg, Virginia during the Civil War." *William and Mary College Quarterly Historical Magazine*, 2nd ser., 23.3 (July 1943): 292–97.

Ahnlund, Nils. *Gustavus Adolphus the Great.* Originally published as *Gustav Adolf the Great.* (American-Scandinavian Foundation, 1940). Translated by Michael Roberts. Foreword by Dennis E. Showalter. New York: History Book Club, 1999.

Aikin, Roger. "Christian Soldiers in the Sala Dei Capitani." *Sixteenth Century Journal* 16.2 (Summer 1985): 206–28.

Ailes, Marianne J. *The Song of Roland — on Absolutes and Relative Values.* Studies in Mediaeval Literature vol. 20. Lewiston, NY: Mellen, 2001.

Alexander, Gen. Edward Porter. *Military Memoirs of a Confederate: A Critical Narrative.* Introduction by Gary W. Gallagher. New York: Da Capo, 1993.

Allan, Elizabeth Randolph Preston. *A March Past: Reminiscences of Elizabeth Randolph Preston Allan.* Janet Allan Bryan, ed. Richmond: Dietz, 1938.

Allen, Ujanirtus. *Campaigning with "Old Stonewall": Confederate Captain Ujanirtus Allen's Letters to His Wife.* Randall A. Allen. and Keith S. Bohannon, eds. Baton Rouge: Louisiana State University Press, 1998.

Altick, Richard D. *Victorian People and Ideas.* New York: W.W. Norton, 1973.

Anderson, Olive. "The Growth of Christian Militarism in Mid-Victorian Britain." *English Historical Review* 86.338 (January 1971): 46–72.

Anonymous. *Poema de Fernan Gonçalez. Texto crítico con introducción, notas y glosario.* 1904. Introduction by C. Carroll Marden, ed. Baltimore: Johns Hopkins, 1930.

_____. *Romancero del Cid.* Compiled by Felipe C. R. Maldonado. Madrid: Taurus, 1970.

_____. *The Song of Roland.* Translated by Glyn Burgess. London: Penguin, 1990.

Apuleius. *Rhetorical Works.* Translated and edited by Stephen Harrison, John Hilton, and Vincent Hunink. Oxford: Oxford University Press, 2001.

Auslander, Joseph. "A Poet Writes Biography." *College English* 1.8 (May 1940): 649–57.

Austin, Aurelia. *Georgia Boys with "Stonewall" Jackson: James Thomas Thompson and the Walton Infantry.* Athens: University of Georgia Press, 1967.

Ayer, Fred Jr. *Before the Colors Fade: Portrait of a Soldier. George S. Patton, Jr.* 1964. Foreword by Omar N. Bradley. Dunwoody, GA: Norman S. Berg, 1971.

Bailey, Matthew. "From Latin Chronicle to Hollywood Extravaganza: The Young Cid Stirs Hearts." *Olifant* 22.1–4 (Spring–Fall 1998–2003): 89–102.

Bainton, Roland H. *The Reformation of the Sixteenth Century.* Boston: Beacon, 1952.

Baker, Denise N. "The Priesthood of Genius: A Study of the Medieval Tradition." *Speculum* 51.2 (April 1976): 277–91.

Baker, Roy Ward, director. *Quatermass and the Pit [Five Million Years to Earth].* 1967. DVD. Hammer-Anchor Bay, 1998.

Bakhtin, Mikhail. *Rabelais and His World.*

Translated by Helene Iswolsky. Bloomington: Indiana University Press, 1984.

Ballesteros Gaibrois, Manuel. *Don Rodrigo
Jiménez de Rada*. Barcelona: Labor, 1936.

Bartlett, John. *Familiar Quotations: A Collection of Passages, Phrases and Proverbs Traced
to Their Sources in Ancient and Modern Literature*. 16th ed. Justin Kaplan, gen. ed.
Boston: Little, Brown, 1992.

Basinger, Jeanine. *Anthony Mann*. Boston:
Hall, 1979.

Beckett, Samuel. *Three Novels by Samuel Beckett: Molloy, Malone Dies, The Unnamable*.
New ed. 1956. Translated by Patrick Bowles,
with Samuel Beckett. New York: Evergreen
Black Cat-Grove, 1965.

Benton, John F. "'Nostre Franceis n'Unt
Talent de Fuïr': The *Song of Roland* and the
Enculturation of a Warrior Class." *Olifant*
21.6 (1979): 237–58.

Bergson, Henri. "Laughter." *Comedy: "Laughter" and "An Essay on Comedy."* Introduction by Wylie Sypher. Garden City, NY:
Doubleday, 1956. 59–190.

Bergmann, Emilie. "The Painting's Observer
in the Epic Canvas: *La hermosura de Angélica*." *Comparative Literature* 38.3 (Summer
1986): 270–88.

Beye, Charles Rowan. *Ancient Greek Literature
and Society*. New York: Anchor-Doubleday,
1975.

Bèze, Theodore de. *Icones*. 1580. Compiled and
edited by John Horden. Introduction by
R. M. Cummings. Continental Emblem
Books. Menston, UK: Scolar, 1971.

Birdwell, Michael E. *Celluloid Soldiers: Warner
Bros.'s Campaign against Nazism*. New York:
New York University Press, 1999.

Blackford, Susan Leigh, comp. *Letters from
Lee's Army: Or Memoirs of Life in and out of
the Army in Virginia during the War Be-
tween the States*. Edited and abridged by
Charles Minor Blackford III. New York:
Scribner's, 1947.

Bloch, Marc. *Feudal Society*. 1961. Translated
by L. A. Manyon. Foreword by M. M.
Postan. Chicago: University of Chicago
Press, 1968.

Blumenson, Martin. *Patton: The Man behind
the Legend, 1885–1945*. New York: Quill-
Morrow, 1985.

Boteler, Alexander Robinson. "At Fredericksburg with Stonewall." *Civil War Times
Illustrated* 36.6 (1997): 20, 22, 78–79, 81–
83.

Bowen, Marjorie. *Sundry Great Gentlemen:
Some Essays in Historical Biography*. 1928.

Essay Index Reprint Series. New York:
Books for Libraries Press, 1968.

Bowers, John. *Stonewall Jackson: Portrait of a
Soldier*. New York: Morrow, 1989.

Braden, Charles S. *Religious Aspects of the Conquest of Mexico*. 1930. New York: AMS, 1966.

Bradford, Gamaliel. *Lee the American*. Boston:
Riverside-Houghton, 1940.

Brandi, Karl. *The Emperor Charles V: The
Growth and Destiny of a Man and of a
World-Empire*. 1939. Translated by C. V.
Wedgwood. London: Jonathan Cape, 1968.

Brault, Gerard J. "The Cult of Saint Peter in
the Cycle of William of Orange." *French
Forum* 6.2 (May 1981): 101–08.

Bridges, Hal. "D.H. Hill's Anti-Yankee Algebra." *Journal of Southern History* 22.2 (May
1956): 220–22.

_____. *Lee's Maverick General: Daniel Harvey
Hill*. New York: McGraw, 1961.

Brock, Rev. William. *A Biographical Sketch of
Sir Henry Havelock, K. C. B*. New York:
Robert Carter and Bros., 1858.

Brooks, Mary Francis. *A King for Portugal: The
Madrigal Conspiracy, 1594–95*. Madison:
University of Wisconsin Press, 1964.

Brown, Laura Morrison. *Historical Sketch of
the Morrison Family*. Charlotte: Presbyterian Standard, 1919.

Bruerton, Courtney. "The Chronology of the
Comedias of Guillén de Castro." *Hispania*
12.2 (April 1944): 89–151.

Brundage, James A. "The Crusade of Richard
I: Two Canonical *Quaestiones*." *Speculum*
38.3 (July 1963): 443–52.

_____. *Medieval Canon Law and the Crusader*.
Madison: University of Wisconsin Press,
1969.

Burton, Alan, Tim O'Sullivan, and Paul Wells,
eds. *Liberal Directions: Basil Dearden and
Postwar British Film Culture*. Trowbridge,
UK: Flicks Books, 1997.

Byrd, Max. *Grant: A Novel*. New York: Ban-
tam, 2001.

Calderón de la Barca, Pedro. *Judas Macabeo*.
Dramas. Vol. 1 of *Obras completas*. Edited by
Ángel Valbuena Briones. Madrid: Aguilar,
1959. 3 vols. 1952–59. 37–68.

Callaway, Mary Chilton, ed. *1 Maccabees. The
New Oxford Annotated Apocrypha*. 3rd ed.
New Revised Standard Version. Michael D.
Coogan, ed. New York: Oxford University
Press, 2001. 201–44.

Camões, Luís de. *Os Lusíadas*. Frank Pierce,
ed. Oxford: Clarendon-Oxford University
Press, 1973.

Carpenter, John A. *Sword and Olive Branch:*

Oliver Otis Howard. Pittsburgh: University of Pittsburgh Press, 1964.

Casler, John O. *Four Years in the Stonewall Brigade.* 2nd ed. Major Jed Hotchkiss, ed. Girard, KS: Appeal, 1906.

Catton, Bruce. 1969. *Grant Takes Command.* Boston: Back Bay-Little, 1988.

Clissold, Stephen. *In Search of the Cid.* New York: Barnes, 1994.

Comnena, Anna. *The Alexiad of Anna Comnena.* Translated by E. R. A. Sewter. London: Penguin, 1969.

Connelly, Thomas Lawrence. 1967. *Army of the Heartland: The Army of Tennessee, 1861–1862.* Baton Rouge: Louisiana State University Press, 2001.

Cooke, John Esten. *Outlines from the Outpost.* Richard Harwell, ed. Chicago: Donnelly-Lakeside, 1961.

Cozzens, Peter. *No Better Place to Die: The Battle of Stones River.* 1990. Champaign: University of Illinois Press, 1991.

Curtius, Ernst Robert. *European Literature and the Latin Middle Ages.* Translated by Willard R. Trask. Afterword by Peter Godman. Bollingen Series. 36. Princeton: Princeton University Press, 1983.

Curtiz, Michael, director. *The Adventures of Robin Hood.* 1938. DVD. Warner, 2003.

Dabney, R.L. *Life and Campaigns of Lieut.-Gen. Thomas J. Jackson, (Stonewall Jackson).* New York: Blelock, 1866.

Dall, John. "Presbyterianism." James Hastings, ed. *Encyclopaedia of Religion and Ethics.* Bibliography by John Herkless. Vol. 9. New York: Scribner's, 1951. 13 vols. 244–71.

Daniel, John W. *Character of Stonewall Jackson.* Richmond: Schaffter and Bryant, 1868.

Daniel, W. Harrison. *Southern Protestantism in the Confederacy.* Bedford, VA: The Print Shop-Virginia Baptist Historical Society, 1989.

Daugherty, George H., Jr. "The Last Battle of El Cid." *College English* 7.3 (December 1945): 154–57.

Davis, Burke. *They Called Him Stonewall: A Life of General T. J. Jackson, C. S. A.* 1954. New York: Fairfax, 1988.

Davis, Gifford. "National Sentiment in the *Poema de Fernán Gonçález* and in the *Poema de Alfonso Onceno.*" *Hispanic Review* 16.1 (January 1948): 61–68.

Davis, Michael. *The Image of Lincoln in the South.* Knoxville: University of Tennessee Press, 1971.

Deavenport, Thomas Hopkins. "The Wartime Diary of Reverend Thomas Hopkins Deavenport. Chaplain of Third Tennessee Regiment, CSA." *Journal of Confederate History* 1.1 (Summer 1988): 35–48.

Del Río, Angel. *Desde los orígenes hasta 1700.* Vol. 1 of *Historia de la literatura española,* rev. ed. 2 vols. New York: Holt, 1963.

DeMolen, Richard L., ed. *Leaders of the Reformation.* Selinsgrove: Susquehanna University Press-Associated University Presses, 1984.

Denhardt, Robert Moorman. "The Equine Strategy of Cortés." *Hispanic American Historical Review* 18.4 (November 1938): 550–59.

D'Este, Carlo. *Patton: A Genius for War.* New York: HarperCollins, 1995.

Díaz, J., A. Tapia, B. Vázquez, and F. Aguilar. *La conquista de Tenochtitlan.* Germán Vázquez, ed. Madrid: Historia 16, 1988.

Díaz del Castillo, Bernal. *Historia verdadera de la conquista de la Nueva España.* Genaro García, ed. 2 vols. México: Oficina Tipográfica de la Secretaría de Fomento, 1904.

Dobson, R. B., and J. Taylor. *Rymes of Robin Hood: An Introduction to the English Outlaw.* Pittsburgh: University of Pittsburgh Press, 1976.

Dooley, John Edward. *John Dooley, Confederate Soldier, His War Journal.* Edited by Joseph T. Durkin, S.J. Foreword by Douglas Southall Freeman. Georgetown: Georgetown University Press, 1945.

Dubois, Gene. Telephone conversation with the author, December 3, 2003.

Duff, J. D. "Introduction." *The Civil War* (Pharsalia). By Lucan, translated by J. D. Duff. 1928. Loeb Classical Library. Cambridge: Harvard University Press, 1969. ix–xvi.

Dunaway, Rev. Wayland Fuller. *Reminiscences of a Rebel.* New York: Neale, 1913.

Dunbabin, Jean. "The Maccabees as Exemplars in the Tenth and Eleventh Centuries." *The Bible in the Medieval World: Essays in Memory of Beryl Smalley.* Edited by Katherine Walsh and Diana Wood. Studies in Church History 4. Subsidia. Oxford: Blackwell-Ecclesiastical History Society, 1985. 31–41.

Durán, Agustín, comp. and ed. *Romancero general o Colección de romances castellanos anteriores al siglo XVIII.* Biblioteca de autores españoles desde la formación del lenguaje hasta nuestros días. 10.1. Madrid: Librería de los Sucesores de Hernando, 1916.

_____, comp. and ed. *Romancero general o*

Colección de romances castellanos anteriores al siglo XVIII. Biblioteca de autores españoles desde la formación del lenguaje hasta nuestros días. 16.2. Madrid: Librería de los Sucesores de Hernando, 1921.

Earle, Peter. *Robert E. Lee*. New York: Saturday Review Press, 1973.

Easton's Bible Dictionary. Theophilos Bible Software ver. 3.1.5. 2003. <http://www.theophilos.sk>.

Eisenhower, John S. D. *The Bitter Woods: The Dramatic Story, Told at All Echelons — from Supreme Command to Squad Leader — of the Crisis That Shook the Western Coalition: Hitler's Surprise Ardennes Offensive*. New York: Putnam's, 1969.

Elliott, J.H. "The Spanish Conquest and Settlement of America." *Colonial Latin America*. Vol. 1 of *The Cambridge History of Latin America*. Leslie Bethell, ed. 11 vols. to date. Cambridge, UK: Cambridge University Press, 1984–. 149–206.

Elliott, Stephen. "Funeral Services at the Burial of the Right Rev. Leonidas Polk, D.D. Together with the Sermon Delivered in St. Paul's Church, Augusta, Ga., on June 29, 1864: Being the Feast of St. Peter the Apostle." Text scanned (OCR) by Elizabeth Wright, images scanned by Elizabeth Wright, text encoded by Christie Mawhinney and Natalia Smith. Chapel Hill: Academic Affairs Library, University of North Carolina, 1999. http://docsouth.unc.edu/elliotts/elliott.html. Call number 2559 Conf. (Rare Book Collection, UNC-CH).

Emmerich, Roland, director. *The Patriot*. DVD. Mutual/Centropolis-Columbia, 2000.

Erasmus, Desiderius. *The Julius Exclusus of Erasmus*. Translated by Paul Pascal. Introduction and notes by J. Kelley Sowards. Bloomington: Indiana University Press, 1968.

Erasmus of Rotterdam. *Praise of Folly and Letter to Martin Dorp 1515*. 1971. Translated by Betty Radice. Introduction and notes by A. H. T. Levi. Harmondsworth, UK: Penguin, 1973.

European. 1969. Anthony Thorlby, ed. Vol. 2 of *The Penguin Companion to Literature*. 4 vols. 1969–. Harmondsworth, UK: Penguin, 1976.

Faison, Frankie. Telephone interview, October 17, 2003.

Fast, Howard. *My Glorious Brothers*. Boston: Little, Brown, 1948.

Faust, Drew Gilpin. "Christian Soldiers: The Meaning of Revivalism in the Confederate Army." *Journal of Southern History* 53.1 (February 1987): 63–90.

Ferguson, Niall. *Empire: How Britain Made the Modern World*. Allen Lane, 2003. Rpt. London: Penguin, 2004.

Fichter, Andrew. *Poets Historical: Dynastic Epic in the Renaissance*. New Haven, CT: Yale University Press, 1982.

Field, Sean. "Devotion, Discontent, and the Henrician Reformation: The Evidence of the Robin Hood Stories." *Journal of British Studies* 41.1 (January 2002): 6–22.

Filson, Floyd V., introd. and exegesis by. *The Second Epistle to the Corinthians*. George Arthur Buttrick, gen. ed. Vol. 10 of *The Interpreter's Bible: The Holy Scriptures in the King James and Revised Standard Versions with General Articles and Introduction, Exegesis, Exposition for Each Book of the Bible*. 263–425. 12 vols. 1951–57. New York: Abingdon, 1953.

Fischer, David Hackett. *Albion's Seed: Four British Folkways in America*. Vol. 1 of *America: A Cultural History*. 1989–. New York: Oxford University Press, 1989.

Fisher, Terence, director. *Dracula: Prince of Darkness*. 1965. DVD. Hammer-Anchor Bay, 1998.

_____, director. *Horror of Dracula*. 1958. DVD. Hammer-Warner, 2002.

Fishwick, Marshall W. "F.F.V.'s." *American Quarterly* 11.2 (1959): 147–56.

Fletcher, R. A. "Reconquest and Crusade in Spain *c*. 1050–1150." *Transactions of the Royal Historical Society* 37 (1987): 31–47.

Fletcher, Richard. *The Quest for El Cid*. 1989. New York: Oxford University Press, 1991.

Freeman, Douglas Southall. *R. E. Lee: A Biography*. 1935. Vol. 3. 4 vols. 1934–35. New York: Scribner's, 1940.

French, Samuel Bassett. *Centennial Tale: Memoirs of Colonel "Chester" S. Bassett French, Extra Aide-de-Camp to Generals Lee and Jackson, the Army of Northern Virginia, 1861–1865*. Compiled by Glenn C. Oldaker. New York: Carlton, 1962.

Gallagher, Gary W. *Stephen Dodson Ramseur: Lee's Gallant General*. Chapel Hill: University of North Carolina Press, 1985.

Gittings, John G. *Personal Reminiscences of Stonewall Jackson, Also: Sketches and Stories*. Cincinnati: Editor Publishing, 1899.

Gontard, Friedrich. *The Chair of Peter: A History of the Papacy*. Translated by A.J. Peeler and E.F. Peeler. New York: Holt, 1964.

Grant, Michael. *The Jews in the Roman World*. New York: Scribner's, 1973.

Hamilton, C. I. "Naval Hagiography and the Victorian Hero." *Historical Journal* 23.2 (June 1980): 381–98.

Hamilton, Edith. *Mythology.* New York: Mentor-Penguin, 1942.

"Havelock." *Merriam-Webster's Biographical Dictionary.* Rev. ed. Springfield, MA: Merriam-Webster, 1995. 470.

Haythornthwaite, Philip J. *Invincible Generals: Gustavus Adolphus, Marlborough, Frederick the Great, George Washington, Wellington.* Bloomington: Indiana University Press, 1992.

Herman, Gerald. "Why Does Olivier Die before the Archbishop Turpin?" *Romance Notes* 14 (1972): 376–82.

Herman, William R. "Heroism and *Paradise Lost.*" *College English* 21.1 (October 1959): 13–17.

Herran, Kathy Neill. *They Married Confederate Officers: The Intimate Story of Anna Morrison, Wife of Stonewall Jackson and Her Five Sisters.* 2nd ed. Davidson, NC: Warren, 2000.

Hill, D.H. "General Orders, Hdqrs. Dept. of North Carolina, No. 20." *Official Records* 18. 1 (26 May 1863): Ch. 30: Correspondence, etc.-Confederate, p. 1073. 1. http://www.ehistory.com/uscw/library/or/026/1073.cfm.

_____. "The Real Stonewall Jackson." *The Century* ns 25.47 (November–April 1893–94): 623–28.

Hill, Maj. D.H. *A Consideration of the Sermon on the Mount.* Philadelphia: William S. and Alfred Martien, 1858.

_____. *Elements of Algebra.* Philadelphia: Lippincott, 1857.

Hoge, Rev. Moses D., and Governor Kemper. "Inauguration of the Jackson Statue. Introductory Address of Governor Kemper and Oration by Rev. Moses D. Hoge, D. D., on Tuesday, October 26, 1875." Richmond: R.F. Walker, superintendent of public printing, 1875.

Holsworth, Jerry W. "Quiet Courage: The Story of Winchester, Va., in the Civil War." *Blue and Gray Magazine* 15.2 (December 1997): 6–26, 47–54.

Hook, Judith. *The Sack of Rome 1527.* London: Macmillan, 1972.

Houghton, Walter E. *The Victorian Frame of Mind 1830–1870.* New Haven, CT: Yale University Press, 1957.

Howard, McHenry. *Recollections of a Maryland Confederate Soldier and Staff Officer under Johnston, Jackson and Lee.* Introduction by James I. Robertson Jr. Dayton: Morningside, 1975.

Howarth, David. *The Voyage of the Armada: The Spanish Story.* 1981. New York: Penguin, 1987.

Imboden, Brig.-Gen. John D. "Stonewall Jackson in the Shenandoah." *Battles and Leaders of the Civil War: Being for the Most Part Contributions by Union and Confederate Officers, Based upon "The Century War Series," Edited by Robert Underwood Johnson and Clarence Clough Buel, of the Editorial Staff of "The Century Magazine."* Vol. 2. 4 vols. Edison, NJ: Castle-Book Sales, n. d. 282–98.

Isidore. *Isidori Hispalensis Episcopi Etymologiarum Sive Originum Libri XX.* 1911. W. M. Lindsay, ed. Oxford: Clarendon-Oxford University Press, 1987.

Jackson, Mary Anna. *Life and Letters of General Thomas J. Jackson (Stonewall Jackson), by His Wife Mary Anna Jackson.* Introduction by Henry M. Field. New York: Harper, 1891.

Jaeger, Werner. *Archaic Greece: The Mind of Athens.* 2nd ed. Translated by Gilbert Highet. Vol. 1 of *Paideia: The Ideals of Greek Culture.* 3 vols. 1944–45. New York: Oxford University Press, 1945.

Jancovich, Mark. "'The Purest Knight of All': Nation, History, and Representation in *El Cid* (1960)." *Cinema Journal* 40.1 (Summer 2000): 79–103.

Jefferson Davis and "Stonewall Jackson" (Thomas Jonathan Jackson): The Life and Public Services of Each, with the Military Career and Death of the Latter. Philadelphia: John E. Potter, 1866.

Jewett, Robert. *The Captain America Complex: The Dilemma of Zealous Nationalism.* Philadelphia: Westminster, 1973.

Kamen, Henry. "The Decline of Spain: A Historical Myth?" *Past and Present* 81 (November 1978): 24–50.

_____. *Spain 1469–1714: A Society of Conflict.* 2nd ed. New York: Longman, 1991.

Keegan, John. *The Mask of Command.* New York: Viking, 1987.

Keen, Maurice. *The Outlaws of Medieval Legend.* Rev. ed. London: Routledge, 2000.

Keller, J. P. "The Hunt and Prophecy Episode of the *Poema de Fernán González.*" *Hispanic Review* 23.4 (October 1955): 251–58.

_____. "The Structure of the *Poema de Fernán González.*" *Hispanic Review* 25.4 (Oct. 1957): 235–46.

Kendrick, T.D. *St. James in Spain.* London: Methuen, 1960.

Knowlton, E.C. "The Allegorical Figure Genius." *Classical Philology* 15.4 (October 1920): 380–84.

_____. "Genius as an Allegorical Figure." *Modern Language Notes* 39.2 (February 1924): 89–95.

Krick, Robert K. "Stonewall Jackson's Deadly Calm." *American Heritage* 47.8 (December 1996): 56–69.

Kurman, George. "Ecphrasis in Epic Poetry." *Comparative Literature* 26.1 (Winter 1974): 1–13.

Lang, Stephen. Telephone interview, January 10, 2002.

Lawrence, Elizabeth A. "His Very Silence Speaks: The Horse Who Survived Custer's Last Stand." *Digging into Popular Culture: Theories and Methodologies in Archeology, Anthropology and Other Fields.* Ray B. Browne and Pat Browne, eds. Bowling Green, KY: Bowling Green State University Popular Press, 1991. 84–94.

Lee, William Mack. *History of the Life of Rev. Wm. Mack Lee, Body Servant of General Robert E. Lee through the Civil War: Cook from 1861 to 1865.* Text scanned (OCR) by Fiona Mills, images scanned by Fiona Mills, text encoded by Carlene Hempel and Natalia Smith. Chapel Hill: Academic Affairs Library, University of North Carolina, 1999. http://docsouth.unc.edu/leewilliam/menu.html. Call number E185.97.L48 1918 (Rare Book Colletion, UNC-CH).

Linderman, Gerald F. *Embattled Courage: The Experience of Combat in the American Civil War.* New York: Macmillan-Free Press, 1987.

Linenthal, Edward Tabor. *Changing Images of the Warrior Hero in America: A History of Popular Symbolism.* Studies in American Religion 6. New York: Mellen, 1982.

Lockhart, J.G., and Robert Southey, trans. *The Spanish Ballads, Translated by J. G. Lockhart, LL.B.; and the Chronicle of the Cid, Translated by Robert Southey.* New York: Century, 1907.

Longacre, Edward G. *General William Dorsey Pender: A Military Biography.* Conshohocken, PA: Combined Publishing, 2001.

Longhurst, John E., introduction. *Alfonso de Valdés and the Sack of Rome:* Dialogue of Lactancio and the Deacon. Trans. and ed. by John E. Longhurst. Hispanic Sources Series. 1. Albuquerque: University of New Mexico Press, 1952. 1–16.

Loomis, Roger Sherman. "Verses on the Nine Worthies." *Modern Philology* 15.4 (August 1917): 211–19.

López de Gómara, Francisco. *Conquista de México. Segunda parte de la* Crónica general de las Indias *por Francisco López de Gómara.*

Vol. 1. 2 vols. Biblioteca histórica de la Iberia 2. México: I. Escalante, 1870.

López de Velorado, Juan, ed. *Cronica del famoso cauallero Cid Ruy Diez Campeador.* Burgos, 1512. Facsim. Ed. Archer M. Huntington, ed. New York: Hispanic Society of America-Kraus Reprints, 1967.

López Estrada, Francisco. *Panorama crítico sobre el* Poema del Cid. Madrid: Castalia, 1982.

Lovelace, Richard. *The Poems of Richard Lovelace.* C.H. Wilkinson, ed. Oxford: Clarendon, 1930.

Lucan. *The Pharsalia of Lucan. Literally Translated into English Prose with Copious Notes.* Translated by H.T. Riley. London: George Bell and Sons, 1903.

Lyle, Royster Jr. "John Blair Lyle of Lexington and His 'Automatic Bookstore.'" *Virginia Cavalcade* 21.2 (1971): 20–27.

Lynch, John. *Empire and Absolutism, 1516–1598.* Vol. 1 of *Spain under the Habsburgs.* 2 vols. 1964. Oxford: Blackwell, 1964.

MacCormack, S. "Roma, Constantinoplis, the Emperor, and His Genius." *Classical Quarterly* 25.1 (May 1975): 131–50.

Maltby, William S. *The Reign of Charles V.* Basingstoke, UK: Palgrave, 2002.

Mann, Anthony, director. *El Cid.* Samuel Bronston-Ear Films-Allied Artists, 1961.

Marañón, Gregorio. *Antonio Pérez: "Spanish Traitor."* Translated by Charles David Ley. London: Hollis and Carter, 1954.

Martel, José; Hymen Alpern, eds. *Diez comedias del Siglo de Oro.* 2nd ed. 1968. Rev. Leonard Mades. Prospect Park, IL: Waveland, 1985.

Matulka, Barbara. *The Cid as a Courtly Hero: From the* Amadís *to* Corneille. New York: Institute of French Studies-Columbia University, 1928.

Matzke, John E. "The Legend of Saint George; Its Development into a Roman d'Aventure." *PMLA* 19.3 (1904): 449–78.

Maugham, Robin. *The Last Encounter.* 1972. New York: McGraw, 1973.

Maxwell, Ronald F., director. *Gettysburg.* 1993. DVD. New Line-Ted Turner, 2000.

_____, director *Gods and Generals.* DVD. Antietam Filmworks-Ted Turner, 2003.

McCorkle, Henry L. "Stonewall — a 'Rare and Eminent Christian.'" *Presbyterian Life* 2 (May 29, 1954): 15–17, 29.

McGuire, Hunter. "The Memory of 'Stonewall' Jackson." Address delivered at the Eighth Annual Banquet of the Confederate Veteran Camp of New York at the St. Denis Hotel, January 22, 1898. New York: A. H. Kellogg, 1898.

McGuire, Hunter Holmes. "Last Wound of the Late Gen. Jackson (Stonewall)." *Richmond Medical Journal* 1 (May 1866): 403–12.

McKim, Randolph H. *A Soldier's Recollections: Leaves from the Diary of a Young Confederate, with an Oration on the Motives and Arms of the Soldiers of the South.* New York: Longmans, 1911.

McWhiney, Grady. "Confederate Crackers and Cavaliers." *Plain Folk of the South Revisited.* Abilene, TX: McWhiney Foundation Press, 2002.

Megged, Aharon. "Stories without Heroes: The Singularity of the Hebrew Story." *Partisan Review* 51.3 (1984): 417–23.

Menéndez Pidal, Ramón. *Texto del Cantar y adiciones. Abreviaturas bibliográficas (p. 1225–1231).* Vol. 3 of *Cantar de mío Cid: texto, gramática y vocabulario.* 3 vols. 1944–46. Madrid: Espasa-Calpe, 1946.

_____. *Vocabulario.* Madrid: Espasa-Calpe, 1945. Vol. 2 of *Cantar de mío Cid : texto, gramática y vocabulario.* 3 vols. 1944–46. Madrid: Espasa-Calpe, 1945.

Merriman, Roger B. "Charles V's Last Paper of Advice to His Son." *American Historical Review* 28.3 (April 1923): 489–91.

Moore, Edward A. *The Story of a Cannoneer under Stonewall Jackson: In Which Is Told the Part Taken by the Rockbridge Artillery in the Army of Northern Virginia.* Introduction by Capt. Robert E. Lee Jr., and Hon. Henry St. George Tucker. New York: Neale, 1907.

Moore, R. Laurence. "Spiritualism and Science: Reflections on the First Decade of the Spirit Rappings." *American Quarterly* 24.4 (October 1972): 474–500.

Muhlenberg, Henry A. *The Life of Major-General Peter Muhlenberg of the Revolutionary Army.* Philadelphia, 1849. Facsim. ed. Ann Arbor: Xerox University Microfilms, 1975.

Nebrija, Antonio de. *Gramática de la lengua castellana.* Antonio Quilis, ed. Madrid: Editora Nacional, 1980.

Nye, Roger H. *The Patton Mind: The Professional Development of an Extraordinary Leader.* Garden City Park, NY: Avery, 1993.

O'Callaghan, Joseph F. *A History of Medieval Spain.* Ithaca: Cornell University Press, 1975.

Opie, John N. *A Rebel Cavalryman with Lee, Stuart, and Jackson.* Chicago: W. B. Conkey, 1899.

Palmer, John Williamson. "Stonewall Jackson's Way: Electronic Edition." Text scanned (OCR) by Gretchen Fricke, images scanned by Gretchen Fricke, text encoded by Elizabeth Wright and Natalia Smith. Chapel Hill: Academic Affairs Library, University of North Carolina, 1999. http://docsouth.unc. edu/palmer/palmer.html. Call number 3193.8 Conf. (Rare Book Colletion, UNC-CH).

Parkes, Henry Bamford. *A History of Mexico.* 1960. New York: American Heritage-Houghton, 1988.

Partridge, Loren, and Randolph Starn. *A Renaissance Likeness: Art and Culture in Raphael's Julius II.* Berkeley: University of California Press, 1980.

Payne, Stanley G. *Spanish Catholicism: An Historical Overview.* Madison: University of Wisconsin Press, 1984.

Pender, Samuel Turner. "General Pender." *The South-Atlantic* 1 (January 1878): 228–35.

Phillips, William D., Jr., and Carla Rahn Phillips. *The Worlds of Christopher Columbus.* Cambridge: Cambridge University Press, 1992.

Pieper, Josef. *Prudence.* Translated by Richard Winston and Clara Winston. New York: Pantheon, 1959.

Place, Edwin B. "Does Lope de Vega's *Gracioso* Stem in Part from Harlequin?" *Hispania* 17.3 (October 1934): 257–70.

Poague, William Thomas. *Gunner with Stonewall: Reminiscences of William Thomas Poague.* Edited by Monroe F. Cockrell. Introduction by Bell Irvin Wiley. Jackson, TN: McCowat-Mercer, 1957.

Pollard, Edward A. *Lee and His Lieutenants; Comprising the Early Life, Public Services, and Campaigns of General Robert E. Lee and His Companions in Arms, with a Record of Their Campaigns and Heroic Deeds.* 1867. Augusta, GA: Southern Publishing, 1870.

Pollock, J.C. *Way to Glory: The Life of Havelock of Lucknow.* London: John Murray, 1957.

Porges, Walter. "The Clergy, the Poor, and the Non-Combatants on the First Crusade." *Speculum* 21.1 (January 1946): 1–23.

Pryor, Mrs. Roger A. [Sara Agnes]. *Reminiscences of Peace and War.* Rev. ed. New York: Macmillan, 1905.

Pye, Douglas. "The Collapse of Fantasy: Masculinity in the Westerns of Anthony Mann." *The Book of Westerns.* Ian Cameron and Douglas Pye, eds. New York: Continuum, 1996. 167–73.

Quintanilha, F.E.G. "Introduction: Fernando Pessoa: The Man and His Work." *Fernando Pessoa: Sixty Portuguese Poems.* Introduced and translated by F. E. G. Quintanilha. Cardiff: University of Wales Press, 1971. xi–xlix.

Randolph, W. F. "With Stonewall Jackson at Chancellorsville." Photocopy. [n.p.]: [n.p.], 1863.

Reedy, Gerard. "'An Horatian Ode' and 'Tom May's Death.'" *Studies in English Literature, 1500–1900* 20.1 (Winter 1980): 137–51.

Reeves, Marjorie. *The Influence of Prophecy in the Later Middle Ages: A Study in Joachimism.* Oxford: Clarendon-Oxford University Press, 1969.

Reid, James, exposition by. *The Second Epistle to the Corinthians.* George Arthur Buttrick, gen. ed. Vol. 10 of *The Interpreter's Bible: The Holy Scriptures in the King James and Revised Standard Versions with General Articles and Introduction, Exegesis, Exposition for Each Book of the Bible.* 263–425. 12 vols. 1951–57. New York: Abingdon, 1953.

Reid, W. Stanford. *Trumpeter of God: A Biography of John Knox.* New York: Scribner's, 1974.

Reynolds, Kevin, director. *Robin Hood: Prince of Thieves.* 1991. DVD. Morgan Creek-Warner, 2003.

Riley, Elihu S. *"Stonewall Jackson": A Thesaurus of Anecdotes of and Incidents in the Life of Lieut.-General Thomas Jonathan Jackson, C.S.A.* Annapolis: Riley's Historic Series, 1920.

Riley-Smith, Jonathan. "Crusading as an Act of Love." *History* 65.214 (June 1980): 177–92.

Riquer, Martín de. "Bavieca, caballo del Cid Campeador, y Bauçan, caballo de Guillaume d'Orange." *La leyenda del Graal y temas épicos medievales.* Madrid: Prensa Española, 1968. 227–47.

Roberts, Michael. *Gustavus Adolphus and the Rise of Sweden.* London: English Universities Press, 1973.

Roberts, William H. "The Figure of King Sebastian in Fernando Pessoa." *Hispanic Review* 34.4 (October 1966): 307–16.

Robertson, James I., Jr. Foreword. *Recollections of a Maryland Confederate Soldier and Staff Officer under Johnston, Jackson and Lee.* By McHenry Howard. Dayton: Morningside, 1975. i–xx.

_____. *Stonewall Jackson: The Man, the Soldier, the Legend.* New York: Macmillan, 1997.

Rocha, Kali. Telephone interview, July 25, 2003.

Rogers, Paul Patrick. "Spanish Influence on the Literature of France." *Hispania* 9.4 (October 1926): 205–35.

Rose, Susan. "Islam Versus Christendom: The Naval Dimension, 1000–1600." *Journal of Military History* 63.3 (July 1999): 561–78.

Royster, Charles. *The Destructive War: William Tecumseh Sherman, Stonewall Jackson, and the Americans.* 1991. New York: Vintage-Random, 1993.

Rozear, Marvin P., and Joseph C. Greenfield, Jr. "'Let Us Cross over the River': The Final Illness of Stonewall Jackson." *Virginia Magazine of History and Biography* 103.1 (January 1995): 29–46.

Rummel, Erika. *Jiménez de Cisneros: On the Threshold of Spain's Golden Age.* Medieval and Renaissance Texts and Studies 212. Medieval and Renaissance Texts and Studies. Renaissance Masters 3. Tempe: Arizona Center for Medieval and Renaissance Studies, 1999.

Russell, Frederick H. *The Just War in the Middle Ages.* Cambridge: Cambridge University Press, 1975.

Sale, William. "Achilles and Heroic Values." *Arion* 2.3 (Autumn 1963): 87–100.

Samito, Christian G. "'Patriot by Nature, Christian by Faith': Major General William Dorsey Pender, C.S.A." *North Carolina Historical Review* 76.2 (April 1999): 162–201.

Sánchez-Albornoz, Claudio. "La auténtica batalla de Clavijo." *Cuadernos de Historia de España* 9 (1948): 94–136.

Schaffner, Franklin J., director. *Patton.* 1969. DVD. Fox, 2003.

Schafler, Norman. "'Sapientia et Fortitudo' in 'The Poema de Mío Cid.'" *Hispania* 60.1 (March 1977): 44–50.

Schildt, John W. *Jackson and the Preachers.* Parsons, WV: McClain, 1982.

Schilling, Heinz. "The Cold Hero of the Retreat." Translated by Anne Mattson. *Journal of Early Modern History* 4.3–4 (2000): 431–41.

Scott, Jeffery Warren, and Mary Ann Jeffreys. "Fighters of Faith." *Christian History Magazine* 11.1 (1992): 34–37.

Shaara, Jeff. E-mail to the author, August 6, 2002.

_____. E-mail to the author, August 7, 2002.

_____. *Gods and Generals.* New York: Ballantine-Random, 1996.

Shaara, Michael. *The Killer Angels.* 1974. New York: Ballantine-Random, 1975.

Shattuck, Gardiner H., Jr. *A Shield and Hiding Place: The Religious Life of the Civil War Armies.* Macon: Mercer University Press, 1987.

Shaw, Christine. *Julius II: The Warrior Pope.* 1993. Oxford: Blackwell, 1996.

Shifflett, Andrew. "'By Lucan Driv'n About':

A Jonsonian Marvell's Lucanic Milton." *Renaissance Quarterly* 49.4 (Winter 1996): 803–23.

Singman, Jeffrey L. *Robin Hood: The Shaping of the Legend. (Contributions to the Study of World Literature* 92.) Westport: Greenwood, 1998.

Smith, Colin. "Did the Cid Repay the Jews?" *Romania* 86 (1965): 520–38.

Smith, Gene. *Lee and Grant: A Dual Biography.* New York: McGraw, 1984.

Smith, Herbert Greenhough. *The Romance of History.* 1891. Essay Index Reprint Series. Freeport, NY: Books for Libraries Press, 1972.

Smith, James Power. "The Religious Character of Stonewall Jackson." Address delivered at the Inauguration of the Stonewall Jackson Memorial Building, Virginia Military Institute, June 23, 1897. Lexington, VA: Stonewall Jackson Memorial, 1900. 29–46.

_____. *With Stonewall Jackson in the Army of Northern Virginia.* Gaithersburg, MD: Zullo and Van Sickle, 1982.

Smith, Richard J. *Mercenaries and Mandarins: The Ever-Victorious Army in Nineteenth Century China.* John K. Fairbank, ed. Millwood, NY: KTO, 1978.

Sowards, J.K. "Erasmus and the 'Other' Pope Julius." University Studies 90. *Wichita State University Bulletin* 48.1 (February 1972): 3–26.

Sowards, J. Kelley. "Introduction: The *Julius Exclusus* and the Authorship Question." *The Julius Exclusus of Erasmus.* Translated by Paul Pascal. Introduction by J. Kelley Sowards. Bloomington: Indiana University Press, 1968. 7–32.

Starnes, D.T. "The Figure Genius in the Renaissance." *Studies in the Renaissance* 11 (1964): 234–44.

Starnes, Richard D. "Forever Faithful: The Southern Historical Society and Confederate Historical Memory." *Southern Cultures* 2.2 (1996): 177–94.

Steele, David N., and Curtis C. Thomas. *The Five Points of Calvinism Defined, Defended, Documented.* Preface by Nicole Roger. Philadelphia: Presbyterian and Reformed, 1963.

Strickland, Matthew. *War and Chivalry: The Conduct and Perception of War in England and Normandy, 1066–1217.* Cambridge: Cambridge University Press, 1996.

Strindberg, August. *Gustav Adolf.* Translated by Walter Johnson. Seattle: University of Washington Press, 1957.

Sword, Wiley. *Mountains Touched with Fire: Chattanooga Besieged, 1863.* New York: St. Martin's, 1995.

Syfret, R.H. "Marvell's 'Horatian Ode.'" *Review of English Studies* ns 12.46 (May 1961): 160–72.

Sypher, Wylie. "Introduction." *Comedy: "Laughter" and "An Essay on Comedy."* Introduction by Wylie Sypher. Garden City, NY: Doubleday, 1956. vii–xvi.

Tapia, Andrés de. "The Chronicle of Andrés de Tapia." *The Conquistadors: First-Person Accounts of the Conquest of Mexico.* Translated and edited by Patricia de Fuentes. Preface by Howard F. Cline. New York: Orion, 1963. 17–48.

Tate, Allen. *Stonewall Jackson: The Good Soldier.* 2nd ed. Preface by Thomas Landess. Nashville: J. S. Sanders, 1991.

Taylor, Lonn. "Blue-Light Presbyterians." Online posting. August 15, 1998. Texas History Forum, 1998. http://www.lsjunction.com/forum98.htm.

Tingsten, Herbert. *Victoria and the Victorians.* Translated and edited by David Grey and Eva Leckström. New York: Delacorte, 1972.

Trela, D.J. "Carlyle, the Just War and the Crimean War." *Carlyle Newsletter* 9 (Spring 1988): 2–11.

Trevor-Roper, Hugh. "Prince Rupert, 1619–82." *History Today* 33 (March 1982): 4–11.

Turville-Petre, T.F.S. "A Poem on the Nine Worthies." *Nottingham Mediaeval Studies* 27 (1983): 79–84.

Valbuena Briones, A. "El simbolismo en el teatro de Calderón: la caída del caballo." *Romanische Forschungen* 74 (1962): 60–76.

Vandiver, Frank E. *Mighty Stonewall.* 1957, 1988. College Station: Texas A&M University Press, 1995.

Van Tyne, C.H. "Influence of the Clergy, and of Religious and Sectarian Forces, on the American Revolution." *American Historical Review* 19.1 (October 1913): 44–64. Vandiver, *Mighty Stonewall.*

Wallace, Randall, director and screenwriter. *We Were Soldiers.* DVD. Icon/Wheelhouse-Paramount-Icon, 2002.

Waugh, John C. *The Class of 1846 from West Point to Appomattox: Stonewall Jackson, George McClellan and Their Brothers.* 1994. Foreword by James M. McPherson. New York: Ballantine-Random, 1999.

Weckmann, Luis. "The Middle Ages in the Conquest of America." *Speculum* 26.1 (January 1951): 130–41.

Whallon, William. "Old Testament Poetry and Homeric Epic." *Comparative Literature* 18.2 (Spring 1966): 113–31.

Wharton, H.M., comp. and ed. *War Songs and Poems of the Southern Confederacy 1861–*

1865: A Collection of the Most Popular and Impressive Songs and Poems of War Times, Dear to Every Southern Heart. Collected and Retold with Personal Reminiscences of the War. N.p.: n.p., 1904.

Willemen, Paul. "Anthony Mann: Looking at the Male." *Framework* (Summer 1981): 16–20.

Williams, Patrick. *Philip II.* Basingstoke, UK: Palgrave, 2001.

Wise, John S. "Stonewall Jackson As I Knew Him." *The Circle* (March 1908): 143–45.

Worden, Blair. "The Politics of Marvell's Horatian Ode." *Historical Journal* 27.3 (September 1984): 525–47.

Worsham, John H. *One of Jackson's Foot Cavalry.* James I. Robertson, Jr., ed. Wilmington, NC: Broadfoot, 1987.

Yates, Frances A. *Astraea: The Imperial Theme in the Sixteenth Century.* London: Routledge, 1975.

Additional Sources

Aamodt, Terrie Dopp. *Righteous Armies: Holy Cause Apocalyptic Imagery and the Civil War.* PhD diss., Boston University. Ann Arbor: UMI, 1986.

Abella, Olga. *Toward the True Balance of Love: The Role of the Women in Defining the Epic Hero, from Symbolic Object to Co-Hero.* PhD diss., State University of New York at Stony Brook, 1989.

Adams, Fannie Lewis Gwathmey. "Reminiscences of a Childhood Spent at Hayfield Plantation near Fredericksburg, Virginia during the Civil War." *William and Mary College Quarterly Historical Magazine* 2nd ser. 23.3 (July 1943): 292–97.

Adams, Michael C.C. "Review Essay: Robert E. Lee and Perspective over Time." *Civil War History* 49.1 (2003): 64–70.

Adams, Robert P. *The Better Part of Valor: More, Erasmus, Colet, and Vives, on Humanism, War, and Peace, 1496–1535.* Translated by Paul Pascal. Introduction and notes by J. Kelley Sowards. Seattle: University of Washington Press, 1962.

Adcock, F.E. *The Greek and Macedonian Art of War.* Berkeley: University of California Press, 1957.

Addicott, Jeffrey F. "Desert Storm: Robert E. Lee or William Tecumseh Sherman?" *Command* Seq. 349. 17 (July–August 1992): 38–43.

Aguado, Joseph. "La historia, la Reconquista y el protonacionalismo en el *Poema de Fer-*nán González." *Arizona Journal of Hispanic Cultural Studies* 3 (1999): 17–32.

Aguirre, J.M. "El nombre propio como fórmula oral en el *Cantar de Mío Cid.*" *La Corónica* 9.2 (Spring 1981): 107–19.

Aili, Hans. "Swedish War Propaganda in Latin, German, and Swedish." *Acta Conventus Neo-Latini Hafniensis.* Edited by Rhoda Schnur et al. Medieval and Renaissance Texts and Studies 120. Binghamton: Medieval and Renaissance Texts and Studies, 1994. 271–83.

Alexander, Gen. Edward Porter. *Fighting for the Confederacy: The Personal Recollections of General Edward Porter Alexander.* Gary W. Gallagher, ed. Chapel Hill: University of North Carolina Press, 1989.

Alexander, Ted. "Destruction, Disease, and Death: The Battle of Antietam and the Sharpsburg Civilians." *Civil War Regiments* 6.2 (1998): 143–73.

Alkon, Paul. "Alternate History and Postmodern Temporality." *Time, Literature, and the Arts: Essays in Honor of Samuel L. Macey.* ELS Monograph Ser. 61. Victoria, B.C.: University of Victoria, 1994. 65–85.

Allan, Col. William. *Stonewall Jackson, Robert E. Lee, and the Army of Northern Virginia, 1862.* Introduction by Robert K. Krick. New York: Da Capo, 1995.

Alonso, María Nieves. "El héroe de esta historia no es Hernán Cortés." *Signos* 25.31–32 (1992): 17–34.

Altamira, Rafael. *A History of Spain from the Beginnings to the Present Day.* 1949. Translated by Muna Lee. Princeton: Van Nostrand, 1958.

Althauser, Thomas J. "Patton's Honor." *Civil War Times Illustrated* 39.4 (August 2000): 25–27.

Alviar, Lourdes J. "The Soul and Eternal Life in Epic Poetry." *St. Louis University Research Journal* 11.3 (September 1980): 436–48.

Anderson, Andrew Runni. "Bucephalas and His Legend." *American Journal of Philology* 51.1 (1930): 1–21.

_____. "Heracles and His Successors: A Study of a Heroic Ideal and the Recurrence of a Heroic Type." *Harvard Studies in Classical Philology* 39 (1928): 7–58.

Anderson, Earl R. "Warrior-Bishops in *La Chanson de Roland* and *Poema de Mio Cid.*" *War, Literature and the Arts* 1.2 (1989–90): 45–72.

Anderson, Susan C. *"Kein Retter Aus der Ferne*: Ricarda Huch's Image of Gustavus II Adolphus." *Cultura Baltica: Literary Culture around the Baltic, 1600–1700.* Acta Universitatis Upsaliensis 35. Studia Germanistica Upsaliensia 0585–5160. Uppsala: [Ubsaliensis S. Academiae]-Almqvist and Wiksell, 1996. 45–51.

Andrew, Edward. "The Foxy Prophet: Machiavelli versus Machiavelli on Ferdinand the Catholic." *History of Political Thought* 11.3 (Autumn 1990): 409–22.

Andrews, Marietta Minnigerode. *Scraps of Paper.* New York: E.P. Dutton, 1929.

Anonymous. *The Poem of the Cid.* 1975. Translated by Rita Hamilton and Janet Perry. Introduction by Ian Michael. London: Penguin, 1984.

_____. *Poema de Mio Cid.* Edited and introduced by Colin Smith. Oxford: Clarendon-Oxford University Press, 1972.

_____. *The Pseudo-Turpin.* "Edited from *Bibliothèque Nationale, Fonds Latin, MS. 17656* with an additional synopsis." 1937. H. M. Smyser, ed. The Mediaeval Academy of America. Publication no. 30. New York: Kraus Reprint, 1970.

_____. "Stonewall Jackson's Body Passes through Charlottesville." *Magazine of Albemarle County History* 22 (1963–64): 21–22.

Arjona, J.H. "La introducciòn del gracioso en el teatro de Lope de Vega." *Hispanic Review* 7.1 (January 1939): 1–21.

Armistead, Samuel G. "Chronicles and Epics in the 15th Century." *La Corónica* 18.1 (1989): 103–07.

_____. "The Initial Verses of the *Cantar de Mio Cid.*" *La Corónica* 12.2 (Spring 1984): 178–86.

Armour, Peter. "The Prisoner and the Veil: The Symbolism of Michelangelo's Tomb of Julius II." *Italian Studies* 49 (1994): 40–69.

Arrizabalaga, Marie-Pierre. "History and Historiography of the Battle of Roncesvalles." *Journal of Basque Studies in America* 6 (1985): 105–18.

Aspinwall, Bernard. *Portable Utopia: Glasgow and the United States 1820–1920.* Aberdeen: Aberdeen University Press-Pergamon, 1984.

_____. "The Scots in the United States." *The Scots Abroad: Labour, Capital, Enterprise, 1750–1914.* R.A. Cage, ed. London: Croom Helm, 1985. 80–110.

Auerbach, Erich. *Mimesis: The Representation of Reality in Western Literature.* 1968. Translated by Willard R. Trask. Princeton: Princeton University Press, 1974.

Avery, A.C. [Alphonso Calhoun]. "Memorial Address on Life and Character of Lieutenant General D.H. Hill, May 10th, 1893." Raleigh: Edwards and Broughton, 1893.

Ayton, Andrew. "Military Service and the Development of the Robin Hood Legend in the Fourteenth Century." *Nottingham Medieval Studies* 36 (1992): 126–47.

Bachs, Agustí. "Gordon y el Mahdi en Khartum." *Historia y Vida* 20.233 (1987): 104–18.

Baehr, Ted, and Susan Wales, comps. *Faith in God and Generals: An Anthology of Faith, Hope, and Love in the American Civil War.* Foreword by Ron Maxwell. Nashville: Broadman, 2003.

Bailey, Matthew. "Figurative Language in the *Poema de Mío Cid* and the *Poema de Fernán González.*" *Anuario Medieval* 2 (1990): 42–63.

_____. *The Poema de Mío Cid and the Poema de Fernán González: The Transformation of an Epic Tradition.* Spanish Series. 78. Madison: Hispanic Seminary of Medieval Studies, 1993.

Bainton, Roland H. "Interpretations of the Reformation." *American Historical Review* 66.1 (October 1960): 74–84.

Balfour, Mark. "Moses and the Princess: Josephus' *Antiquitates Judaicae* and the *Chansons de Geste.*" *Medium Aevum* 64.1 (Spring 1995): 1–16.

Barbera, Raymond. "The Source and Distribution of Wealth in the *Poema de Mio Cid.*" *Romance Notes* 10 (1969): 393–99.

Barrett, C.K. *A Commentary on the Second Epistle to the Corinthians.* New York: Harper, 1973.

Barton, Simon. "From Tyrants to Soldiers of Christ: The Nobility of Twelfth-Century León-Castile and the Struggle against Islam." *Nottingham Medieval Studies* 44 (2000): 28–48.

Bataillon, Marcel. "Charles-Quint bon pasteur, selon Fray Cipriano de Huerga." *Bulletin Hispanique* 50 (1948): 398–406.

Bates, David R. "The Character and Career of Odo, Bishop of Bayeux (1049/50–1097)." *Speculum* 50.1 (January 1975): 1–20.

Baynes, John. *Morale: A Study of Men and Courage. The Second Scottish Rifles at the Battle of Neuve Chapelle, 1915.* London: Cassell, 1967.

Bean, W.G. "The Unusual War Experience of Lieutenant George G. Junkin, C.S.A." *Virginia Magazine of History and Biography* 76.2 (April 1968): 181–90.

Beck, Roy. "Love and Devotion: A Captivating New Look at the Civil War through Spectacle and Universal Themes." Rev. of *Gods and Generals,* 2002. E-mail from Patrick Gorman. July 26, 2002.

Behrman, Cynthia F. "The After-Life of General Gordon." *Albion* 3.2 (1971): 47–61.

Beidler, Philip. "Ted Turner *et al.* at Gettysburg: Or, Re-Enactors in the Attic." *Virginia Quarterly Review* 75.3 (Summer 1999): 488–503.

Bell, Aubrey F.G. *Portuguese Literature.* 1922. Oxford: Clarendon-Oxford University Press, 1970.

_____. "A Portuguese Mystic: Frei Thomé de Jesus." *Hispanic Review* 1.1 (January 1933): 50–54.

Beltrán, Luis. "The Poet, the King and the Cardinal Virtues in Juan de Mena's *Laberinto.*" *Speculum* 46.2 (April 1971): 318–32.

Bennett, P.E. "Further Reflections on the Luminosity of the *Chanson de Roland.*" *Olifant* 4.3 (March 1977): 191–204.

Berkeley, Henry Robinson. *Four Years in the Confederate Artillery: The Diary of Private Henry Robinson Berkeley.* William H. Runge, ed. Virginia Historical Society Documents. Chapel Hill: Virginia Historical Society-University of North Carolina Press, 1961.

Bertaud, Madeleine. "Rodrigue et Chimène: la formation d'un couple héroïque." *Papers on French Seventeenth Century Literature* 11.21 (1984): 521–45.

Besas, Peter. *Behind the Spanish Lens: Spanish Cinema under Fascism and Democracy.* Denver: Arden, 1985.

Best, Thomas W. *The Humanist Ulrich von Hutten: A Reappraisal of His Humor.* Chapel Hill: University of North Carolina Press, 1969.

Bickerman, Elias. "The Maccabean Uprising: An Interpretation." Edited and translated by Krishna Winston. *The Jewish Expression.* Joshua Goldin, ed. New Haven: CT Yale University Press, 1976. 66–86.

Bierbach, Christine. "'La lengua, compañera del imperio?' ou 'la filología, compañera del imperialismo?' Nebrija (1492) au service de la politique linguistique du Franquisme." *Minorisation Linguistique et Interaction.* Bernard Py and René Jeanneret, eds. Université de Neuchâtel, Recueil de Travaux Publiés par la Faculté des Lettres. 41. Neuchâtel: Faculté des Lettres, Université de Neuchâtel, 1989. 217–32.

Birdwell, Michael E. "'The Devil's Tool': Alvin York and *Sergeant York.*" *Hollywood's World War I: Motion Picture Images.* Peter C. Rollins and John E. O'Connor, eds. Bowling Green, KY: Bowling Green State University Popular Press, 1997. 121–41.

Black, C.F. "The Baglioni as Tyrants of Perugia, 1488–1540." *English Historical Review* 85.335 (April 1970): 245–81.

Blackford, Lt. Col. W[illiam]. W[illis]., C.S.A. *War Years with Jeb Stuart.* Introduction by Douglas Southall Freeman. New York: Scribner's, 1945.

Blaine, Martin E. "Gustavus Adolphus, 'True Englishmen,' and the Politics of Caroline Poetry." *Modern Language Quarterly* 59.3 (September 1998): 279–311.

Bleser, Carol K., and Lesley J. Gordon, eds. *Intimate Strategies of the Civil War: Military Commanders and Their Wives.* Oxford: Oxford University Press, 2001.

Bliese, John R.E. "Courage and Honor, Cowardice and Shame: A Motive Appeal in Battle Orations in *The Song of Roland* and in Chronicles of the Central Middle Ages." *Olifant* 20.1–4 (Fall–Summer 1995–96): 191–212.

_____. "Fighting Spirit and Literary Genre: A Comparison of Battle Exhortations in the 'Song of Roland' and in Chronicles of the Central Middle Ages." *Neuphilologische Mitteilungen* 96.4 (1995): 417–36.

_____. "The Just War as Concept and Motive in the Central Middle Ages." *Medievalia et Humanistica* 17 (1991): 1–26.

Blight, David W. "'What Will Peace among the Whites Bring?' Reunion and Race in the Struggle over the Memory of the Civil War in American Culture." *Massachusetts Review* 34.3 (Fall 1993): 393–410.

Bloom, Robert L. "The Battle of Gettysburg in Fiction." *Pennsylvania History* 43 (1976): 309–27.

Bloomfield, Morton W. "Joachim of Flora: A Critical Survey of His Canon, Teachings, Sources, Biography, and Influence." *Traditio: Studies in Ancient and Medieval History, Thought and Religion.* 13. Edited by Stephan Kuttner et al. New York: Fordham University Press, 1957. 249–311.

Bloomfield, Morton W., and Marjorie E. Reeves. "The Penetration of Joachism into Northern Europe." *Speculum* 29.4 (October 1954): 772–93.

Boldrick, Charles C. "Father Abram J. Ryan, 'the Poet-Priest of the Confederacy.'" *Filson Club History Quarterly* 46.3 (1972): 201–18.

Boney, F. N. "The Military Tradition in the South." *Midwest Quarterly* 21.2 (Winter 1980): 163–74.

Bono, Dianne M. *Cultural Diffusion of Spanish Humanism in New Spain: Francisco Cervantes de Sálazar's* Diálogo de la dignidad del hombre. American University Studies. Series II, Romance Languages and Literature. 174. New York: Lang, 1991.

Boom, Aaron M. "'We Sowed and We Have Reaped': A Postwar Letter from Braxton Bragg." *Journal of Southern History* 31.1 (February 1965): 75–79.

Bowra, C.M. *Heroic Poetry*. 1952. Martin Classical Lectures. 7. London: Macmillan, 1964.

Bratton, Mary Jo. "John Esten Cooke and His 'Confederate Lies.'" *Southern Literary Journal* 13.2 (Spring 1981): 72–91.

Brault, Gerard J. "The French Chansons de Geste." *Heroic Epic and Saga: An Introduction to the World's Great Folk Epics*. Felix J. Oinas, ed. Bloomington: Indiana University Press, 1978. 193–215.

_____. "The Religious Content of the Chansons de Geste: Some Recent Studies." *Continuations: Essays on Medieval French Literature and Language in Honor of John L. Grigsby*. Norris J. Lacy and Gloria Torrini-Roblin, eds. Birmingham, AL: Summa, 1989. 175–86.

_____. "*Sapientia* dans la *Chanson de Roland*." *French Forum* 1.2 (May 1976): 99–118.

Bravo, Antonio. "Prayer as a Literary Device in *The Battle of Maldon* and in *The Poem of the Cid*." *SELIM: Journal of the Spanish Society for Mediaeval English Language and Literature* 2 (1992): 31–46.

Brendon, Piers. *Ike: His Life and Times*. New York: Harper, 1986.

Brooks, Francis J. "Motecuzoma Xocoyotl, Hernán Cortés, and Bernal Díaz del Castillo: The Construction of an Arrest." *Hispanic American Historical Review* 75.2 (May 1995): 149–83.

Brown, Jack I. *The Shade of the Trees: A Narrative Based on the Life and Career of Lieutenant General Thomas Jonathan 'Stonewall' Jackson*. Great Neck, NY: Todd and Honeywell, 1988.

Brown, Katharine L. "Stonewall Jackson in Lexington." *Proceedings of the Rockbridge Historical Society* 9 (1975–79): 197–210.

Brown, Kent Masterson. "The Heroic Agonies of the Colonels Patton." *Virginia Country's Civil War* 1 (1983): 76–78.

Brown, S.A. "The Bayeux Tapestry." *Anglo-Norman Studies*. Proceedings of the Battle Conference on Anglo-Norman Studies. 12. Woodbridge, Suffolk: Boydell, 1989. 7–28.

Brown, S.B. "Fighting Confederate Parsons." *Confederate Veteran* 17.11 (November 1909): 541–42.

Brown, Shirley Anne. "The Bayeux Tapestry

and the *Song of Roland*." *Olifant* 6.3-4 (Spring–Summer 1979): 339–50.

Brumm, Ursula. "Definitions of Southern Identity in the Civil War Novels of John Esten Cooke." *Rewriting the South: History and Fiction*. Edited by Lothar Hönnighausen et al. Tübingen: Francke, 1993. 169–75.

Brundage, James A. "Adhemar of Puy: The Bishop and His Critics." *Speculum* 34.2 (April 1959): 201–12.

Bryant, Shasta M. *The Spanish Ballad in English*. Studies in Romance Languages 8. Lexington: University Press of Kentucky, 1973.

Buchan, John. *Oliver Cromwell*. 1934. London: Hodder and Stoughton, 1967.

Buckler, William E. "The Aesthetic of Seeing/The Morality of Being: Carlyle's Grand and Simple Insight into the Humanness of Heroism." *Prose Studies* 4.3 (December 1981): 287–300.

Buffington, Arthur H. "The Puritan View of War." *Publications of the Colonial Society of Massachusetts* 28 (April 1931): 67–86.

Bungert, Heike. "*Glory* and the Experience of African-American Soldiers in the Civil War: An Attempt at Historical Film Analysis." *Amerikastudien* 40.2 (1995): 271–82.

Burke, James F. "Alfonso X and the Structuring of Spanish History." *Revista Canadiense de Estudios Hispánicos* 9.3 (Spring 1985): 464–71.

_____. "La lógica de la imagen animal en el *Cantar de Mio Cid*." *Actas del X Congreso de la Asociación de Hispanistas, I–IV*. Vol. 1. Antonio Vilanova, ed. Barcelona: Promociones y Publicaciones Universitarias, 1992. 133–37.

Butler, George Frank. "The Spiritual Odyssey and the Renaissance Epic." PhD diss., University of Connecticut, 1988.

Caddies, Kelvin. *Kevin Costner: Prince of Hollywood*. London: Plexus, 1995.

Callaway, Mary Chilton, ed. *2 Maccabees. The New Oxford Annotated Apocrypha*. 3rd ed. New Revised Standard Version. Michael D. Coogan, ed. New York: Oxford University Press, 2001. 245–78.

Callcott, Frank. "The Cid As History Records Him." *Hispania* 17.1 (February 1934): 43–50.

Camerer, Capt. C.B. "The Last Days of 'Stonewall' Jackson." *Military Surgeon* 78 (1936): 135–40.

Campbell, Ian. "James Leslie Mitchell's *Spartacus*: A Novel of Rebellion." *Scottish Literary Journal* 5.1 (1978): 53–60.

Cantarino, Vicente, and Khalil I. Semaan. "The Spanish Reconquest: A Cluniac Holy War against Islam?" *Islam and the Medieval West: Aspects of Intercultural Relations. Papers Presented at the 9th Annual Conference of the Center for Medieval & Early Renaissance Studies, State University of New York at Binghamton.* Khalil I. Semaan, ed. Albany: State University of New York Press, 1980. 82–109

Cantor, George. *Confederate Generals: Life Portraits.* Dallas: Taylor Trade Publishing, 2000.

Carmichael, Peter S. "Christian Warriors." *Columbiad* 3 (Summer 1999): 88–106.

Carnes, Mark C., gen. ed. *Past Imperfect: History According to the Movies.* New York: Agincourt-Henry Holt, 1995.

Carroll, Michael P., and Ada Martinkus. "Col. Travis at Masada, Zealots at the Alamo: Reflections on Myth and History." *Cahiers de Littérature Orale* 16 (1984): 105–20.

Carter, John Marshall. "Sport, War, and the Three Orders of Feudal Society: 700–1300." *Military Affairs* 49.3 (July 1985): 132–39.

Carvalho, David de. "General Charles Gordon: The Making and Meaning of a Cultural Hero." *Melbourne Historical Journal* 20 (1990): 1–24.

Casa, Frank P. "The Self-Realization of the Cid." *Folio* 12 (1980): 1–11.

Casdorph, Paul D. *Lee and Jackson: Confederate Chieftains.* New York: Paragon, 1992.

Castro, Américo. *La realidad histórica de España.* 2nd rev. ed. 1965. Mexico City: Porrúa, 1975.

_____. *Santiago de España.* Buenos Aires: Emecé, 1958.

Catton, Bruce. *Grant Moves South.* 1960. Boston: Back Bay-Little, Brown, 1988.

Chadwick, Bruce. *The Reel Civil War: Mythmaking in American Film.* New York: Knopf, 2001.

Chadwick, Owen. *The Reformation.* The Pelican History of the Church 3. Penguin, 1964.

Chalon, Louis. "Le roi Búcar du Maroc dans l'histoire et dans la poésie épique espagnole." *Le Moyen Age* 75 (1969): 39–49.

Chambers, A.B. "Wisdom and Fortitude in *Samson Agonistes.*" *PMLA* 78.4 (September 1963): 315–20.

Chambers, Lenoir. *The Legend and the Man to Valley V.* Vol. 1 of *Stonewall Jackson.* 2 vols. New York: Morrow, 1959.

_____. *Seven Days I to the Last March.* Vol. 2 of *Stonewall Jackson.* 2 vols. New York: Morrow, 1959.

Chance, Jane. *Woman as Hero in Old English Literature.* Syracuse, NY: Syracuse University Press, 1986.

Chaney, William Franklin. *Duty Most Sublime: The Life of Robert E. Lee As Told through the "Carter Letters."* Baltimore: Gateway, 1996.

Charles, Elizabeth. *Three Martyrs of the Nineteenth Century: Studies from the Lives of Livingstone, Gordon, and Patteson.* New York: Negro Universities Press/Greenwood, 1969.

Chastel, André. *The Sack of Rome, 1527.* The A.W. Mellon Lectures in the Fine Arts, 1977. National Gallery of Art, Washington, D.C., No. 26. Translated by Beth Archer. Bollingen Series. 35. Princeton: Princeton University Press, 1972.

Christopherson, Merrill G., and Adolfo Leon, trans. *El Cid: Cidean Ballads: Ballads about the Great Spanish Hero El Cid.* Fennimore, WI: John Westburg, 1974.

Clark, George. "The Hero of *Maldon*: Vir Pius et Strenuus." *Speculum* 54.2 (April 1979): 257–82.

Clarke, Dorothy C. "The Cid and His Daughters." *La Corónica* 5 (1976–77): 16–21.

Clebsch, William A. *Christian Interpretations of the Civil War.* Historical Series (American Church). Philadelphia: Fortress-Facet, 1969.

Clendinnen, Inga. "Fierce and Unnatural Cruelty: Cortés and the Conquest of Mexico." *Representations* 33 (1991): 65–100.

Codman, Col. Charles R. *Drive.* Boston: Atlantic Monthly-Little, Brown, 1957.

Coe, Ada M. "Vitality of the Cid Theme." *Hispanic Review* 16.2 (April 1948): 120–41.

Cohen, Esther, and Sophia Menaché. "Holy Wars and Sainted Warriors: Christian War Propaganda in the Middle Ages." *Journal of Communication* 36.2 (Spring 1986): 52–62.

Cohen, Stan. "Colonel George S. Patton and the 22nd Virginia Infantry Regiment." *West Virginia History* 26.3 (1965): 178–90.

Comfort, William Wistar. "Notes on the 'Poema del Cid' in Further Proof of its Spanish Nationality." *Modern Philology* 1.2 (1903): 309–15.

Conerly, Porter. "Largesse of the Epic Hero as a Thematic Pattern in the *Cantar de Mio Cid.*" *Kentucky Romance Quarterly* 31.3 (1984): 281–89.

Connelly, Thomas L., and Barbara L. Bellows. *God and General Longstreet: The Lost Cause and the Southern Mind.* 1982. Baton Rouge: Louisiana State University Press, 1995.

Connelly, Thomas Lawrence. *Autumn of*

Glory: The Army of Tennessee, 1862–1865. 1971. Baton Rouge: Louisiana State University Press, 2001.

Cooke, John Esten. *Mohun; Or, the Last Days of Lee and His Paladins. Final Memoirs of a Staff Officer Serving in Virginia. From the Mss. of Colonel Surry, of Eagle's Nest.* 1869. Ridgewood, NJ: Gregg, 1968.

_____. *Stonewall Jackson: A Military Biography.* New York: D. Appleton, 1876.

_____. *Stonewall Jackson and the Old Stonewall Brigade.* Richard B. Harwell, ed. Charlottesville: Tracy W. McGregor Library-University of Virginia Press, 1954.

_____. *Surry of Eagle's Nest; Or, the Memoirs of a Staff-Officer Serving in Virginia. Edited from the Mss. of Colonel Surry, by John Esten Cooke.* Winslow Homer, illustrator. New York: Bunce and Huntington, 1866.

Coolidge, John S. "Marvell and Horace." *Modern Philology* 63.2 (November 1965): 111–20.

Copenhagen, Carol A. "Messages from Kings; Two Letters of Instruction in the Chronicles of Juan II." *La Corónica* 11.1 (Fall 1982): 109–22.

Cormier, Raymond. "From Exile to Restoration: The Cid's Vindication as Heroic Renewal. A New Study of the *Cantar de Mio Cid*." *Language Quarterly* 29.3–4 (Summer–Fall 1991): 44–49.

Cortés, Hernán. *Fernando Cortes: His Five Letters of Relation to the Emperor Charles V.* Translated and edited by Francis Augustus MacNutt. Cleveland: A.H. Clark, 1908.

_____. *Letters from Mexico.* Translated and edited by A. R. Pagden. Introduction by J. H. Elliott. New York: Orion-Grossman, 1971.

Couper, Col. William. *One Hundred Years at V.M.I.* Foreword by Gen. George C. Marshall. Richmond: Garrett and Massie, 1939.

Craig, Simon. "Breaking the Square: Dervishes Vs. Brits at the 1885 Battle of Abu Klea." *Military Heritage* 3.3 (December 2001): 79–84.

Crandell, John. "Winfield Hancock and His Grievous Angels Revisited." *Southern California Quarterly* 79.1 (1997): 1–28.

Crespo, Angel. "Le Sébastianisme de Fernando Pessoa et deux messianismes de l'Asie centrale." *Europe* 710–11 (June–July 1988): 78–87.

Crewdson, Robert L. "Bishop Polk and the Crisis in the Church: Separation or Unity?" *Historical Magazine of the Protestant Episcopal Church* 52.1 (March 1983): 43–51.

The Critical Response to Thomas Carlyle's Major Works. D.J. Trela and Rodger L. Tarr, eds. Critical Responses in Arts and Letters 27. Westport: Greenwood, 1997.

Cropp, Glynnis M. "Les vers sur les Neuf Preux." *Romania* 120.3–4 [479–480] (2002): 449–82.

Cullen, Jim. *The Civil War in Popular Culture: A Reusable Past.* Washington: Smithsonian, 1995.

Cumming, Kate. *Kate: The Journal of a Confederate Nurse.* Rev. ed. Richard Barksdale Harwell, ed. Baton Rouge: Louisiana State University Press, 1987.

Cutler, A. "The First Crusade and the Idea of Conversion." *The Muslim World* 58 (1968): 57–71, 155–64.

Dabney, Robert Lewis. *Philosophical.* 1892. C.R. Vaughan, ed. Vol. 3 of *Discussions.* Richmond: Presbyterian Committee of Publication, 1890–97.

Daniel, W. Harrison. "Protestantism and Patriotism in the Confederacy." *Mississippi Quarterly* 24.2 (Spring 1971): 117–34.

Danielou, Jean. *From Shadows to Reality: Studies in the Biblical Typology of the Fathers.* Dom Wulstan Hibberd, translator. Westminster, MD: Newman, 1960.

Davidson, Donald. *Lee in the Mountains and Other Poems, Including "The Tall Men."* New York: Scribner's, 1949.

_____. *Poems 1922–1961.* Minneapolis: University of Minnesota Press, 1966.

_____. *Still Rebels, Still Yankees and Other Essays.* Theresa Sherrer Davidson, illustrator. Baton Rouge: Louisiana State University Press, 1957.

Davidson, Lola Sharon. "Dreams, History and the Hero in the *Chansons de Geste*." *The Epic in History.* Edited by Lola Sharon Davidson et al. Sydney Studies in Society and Culture. 11. Sydney: Sydney Association for Studies in Society and Culture, 1994. 125–37.

Davis, Gifford. "The Debt of the *Poema de Alfonso Onceno* to the *Libro de Alexandre*." *Hispanic Review* 15.4 (Oct. 1947): 436–52.

_____. "The Development of a National Theme in Medieval Castilian Literature." *Hispanic Review* 3.2 (Apr. 1935): 149–61.

Davis, Stephen. "Southern Writers and the Image of Johnny Reb: Reflections of Regional Change Since Appomattox." *From the Old South to the New: Essays on the Transitional South.* Edited by Walter J. Fraser Jr. and Winfred B. Moore Jr. Contributions in American History. 93. Westport: Greenwood, 1981. 135–41.

Davis, Steve. "Turning to the Immoderate Past: Allen Tate's *Stonewall Jackson.*" *Mississippi Quarterly* 32.2 (Spring 1979): 241–51.

Davis, William C. *The Cause Lost: Myths and Realities of the Confederacy.* Lawrence: University Press of Kansas, 1996.

Dawson, Graham. *Soldier Heroes: British Adventure, Empire and the Imagining of Masculinities.* London: Routledge, 1994.

Dawson, Jan C. "The Puritan and the Cavalier: The South's Perception of Contrasting Traditions." *Journal of Southern History* 44.4 (November 1978): 597–614.

Dazey, Mary Ann. "Truth in Fiction and Myth in Political Rhetoric: The Old South's Legacy." *Southern Studies* 25.3 (Fall 1986): 305–10.

De Chasca, Edmund. "The King-Vassal Relationship in *El Poema de Mio Cid.*" *Hispanic Review* 21.3 (July 1953): 183–92.

_____. *The Poem of the Cid.* Twayne's World Authors Series 378: Spain. Boston: Hall, 1976.

Dederer, John Morgan. "The Origins of Robert E. Lee's Bold Generalship: A Reinterpretation." *Military Affairs* 49.3 (July 1985): 117–23.

De Groot, Gerard J. "Educated Soldier or Cavalry Officer? Contradictions in the Pre–1914 Career of Douglas Haig." *War and Society* 4.2 (1986): 51–69.

Delgado, J. "Hernán Cortés en la poesía española de los siglos XVIII y XIX." *Revista de Indias* 8 (1948): 393–469.

DeMolen, Richard L., ed. *Leaders of the Reformation.* Selinsgrove, PA: Susquehanna University Press-Associated University Presses, 1984.

Denhardt, Robert M. "The Truth about Cortés's Horses." *Hispanic American Historical Review* 17.4 (November 1937): 525–32.

De Ville, Oscar. "The Deyvilles and the Genesis of the Robin Hood Legend." *Nottingham Medieval Studies* 43 (1999): 90–109.

DeVries, Kelly. "A Woman as Leader of Men: Joan of Arc's Military Career." *Fresh Verdicts on Joan of Arc.* Edited by Bonnie Wheeler and Charles T. Wood. The New Middle Ages. 2. Garland Reference Library of the Humanities. 1976. New York: Garland, 1996. 3–18.

Deyermond, A. D. *Epic Poetry and the Clergy: Studies on the "Mocedades de Rodrigo."* London: Tamesis, 1968.

Deyermond, Alan. "Medieval Spanish Epic Cycles: Observations on Their Formation and Development." *Kentucky Romance Quarterly* 23 (1976): 282–303.

_____. *"Mio Cid" Studies.* Alan Deyermond, ed. Colección Támesis. Serie A — Monografías. 59. London: Tamesis, 1977.

Dietrich, Steve E. "The Professional Reading of General George S. Patton, Jr." *Journal of Military History* 53.4 (October 1989): 387–418.

Diffley, Kathleen. "The Roots of Tara: Making War Civil." *American Quarterly* 36.3 (1990): 359–72.

_____. "Where My Heart is Turning Ever: Civil War Stories and National Stability from Fort Sumter to the Centennial." *American Literary History* 2.4 (Winter 1990): 627–58.

Dobson, R.B., and J. Taylor. *Rymes of Robin Hood: An Introduction to the English Outlaw.* Pittsburgh: University of Pittsburgh Press, 1976.

Dodwell, C.R. "The Bayeux Tapestry and the French Secular Epic." *Burlington Magazine* 108.764 (November 1966): 549–60.

Donald, David. *An Excess of Democracy: The American Civil War and the Social Process.* An inaugural lecture delivered before the University of Oxford on May 2, 1960. Oxford: Clarendon-Oxford University Press, 1960.

Donald, Dorothy, and Elena Lázaro. *Alfonso de Valdés y su época.* Cuenca, Sp.: Excma. Diputación Provincial, 1983.

Dooley, Louise K. "Little Sorrel: A War-Horse for Stonewall." *Army* 25 (April 1975): 34–39.

Dorsey, Chris. "Of Iron and Stone: A Comparison of the Iron and Stonewall Brigades." *Journal of America's Military Past* 27.3 (Winter 2001): 48–67.

Douglas, D.C. "Companions of the Conqueror." *History* 28 (September 1943): 129–47.

Douglas, David. "The 'Song of Roland' and the Norman Conquest of England." *French Studies* 14.2 (April 1960): 99–116.

Dubois, G. W. "The *Poema de Fernán González* and the Waning of the Heroic Ideal." *Revue Bénédictine* 110.1–2 (2000): 124–34.

Dubois, Gene W. "Decisions, Consequences, and Characterization in the *Poema de Mio Cid.*" *Olifant* 21.3–4 (Spring–Summer 1997): 85–106.

Du Gard, René Coulet. "Victor Hugo's *Cromwell.*" *Literary Onomastics Studies* 3 (1976): 94–101.

Duggan, Joseph J. "Elpha and Alamos in the Cantar de Mio Cid, with Some Observations on Tizon." *Olifant* 17.1–2 (Spring–Summer 1992): 29–50.

———. "Legitimation and the Hero's Exemplary Function in the *Cantar de Mio Cid* and the *Chanson de Roland*." *Oral Traditional Literature: A Festschrift for Albert Bates Lord.* John Miles Foley, ed. Columbus, OH: Slavica, 1981. 217–34.

———. "Social Functions of the Medieval Epic in the Romance Literatures." *Oral Tradition* 1.3 (October 1986): 728–66.

Dunn, Peter M. "Levels of Meaning in the *Poema de Mio Cid.*" *Modern Language Notes* 85.2 (March 1970): 109–19.

———. "Theme and Myth in the *Poema de Mio Cid.*" *Romania* 83 (1962): 348–69.

Duque, Aquilino. "Camoens y Pessoa: poetas del mito." *Hispanic Review* 56.1 (Winter 1988): 39–52.

Dust, Philip. "Thomas More's Influence on Erasmus' Epigram Against Julius II." *Moreana: Bulletin Thomas More* 65–66 (1980): 99–106.

Duvall, Robert. "An Interview with Robert Duvall." Interview with Laura Schiff. *Creative Screenwriting* 5.2 (1998): 30–31.

———. Telephone interview. March 12, 2002.

Dwyer, John J. *Stonewall: A Novel.* Nashville: Broadman, 1988.

Eaton, Clement. *Freedom of Thought in the Old South.* Durham: Duke University Press, 1940.

Edwards, Kathy, and Esmé Howard. "Monument Avenue: The Architecture of Consensus in the New South, 1890–1930." *Shaping Communities.* Edited by Carter L. Hudgins and Elizabeth Collins Cromley. Shaping Vernacular Architecture. 6. Knoxville: University of Tennessee Press, 1997. 92–110.

Eggleston, George Cary. *A Rebel's Recollections.* Introduction by David Donald. Bloomington: Indiana University Press, 1959.

Elliott, J.H. "The Mental World of Hernán Cortés." *Transactions of the Royal Historical Society* 5th ser. 17 (1967): 41–58.

Elmessiri, Nur. "Burying Eternal Life in Bram Stoker's *Dracula*: The Sacred in an Age of Reason." *Alif: Journal of Comparative Poetics* 14 (1994): 101–35.

The Encyclopedia of Science Fiction. Edited by John Clute and Peter Nicholls. New York: St. Martin's Press, 1993.

Endy, Melvin B., Jr. "Just War, Holy War, and Millennialism in Revolutionary America." *William and Mary Quarterly* 3rd ser. 42.3 (January 1985): 3–25.

Erdmann, Carl. *The Origin of the Idea of Crusade.* Translated by Marshall W. Baldwin and Walter Goffart. Foreword by Marshall W. Baldwin. Princeton: Princeton University Press, 1977.

Essame, H. *Patton: A Study in Command.* New York: Scribner's, 1974.

"Famous Horses". http://www.oup.co.uk/pdf/0-19-860219-7.pdf. Oxford: Oxford University Press. 496.

Farago, Ladislas. *The Last Days of Patton.* New York: McGraw, 1981.

Farmer, William Reuben. *Maccabees, Zealots, and Josephus: An Inquiry into Jewish Nationalism in the Greco-Roman Period.* 1956. Westport: Greenwood, 1973.

Fellman, Michael. "Robert E. Lee: Postwar Southern Nationalist." *Civil War History* 46.3 (September 2000): 185–204.

Fellows, Jennifer. "St. George as Romance Hero." *Reading Medieval Studies: Annual Proceedings of the Graduate Centre for Medieval Studies in the University of Reading.* 19. Reading, Berkshire: Centre for Medieval Studies, 1993. 27–54.

Fernández, José A. "Erasmus on the Just War." *Journal of the History of Ideas* 34.2 (April–June 1973): 209–26.

Finley, C. Stephen. "'Greater Than Tongue Can Tell': Carlyle and Ruskin on the Nature of Christian Heroism." *Christianity and Literature* 34.4 (Summer 1985): 27–40.

Fisher, Elwood. "Lecture on the North and the South: Delivered before the Young Men's Mercantile Association of Cincinnati, Ohio, January 16, 1849." Charleston: A. J. Burke, 1849.

Fishwick, Marshall W. *American Heroes: Myth and Reality.* Washington: Public Affairs, 1954.

———. *Gentlemen of Virginia.* New York: Dodd, 1961.

———. *The Hero, American Style.* New York: D. McKay, 1969.

———. "Robert E. Lee, Churchman." *Historical Magazine of the Protestant Episcopal Church* 30.4 (1961): 251–65.

———. *Virginians on Olympus: A Cultural Analysis of Four Great Men.* Richmond: n.p., 1951.

Fletcher, C.R.L. *Gustavus Adolphus and the Thirty Years War.* New York: Capricorn, 1963.

Fletcher, R.A. *Saint James's Catapult: The Life and Times of Diego Gelmírez of Santiago de*

Compostela. Oxford: Clarendon-Oxford University Press, 1984.

Fletcher, Richard. 1992. *Moorish Spain.* Berkeley: University of California Press, 1993.

Forbes, Archibald. *Havelock.* London: Macmillan, 1903.

Foster, Gaines M. *Ghosts of the Confederacy: Defeat, the Lost Cause, and the Emergence of the New South 1865 to 1913.* New York: Oxford University Press, 1987.

Fraker, Charles A. "Sancho II: Epic and Chronicle." *Romania* 95 (1974): 467–507.

France, John. "Anna Comnena, the Alexiad and the First Crusade." *Reading Medieval Studies* 10 (January 1984): 20–38.

Fraser, Antonia. *Cromwell: The Lord Protector.* Reprint of *Cromwell: Our Chief of Men.* New York: Grove, 1973.

Freeman, Douglas Southall. *Cedar Mountain to Chancellorsville.* 1943. Vol. 2 of *Lee's Lieutenants: A Study in Command.* 3 vols. 1942–44. New York: Scribner's, 1971.

_____. *Gettysburg to Appomattox.* 1944. Vol. 3 of *Lee's Lieutenants: A Study in Command.* 3 vols. 1942–44. New York: Scribner's, 1972.

_____. *Manassas to Malvern Hill.* 1942. Vol. 1 of *Lee's Lieutenants: A Study in Command.* 3 vols. 1942–44. New York: Scribner's, 1970.

_____. *The South to Posterity: An Introduction to the Writing of Confederate History.* New York: Scribner's, 1939.

Friedrich, Paul, and James Redfield. "Speech as a Personality Symbol: The Case of Achilles." *Language* 54.2 (June 1978): 263–88.

Fries, Maureen. "How Many Roads to Camelot? The Married Knight in Malory's *Morte Darthur.*" *Culture and the King: The Social Implications of the Arthurian Legend. Essays in Honor of Valerie M. Lagorio.* Martin B. Schichtman and James P. Carley, eds. SUNY Series in Medieval Studies. Albany: State University of New York Press, 1994. 196–207.

Fuller, Maj.-Gen. J. F. C. *The Conduct of War: 1789–1961.* 1961. New Brunswick, NJ: Rutgers University Press, 1962.

Gallagher, Gary. "In the Shadow of Stonewall Jackson: Richard S. Ewell in the Gettysburg Campaign." *Virginia Country's Civil War* 5 (1986): 54–59.

_____. "The Making of a Hero and the Persistence of a Legend: Stonewall Jackson during the Civil War and in Popular Memory." *Lee and His Generals in War and Memory.* Gary W. Gallagher, ed. Baton Rouge: Louisiana State University Press, 1998. 101–17.

Gallagher, Gary W., ed. *The Confederate War: How Popular Will, Nationalism, and Military Strategy Could Not Stave off Defeat.* Cambridge: Harvard University Press, 1997.

_____. *Lee and His Army in Confederate History.* Chapel Hill: University of North Carolina Press, 2001.

_____. *The Third Day at Gettysburg and Beyond.* Chapel Hill: University of North Carolina Press, 1994.

García de Santa María, Alvar. *Crónica de Juan II de Castilla.* Juan de Mata Carriazo y Arroquía, ed. Madrid: Real Academia de la Historia, 1982.

García Gómez, Emilio. "El 'Rey Búcar' del *Cantar de Mío Cid.*" *Studi Orientalistici in Onore di Giorgio Levi Della Vida* 1 (1956): 371–77.

García Oro, José. "De Granada a Jerusalén: La cruzada del Cardenal Cisneros." *Archivo Iberoamericano* 51.203-04 (1991): 553–766.

Gardner, Sarah E. "'A Sweet Solace to My Lonely Heart': 'Stonewall' and Mary Anna Jackson and the Civil War." *Intimate Strategies of the Civil War: Military Commanders and Their Wives.* Ed. Carol K. Bleser and Lesley J. Gordon, eds. Oxford: Oxford University Press, 2001. 49–68, 253–58.

Gariano, Carmelo. "Lo religioso y lo fantástico en el 'Poema de Mio Çid.'" *Hispania* 47.1 (March 1964): 69–78.

Geary, John S. "The Death of the Count: Novelesque Invention in the *Crónica de Fernán González.*" *Bulletin of Hispanic Studies* 69.4 (October 1992): 321–34.

_____. "The 'Tres Monjes' of the *Poema de Fernán González:* Myth and History." *La Corónica* 19.2 (Spring 1991): 24–42.

Geerken, John H. "Homer's Image of the Hero in Machiavelli: A Comparison of Areté and Virtù." *Italian Quarterly* 53 (1970): 45–90.

Gerli, E. Michael. "Individualism and the Castilian Epic: A Survey, Synthesis, and Bibliography." *Olifant* 9.3–4 (Spring–Summer 1982): 129–50.

_____. "Nun'Alvares Pereira and the *Topos* of the Seven Virtues in the *Crónica de D. João I.*" *Romance Notes* 14 (1972): 203–06.

Gerlo, Aloïs. "Le *Iulius Exclusus e coelis* dans la correspondance d'Erasme." *La Satire Humaniste: Actes Du Colloque International Des 31 Mars, 1er et 2 Avril 1993.* Rudolf De Smet, ed. Travaux de l'Institut Interuniversitaire pour l'Étude de la Renaissance et de l'Humanisme. 11. Louvain, Belg.: Peeters, 1994. 165–87.

Gilly, Carlos. "The 'Midnight Lion,' the 'Eagle' and the 'Antichrist': Political, Religious and

Chiliastic Propaganda in the Pamphlets, Illustrated Broadsheets and Ballads of the Thirty Years War." *Nederlandsch Archief Voor Kerkgeschiedenis* 80.1 (2000): 46–62.

Gilman, Owen W., Jr. *Vietnam and the Southern Imagination*. Jackson: University Press of Mississippi, 1992.

Gimeno, Joaquín. "Las espadas del Cid en el *Poema*." *Mester* 9.1 (January 1980): 49–56.

Gimeno Casalduero, Joaquín. "La profecía medieval en la literatura castellana y su relación con las corrientes proféticas europeas." *Nueva Revista de Filología Hispánica* 20 (1971): 64–89.

Gobineau, Count Arthur. *The Golden Flower*. 1924. Translated and introduced by Ben Ray Redman. Essay Index Reprint Series. Freeport, NY: Books for Libraries Press, 1968.

Goldberg, Harriet. "The Dream Report as a Literary Device in Medieval Hispanic Literature." *Hispania* 66.1 (March 1983): 21–31.

Gómez de Castro, Alvar. *De las hazañas de Francisco Jiménez de Cisneros*. Edited and translated by José Oroz Reta. Madrid: Fundación Universitaria Española, 1984.

González, Cristina. "El conflicto entre el héroe y el rey en el *Poema de mio Cid* y en el *Libro del Cavallero Zifar*." *Studies on Medieval Spanish Literature in Honor of Charles F. Fraker*. Mercedes Vaquero and Alan Deyermond, eds. Madison: Hispanic Seminary of Medieval Studies, 1995.

Gonzalo, Pedro, and Antonio Bravo. "*Sapientia et Fortitudo* in the Anglo-Saxon Epic Heroes and in Ælfric's English Saints." *SELIM: Journal of the Spanish Society for Mediaeval English Language and Literature* 3 (1993): 72–102.

Goodman, Mark. "A Hood for the Ages: Robin: Hero, Martyr or Sherwood Forest's Prime Poacher?" *People* (July 8, 1991): 47–48.

Gordon, Charles E. *General Gordon's Khartoum Journal*. Lord Elton, ed. New York: Vanguard, 1961.

_____. *Letters of General C.G. Gordon to His Sister M.A. Gordon*. London: Macmillan, 1888.

Gorman, Patrick. E-mail to the author. October 30, 2001.

_____. E-mail to the author. December 29, 2001.

_____. E-mail to the author. May 20, 2003.

Gorosterratzu, Javier. *Don Rodrigo Jiménez de Rada: gran estadista, escritor y prelado. Estudio documentado de su vida, de los cuarenta años de su Primacía en la Iglesia de España y de su Cancillerato en Castilla; y en particular, la prueba de su asistencia al Concilio IV de Letrán, tan debatida en la controversia de la venida de Santiago a España*. Pamplona: Viuda de T. Bescansa, 1925.

Gow, June I. "Military Administration in the Confederate Army of Tennessee." *Journal of Southern History* 40.2 (May 1974): 183–98.

Graevell, Dr. *Die Charakteristik der Personen Im Rolandsliede. Ein Beitrag zur Kenntniss seiner poetischen Technik*. Heilbronn: Gebrüder Henninger, 1880.

Graham, Colin. *Ideologies of Epic: Nation, Empire and Victorian Epic Poetry*. Manchester: Manchester University Press, 1998.

Grammer, Tim. "The Myth of Wellington." The E.C. Barksdale Memorial Essays in History. 15. Arlington: Omicron Kappa Chapter of Phi Alpha Theta, University of Texas at Arlington, 1997–98. 105–51.

Grant, Carl E. "Partisan Warfare, Model 1861–1865." *Military Review* 8 (November 1958): 43–56.

Grant, Lee, Lincoln and the Radicals: Essays on Civil War Leadership by Bruce Catton, Charles P. Roland, David Donald, T. Harry Williams. Grady McWhiney, ed. Chicago: Northwestern University Press, 1964.

Grant's Lieutenants from Cairo to Vicksburg. Steven E. Woodworth, ed. Lawrence: University Press of Kansas, 2001.

Grauke, Kevin. "Vietnam, Survivalism, and the Civil War: The Use of History in Michael Shaara's *The Killer Angels* and Charles Frazier's *Cold Mountain*." *War, Literature and the Arts* 14.1–2 (2002): 45–58.

Gray, Richard. *Writing the South: Ideas of an American Region*. Cambridge: Cambridge University Press, 1986.

Greenblatt, Stephen. *Marvelous Possessions: The Wonder of the New World*. Chicago: University of Chicago Press, 1991.

Grindon, Leger. *Shadows on the Past: Studies in the Historical Fiction Film*. Philadelphia: Temple University Press, 1994.

Gross, Theodore L. "The Southern Hero." Pt. 2. *The Heroic Ideal in American Literature*. New York: The Free Press, 1971. 87–122.

Guendling, John E. "Arete: The Civilizing of an Idea." *Ball State University Forum* 12.4 (1971): 3–12.

Guild, Nicholas. "The Context of Marvell's Allusion to Lucan in 'An Horatian Ode.'" *Papers on Language and Literature* 14.4 (Fall 1978): 406–13.

Guillaume d'Orange. *Guillaume d'Orange, Four Twelfth-Century Epics*. Translated by Joan M. Ferrante. New York: Columbia University Press, 1974.

Guzmán Betancourt, Ignacio. "La lengua, ¿compañera del imperio? Destino de un 'presagio' nebrisiense en la Nueva España." *Cuadernos Americanos* 7.37 (January–February 1993): 148–64.

Gwynne, Paul. "'Tu Alter Caesar Eris': Maximilian I, Vladislav II, Johannes Michael Nagonius and the *Renovatio Imperii*." *Renaissance Studies* 10.1 (1996): 56–71.

Hall, Robert A., Jr. "'A Roland for an Oliver': Their Quarrel Again (*La Chanson de Roland, Laisses* 130–31)." *Olifant* 20.1–4 (Fall–Summer 1995–96): 109–44.

Hall, T.W. "Religion in the Army of Tennessee." *The Land We Love* 4 (1867): 127–31.

Halsey, Ashley. "Ancestral Gray Cloud over Patton." *American History Illustrated* 19.1 (Mar. 1984): 42–48.

Hamilton, Rita. "Epic Epithets in the *Poema de Mío Cid*." *Revue de Littérature Comparée* 36 (1962): 161–78.

Hansen, Harry. *The Civil War: A History*. Foreword by Richard Wheeler. New York: Penguin Putnam-New American Library, 1991.

Happel, Ralph. *Jackson*. Richmond: Eastern National Park and Monument Association, 1971.

Harney, Michael. "Movilidad social, rebelión primitiva y la emergencia del estado en el *Poema de Mio Cid*." *Mythopoesis: literatura, totalidad, ideología: ofrecido a Joseph J. Duggan por su distinguida aportación a los estudios literarios*. Juan Ramón Resina, ed. Ambitos Literarios/Ensayo. 42. Barcelona: Anthropos, 1992. 65–101.

Harris, Joseph. "Beowulf's Last Words." *Speculum* 67.1 (1992): 1–32.

Harrison, Harry. *Stars & Stripes Forever*. 1998. New York: Del Rey-Ballantine-Random, 1999.

_____. *Stars & Stripes in Peril*. 2000. New York: Del Rey-Ballantine-Random, 2001.

Hart, Thomas R. "The Author's Voice in *The Lusiads*." *Hispanic Review* 44.1 (Winter 1976): 45–55.

Hartigan, Richard Shelly. "Saint Augustine on War and Killing: The Problem of the Innocent." *Journal of the History of Ideas* 27.2 (April–June 1966): 195–204.

Harty, Kevin J. "Robin Hood on Film: Moving beyond a Swashbuckling Stereotype." *Robin Hood in Popular Culture: Violence,*

Transgression, and Justice. Thomas Hahn, ed. Cambridge, UK: Brewer, 2000. 87–100.

Harwell, Richard B., ed. *The Confederate Reader*. New York: Longmans, Green, 1957.

Haspel, Paul. "From Hero to Villain to Unknown Other: The Confederate Soldier in American Film." *Studies in Popular Culture* 19.2 (October 1996): 131–40.

Hassler, William W., ed. *The General to His Lady: The Civil War Letters of William Dorsey Pender to Fanny Pender*. Chapel Hill: University of North Carolina Press, 1965.

_____. "The Religious Conversion of General W. Dorsey Pender, C.S.A." *Historical Magazine of the Protestant Episcopal Church* 33.2 (1964): 171–78.

Hathaway, Robert L. "The Art of the Epic Epithets in the *Cantar de Mio Cid*." *Hispanic Review* 42.3 (Summer 1974): 311–21.

Hattaway, Herman, and Archer Jones. *How the North Won: A Military History of the Civil War*. Champaign: University of Illinois Press, 1991.

"Havelock." *Merriam-Webster's Biographical Dictionary*. Rev. ed. Springfield, MA: Merriam-Webster, 1995. 470.

Hay, Thomas Robson. "Braxton Bragg and the Southern Confederacy." *Georgia Historical Quarterly* 9.4 (December 1925): 267–316.

_____. "The Campaign and Battle of Chickamauga." *Georgia Historical Quarterly* 7.3 (September 1923): 213–50.

_____. "Davis, Bragg, and Johnston in the Atlanta Campaign." *Georgia Historical Quarterly* 8.1 (March 1924): 38–48.

Healy, Mark. *Heroes and Warriors: Judas Maccabeus, Rebel of Israel*. Richard Hook, illustrator. Poole, UK: Firebird, 1989.

Heath-Stubbs, John. "The Hero as a Saint: St. George." *The Hero in Tradition and Folklore; Papers Read at a Conference of the Folklore Society Held at Dyffryn House, Cardiff, July 1982*. London: Folklore Society, 1984. 1–15.

Heffner, David. "*Regnum Vs. Sacerdotium* in a Reformation Pamphlet." *Sixteenth Century Journal* 20.4 (Winter 1989): 617–30.

Hellekson, Karen. "Refiguring Historical Time: The Alternate History." Ph.D. diss., University of Kansas, 1991.

Hemelryck, T. Van. "Où Sont les 'Neuf Preux?' Variations sur un Thème Médiéval." *Studi Francesi* 41.1 (1988): 1–8.

Henderson, G.F.R. *Stonewall Jackson and the American Civil War*. Introduction by Thomas Connelly. New York: Da Capo, 1988.

Hendrickson, Kenneth E. III. *Making Saints: Religion and the Public Image of the British Army, 1809–1885.* Cranbury, NJ: Associated University Presses, 1998.

Henrickson, Bruce. "*Gettysburg*: The Killer Angels Comes to the Screen." With Ronald F. Maxwell. *Pennsylvania Heritage* 19.2 (1993): 24–31.

Hergenhan, Laurie. "Interview with Thomas Keneally." *Australian Literary Studies* 12.4 (October 2000): 453–57.

Hergesheimer, Joseph. *Swords and Roses.* New York: Knopf, 1929.

Herman, Arthur. *How the Scots Invented the Modern World: The True Story of How Europe's Poorest Nation Created Our World and Everything in It.* New York: Three Rivers-Crown-Random, 2001.

Hernon, Joseph M., Jr. *Celts, Catholics and Copperheads: Ireland Views the American Civil War.* N.p.: Ohio State University Press, 1968.

Herwaarden, Jan van. "The Origins of the Cult of St. James of Compostela." *Journal of Medieval History* 6 (1980): 1–35.

Hess, Andrew C. "The Moriscos: An Ottoman Fifth Column in Sixteenth-Century Spain." *American Historical Review* 74.1 (October 1968): 1–25.

Hess, Earl J. *Lee's Tar Heels: The Pettigrew-Kirkland-MacRae Brigade.* Chapel Hill: University of North Carolina Press, 2002.

Hibbert, Christopher. *The Great Mutiny: India 1857.* New York: Viking, 1978.

Hieatt, Constance. "Roland's Christian Heroism." *Traditio: Studies in Ancient and Medieval History, Thought and Religion.* 24. Edited by Stephan Kuttner et al. New York: Fordham University Press, 1968. 420–29.

Higginbotham, R. Don. "The Martial Spirit in the Antebellum South: Some Further Speculations in a National Context." *Journal of Southern History* 58.1 (February 1992): 3–26.

Higginbotham, Virginia. *Spanish Film under Franco.* Austin: University of Texas Press, 1988.

Hill, Maj.-Gen. D. H. *The Confederate Soldier in the Ranks: An Address by Major-General D. H. Hill, of North Carolina. Before the Virginia Division of the Association of the Army of Northern Virginia, at Richmond, Virginia, on Thursday Evening, October 22d, 1885. Also Some Account of the Banquet, including the Response of the Hon. D. B. Lucas, of West Virginia, to the Toast "Our Dead."* Richmond: Wm. Ellis Jones, 1885.

Hill, Samuel S., Jr. "The South's Two Cultures." *Religion and the Solid South.* Compiled and edited by Samuel S. Hill, Jr. Nashville: Abingdon, 1972. 24–56.

Hilton, R.H., ed. *Peasants, Knights, and Heretics: Studies in Medieval English Social History.* Cambridge: Cambridge University Press, 1976.

Hinton, Norman D. "Lucan and the *Man of Law's Tale.*" *Papers on Language and Literature* 17.4 (Fall 1981): 339–46.

Hirshson, Stanley P. *General Patton: A Soldier's Life.* New York: HarperCollins-Perennial, 2002.

The Historian's Lincoln: Pseudohistory, Psychohistory, and History. Gabor S. Boritt, ed. Champaign: University of Illinois Press, 1988.

Hobson, Fred. *Tell About the South: The Southern Rage to Explain.* Baton Rouge: Louisiana State University Press, 1983.

Holman, Andrew C. "Thomas J. Jackson and the Idea of Health: A New Approach to the Social History of Medicine." *Civil War History* 38.2 (June 1992): 131–55.

Holman, C. Hugh. "'Time … The Sheath Enfolding Experience': The Past as a Way of Life." *The Immoderate Past: The Southern Writer and History.* The 1976 Lamar Lectures at Wesleyan College. Athens: University of Georgia Press, 1977. 38–65.

Holt, J.C. *Robin Hood.* London: Thames and Hudson, 1982.

Hoover, John E. "Edward Porter Alexander." *Richmond County History* 31.1 (2000): 11–20.

Horrent, Jules. "Sur deux romances cidiens: Hélo, hélo por do viene." *Hommage au Professeur Maurice Delbouille.* Edited by Jeanne Wathelet-Willem and Madeleine Tyssens. Liège: Cahiers de l'A.R.U.Lg, 1973. 79–88.

Houghton, Walter E. *The Victorian Frame of Mind 1830–1870.* New Haven, CT: Yale University Press, 1957.

Howard, McHenry. *Recollections of a Maryland Confederate Soldier and Staff Officer Under Johnston, Jackson and Lee.* Introduction by James I. Robertson Jr. Dayton: Morningside, 1975.

Hungerford, Harold R. "'That Was at Chancellorsville': The Factual Framework of *The Red Badge of Courage.*" *American Literature* 34 (1963): 520–31.

Hunt, Frazier, and Robert Hunt. *Horses and Heroes: The Story of the Horse in America for 450 Years.* New York: Scribner's, 1949.

Hunter, Robert. "Stonewall's Church: The First Two Centuries." *Proceedings of the*

Rockbridge Historical Society 11 (1990–94): 25–40.

Hutchings, Peter. *Terence Fisher.* Manchester: Manchester University Press-Palgrave, 2001.

_____. "'We're the Martians Now': British Sf Invasion Fantasies of the 1950s and 1960s." *British Science Fiction Cinema.* Ed. I.Q. Hunter. London: Routledge, 1999. 33–47.

Hutton, Lewis J. *The Christian Essence of Spanish Literature: An Historical Study.* Studies in Art and Religious Interpretation 9. Lewiston, NY: Mellen, 1988.

Hyman, Lawrence W. "Politics and Poetry in Andrew Marvell." Part 1. *PMLA* 73.5 (December 1958): 475–79.

Inman, Arthur Crew, ed. *Soldier of the South: General Pickett's War Letters to His Wife.* Boston: Riverside, 1928.

Jackson, Mary Anna. *Life and Letters of General Thomas J. Jackson (Stonewall Jackson), by His Wife Mary Anna Jackson.* 1891. Introduction by Henry M. Field. Harrisonburg, VA: Sprinkle, 1995.

Jaeger, Werner. *The Conflict of Cultural Ideals in the Age of Plato.* Gilbert Highet, translator. Vol. 3 of *Paideia: The Ideals of Greek Culture.* 3 vols. 1944–45. New York: Oxford University Press, 1944.

_____. *In Search of the Divine Centre.* 2nd ed. Gilbert Highet, translator. Vol. 2 of *Paideia: The Ideals of Greek Culture.* 3 vols. 1944–45. New York: Oxford University Press, 1945.

Janas, John Michael. "Rhetoric, History, and the Collective Memory: The Civil War in Contemporary America." PhD diss. University of Iowa, 1994.

Jervey, James Postell. "The Confederate General." *Historical Magazine of the Protestant Episcopal Church* 7 (1938): 389–404.

Jewett, Robert, and John Shelton Lawrence. *The American Monomyth.* Garden City, NJ: Anchor, 1977.

The Jewish Expression. Joshua Goldin, ed. New Haven, CT: Yale University Press, 1976.

Jewish Society through the Ages. H.H. Ben-Sasson and S. Ettinger, eds. London: Vallentine, Mitchell, 1971.

Jiménez de Rada, Rodrigo. *Historia de los hechos de España.* Edited and translated by Juan Fernández Valverde. Madrid: Alianza, 1989.

Johnson, Clint. *Touring the Carolinas' Civil War Sites.* Winston-Salem: John F. Blair, 1996.

Johnson, Paul. "God and the Americans." *Commentary* 99.1 (January 1995): 25–45.

Johnson, Walter. Preface. *August Strindberg. Gustav Adolf.* Walter Johnson, translator. Seattle: University of Washington Press, 1957. i–ix.

Johnson, William. "Mars Attacks." *Film Comment* 33.2 (March–April 1997): 64–67.

Johnston, Mary. *Cease Firing.* N. C. Wyeth, illustrator. Boston: Houghton, 1912.

_____. *The Long Roll.* N. C. Wyeth, illustrator. Boston: Houghton, 1911.

Jones, Archer. *Civil War Command and Strategy: The Process of Victory and Defeat.* New York: The Free Press-Macmillan, 1992.

_____. *Confederate Strategy from Shiloh to Vicksburg.* Baton Rouge: Louisiana State University Press, 1961.

_____. "Jomini and the Strategy of the American Civil War, a Reinterpretation." *Military Affairs* 34.4 (December 1970): 127–31.

_____. "What Should We Think about Lee's Thinking?" *Columbiad* 1.2 (Summer 1997): 73–85.

Jones, George Fenwick. "Lov'd I not Honour More: The Durability of a Literary Motif." *Comparative Literature* 11.2 (Spring 1959): 131–43.

Jones, J. William, Rev., comp. *Army of Northern Virginia Memorial Volume.* James I. Robertson, Jr., ed. Dayton: Morningside, 1976.

_____. *Christ in the Camp, or Religion in the Confederate Army.* 1904. Introduction by Rev. J.C. Granberry. Harrisonburg, VA: Sprinkle, 1986.

Jones, Peter G. *War and the Novelist: Appraising the American War Novel.* Foreword by M.L. Rosenthal. Columbia: University of Missouri Press, 1976.

Jones, R. Tudur. "Preacher of Revolution." *Christian History* 14.2 (1995): 8–16.

Jordan, William Chester. "Saint Louis in French Epic and Drama." *Studies in Medievalism* 8 (1996): 174–94.

Jorquera, Cecilia. "*Naves quemadas:* la demitificación de un héroe histórico." *Revista Chilena de Literatura* 29 (April 1987): 171–77.

"Julius II." *Microsoft Encarta Reference Library 2003.* CD-ROM. Redman, WA: Microsoft, 1993–2002.

Kaler, Anne K. "Who Is That Monk in the Hood?: Friar Tuck, Francis of Assisi, and Robin Hood." *Journal of Popular Culture* 30.4 (Spring 1997): 51–75.

Kaske, R.E. "*Sapientia et Fortitudo* as the Controlling Theme of *Beowulf.*" *Studies in Philology* 55 (July 1958): 423–57. Reprinted in *An Anthology of Beowulf Criticism.* 1963. Lewis E. Nicholson, ed. Notre Dame: University of Notre Dame Press, 1980. 269–310.

_____. "*Sapientia et Fortitudo* in the Old English *Judith.*" *The Wisdom of Poetry: Essays in Early English Literature in Honor of Morton W. Bloomfield.* Larry D. Benson and Siegfried Wenzel, eds. Kalamazoo: Medieval Institute Publications, 1982. 15–29, 264–68.

Kaufman, Will. "'Our Rancorous Cousins': British Literary Journals on the Approach of the Civil War." *Symbiosis* 4.1 (April 2000): 35–50.

Kay, H.S. "Topography and the Relative Realism of Battle Scenes in Chansons de Geste." *Olifant* 4 (1977): 259–78.

Kedar, Benjamin Z. *Crusading and Mission: European Approaches toward the Muslims.* Princeton: Princeton University Press, 1984.

Keegan, John. "The Breaking of Armies." *MHQ: The Quarterly Journal of Military History* 11.4 (1999): 30–39.

Keen, M.H. "Chivalry and Courtly Love." *Peritia* 2 (1983): 149–69.

Keidel, George C. "Colonel Magnus Thompson's Little Confederate Museum, Leesburg, Virginia." *William and Mary Quarterly Historical Magazine* 2nd ser. 14.2 (April 1934): 171–72.

Keller, Jean Paul. *The Poet's Myth of Fernán González.* Scripta Humanistica. 81. Potomac, MD: Scripta Humanistica, 1990.

Kelso, Sylvia. "Connie Willis's Civil War: Re-Dreaming America as Science Fiction." *Foundation* 73 (Summer 1998): 67–76.

Kennedy, Billy. *The Scots-Irish in the Shenandoah Valley.* Londonderry: Causeway, 1996.

Kennedy, Patrick. *Legendary Fictions of the Irish Celts.* 1866. Detroit: Singing Bird, 1968.

Kennett, Lee. *Sherman: A Soldier's Life.* New York: HarperCollins, 2001.

Kim, Erwin. *Franklin J. Schaffner.* Metuchen, NJ: Scarecrow, 1985.

Kinder, A. Gordon. "Religious Literature as an Offensive Weapon: Cipriano de Valera's Part in England's War with Spain." *Sixteenth Century Journal* 19.2 (Summer 1988): 223–35.

King, Benjamin. *A Bullet for Stonewall.* Gretna, LA: Pelican, 1990.

King, Katherine Callen. *Achilles: Paradigms of the War Hero from Homer to the Middle Ages.* Berkeley: University of California Press, 1987.

Kinney, Martha E. "'If Vanquished I Am Still Victorious': Religious and Cultural Symbolism in Virginia's Confederate Memorial Day Celebrations, 1866–1930." *"To Perpetuate Holy Memory": Commemorating the Lost Cause in the Old Dominion.* Spec. issue. *Virginia Magazine of History and Biography* 106.3 (Summer 1998): 237–66.

Kinsolving, Mrs. Roberta Cary Corbin. "Stonewall Jackson in Winter Quarters: Memories of Moss Neck in the Winter of 1862–63." *Confederate Veteran* 20.1 (January 1912): 24–26.

Knight, Stephen. "Bold Robin Hood: The Structures of a Tradition." *Southern Review* 20.2 (July 1987): 152–67.

_____. "Robin Hood and the Royal Restoration." *Critical Survey* 5.3 (Spring 1993): 298–312.

Knoppers, Laura Lunger. "The Politics of Portraiture: Oliver Cromwell and the Plain Style." *Renaissance Quarterly* 51.4 (Winter 1998): 1282–319.

Kornweibel, Theodore, Jr. "Humphrey Bogart's *Sahara*: Propaganda, Cinema and the American Character in World War II." *American Studies* 22.1 (Spring 1981): 5–19.

Krappe, Alexander H. "Guiding Animals." *Journal of American Folklore* 55.218 (1942): 228–46.

Krappe, Alexander Haggerty. "The Dreams of Charlemagne in the *Chanson de Roland.*" *PMLA* 36.2 (June 1921): 134–41.

Kreyling, Michael. "Lee Agonistes: The Southern Hero in Midpassage." *Figures of the Hero in Southern Narrative.* Baton Rouge: Louisiana State University Press, 1987. 103–24.

Krick, Robert K. *The Smoothbore Volley That Doomed the Confederacy: The Death of Stonewall Jackson and Other Chapters on the Army of Northern Virginia.* Baton Rouge: Louisiana State University Press, 2002.

Kuter, Gen. Laurence S. "Goddammit, Georgie!" *Air Force Magazine* 56.2 (Feb. 1973): 51–56.

Kyle, David Joseph, 9th Virginia Cavalry. "How a Private Soldier Saw the Wounding of General Thomas J. Jackson." Typescript June 1994. Fredericksburg: Fredericksburg/Spotsylvania National Military Park Archives, 1895.

Kyle, Richard. "John Knox and Apocalyptic Thought." *Sixteenth Century Journal* 15.4 (1984): 449–69.

Kyle, Richard G. "John Knox Confronts the

Anabaptists." *Mennonite Quarterly Review* 75.4 (2001): 493–515.

Lacarra, María Eugenia. "El significado histórico del *Poema de Fernán González.*" *Studi Ispanici* (1979): 9–41.

Lacy, Al. *Turn of Glory.* Sisters, OR: Multnomah, 1998.

LaFantasie, Glenn W. "Becoming Joshua Lawrence Chamberlain." *North and South* 5.2 (February 2002): 29–38.

Lamers, William M. *The Edge of Glory: A Biography of General William S. Rosecrans, U.S.A.* New York: Harcourt, 1961.

Landon, Philip J. "From Cowboy to Organization Man: The Hollywood War Hero, 1940–1955." *Studies in Popular Culture* 12.1 (1989): 28–41.

Lang, Andrew. *John Knox and the Reformation.* New York: Longmans, Green, 1905.

"Last Words of Jackson." *Macon [Ga.] Telegraph,* May 25, 1863.

Lauwers, Michel. "La mort et le corps des saints: la scène de la mort dans les *Vitae* du haut Moyen Age." *Le Moyen Age* 94.1 (1988): 21–50.

Lawson, M.K. *The Battle of Hastings 1066.* Stroud, UK: Tempus, 2002.

Leavitt, Sturgis E. "Divine Justice in the *Hazañas del Cid.*" *Hispania* 12.2 (March 1929): 141–46.

Lee, David D. *Sergeant York: An American Hero.* Lexington: University Press of Kentucky, 1985.

Lee, Susan P. *Memoirs of William Nelson Pendleton, D.D.* Harrisonburg, VA: Sprinkle, 1991.

Leenhoouts, Anneke. "Forever Riding with Stonewall: Three Approaches to Henry Kyd Douglas." *Writing Lives: American Biography and Autobiography.* European Contributions to American Studies 39. Amsterdam: VU University Press, 1998. 165–71.

Lewis, C.S. "Genius and Genius." *Review of English Studies* 12.46 (April 1936): 189–94.

Liddell Hart, B. H. "How Myths Grow — Passchendaele." *Military Affairs* 28.4 (Winter 1964–65): 184–86.

Liebler, Naomi C. "Elizabethan Pulp Fiction: The Example of Richard Johnson." *Critical Survey* 12.2 (2000): 71–87.

Linenthal, Edward Tabor. *Sacred Ground: Americans and Their Battlefields.* 2nd ed. Foreword by Robert M. Utley. Urbana: University of Illinois Press, 1993.

Lintott, A.W. "Lucan and the History of the Civil War." *Classical Quarterly* ns [new series] 21.2 (November 1971): 488–505.

Ljubarskij, Jakov. "Why Is the *Alexiad* a Masterpiece of Byzantine Literature?" *Anna Komnene and Her Times.* Edited by Thalia Gouma-Peterson. Introduction by Angeliki Laiou. Garland Medieval Casebooks 29. New York: Garland, 2000. 169–85.

Loetscher, Lefferts Augustine. *A Brief History of the Presbyterians.* Rev. and enl. ed. Philadelphia: Westminster, 1958.

Long, A.L. *Memoirs of Robert E. Lee: His Military and Personal History, Embracing a Large Amount of Information Hitherto Unpublished, Together with Incidents relating to His Private Life subsequent to the War, Collected and Edited with the Assistance of Marcus J. Wright.* New York: J.M. Stoddart, 1887.

Long, Andrew Davidson. *Stonewall's "Foot Cavalryman."* Walter E. Long, ed. Austin, TX: n.p., 1965.

Longacre, Edward G. "A 'Christian Warrior' in Winter Quarters." *Manuscripts* 33.3 (Summer 1981): 241–44.

Loomie, Albert J., "Philip II's Armada Proclamation of 1597." *Recusant History* 12.5 (1974): 216–25.

Loomis, Roger Sherman. "The Heraldry of Hector or Confusion Worse Confounded." *Speculum* 42.1 (January 1967): 32–35.

López de Gómara, Francisco. *Conquista de Méjico. Segunda parte de la Crónica General de las Indias. Historiadores primitivos de Indias.* Vol. 1. Biblioteca de autores españoles desde la formación del lenguaje hasta nuestros días 22. Compiled and edited by Enrique de Vedia. Madrid: Real Academia Española, 1946. 295–455.

_____. *Cortés: The Life of the Conqueror by His Secretary.* Translated and edited by Lesley Byrd Simpson. Berkeley: University of California Press, 1965.

Louis, René. "La grande douleur pour la mort de Roland." *Cahiers de Civilisation Médiévale* 3 (1960): 62–67.

Lourie, Elena. "A Society Organized for War: Medieval Spain." *Past and Present* 35 (December 1966): 54–76.

Lovelace, Richard. *Selected Poems.* Edited and introduced by Gerald Hammond. Manchester, UK: Fyfield, 1987.

Luvaas, Jay. "Lee and the Operational Art: The Right Place, the Right Time." *Parameters* 22.3 (Autumn 1992): 2–18.

_____. *The Military Legacy of the Civil War: The European Inheritance.* Lawrence: University Press of Kansas, 1988.

Lynch, John. *Spain and America, 1598–1700.*

Spain under the Habsburgs. Vol. 2. Oxford: Blackwell, 1969.

Lytle, Andrew. *The Hero with the Private Parts: Essays by Andrew Lytle.* Baton Rouge: Louisiana State University Press, 1966.

_____. "R.E. Lee." *The Hero with the Private Parts: Essays by Andrew Lytle.* Baton Rouge: Louisiana State University Press, 1966. 227–39.

MacCormack, Sabine. "Ubi Ecclesia? Perceptions of Medieval Europe in Spanish America." *Speculum* 692.1 (January 1994): 74–100.

Macdonald, Andrew. *Howard Fast: A Critical Companion.* Westport: Greenwood, 1996.

Macedo, Hélder. "The Lusiads: Epic Celebration and Pastoral Regret." *Portuguese Studies* 6 (1990): 32–37.

Mackenzie, Donald. "Rhetoric *Versus* Apocalypse: The Oratory of the *Holy War.*" *Bunyan Studies* 2.1 (Spring 1990): 33–45.

MacKenzie, John M. "Heroic Myths of Empire." *Popular Imperialism and the Military 1850–1950.* John M. MacKenzie, ed. Manchester: Manchester University Press, 1992. 109–38.

Maddex, Jack P., Jr. "'The Southern Apostasy' Revisited: The Significance of Proslavery Christianity." *Marxist Perspectives* 2 (Fall 1979): 132–41.

Malvasi, Mark G. *The Unregenerate South: The Agrarian Thought of John Crowe Ransom, Allen Tate, and Donald Davidson.* Baton Rouge: Louisiana State University Press, 1997.

Manigault, Gabriel. "The Decay of Religion in the South." *The Land We Love* 5 (July 1868): 202–14.

Manzanares de Cirre, M. "Las cien doncellas: trayectoria de una leyenda." *PMLA* 81.3 (June 1966): 179–84.

Maravall, José Antonio. *Carlos V y el pensamiento político del Renacimiento.* Madrid: Instituto de Estudios Políticos, 1960.

_____. "La idea de Reconquista en España durante la Edad Media." *Arbor* 28 (1954): 1–37.

Margolis, Nadia. *Joan of Arc in History, Literature, and Film: A Select, Annotated Bibliography.* New York: Garland, 1990.

Markus, R.A. "Saint Augustine's Views on the 'Just War.'" *The Church and War: Papers Read at the Twenty-First Summer Meeting and the Twenty-Second Winter Meeting of the Ecclesiastical History Society.* Studies in Church History 20. N.p.: Blackwell, 1983. 1–13.

Marsh, Catherine. *Sketch of the Life of Capt. Hedley Vicars, the Christian Soldier.* Text and images scanned (OCR) by Jeanine Cali, text encoded by Melissa Maxwell Edwards and Natalia Smith. Chapel Hill: Academic Affairs Library, University of North Carolina, 1999. http://docsouth.unc.edu/marsh/marsh.html. Call number VCp970.79 M36s (North Carolina Collection, UNC-CH).

Marshall, Gen. S.L.A. "Leaders and Leadership." Reprinted from *The Armed Forces Officer* (Washington: GPO, 1975): 47–57. *Military Leadership: In Pursuit of Excellence.* Robert L. Taylor and William E. Rosenbach, eds. Foreword by Malham M. Wakin. Boulder, CO: Westview, 1984. 37–48.

Martínez, J. Victorio. "Nota sobre la épica medieval española: el motivo de la rebeldía." *Revue Belge de Philologie et d'Histoire* 50 (1972): 777–92.

Martínez Mata, Emilio. "El romance del Conde Arnaldos y el más allá." *Actas del III Congreso de la Asociación Hispánica de Literatura Medieval, I-II.* María Isabel Toro Pascua, ed. Biblioteca Española del Siglo XV. Salamanca: Departamento de Literatura Española e Hispanoamericana, 1994. 605–11.

Marvell, Andrew. *The Complete Poems.* Rev. ed. Elizabeth Story Donno, ed. London: Penguin, 1996.

Mason, Roger A. "Knox, Resistance and the Moral Imperative." *History of Political Thought* 1.3 (Autumn 1980): 411–36.

Mathews, Donald G. *Religion in the Old South.* Chicago: University of Chicago Press, 1977.

Matthews, John. *Robin Hood: Green Lord of the Wildwood.* Foreword by Richard Carpenter. Afterword by Chesca Potter. Glastonbury, UK: Gothic Image, 1993.

Mattingly, Gerald. *Renaissance Diplomacy.* Boston: Riverside-Houghton, 1955.

Matzke, John E. "Contributions to the History of the Legend of Saint George, with Special Reference to the Sources of the French, German and Anglo-Saxon Metrical Versions." *PMLA* 17.4 (1902): 464–535.

Maurer, Christopher. "Un monarca, un imperio y una espada: Juan Latino y el soneto de Hernando de Acuña sobre Lepanto." *Hispanic Review* 61.1 (Winter 1993): 35–51.

Maurice, Maj.-Gen. Sir Frederick. *Robert E. Lee the Soldier.* 1925. Freeport, NY: Books for Libraries Press, 1975.

Maxwell, Jerry H. "Lewis A. Armistead: 'The Bravest of the Brave.'" *Lincoln Herald* 90.1 (Spring 1988): 2–9.

Mazzeo, Joseph Anthony. "Cromwell as Machiavellian Prince in Marvell's 'An Horatian Ode.'" *Journal of the History of Ideas* 21.1 (January–March 1960): 1–17.

McCaslin, Robert B. *Lee in the Shadow of*

Washington. Baton Rouge: Louisiana State University Press, 2001.

McClellan, H[enry]. B. *I Rode with Jeb Stuart: The Life and Campaigns of Major General J.E.B. Stuart*. 1958. Introduction by Burke Davis. [New York]: Da Capo, 1994.

McCullough, W. Stewart. *The History and Literature of the Palestinian Jews from Cyrus to Herod: 550 B C to 4 B C*. Toronto: University of Toronto Press, 1975.

McDonald, Forrest, and Grady McWhiney. "[Celtic Mist over the South]: A Response." *Journal of Southern History* 52.4 (November 1986): 547–48.

McGuire, Judith. *Diary of a Southern Refugee during the War*. New York: New York Times-Arno, 1972. Reprint of *Diary of a Southern Refugee during the War, by a Lady of Virginia*. 1867.

McKim, Randolph H. *A Soldier's Recollections: Leaves from the Diary of a Young Confederate, with an Oration on the Motives and Arms of the Soldiers of the South*. Text and images scanned (OCR) by Carlene Hempel, text encoded by Jill Kuhn and Natalia Smith. Chapel Hill: Academic Affairs Library, University of North Carolina, 1999. http://docsouth.unc.edu/mckim/mckim. html. Call number 973.78 M15s 1910 (Davis Library, UNC-CH).

_____. *The Soul of Lee: By One of His Soldiers*. New York: Longmans, Green, 1918.

McMurry, Richard M. *John Bell Hood and the War for Southern Independence*. 1982. Lincoln: University of Nebraska Press, 1992.

McWhiney, Grady. "Crackers and Cavaliers: Shared Courage." *Plain Folk of the South Revisited*. Samuel C. Hyde, Jr., ed. Baton Rouge: Louisiana State University Press, 1997. 187–202.

_____. "Saving the Best from the Past." *Alabama Review* 32 (October 1979): 243–72.

Mejías-López, William. "Hernán Cortés y su intolerancia hacia la religión azteca en el contexto de la situación de los conversos y moriscos." *Bulletin Hispanique* 95.2 (1993): 623–46.

Mendeloff, Henry. "What Did the Bishop Say? (*Cantar de Mio Cid*, 1294–95)." *Romance Notes* 11 (1970): 670–73.

Menéndez Pidal, Ramón. *Crítica del texto. Gramática*. Vol. 1 of *Cantar de mío Cid: texto, gramática y vocabulario*. 3 vols. 1944–46. Madrid: Espasa-Calpe, 1944.

_____. *La España del Cid*. Abbr. ed. 1939. Obras de Menéndez Pidal 6–7. 2 vols. Madrid: Espasa-Calpe, 1969.

_____. *Idea imperial de Carlos V*. 5th ed. Madrid: Espasa-Calpe, 1963.

_____. "Poesía e historia en el *Mio Cid*." *Nueva Revista de Filología Hispánica* 3.2 (1949): 113–29.

_____. "La política y la Reconquista en el siglo XI." *Revista de Estudios Políticos* 19 (1947): 1–35.

_____. "The Significance of the Reign of Isabella the Catholic, according to Her Contemporaries." *Spain in the Fifteenth Century 1369–1516: Essays and Extracts by Historians of Spain*. Edited by Roger Highfield. Translated by Frances M. López-Morillas. London: Macmillan, 1972. 380–404.

Mertz, Gregory A. "'A Severe Day on All the Artillery': Stonewall Jackson's Artillerists and the Defense of the Confederate Right." *Civil War Regiments* 4 (1995): 70, 75, 94–95.

Michel, Alain. "Du héros antique au Roland furieux: le chevalier, le courtisan, le saint." *Le Roman de Chevalerie au Temps de la Renaissance*. Centre de Recherche sur la Renaissance. 12. Paris: J. Touzot, 1987. 11–27.

Miletich, John S. "The Religious-Heroic/Human Tension in Berceo's *Vida de Santo Domingo*." *Studia in Honorem Prof. M. de Riquer*. 4. Barcelona: Quaderns Crema, 1991. 263–08.

Miller, Richard F., and Robert F. Mooney. "Across the River and into the Streets: The 20th Massachusetts Infantry and the Street Fight for Fredericksburg." *Civil War Regiments* 4.4 (1994): 101–26.

Miller, William J. "'And Ye Shall Chase Your Enemies': Jed Hotchkiss, Stonewall Jackson, and the Valley Campaign." *Virginia Cavalcade* 43.3 (Winter 1994): 112–31.

Misrahi, Jean, and William L. Hendrickson. "Roland and Oliver: Prowess and Wisdom, the Ideal of the Epic Hero." *Romance Philology* 33.3 (February 1980): 357–72.

Mommsen, Theodor E. "The Accession of the Helvetian Federation to the Holy League: An Unpublished Bull of Pope Julius II of March 17, 1512." *Journal of Modern History* 20.2 (June 1948): 123–32.

Montgomery, Walter Alexander. "Life and Character of Major-General W.D. Pender: Memorial Address, May 10, 1894." Raleigh: Edwards and Broughton, 1894.

Moore, F.G. "On Urbs Aeterna and Urbs Sacra." *Transactions of the American Philological Association (1869–1896)* 25 (1894): 34–60.

Moore, Lt. Gen. Harold G., and Joseph L. Galloway. *We Were Soldiers Once ... and Young*.

Ia Drang— the Battle That Changed the War in Vietnam. HarperTorch-HarperCollins, 2002.

Morley, John. Oliver Cromwell: Fully Illustrated with Carefully Authenticated Portraits in Public and Private Galleries, and with Reproductions of Contemporaneous Prints in the British Museum and the University of Oxford. New York: Century, 1901.

Morreale, Margharita. "Para la interpretación de los versos 'Allí hablara el cavallo, bien oiréis lo que hablara: —1Rebentar devía la madre que a su hijo no esperava!' en El Romance del Cid y Búcar." Thesaurus 27 (1972): 122–27.

Morrill, John, ed. Oliver Cromwell and the English Revolution. London: Longman, 1990.

Moynahan, Brian. The Faith: A History of Christianity. New York: Doubleday, 2002.

Muir, Edwin. John Knox: Portrait of a Calvinist. 1929. Freeport, NY: Books for Libraries Press, 1971.

Mullen, Edward J. "The Role of the Supernatural in El Libro del Cavallero Zifar." Revista de Estudios Hispánicos 5 (1971): 257–68.

Musto, Ronald G. "Just Wars and Evil Empires: Erasmus and the Turks." Renaissance Society and Culture: Essays in Honor of Eugene F. Rice, Jr. New York: Italica, 1991. 197–216.

Napier, Lt. Col. John Hawkins, III. "The Militant South Revisited: Myths and Realities." Alabama Review 33 (October 1980): 243–65.

Neely, Mark E., Jr., Harold Holzer, and Gabor S. Boritt. The Confederate Image: Prints of the Lost Cause. Chapel Hill: University of North Carolina Press, 1987.

Nelson, Lynn H., and Arnold H. Weiss. "An Early Life of Francisco Jiménez de Cisneros." Franciscan Studies 42.20 (1982): 156–65.

Nelson, Ralph. "Erasmus and Grotius on Just War Theory." Canadian Journal of Netherlandic Studies 6.1 (Spring 1985): 40–60.

Nevinson, John L. "A Show of the Nine Worthies." Shakespeare Quarterly 14.2 (Spring 1963): 103–07.

The New Oxford Annotated Apocrypha. 3rd ed. New Revised Standard Version. Michael D. Coogan, ed. New York: Oxford University Press, 2001.

Niven, Alexander C., ed. and introd. "The War Time Reminiscences of Thomas Julian Skinker II." Journal of Confederate History 7 (1991): 19–31.

Nock, Arthur Darby. "The Emperor's Divine Comes." Journal of Roman Studies 37.1–2 1947): 102–16.

Nofi, Albert A. "Stonewall in the Shenandoah, 1862." Strategy and Tactics 67 (1978): 4–11.

Nolan, Alan T. Lee Considered: General Robert E. Lee and Civil War History. 1991. Chapel Hill: University of North Carolina Press, 1995.

Northup, George Tyler. "The Cloak Episode in Spanish." Modern Language Notes 23.3 (March 1908): 92.

Nye, Roger H. "The Patton Library Comes to West Point." Assembly 46 (February 1988): 18–19.

Nyrop, Cristoforo [Nyrop, Kristoffer]. Storia dell'epopea francese nel medio evo. Translated by Egidio Gorra. Torino: Ermanno Loescher, 1888.

O'Brien, Kevin E. "'Blaze Away and Stand to It, Boys': Captain Jack Donovan and the Irish Brigade at Fredericksburg." The Irish Sword 20.80 (1996): 121–30.

O'Brien, Matthew C. "John Esten Cooke, George Washington, and the Virginia Cavaliers." Virginia Magazine of History and Biography 84.3 (July 1976): 259–65.

_____. "'The Sweet Teaching of the Heavens': The Significance of the Sun in Civil War Literature." Helios: From Myth to Solar Energy: Images of the Sun in Myth and Legend; the Sun in Literature, Art, and Music; Solar Energy Projections— Social, Economic, Legal, and Political. Albany: Institute for Humanistic Studies, State University of New York, 1978. 411–20.

O'Grady, Kelly J. Clear the Confederate Way! The Irish in the Army of Northern Virginia. Foreword by Robert K. Krick. Mason City, IA: Savas, 2000.

Oliveira, Vítor de. "Les epithètes de D. Sébastien, Roi du Portugal (1554–1578)." Quadrant 7 (1988): 25–66.

Olsson, Kurt. "The Cardinal Virtues and the Structure of John Gower's Speculum Meditantis." Journal of Medieval and Renaissance Studies 7.1 (Spring 1977): 113–48.

O'Reilly, Clare. "'Maximus Caesar et Pontifex Maximus': Giles of Viterbo Proclaims the Alliance between the Emperor Maximilian and Pope Julius II." Augustiniana 22 (1972): 80–117.

Oroz, Rodolfo. "Los animales en el Cantar de Mio Cid." Miscelânea de Filologia, Literatura e História Cultural, à Memória de Francisco Adolfo Coelho (1847–1919). Boletim de Filologia. Lisbon: Centro de estudos filológicos (Portugal) 44.10-11 (1949–50): 273–78.

Oses, Boris. "Santa Cruz y Medina-Sidonia, almirantes de la Gran Armada." *Revista de Marina* 3 (1983): 347–66.

Osterweis, Rollin G. *The Myth of the Lost Cause 1865–1900*. Hamden, CT: Archon-Shoe String, 1973.

Owen, D.D.R. "The Secular Inspiration of the *Chanson de Roland*." *Speculum* 37.3 (July 1962): 390–400.

Painter, Sidney. *French Chivalry: Chivalric Ideas and Practices in Mediaeval France*. Ithaca: Great Seal-Cornell University Press, 1957.

_____. "The Ideas of Chivalry." *Johns Hopkins Alumni Magazine* 23 (1935): 218–32.

Parks, Joseph H. *General Leonidas Polk C.S.A.: The Fighting Bishop*. Baton Rouge: Louisiana State University Press, 1962.

Parry, Richard. *That Fateful Lightning: A Novel of Ulysses S. Grant*. New York: Ballantine, 2000.

Pastor, Ludwig. *The History of the Popes, from the Close of the Middle Ages: Drawn from the Secret Archives of the Vatican and Other Original Sources*. Frederick Ignatius Antrobus, ed. Vol. 6. 40 vols. London: Routledge, 1938–61.

Patton, Beatrice Ayer. "A Soldier's Reading." *Armor* 61 (November–December 1952): 10–11.

Pearsall, Cornelia D.J. "Burying the Duke: Victorian Mourning and the Funeral of the Duke of Wellington." *Victorian Literature and Culture* 27.2 (1999): 365–93.

Pease, Arthur Stanley. "Some Aspects of Invisibility." *Harvard Studies in Classical Philology* 53 (1942): 1–36.

Pélaprat, Jean-Marie. "Chimène et le Cid, pour de vrai." *Historama* 8 (October 1984): 72–75.

Pérez de Urbel, Justo. "Notas histórico-críticas sobre el poema de 'Fernán González.'" *Boletín* 174 (1970): 42–75.

Perret, Geoffrey. *A Country Made by War: From the Revolution to Vietnam — the Story of America's Rise to Power*. Tricentennial Booklet. 2. New York: Random, 1989.

Perry, Mark. *Conceived in Liberty: Joshua Chamberlain, William Oates, and the American Civil War*. 1997. New York: Penguin, 1999.

Pettegrew, John. "'The Soldier's Faith': Turn-of-the-Century Memory of the Civil War and the Emergence of Modern American Nationalism." *Journal of Contemporary History* 31.1 (January 1996): 49–73.

Phillips, E.C. *Sir Henry Havelock and Colin Campbell, Lord Clyde*. London: Cassell, 1885.

Phillips, Kevin. *The Cousins' Wars: Religion, Politics, and the Triumph of Anglo-America*. New York: Basic-Perseus, 1999.

Pierce, Frank. "Ancient History in 'Os Lusíadas.'" *Hispania* 57.2 (May 1974): 220–30.

_____. "Camões' Adamastor." *Hispanic Studies in Honour of Joseph Manson*. Dorothy M. Atkinson and Anthony H. Clarke, eds. Oxford: Dolphin, 1972. 207–15.

_____. "The Place of Mythology in the Lusiads." *Comparative Literature* 6.2 (Spring 1954): 97–122.

_____. "Some Themes and Their Sources in the Heroic Poem of the Golden Age." *Hispanic Review* 14.2 (April 1946): 95–103.

Pierce, Peter. "The Sites of War in Thomas Keneally." *Australian Literary Studies* 12.4 (October 1986): 442–52.

Place, Edwin B. "Once More, Durendal." *Modern Language Notes* 64.3 (March 1949): 161–64.

Polk, William M. *Leonidas Polk: Bishop and General*. 2nd ed. New York: Longmans, Green, 1915.

Porter, Jean. "Heroism Reclaimed: Three Medieval Perspectives on Heroism and Christian Virtue." *Providence: Studies in Western Civilization* 6.1 (Spring–Summer 2001): 109–26.

Porter, Roy. "Heroes in the Old Testament: The Hero As Seen in the Book of Judges." *The Hero in Tradition and Folklore; Papers Read at a Conference of the Folklore Society Held at Dyffryn House, Cardiff, July 1982*. London: Folklore Society, 1984. 90–111.

Posey, Walter Brownlow. "Influence of Slavery Upon the Methodist Church in the Early South and Southwest." *Mississippi Valley Historical Review* 17.4 (March 1931): 530–42.

Potter, William. *Beloved Bride: The Letters of Stonewall Jackson to His Wife, 1857–1863*. San Antonio: Vision Forum, 2002.

Powell, Brian. *Epic and Chronicle: The Poema de Mio Cid and the Crónica de Veinte Reyes*. R. M. Walker, ed. Texts and Dissertations. 18. London: Modern Humanities Research Assn., 1983.

Power, J. Tracy. "'There Stands Jackson Like a Stone Wall': The Image of General Thomas J. 'Stonewall' Jackson in the Confederate Mind, July 1861–November 1862." MA thesis. Emory University, 1984.

Power, Mary. "The Uniqueness of Rocinante." *Romance Languages Annual*. Purdue University Monographs in Romance Languages. 2. West Lafayette, IN: Purdue Research Foundation, 1990. 520–23.

Prado Coelho, Jacinto do. "O nacionalismo utópico de Fernando Pessoa." *Colóquio* 31 (December 1964): 53–57.

Prados, John. "Cobra: Patton's 1944 Summer Offensive in France." *Strategy and Tactics* 65 (1977): 4–8.

Prestage, Edgar, ed. *Chivalry: A Series of Studies to Illustrate Its Historical Significance and Civilizing Influence, by Members of King's College, London.* 1928. New York: AMS, 1974.

Prien, Hans-Jürgen. "La justificación de Hernán Cortés de su conquista de México y de la conquista española de América." Translated by María-Rosa Fernández Cuesta. *Revista Complutense de Historia de América* 22 (1996): 11–31.

Prinz, Friedrich E. "King, Clergy and War at the Time of the Carolingians." *Saints, Scholars and Heroes: Studies in Medieval Culture in Honour of Charles W. Jones.* Margot H. King and Wesley M. Stevens, eds. Carolingian Studies 2. Collegeville, MN: Hill Monastic Manuscript Library, Saint John's Abbey and University-UMI Research Press, 1979. 301–29.

Prioli, Carmine A. "King Arthur in Khaki: The Medievalism of General George S. Patton, Jr." *Studies in Popular Culture* 10.1 (1987): 42–50.

Pryor, J.H. "The Oaths of the Leaders of the First Crusade to Emperor Alexius I Comnenus: Fealty, Homage — Pistis, Douleia." *Parergon* 2 (1984): 111–41.

Pryor, John H. "The Naval Battles of Roger of Lauria." *Journal of Medieval History* 9.3 (September 1983): 179–216.

Puhvel, Martin. "*Beowulf* and Irish Battle Rage." *Folklore* 79 (1968): 40–47.

Pullen, John J. *Joshua Chamberlain: A Hero's Life and Legacy.* Mechanicsburg, PA: Stackpole, 1999.

Quint, David. "Voices of Resistance: The Epic Curse and Camões's Adamastor." *Representations* 27 (Summer 1989): 111–41.

Rabil, Albert, Jr., ed. *Humanism beyond Italy.* Vol. 2 of *Renaissance Humanism: Foundations, Forms, and Legacy.* 3 vols. 1988. Philadelphia: University of Pennsylvania Press, 1988.

Raible, Christopher Gist. "Dracula: Christian Heretic." *Christian Century* 96.4 (1979). Rpt. in Dracula: *The Vampire and the Critics.* Margaret L. Carter, ed. Studies in Spec-ulative Fiction. 19. Ann Arbor; London: UMI Research Press, 1988. 105–07.

Ramsey, Rev. James B. "True Eminence Founded on Holiness. A Discourse Occasioned by the Death of Lieut. Gen. T.J. Jackson. Preached in the First Presbyterian Church of Lynchburg, May 24th, 1863." Text scanned (OCR) by Allen Vaughn, images scanned by Allen Vaughn and Christie Mawhinney; text encoded by Christie Mawhinney and Jill Kuhn. Chapel Hill: Academic Affairs Library, University of North Carolina, 1999. http://docsouth. unc.edu/ramsey/ramsey.html. Call number 2600 Conf. (Rare Book Collection, UNC-CH).

Randall, J.G. "The Civil War Restudied." *Journal of Southern History* 6.4 (November 1940): 439–57.

Randall, J.G., and Richard N. Current. *Lincoln the President: Last Full Measure.* Introduction by Richard N. Current. Champaign: University of Illinois Press, 1991.

Randle, Brig. Gen. Edwin W. "The General and the Movie." *Army* (September 1971): 17–22.

Ratcliffe, Marjorie. "Women and Marriage in the Medieval Spanish Epic." *Journal of the Rocky Mountain Medieval and Renaissance Association* 8 (January 1987): 1–14.

Raugh, Capt. Harold E., Jr. "Garnet Joseph Wolseley and the Gordon Relief Expedition." *Army Quarterly and Defence Journal* 117.4 (1987): 441–51.

Ray, William E., Jr. "Pairing and Temporal Perspective in the *Chanson de Roland.*" *French* 50.2 (December 1976): 243–50.

Reardon, Carol. "Chipping Away at 'the Marble Man': Robert E. Lee in Civil War History." *Reviews in American History* 21.3 (September 1993): 415–23.

_____. *Pickett's Charge in History and Memory.* Chapel Hill: University of North Carolina Press, 1997.

Reeves, Marjorie E. *Medieval and Renaissance Studies.* Richard Hunt and Raymond Klibansky, eds. Vol. 1, 1941–43 (London: Warburg Inst., 1943). Rpt. in The Liber Figurarum *of Joachim of Fiore.* Nendeln, Lichtenstein: Kraus Reprint, 1969. 57–81.

Reid, W. Stanford. "John Knox's Theology of Political Government." *Sixteenth Century Journal* 19.4 (Winter 1988): 529–40.

Reidenbaugh, Lowell. "Mary Anna Morrison Jackson." *Lincoln Herald* 85.2 (Summer 1983): 100–08.

Reilly, Timothy. "Genteel Reform versus

Southern Allegiance: Episcopalian Dilemma in Old New Orleans." *Historical Magazine of the Protestant Episcopal Church* 44.4 (1975): 437–50.

Reynolds, Winston A. "Gonzalo de Illescas and the Cortés-Luther Confrontation." *Hispania* 45.3 (September 1962): 402–04.

_____. "Hernán Cortés y los héroes de la antigüedad." *Revista de Filología Española* 45 (1962): 259–71.

_____. "Martin Luther and Hernán Cortés: Their Confrontation in Spanish Literature." *Hispania* 42.1 (March 1959): 66–70.

Richards, Warren J. *God Blessed Our Arms with Victory: The Religious Life of Stonewall Jackson.* Introduction by Henry M. Field. New York: Vantage, 1986.

Riley, John Allen. "John Esten Cooke: A Comparative Study of His Non-Fiction Writings on the Civil War." PhD diss., University of Georgia, 1967.

Rilliet, Jean. *Zwingli: Third Man of the Reformation.* Translated by Harold Knight. Philadelphia: Westminster, 1964.

Ritson, Joseph. *Robin Hood: A Collection of All the Ancient Poems, Songs, and Ballads.* 1795, 1823. Introduction by Jim Lees. Totowa, NJ: Rowman and Littlefield, 1972.

Roberts, John Hawley. "The Nine Worthies." *Modern Philology* 19.3 (February 1922): 297–305.

Roberts, Kenneth. *Trending into Maine.* Illustrated by N.C. Wyeth. Boston: Little, Brown, 1938.

Roberts, Michael. *Essays in Swedish History.* Minneapolis: University of Minnesota Press, 1967.

Roberts, William H. "The Figure of King Sebastian in Fernando Pessoa." *Hispanic Review* 34.4 (October 1966): 307–16.

Robertson, James I., Jr. "Chaplain William E. Wiatt: Soldier of the Cloth." *Rank and File: Civil War Essays in Honor of Bell Irvin Wiley.* James I. Robertson, Jr. and Richard M. McMurry, eds. San Rafael, CA: Presidio, 1976. 113–36.

_____. "Soldiers." *Encyclopedia of the Confederacy.* Richard N. Current, gen. ed. Vol. 4. New York: Simon, 1993. 1494–1501.

Robinson, I. S. *Authority and Resistance in the Investiture Contest: The Polemical Literature of the Late Eleventh Century.* Manchester: Manchester University Press-Holmes and Meier, 1978.

_____. "Gregory VII and the Soldiers of Christ." *History* 58 (1973): 169–92.

Robinson-Durso, Pamela. "Chaplains in the Confederate Army." *Journal of Church and State* 33.4 (Autumn 1991): 747–63.

Robson, C.A. "The Character of Turpin in the Chanson de Roland." *Medium Aevum* 10 (1941): 97–100.

Rogers, Edith Randam. *The Perilous Hunt: Symbols in Hispanic and European Balladry.* Studies in Romance Languages 22. Lexington: University Press of Kentucky, 1980.

Rojinsky, David M. "Grammatical Rule for a 'Scriptural' Empire: A Reading of the Prologue to Nebrija's *Gramática Castellana.*" *Hispanic Journal* 21.1 (Spring 2000): 151–63.

Roland, Charles P. "The Generalship of Robert E. Lee." *Grant, Lee, Lincoln and the Radicals: Essays on Civil War Leadership by Bruce Catton, Charles P. Roland, David Donald, T. Harry Williams.* Grady McWhiney, ed. Chicago: Northwestern University Press, 1964. 31–71.

Rolinson, Dave, and Nick Cooper. "'Bring Something Back': The Strange Career of Professor Bernard Quatermass." *Journal of Popular Film and Television* 30.3 (Fall 2002): 158–65.

Rollins, Richard. "Pickett's Charge and the Principles of War." *North and South* 4.5 (June 2001): 12–24.

Ronnick, Michele Valerie. "Classical Elements in Edward Pollard's Idea of Southern Honor and 'The Lost Cause' 1865–66." *Classical and Modern Literature* 18.1 (1997): 15–23.

Roosevelt, Theodore. "The Sword of the Lord and of Gideon." *Rank and File: True Stories of the Great War.* Illustrated by Capt. John W. Thomason Jr. New York: Scribner's, 1928. 31–59.

Rose, H.J. "On the Original Significance of the Genius." *Classical Quarterly* 17.2 (April 1923): 57–60.

Rose, William. "El número en el 'Romancero del Cid.'" *Hispania* 44.3 (September 1961): 454–56.

Rosenberg, Bruce A. *Custer and the Epic of Defeat.* University Park: Pennsylvania State University Press, 1974.

Rosenstone, Robert A., ed. *Revisioning History: Film and the Construction of a New Past.* Princeton, NJ: Princeton University Press, 1995.

Rosenzweig, Sidney. *Casablanca and Other Major Films of Michael Curtiz.* Ann Arbor: UMI Research Press, 1982.

Rossi, Giuseppe Carlo. "La 'verità' su D. Sebastiao Re di Portogallo." *Annali Istituto Universitario Orientale, Napoli, Sezione Romanza* 25.2 (July 1983): 693–707.

Rossi-Ross, Elena. "Style and Pathos in the Spanish Epic *Planctus*: An Aesthetic Critique of *Roncesvalles*." *Revista Canadiense de Estudios Hispánicos* 12.3 (Spring 1988): 429–45.

Rubel, Capt. Robert C. "Gettysburg and Midway: Historical Parallels in Operational Command." *Naval War College Review* seq. 349. 48.1 (Winter 1995): 96–110.

Rubin, Louis D. "The Image of an Army." *Southern Writers: Appraisals in Our Time*. R. L. Simonini, ed. Charlottesville, VA: Ayer, 1964. Rpt. in *The Curious Death of the Novel: Essays in American Literature*. Baton Rouge: Louisiana State University Press, 1967. 183–206.

Rubin, Louis D., ed. *The American South: Portrait of a Culture*. Baton Rouge: Louisiana State University Press, 1980. 245–53.

_____. *The Curious Death of the Novel: Essays in American Literature*. Baton Rouge: Louisiana State University Press, 1967.

Runge, William H., ed. *Four Years in the Confederate Artillery: The Diary of Private Henry Robinson Berkeley*. Virginia Historical Society Documents. Chapel Hill: U of North Carolina Press, 1961.

Russell, D.S. *The Jews from Alexander to Herod*. The New Clarendon Bible. Old Testament 5. Oxford: Oxford University Press, 1967.

Russell, P. E. "San Pedro de Cardeña and the Heroic History of the Cid." *Medium Aevum* 27.2 (1958): 57–79.

Ryan, Edward A. "The Rejection of Military Service by the Early Christians." *Theological Studies* 13 (1952): 1–32.

Samet, Elizabeth D. "'Adding to My Book and My Coffin': The Unconditional Memoirs of Ulysses S. Grant." *PMLA* 115.5 (October 2000): 1117–24.

Sargeant, Amy. "Making and Selling Heritage Culture: Style and Authenticity in Historical Fictions on Film and Television." *British Cinema, Past and Present*. Justine Ashby and Andrew Higson, eds. London: Routledge, 2000. 301–15.

Savage, Douglas. *The Court Martial of Robert E. Lee: A Historical Novel*. Mechanicsburg, PA: Combined-Stackpole, 1993.

Sánchez Alonso, B. "Nebrija, historiador." *Revista de Filología Española* 29 (1945): 129–52.

Scarborough, Connie L. "Characterization in the *Poema de Fernán González*: Portraits of the Hero and the Heroine." *Literary and Historical Perspectives of the Middle Ages*. Proceedings of the 7th Southeastern Medieval Association Meeting, 1981. Edited by Patricia W. Cummins et al. Morgantown: West Virginia University Press, 1982. 52–65.

Schackel, Paul A. "Memorializing Landscapes and the Civil War in Harpers Ferry." *Look to the Earth: Historical Archaeology and the American Civil War*. Clarence R. Geier, Jr. and Susan E. Winter, eds. Knoxville: University of Tennessee Press, 1994. 256–70.

Schenck, Martin. *Up Came Hill: The Story of the Light Division and Its Leaders*. Harrisburg, PA: Stackpole, 1958.

Schevill, Rudolph. "Erasmus and the Fate of a Liberalistic Movement prior to the Counter Reformation." *Hispanic Review* 5.2 (April 1937): 103–23.

Schroeder, Horst. "The Nine Worthies: A Supplement." *Archiv Für das Studium der Neueren Sprachen und Literaturen* 218.133 (1981): 330–40.

Schwetman, John W. "The Appearance of Saint George above the English Troops at Agincourt: The Source of a Detail in the Historical Record." *Notes and Queries* 41.3 (September 1994): 304–07.

Scott, Jeffery Warren. "Fighters of Faith." With Mary Ann Jeffreys. *Christian History Magazine* 11.1 (1992): 34–37.

Scully, Terence. "The Ordeal at Roncesvalles: *Francs e paiens, as les vus ajustez*." *Olifant* 7.3 (Spring 1980): 213–34.

Seabra, José Augusto. "Sampaio Bruno, the Inquisition, and Sebastianism." Translated by Maria do Carmo Ponte. *Portuguese Studies* 4 (1988): 176–80.

Sears, Stephen W. *Chancellorsville*. Boston: Houghton Mifflin, 1996.

_____. *Landscape Turned Red: The Battle of Antietam*. Boston: Houghton Mifflin, 1983.

_____. *To the Gates of Richmond: The Peninsula Campaign*. Boston: Mariner-Houghton, 2001.

Sears, Theresa Ann. "The Blood of Innocents: War, Law, and Violence in the *Poema de Mio Cid*." *Medieval Perspectives* 4–5 (1989–90): 172–84.

_____. "Spain's Medievalist Project in the New World." *Studies in Medievalism* 5 (1993): 200–08.

Semmes, Brig. Gen. Harry H. "General George S. Patton, Jr.'s Psychology of Leadership." *Quartermaster Review* 35 (September–October 1955): 8–9, 144–64.

Setton, K.M. "Lutheranism and the Turkish Peril." *Balkan Studies* 3 (1962): 136–65.

Severino, Alexandrino P. "Fernando Pessoa: A Modern Lusiad." *Hispania* 67.1 (March 1984): 52–60.

Seward, Desmond. *The Monks of War: The Military Religious Orders.* Rev. ed. Harmondsworth, UK: Penguin, 1995.

Shaara, Jeff. *The Last Full Measure.* 1998. New York: Ballantine-Random, 2000.

Shamkovich, Tatyana Ivanovna. "Saintly Hero: Mythological, Epic and Ecclesiastical Perspectives on the Image of the Saint in Medieval Hagiography." PhD diss., State University of New York at Stony Brook, 1991.

Sharma, K.N. "Spartacus: Variations on a Theme." *Modern Studies and Other Essays in Honour of Dr. R.K. Sinha.* ed. R.C. Prasad and A.K. Sharma, eds. New Delhi: Vikas, 1987. 261–72.

Shattuck, Gardiner H., Jr. "'Appomattox as a Day of Blessing': Religious Interpretations of Confederate Defeat in the New South Era." *Journal of Confederate History* 7 (1991): 1–18.

Shields, Randolph Tucker, Jr. "Recollections of a Liberty Hall Volunteer." *Proceedings of the Rockbridge Historical Society* 9 (1975–79): 9–23.

Shoop, Michael I., comp. *The Genealogies of the Jackson, Junkin, and Morrison Families.* 2nd ed. Lexington, VA: Garland Gray Memorial Research Center, Stonewall Jackson House, Historic Lexington Foundation, 1981.

Shrader, Charles R. "The Influence of Vegetius' *De Re Militari*." *Military Affairs* 45.4 (December 1981): 167–72.

Siberry, Elizabeth. *The New Crusaders: Images of the Crusades in the Nineteenth and Early Twentieth Centuries.* Aldershot, UK: Ashgate, 2000.

Silver, James W. 1957. *Confederate Morale and Church Propaganda.* New York: Norton, 1967.

Simmons, Merle E. "The Spanish Epics." *Heroic Epic and Saga: An Introduction to the World's Great Folk Epics.* Felix J. Oinas, ed. Bloomington: Indiana University Press, 1978. 216–35.

Simms, L. Moody, Jr. "Father Abram Joseph Ryan: Poet of the Lost Cause." *Lincoln Herald* 73.1 (1971): 3–7.

Simpson, John A. "The Cult of the 'Lost Cause.'" *Tennessee Historical Quarterly* 34.4 (Winter 1975): 350–61.

Simpson, John Mack. "Sapientia et Fortitudo: The Drama of Athalsteinn." *Journal of Indo-European Studies* 7 (1979): 113–20.

Skeyhill, Tom, ed. *Sergeant York: His Own Life Story and War Diary.* Garden City, NY: Doubleday, 1928.

Skinner, Quentin. "The Origins of the Calvinist Theory of Revolution." *After the Reformation: Essays in Honor of J.H. Hexter.* Barbara C. Malament, ed. Philadelphia: University of Pennsylvania Press, 1980. 309–30.

Smail, R.C. *Crusading Warfare (1097–1193).* 1956. Cambridge, UK: Cambridge University Press, 1967.

Smalley, Beryl. *Historians in the Middle Ages.* London: Thames and Hudson, 1974.

Smith, Bradley. *Spain: A History in Art.* Garden City, NY: Gemini-Smith-Doubleday, n.d.

Smith, Catherine B. R. "Death and Funerals of Bishop-General Leonidas Polk." *Richmond County History* 15.1 (Winter 1983): 31–41.

Smith, Colin. "The Cid as Charlemagne in the *Leyenda de Cardeña.*" *Romania* 97 (1976): 510–31.

_____. "The Diffusion of the Cid Cult: A Survey and a Little-Known Document." *Journal of Medieval History* 6 (1980): 37–60.

_____. "Further French Analogues and Sources for the *Poema de Mio Cid.*" *La Corónica* 6 (1977): 14–21.

_____. "Historiadores de Cardeña." *Studia in Honorem Prof. M. de Riquer.* 2. Barcelona: Quaderns Crema, 1987. 433–52.

_____. *The Making of the* Poema de Mio Cid. Cambridge: Cambridge University Press, 1983.

_____. "On the Distinctiveness of the 'Poema de Mio Cid.'" *'Mio Cid' Studies.* Alan Deyermond, ed. Colección Támesis. Serie A—Monografías. 59. London: Tamesis, 1977. 161–94.

_____. "A Reading Public for the *Poema de Mio Cid*?" *La Corónica* 22.1 (Fall 1993): 1–14.

Smith, Francis H. *Discourse on the Life and Character of Lt. Gen. Thos. J. Jackson, (C. S. A.), Late Professor of Natural and Experimental Philosophy in the Virginia Military Institute. By Francis H. Smith, A. M. Read before the Board of Visitors, Faculty and Cadets, July 1ˢᵗ, 1863. With Proceedings of the Institution, in Honor of the Illustrious Deceased.* Richmond: Ritchie and Dunaway, 1863. 29–46.

Sobchack, Vivian. "'Surge and Splendor': A Phenomenology of the Hollywood Historical Epic." *Representations* 29 (Winter 1990): 24–49.

Socarrás, Cayetano J. "The Cid and the Bishop of Valencia (An Historical Interpretation)." *Iberoromania* 3 (1971): 101–11.

Somville, Pierre. "Un ancêtre mythique de

Saint Georges: Héraklès." *Cahiers Internationaux de Symbolisme* 95–97 (2000): 301–05.

Sorrel, Gen. G. Moxley. *Recollections of a Confederate Staff Officer*. Introduction by Sen. John W. Daniel. New York: Neale, 1905.

South, Betty. "We Called Him 'Uncle Georgie.'" *Quartermaster Review* 33 (January–February 1954): 28–29, 122–25.

Sowards, J. K. "Erasmus and the Making of *Julius Exclusus*." University Studies 60. *Wichita State University Bulletin* 40.3 (August 1964): 3–16.

_____. "Thomas More, Erasmus and Julius II: A Case of Advocacy." *Moreana* 24 (1969): 81–99.

Spears, Jack. *The Civil War on Screen and Other Essays*. Cranbury, NJ: Barnes, 1977.

Spitzer, Leo. "The Name of Roland's Sword." *Language* 15.1 (January–March 1939): 48–50.

Spivakovsky, Erika. "The Legendary 'First' Military Campaign of Philip II." *Renaissance Quarterly* 21.4 (Winter 1968): 413–19.

Squire, J. C., ed. *If It Had Happened Otherwise*. Introduction by Sir John Wheeler-Bennett. 2nd ed. London: Sedgwick and Jackson, 1972.

Stableford, Brian. "Speculative Fiction in Europe and America: The Past and the Future." *New York Review of Science Fiction* 10.7 [115] (March 1998): 1, 8–12.

Stablein, Patricia Harris. "The Structure of the Hero in the *Chanson de Roland*: Heroic Being and Becoming." *Olifant* 5 (1977): 105–19.

Stace, C. "The Slaves of Plautus." *Greece and Rome* 2nd ser. 15.1 (April 1968): 64–77.

Stackpole, E.J. "Generalship in the Civil War." *Military Affairs* 24.2 (Summer 1960): 57–67.

Stallybrass, Peter. "'Drunk with the Cup of Liberty': Robin Hood, the Carnivalesque, and the Rhetoric of Violence in Early Modern England." *The Violence of Representation: Literature and the History of Violence*. Nancy Armstrong and Leonard Tennenhouse, eds. London: Routledge, 1989. 45–76.

Stammerjohan, George R. "Captain Winfield Scott Hancock in Los Angeles?" *Periodical* 19.1 (Fall 1992): 128–35.

Stanchak, John E. "*Gods and Generals*." Van Redin, photog. *Civil War Times Illustrated* 41.6 (December 2002): 30–37.

Stanford, W.B. "Ghosts and Apparitions in Homer, Aeschylus, and Shakespeare." *Hermathena* 56 (1940): 84–92.

Stanley, Brian. "Christian Responses to the Indian Mutiny of 1857." *The Church and War: Papers Read at the Twenty-First Summer Meeting and the Twenty-Second Winter Meeting of the Ecclesiastical History Society*. W.J. Sheils, ed. 23. N.p.: Blackwell, 1983. 277–89.

Staples, W.E. "Some Aspects of Sin in the Old Testament." *Journal of Near Eastern Studies* 6.2 (April 1947): 56–79.

Starkie, Walter. *Grand Inquisitor: Being an Account of Cardinal Ximenez de Cisneros and His Times*. London: Hodder and Stoughton, 1940.

Steckmesser, Kent L. "Robin Hood and the American Outlaw: A Note on History and Folklore." *Journal of American Folklore* 79 (1966): 348–55.

Steiner, Paul E. *Medical-Military Portraits of Union and Confederate Generals*. Philadelphia: Whitmore, 1968.

Stern, Philip Van Doren. *Robert E. Lee: The Man and the Soldier*. New York: Bonanza, 1963.

Stokesbury, James L. "Leadership as an Art." *Military Leadership*. James H. Buck and Lawrence J. Korb, eds. (Beverly Hills, CA: Sage, 1981): 23–40. Rpt. in *Military Leadership: In Pursuit of Excellence*. Robert L. Taylor and William E. Rosenbach, eds. Foreword by Malham M. Wakin. Boulder: Westview, 1984. 5–21.

Sullivan, Walter. "The Fading Memory of the Civil War." *The American South: Portrait of a Culture*. Louis D. Rubin, ed. Baton Rouge: Louisiana State University Press, 1980. 245–53.

Sutherland, Daniel E. "Abraham Lincoln, John Pope, and the Origins of Total War." *Journal of Military History* 56.4 (October 1992): 567–86.

Tanner, John S. "When God Is Hero: Worshipping God as Hero in Carlyle and Hopkins." *Hopkins Quarterly* 10.4 (Winter 1984): 145–63.

Tanner, Robert G. *Retreat to Victory? Confederate Strategy Reconsidered*. Wilmington, DE: Scholarly Resources, 2001.

Tate, Allen. *Memoirs and Opinions, 1926–1974*. Chicago: Swallow, 1975.

_____."Ode to the Confederate Dead." *Collected Poems, 1919–1976*. New York: Farrar, 1977. 20–23.

_____. "A Southern Mode of the Imagination." *Essays of Four Decades*. Chicago: Swallow, 1968. 577–92.

Tate, Robert B. "Mythology in Spanish Historiography of the Middle Ages and the Renaissance." *Hispanic Review* 22.1 (January 1954): 1–18.

_____. "Nebrija the Historian." *Bulletin of Hispanic Studies* 34 (1957): 125–46.

Taylor, Gen. Richard. *Deconstruction and Reconstruction: Personal Experiences of the Civil War*. 1879. New introd. by T. Michael Parrish. New York: Da Capo, 1995.

Taylor, John M. *Duty Faithfully Performed: Robert E. Lee and His Critics*. Foreword by Rod Paschall. Dulles, VA: Brassey's, 1999.

_____. "General Hancock: Soldier of the Gilded Age." *Pennsylvania History* 32.2 (1965): 187–96.

Taylor, Mark. "From Agincourt to Bastogne: George S. Patton and the Rhetoric of Saint Crispin's Day." *Upstart Crow* 19 (1999): 98–109.

Taylor, Michael W., ed. *The Cry Is War, War, War: The Civil War Correspondence of Lts. Burwell Thomas Cotton and George Job Huntley, 34th Regiment North Carolina Troops, Pender-Scales Brigade of the Light Division, Stonewall Jackson's and A. P. Hill's Corps, Army of Northern Virginia, CSA*. Dayton: Morningside, 1994.

_____. *To Drive the Enemy from Southern Soil: The Letters of Col. Francis Marion Parker and the History of the 30th Regiment North Carolina Troops*. Dayton: Morningside, 1998.

Taylor, William R. *Cavalier and Yankee: The Old South and American National Character*. 1979. New York: Oxford University Press, 1993.

Tetel, Marcel. "Gobineau et Rabelais: symbolisme et Renaissance." *Symbolism and Modern Literature: Studies in Honor of Wallace Fowlie*. Marcel Tetel, ed. Durham: Duke University Press, 1978. 113–29.

Thomas, Emory M. *Robert E. Lee: A Biography*. New York: Norton, 1995.

Thomas, Hugh. *Conquest: Montezuma, Cortés, and the Fall of Old Mexico*. 1993. New York: Touchstone-Simon, 1995.

Thomason, Lt. Col. John W., Jr. *Lone Star Preacher: Being a Chronicle of the Acts of Praxiteles Swan, M.E. Church South Sometime Captain, 5th Texas Regiment Confederate States Provisional Army*. New York: Scribner's, 1941.

Thompson, Billy Bussell. "Chivalric Transformations of the Cid." *Studies on Medieval Spanish Literature in Honor of Charles F. Fraker*. Mercedes Vaquero and Alan Deyermond, eds. Madison: Hispanic Seminary of Medieval Studies, 1995. 259–64.

Thompson, Ernest Trice. *1607–1861*. Vol. 1 of *Presbyterians in the South*. 3 vols. 1963–73. Richmond: John Knox Press, 1963.

_____. *1861–1890*. Vol. 2 of *Presbyterians in the South*. 3 vols. 1963–73. Richmond: John Knox Press, 1973.

_____. *1890–1972*. Vol. 3 of *Presbyterians in the South*. 3 vols. 1963–73. Richmond: John Knox Press, 1973.

Thompson, I.A.A. "The Appointment of the Duke of Medina Sidonia to the Command of the Spanish Armada." *Historical Journal* 12.2 (1969): 197–216.

Thomson, John A.F. *Popes and Princes, 1417–1517: Politics and Polity in the Late Medieval Church*. London: Allen, 1980.

Tindall, George. "Mythology: A New Frontier in Southern History." *Myth and Southern History*. 2nd ed. Patrick Gerster and Nicholas Cords, eds. Urbana: University of Illinois Press, 1989. 1–15.

Torre Villar, Ernesto de la. "El hallazgo espiritual de Hernán Cortés." *Missionalia Hispánica* 42.121 (1985): 77–88.

Trulock, Alice Rains. *In the Hands of Providence: Joshua Chamberlain and the American Civil War*. Foreword by Alan T. Nolan. Chapel Hill: University of North Carolina Press, 1992.

Turner, Charles W. *Captain Greenlee Davidson, C.S.A.: Diary and Letters, 1851–1863*. Verona, VA: McClure, 1975.

Turner, Rory. "The Play of History: Civil War Reenactments and Their Use of the Past." *Folklore Forum* 22.1–2 (1989): 54–61.

Turtledove, Harry. *The Guns of the South: A Novel of the Civil War*. 1992. New York: Del Rey-Ballantine-Random, 1993.

Tuve, Rosemond. "The Red Crosse Knight and the Mediaeval Demon Stories." *PMLA* 44.3 (September 1929): 706–14.

Ullmann, Walter. *Medieval Papalism: The Political Theories of the Medieval Canonists*. London: Methuen, 1949.

_____. *The Papacy and Political Ideas in the Middle Ages*. London: Variorum Reprints, 1976.

_____. "The Pontificate of Adrian IV." *Cambridge Historical Journal* 11.3 (1955): 233–52.

Vagts, Alfred. "Battle-Scenes and Picture-Politics." *Military Affairs* 5.2 (Summer 1941): 87–103.

Valbuena-Briones, A. "A Critique of Calderón's *Judas Macabeo*." *Estudios en homenaje a Enrique Ruiz-Fornells*. Edited by Juan Fernández Jiménez et al. Homenajes. 1.

Erie, PA: Asociación de Licenciados y Doctores Españoles en Estados Unidos, 1990. 658–65.

Valverde Morán, Juan Pablo. "Geografía e ideología de Castilla en el *Poema de Fernán González*." *Caminería hispánica*. Manuel Criado de Val, ed. *Actas del II Congreso Internacional de Caminería Hispánica*. 2. Guadalajara: AACHE, with Patronato Arcipreste de Hita, Asociación Técnica de Carreteras, 1996. 255–71.

Vandiver, Frank E. "The Confederacy and the American Tradition." *Journal of Southern History* 28.3 (August 1962): 277–86.

_____. "The Confederate Myth." *Myth and Southern History*. 2nd ed. Patrick Gerster and Nicholas Cords, eds. Urbana: University of Illinois Press, 1989. 147–53.

_____. "Jefferson Davis— Leader without Legend." *Journal of Southern History* 43.1 (February 1977): 3–18.

Vaquero, Mercedes. "El cantar de la jura de Santa Gadea y la tradición del Cid como vasallo rebelde." *Olifant* 15 (1990): 47–84.

_____. "La Devotio Moderna y la poesía del siglo XV: elementos hagiográficos en la *Vida rimada de Fernán González*." *Saints and Their Authors: Studies in Medieval Hispanic Hagiography in Honor of John K. Walsh*. Edited by Jane E. Connolly et al. Madison: Hispanic Seminary of Medieval Studies, 1990. 107–19.

_____. "Spanish Epic of Revolt." *Epic and Epoch: Essays on the Interpretation and History of a Genre*. Edited by Steven M. Oberhelman, Van Kelly, and Richard J. Golsan. Studies in Comparative Literature 24. Lubbock: Texas Tech University Press, 1994. 146–63.

Vasiliev, Alexander A. "Medieval Ideas of the End of the World." *Byzantion* 16.2 (1942–43): 462–502.

Vaux, Sarah Anson. *Finding Meaning in the Movies*. Nashville: Abingdon, 1999.

Vaz, Katherine. "My Hunt for King Sebastião; How We Invite Miracles into Art and Everyday Life." Edited and introduced by Asela Rodríguez de Laguna. *Global Impact of the Portuguese Language*. New Brunswick NJ: Transaction, 20001. 51–60.

Veder, Robin. "'Julia, Daughter of Stonewall': Julia Thomas Jackson." *Virginia Cavalcade* 46.1 (1996): 4–19.

Villacorta Baños-García, Antonio. *Don Sebastián, rey de Portugal*. Barcelona: Ariel, 2001.

Wagner, Henry R. "The Lost First Letter of Cortés." *Hispanic American Historical Review* 21.4 (November 1941): 669–72.

Waldrep, B. Dwain. "John Jefferson DeYampert Renfroe: Alabama's Prophet of the Lost Cause." *Indian Journal of American Studies* 25.1 (Winter 1995): 93–106.

Walker, Eric C. "Wordsworth, Wellington, and Myth." *History and Myth: Essays on English Romantic Literature*. Stephen C. Behrendt, ed. Detroit: Wayne State University Press, 1990. 100–15.

_____. "Wordsworth, Wellington, and Naming." *Studies in Romanticism* 29.3 (Summer 1990): 223–40.

Walker, Roger M. "The Role of the King and the Poet's Intentions in the *Poema de Mio Cid*." *Medieval Hispanic Studies Presented to Rita Hamilton*. A.D. Deyermond, ed. London: Tamesis, 1976. 257–66.

Walker, Roger M., and Milija N. Pavlovic. "War Horses and Their Epithets in the *Poema de Mio Cid* and French Epic: Some Observations and Tentative Conclusions." *Neophilologus* 65.1 (January 1991): 76–85.

Wallace, John M. "Marvell's Horatian Ode." *PMLA* 77.1 (March 1962): 33–45.

Walsh, Elizabeth. "Hary's Wallace: The Evolution of a Hero." *Scottish Literary Journal* 11.1 (May 1984): 5–19.

Walsh, John K. "The Chivalric Dragon: Hagiographic Parallels in Early Spanish Romances." *Bulletin of Hispanic Studies* 54 (1977): 189–98.

_____. "Epic Flaw and Final Combat in the *Poema de Mío Cid*." *La Corónica* 5 (Spring 1977): 100–09.

_____. "Religious Motifs in the Early Spanish Epic." *Revista Hispánica Moderna* 36.4 (1970–71): 165–72.

Walston, Mark L. "Voices of the Holy War: Occasional Verse of the American Civil War." *Victorians Institute Journal* 15 (1987): 93–104.

Walton, Robert C. "Zwingli: Founding Father of the Reformed Churches." *Leaders of the Reformation*. Richard L. DeMolen, ed. Selinsgrove: Susquehanna University Press-Associated University Presses, 1984. 69–98.

Walzer, Michael. *The Revolution of the Saints: A Study in the Origins of Radical Politics*. Cambridge: Harvard University Press, 1965.

Warren, Craig A. "'Oh, God, What a Pity!': The Irish Brigade at Fredericksburg and the Creation of Myth." *Civil War History* 47.3 (1997): 193–221.

Warren, F.M. "An Earlier Version of the

Roland Miracle." *Modern Language Notes* 29.1 (January 1914): 3–4.

Watson, A.T. "Calderón's King Sebastian: Fool or Hero?" *Bulletin of Hispanic Studies* 61.3 (July 1984): 407–18.

Watson, J.R. "Soldiers and Saints: The Fighting Man and the Christian Life." *Masculinity and Spirituality in Victorian Culture*. Edited by Andrew Bradstock et al. New York: St. Martin's, 2000. 10–26.

Watson, Richie Devon, Jr. *The Cavalier in Virginia Fiction*. Baton Rouge: Louisiana State University Press, 1985.

Watson, Samuel J. "Religion and Combat Motivation in the Confederate Armies." *Journal of Military History* 58.1 (January 1994): 29–55.

Webb, Max. "The Self, Fortune, and Providence: Allen Tate on Stonewall Jackson." *Mississippi Quarterly* 30.2 (Spring 1977): 249–58.

Weigley, Russell F. *The Partisan War: The South Carolina Campaign of 1780–1782*. Tricentennial Booklet No. 2. Columbia: University of South Carolina Press, 1970.

Wert, Jeffry. "'I Am So Unlike Other Folks.'" *Civil War Times Illustrated* 28.2 (April 1989): 14–21.

_____. "Sandie Pendleton: Stonewall Jackson's Aide." *Virginia Cavalcade* 36.4 (1987): 158–69.

Wert, Jeffry D. *General James Longstreet: The Confederacy's Most Controversial Soldier — a Biography*. New York: Simon, 1993.

_____. "'The Tycoon': Lee and His Staff." *Civil War Times Illustrated* 11.4 (1972): 11–19.

_____. "The Valley Campaign of 1862: Part 1." *Virginia Cavalcade* 34.4 (1985): 150–61.

West, Beverly. *Epic, Folk, and Christian Traditions in the* Poema de Fernán González. Madrid: José Porrúa Turanzas-Scripta Humanitatis, 1983.

West, Geoffrey. "Hero or Saint? Hagiographic Elements in the Life of the Cid." *Journal of Hispanic Philology* 7.2 (Winter 1983): 87–105.

Wetherbee, Winthrop. "The Theme of Imagination in Medieval Poetry and the Allegorical Figure 'Genius.'" *Medieval Poetics*. Paul Maurice Clogan, ed. *Medievalia et Humanistica: Studies in Medieval and Renaissance Culture* ns 1. Cambridge: Cambridge University Press, 1976. 45–64.

Whallon, William. "Formulaic Poetry in the Old Testament." *Comparative Literature* 15.1 (Winter 1963): 1–14.

_____. "Formulas for Heroes in the *Iliad* and in *Beowulf*." *Modern Philology* 63.2 (November 1966): 95–104.

_____. "The Homeric Epithets." *Yale Classical Studies* 17. Harry M. Hubbell and William S. Anderson, eds. New Haven: Yale University Press, 1961. 97–142.

Wheeler, Richard. *We Knew Stonewall Jackson*. New York: Crowell, 1977.

Where These Memories Grow: History, Memory, and Southern Identity. W. Fitzhugh Brundage, ed. Chapel Hill: University of North Carolina Press, 2000.

White, Henry Alexander. *Stonewall Jackson*. Philadelphia: George W. Jacobs, 1909.

White, Gen. I. D. "Patton — the Man and the Film." *Military Affairs* 34.4 (December 1970): 138.

Whiting, Charles. *Patton*. Ballantine's Illustrated History of World War II. New York: Ballantine, 1970.

Williams, T. Harry. "Freeman, Historian of the Civil War: An Appraisal." *Journal of Southern History* 21.1 (February 1955): 91–100.

Wilson, Charles Reagan. "The Religion of the Lost Cause." *Myth and Southern History*. 2nd ed. Patrick Gerster and Nicholas Cords, eds. Urbana: University of Illinois Press, 1989. 169–89.

_____. "Robert Lewis Dabney: Religion and the Southern Holocaust." *Virginia Magazine of History and Biography* 89.1 (January 1981): 79–89.

Wilson, Howard McKnight. *The Lexington Presbytery Heritage: The Presbytery of Lexington and Its Churches in the Synod of Virginia Presbyterian Church in the United States*. Verona, VA: McClure, 1971.

Wilson, William Lynn. *A Borderland Confederate*. Festus P. Summers, ed. Pittsburgh: University of Pittsburgh Press, 1962.

Winkler, Martin M. "Mythic and Cinematic Traditions in Anthony Mann's *El Cid*." *Mosaic* 26.3 (Summer 1993): 89–111.

Wirmark, Margareta. "Strindberg's History Plays: Some Reflections." *Strindberg and Genre*. Michael Robinson, ed. Scandinavian Literary History and Criticism. 9. Norwich: Norvik, 1991. 200–06.

Wise, John Sergeant. *The End of an Era*. Text scanned (OCR) by Jessica Mathewson, images scanned by Carlene Hempel, text encoded by Carlene Hempel and Natalia Smith. Chapel Hill: Academic Affairs Library, University of North Carolina, 1998. http://docsouth.unc.edu/wise/menu.html. Call number E605.W8 1899 (Davis Library, UNC-CH).

Wolff, John. *Great Deaths: Grieving, Religion, and Nationhood in Victorian and Edwardian*

Britain. Oxford: British Academy-Oxford University Press, 2000.

Wood, W.J. *Civil War Generalship: The Art of Command.* New York: Da Capo, 1997.

Woods, Jean M. "Weckherlin's 'Ebenbild' on Gustavus Adolphus and the Swedish Intelligencer." *Daphnis* 3 (1974): 83–88.

Wright, Richardson. *American Wags and Eccentrics from Colonial Times to the Civil War.* New York: Frederick Ungar, 1965. Rpt. of *Grandfather Was Queer.* 1939.

Writing the Civil War: The Quest to Understand. James M. McPherson and William J.

Cooper, Jr., eds. Columbia: University of South Carolina Press, 1998.

Wyatt-Brown, Bertram. "Gentility." *Southern Honor: Ethics and Behavior in the Old South.* New York: Oxford University Press, 1982. 88–114.

Yadin, Yigael. *Bar-Kokhba: The Rediscovery of the Legendary Hero of the Second Jewish Revolt against Rome.* New York: Random, 1971.

Yearout, Maj. Robert D. "Chancellorsville, Mobile Defense." *Infantry* 63 (November–December 1973): 29–32.

Index

Numbers in *boldface italics* indicate photographs

reer before Civil War 17; compared to
  Jackson 60
Shields, Gen. James 26
Shifflett, Andrew 72
Silver, James W. 60
Singman, Jeffrey 163
Sixtus IV 136, 140
Slavery 43, 66, 116–19
Smith, Colin 133
Smith, Gene 21–22
Smith, James Power 11, 44–45, 56–57, 95
Smith, R. J. 100
Smith, Richard J. 101–2
Soldier as Christian hero 93
Sorrel (horse of William III) 32
Song of Roland 110 *see Chanson de
  Roland*
Sorvino, Mira 80
South: view of Lincoln 181n38
South America 153
South Carolina 62, 89, 95
Southern Historical Society 179n21
Southrons 55
Sowards, Kelly 138, 140–41, 143
Spain 1–2, 7–8, 39, 42, 67, 105, 110, 125–
  26, 128–29, 131, 133–35, 142, 144, 147,
  149, 152–53, 156–60, 175n1, 177n10,
  188n88, 189n97, 191n106; decline of 160,
  191n106
Spanish Golden Age drama 142
Spanish language 153, 189n100
Spanish navy 152, 158–59
Spartacus 6, 39–40
Spartacus (film) 40
Sperry, Kate 59
Spiritual Rapping 116–17
Spotsylvania, battle of 14
Stafford Heights, Federal headquarters,
  Fredericksburg 71
Stanley, NC 35
Starn, Randolph 139
Starnes, D.T. 142
Starnes, Richard D. 179n21
Staunton, VA 75, 179n27
Steiger (*Patton*) 188n84
Stewart, James 131, 172
Stone, Irving 140
Stone, Oliver 180n36
Stones River, battle of 5
Stonewall, as nickname for Jackson 48
Stonewall (Dwyer) 182n50
Stonewall Brigade 18–19, 26–28, 31, 48,
  52, 76, 94, 101, 179n27; as "foot-cav-
  alry" 19

Stonewall Jackson Headquarters Museum
  (Winchester) 18
"Stonewall Jackson's Way" 26–28
Strickland, Matthew 110
Strindberg, August 87
Stuart, Gen. James Ewell Brown (Jeb) 21,
  25, 27, 55; in *Gods and Generals* (2003)
  94; and Jackson 70, 183n58; and Prince
  Rupert 55
Sudan 100, 102
Suleiman the Magnificent 158
Sultan of Morocco, and Sebastian 157
Surry of Eagle's Nest (1866) 65
Swamp Fox 89; *see also* Marion, Francis
Sweden 1, 48, 57, 83, 85–87
Swiss Reformation 57
Switzerland 181n40
Sword, Wiley 3–4, 7
"Sword of God," and Jackson 94
Syfret, R.H. 72–74

Tacitus 155
Taipings 6, 98, 100
Tangiers 157–58
Tapia, Andrés de 148
Tarboro, NC 61, 182n48
Tarleton, Col. Banastre 89
Tate, Allen 18–19, 21, 50, 179n19
Tavington, Col. William (*The Patriot*) 89
Taylor, Lonn 47
Taylor, Gen. Richard 57–58, 182n47; crit-
  icism of Jackson 50
Templo Mayor, cleansing of 147–48
Tennessee 49, 180n37, 181n41
Tennyson, Alfred, Lord 24–25
Tenochtitlán 147
Terence 142
Themistocles 101
Thetis 43
Third Army, U.S. 2
33rd Virginia Infantry, CSA, at First
  Manassas 31
Thirty Years' War 83, 85
Thomas, Gen. George 79
Thomas Aquinas, Saint 29
Thompson, James Thomas, 11th Ga. 32
Thornton, VA 9
Tingsten, Herbert 98
Titian 146; portrait of Charles V 149–50
Tizón, Tizona (Sword of the Cid) 134,
  169–70
"To Lucasta, Going to the Wars" 80,
  185n71
Toledo 108, 154